Machine Learning for Social and Behavioral Research

Methodology in the Social Sciences

David A. Kenny, Founding Editor
Todd D. Little, Series Editor
www.guilford.com/MSS

This series provides applied researchers and students with analysis and research design books that emphasize the use of methods to answer research questions. Rather than emphasizing statistical theory, each volume in the series illustrates when a technique should (and should not) be used and how the output from available software programs should (and should not) be interpreted. Common pitfalls as well as areas of further development are clearly articulated.

RECENT VOLUMES

MEASUREMENT THEORY AND APPLICATIONS FOR THE SOCIAL SCIENCES
Deborah L. Bandalos

CONDUCTING PERSONAL NETWORK RESEARCH: A PRACTICAL GUIDE
Christopher McCarty, Miranda J. Lubbers, Raffaele Vacca, and José Luis Molina

QUASI-EXPERIMENTATION: A GUIDE TO DESIGN AND ANALYSIS
Charles S. Reichardt

THEORY CONSTRUCTION AND MODEL-BUILDING SKILLS:
A PRACTICAL GUIDE FOR SOCIAL SCIENTISTS, SECOND EDITION
James Jaccard and Jacob Jacoby

LONGITUDINAL STRUCTURAL EQUATION MODELING WITH Mplus:
A LATENT STATE–TRAIT PERSPECTIVE
Christian Geiser

COMPOSITE-BASED STRUCTURAL EQUATION MODELING:
ANALYZING LATENT AND EMERGENT VARIABLES
Jörg Henseler

BAYESIAN STRUCTURAL EQUATION MODELING
Sarah Depaoli

INTRODUCTION TO MEDIATION, MODERATION, AND CONDITIONAL
PROCESS ANALYSIS: A REGRESSION-BASED APPROACH, THIRD EDITION
Andrew F. Hayes

THE THEORY AND PRACTICE OF ITEM RESPONSE THEORY, SECOND EDITION
R. J. de Ayala

APPLIED MISSING DATA ANALYSIS, SECOND EDITION
Craig K. Enders

PRINCIPLES AND PRACTICE OF STRUCTURAL EQUATION MODELING, FIFTH EDITION
Rex B. Kline

MACHINE LEARNING FOR SOCIAL AND BEHAVIORAL RESEARCH
Ross Jacobucci, Kevin J. Grimm, and Zhiyong Zhang

LONGITUDINAL STRUCTURAL EQUATION MODELING, SECOND EDITION
Todd D. Little

Machine Learning for Social and Behavioral Research

Ross Jacobucci
Kevin J. Grimm
Zhiyong Zhang

Series Editor's Note by Todd D. Little

THE GUILFORD PRESS
New York London

A Division of Guilford Publications, Inc.
370 Seventh Avenue, Suite 1200, New York, NY 10001
www.guilford.com

Printed in the United States of America

This book is printed on acid-free paper.

Last digit is print number: 9 8 7 6 5 4 3 2 1

Library of Congress Cataloging-in-Publication Data

Names: Jacobucci, Ross, author.
Title: Machine learning for social and behavioral research / Ross Jacobucci, Kevin J. Grimm, Zhiyong Zhang.
Description: New York, NY : The Guilford Press, [2023] | Series: Methodology in the social sciences | Includes bibliographical references and index.
Identifiers: LCCN 2023005151 | ISBN 9781462552924 (paperback) | ISBN 9781462552931 (cloth)
Subjects: LCSH: Social sciences—Research.
Classification: LCC H62 .J298 2023 | DDC 300.72–dc23/eng/20230322
LC record available at *https://lccn.loc.gov/2023005151*

Series Editor's Note

As a fellow social and behavioral science researcher, we work in a massively multivariate world. Large-scale data collection is widespread. Finding structure and revealing relationships among the vast number of variables is a challenging goal to achieve. Adding the principles and techniques of machine learning to your toolbox will aid in overcoming the challenges; moreover, this book covers techniques that are applicable to univariate outcomes with multiple predictors (e.g., decision trees, regularized regression). Unlike books on machine learning that come from a computer science perspective, Jacobucci, Grimm, and Zhang bring a social and behavioral sciences perspective to machine learning techniques that are decidedly underutilized in our fields. This dream team of authors walks you through numerous real-world data examples from fields spanning clinical, cognitive, educational, health, and personality sciences.

Given that theory is an analyst's best friend, these authors emphasize the critical interplay between theory and data that is the hallmark of techniques such as structural equation modeling. The authors expand this theory–data interplay by adding and expanding the algorithms that can be utilized beyond the likelihood and Bayesian algorithms that we are quite accustomed to using. Quite importantly, they bring this traditional background to connect new ideas with traditional statistical training principles and practices. In their chapters on multivariate machine learning algorithms, they cover various core techniques such as factor analysis (and principal components analysis), structural equation modeling, mixed-effects modeling, and finite mixture modeling, as well as alternative data types (i.e., text analysis and social networks).

One cool feature of this book's structure is that the authors open each chapter with key terms and definitions to foreshadow the concepts that they cover and offer thoughtful further readings at the end of each chapter as well as a computational time section at the end of the practice chapters. They rely on a broad selection of data examples throughout, spanning early-childhood learning, to Big Five personality traits, to drug use and the like. After explaining and then providing easy-to-follow examples, which you can emulate for your own methods and results sections, the authors then provide coding examples (and all the R code is available on the companion website).

Unlike most approaches to machine learning, Jacobucci, Grimm, and Zhang emphasize the critical need to correct for measurement error. When measurement error is not trivial (and it rarely is), it will wreak havoc on the validity of any findings. Error correction and techniques to ensure the validity of the findings are essential features of any advanced modeling technique. The authors offer best-practice advice and procedures for accomplishing these features for the various algorithms they cover.

As mentioned in the preface, this work was inspired by the late Jack McArdle. Jack was a quintessential scientist and a kindhearted person. His seminal contributions to the literature as well as his generative sharing of his ideas have shaped the entire field of quantitative methodology. Jack is sorely missed but his influence remains tangible, such as the existence of this book.

All the material is presented in an engaging and highly accessible manner. From graduate students to seasoned veterans, *Machine Learning for Social and Behaviorial Research* will be a staple reference work for you to tackle the challenges of modeling data from this massively multivariate world. As always, enjoy!

TODD D. LITTLE
Lubbock, Texas

Preface

Over the past 20 years, there has been an incredible change in the size, structure, and types of data collected in the social and behavioral sciences. Thus, social and behavioral researchers have increasingly been asking the question "What do I do with all of this data?" The goal of this book is to help answer that question.

With advances in data collection, there has been a corresponding expansion in the understanding of the complexity underlying the relationships between variables. Nonlinear effects and interactions are now regularly posed as hypotheses, aided by larger sample sizes that afford adequate statistical power. Further, predicting an outcome with only a few covariates of interest, while only assessing linear relationships, is now recognized as severely limiting. While this approach was common in the past, due to smaller dataset sizes and statistical software limitations, computer-assisted data collection and new software have helped overcome such challenges.

In the past, particularly in academic research, certain types of data were only analyzed with specific types of statistical models such as analysis of variance (ANOVA) and linear regression, which were closely aligned with the theoretical motivation underlying the study. However, the advent of novel data collection methods has resulted in new data types (e.g., text), extracted from a variety of sources (e.g., brain imaging, social network), as well as larger collections of traditional survey data. As a result, there is an incredible degree of flexibility in the choice of algorithms. This complicates modern statistical applications, as researchers and practitioners have to contend with an additional dimension, specifically, "Which algorithm or algorithms should I apply?" and "How does this algorithm align with the theoretical motivations of my study?"

It is our viewpoint that in social and behavioral research, to answer the question "What do I do with all of this data?", one needs to know the latest advances in the algorithms and think deeply about the interplay of statistical algorithms, data, and theory.

An important distinction between this book and most other books in the area of machine learning is our focus on theory. To address the interplay

FIGURE1. The complexity of modern data analysis necessitates a transition from primarily focusing on the interplay of data and theory, to now understanding how data, theory, and algorithms are integrated in practice.

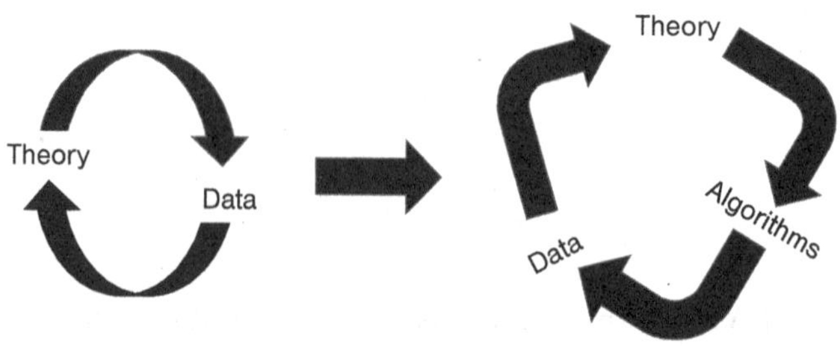

of machine learning, data, and theory (see Figure 1), we start with detailing our perspective in Chapter 2 to address the question we often receive when teaching classes or workshops on machine learning, namely: "Can machine learning analyses be incorporated into my traditional confirmatory research?" The follow-up question is often: "Given the exploratory nature of machine learning, how can we be sure our results are trustworthy?" We address this question specifically in Chapter 3 by providing details on a number of cross-validation strategies that help prevent overfitting.

One glance at the table of contents from any of the recently published books on machine learning, data mining, statistical learning, data science, or artificial intelligence reveals a dizzying array of algorithms not detailed in traditional statistics textbooks. This book is different in a number of ways. The first is our aforementioned focus on theory. While Chapter 1 provides an orientation to the book's organization, the primary substance of our book begins with a focus on theory (Chapter 2)—namely, how machine learning fits into research that has traditionally been done from a hypothesis-driven perspective. This is followed by a chapter (Chapter 3) on principles, specifically, how practitioners can apply machine learning algorithms to produce trustworthy results. These chapters set the stage for our discussion of algorithms for univariate outcomes (Chapters 4–6); however, in contrast to other books, we focus largely on regularization and tree-based methods. This better allows us to discuss the integration of these algorithms with complex models that are commonly applied in social and behavioral research, namely, latent variable models. This enables us to provide additional detail on handling measurement error, an extremely important component of survey data, longitudinal data analysis, and the assessment of heterogeneity through the identification of subgroups. Measurement is the focus of Chapters 7 and 8, followed by a discussion of modeling longitudinal data (Chapter 9), and assessing heterogeneity (Chapter 10). Finally, we focus the last two chapters on alternative data types, with an introduction to text analysis (Chapter 11), where we detail the processing of text data and implementing commonly applied algorithms, and social network data (Chapter 12), with an emphasis on network modeling.

Chapters 1 through 6, 9, and 11 have been used as the primary source material for an advanced undergraduate and graduate course. Further, this book can be used as a supplementary reading for courses on regression, multivariate, longitudinal data, and structural equation modeling, among others. While Chapters 4 through 6 have considerable overlap with content found in other books oriented toward supervised learning, Chapter 7 and the subsequent chapters provide a more detailed/advanced account of machine learning methodologies.

Chapters pair a breadth in coverage of methodologies and algorithms with a depth in focusing on fundamental topics, which are detailed at the beginning of each chapter in a "Key Terminology" section to prepare readers for the fundamental concepts of each chapter. Further, we end Chapters 3–12 with a "Computational Time and Resources" section that discusses how to put each method into practice, denoting the key R packages that can be used. Every application of machine learning detailed in this book was programmed in the R statistical environment. While the book does not detail R code, code for all analyses is provided on the book's website. Readers can apply this code to reproduce every example in the book.

Acknowledgments

Each author of this book became interested in machine learning because of mentorship, collaboration, and friendship with John (Jack) J. McArdle, who passed away before this book was completed. Jack was one of the first psychological researchers who became interested in machine learning, writing a host of papers and an edited book on the topic dating back to the early 2010s. Jack provided the inspiration and motivation for each one of us to pursue research in machine learning, spurred by his novel application of machine learning to understanding attrition in longitudinal studies and heterogeneity in longitudinal trajectories. Simply put, without Jack, this book would never have been written.

In addition, we would like to thank the helpful reviewers of the book who guided us in the development of the manuscript. These reviewers were initially anonymous, but they agreed to have their identities revealed now, and we would like to thank them for their insightful feedback: Sonya K. Sterba, Department of Psychology and Human Development, Vanderbilt University; George Marcoulides, Mays Business School, Texas A&M University; and Alexander Christensen, Department of Psychology and Human Development, Vanderbilt University.

Finally, we would like to thank the staff at The Guilford Press, particularly C. Deborah Laughton, whose patience allowed the writing of this book to continue through the COVID-19 pandemic.

Contents

The companion website (*www.guilford.com/jacobucci-materials*) provides the R programming scripts for the examples used in the book.

Part I

FUNDAMENTAL CONCEPTS

1 Introduction

1.1 Why the Term *Machine Learning*?

In writing this book, we struggled in deciding what term to use: artificial intelligence, machine learning, data mining, statistical learning, data science, big data, among others. There are a number of additional terms that refer to more specific families of algorithms, each of which is less in line with the perspective that this book takes: deep learning, natural language processing, generative modeling, and others. Many of the distinctions in terminology refer to the characteristics of the data that the algorithms are optimized for. For instance, natural language processing refers to the modeling of text data, where the text can be extracted from speech, or the words used to answer an open-ended question. Although distinctions between the terms *machine learning* and *data mining* have been made, we see little benefit in further trying to parse overarching labels. Instead, we use the term *machine learning*, as this has become the common term of use in social and behavioral research. To this end, we believe one can better understand the perspective of this book by assessing the types of data we detail.

The datasets detailed in this book are exclusively observational and include both cross-sectional and longitudinal data. While Chapter 2 highlights the role of theory and the practice of science involved when applying machine learning, Chapter 3 moves directly into all of the steps and methods necessary for producing trustworthy results. Chapters 4 through 6 focus on the research scenario where there is a single outcome and several predictors. We move beyond this and detail methods that can model multivariate (multiple) data, such as factor analysis (Chapter 7), structural equation modeling (Chapter 8), and mixed-effects models (Chapter 9). Further, a theme in this book is the identification of heterogeneity, namely, imposing or searching for some form of group structure to the data. We discuss this in Chapter 10 in relation to mixture models and structural equation model trees. We move beyond these more traditional forms of data in both Chapters 11, where we provide an introduction to text analysis, and Chapter 12, where we provide details on a number of algorithms for modeling social network data.

While there are various definitions of *machine learning*, we find most of them unsatisfactory, as they refer mainly to concepts from computer science. First, we can try to define *machine learning* by the constituent characteristics of the algorithms. For example, we could define machine learning as being a family of nonparametric algorithms, meaning that common probability distributions are not used. Thus, *p*-values, as used in a variety of statistical frameworks (e.g., regression), should not be available in machine learning. However, this fails to hold for a number of algorithms, such as *Gaussian processing*, *ridge regression*, *conditional inference decision trees*, and recent algorithms that pair with structural equation models or multilevel models. Second, *machine learning* as a methodology can be defined by the increase in the degree of complexity compared to traditional statistical models. This definition is difficult to quantify because many algorithms do not have *parameters* that estimate population level quantities. Further, two methods that fall under the umbrella of *machine learning*, namely, *ridge* and *lasso regression*, go against most attempts to define *machine learning* in this way because they result in *less* complex models. Additionally, a number of algorithms, such as *support vector machines* and *neural networks*, can be specified to be quite similar to regression models. The most coherent definition of *machine learning* is a collection of algorithms that are *adaptive*, meaning the number of parameters, types of constraints, or other characteristics are not set a priori, but are developed during their implementation. Algorithmic flexibility is typically implemented by *hyperparameters* or *tuning parameters*, as they are parameters that control various aspects of the algorithm. For instance, the hyperparameters in a *random forest*, which fits a sequence of decision trees, include the *number of trees*, *tree depth*, and the *number of variables to test for each split*. The drawback to this definition of machine learning is that it is seemingly all encompassing, only leaving the *generalized linear model* as not being *machine learning*.

1.1.1 Why Not Just Call It Statistics?

The one distinction we do make is between *traditional inferential statistics* and *machine learning*, with the former being the focus of most statistics courses, specifically with respect to analysis of variance and linear regression. Note that the main difference is parametric (*traditional inferential statistics*) versus nonparametric (*machine learning*), with parametric referring to the use of probability distributions (e.g., normal distribution for continuous outcomes). Instead of providing additional detail on this distinction, we note that the divide between *traditional inferential statistics* and *machine learning* has diminished recently and will likely continue to diminish into the future. Researchers now have access to increasingly varied types of data, thus requiring ever expanding statistical toolboxes. Solely using *traditional inferential statistical* models is now becoming increasingly limiting; however, the same can be said for *machine learning*, as there are a number of research scenarios in which *traditional inferential statistical* models are more appropriate.

1.2 Why Do We Need Machine Learning?

There have been overviews of *machine learning* and calls for its increased use in almost every area of social and behavioral research, such as clinical psychology (e.g., Dwyer, Falkai, & Koutsouleris, 2018), political science (e.g., Grimmer, 2015), economics (Athey, 2018), and sociology (McFarland, Lewis, & Goldberg, 2016). The natural question is why? The easiest explanation is the increased availability of large datasets, which are facilitated by new data collection methodologies, openly available dataset repositories, and distributed laboratories (e.g., see Moshontz et al., 2018). While data represents one piece of the pie, an equally important rationale for the use of *machine learning* is the increasing support for the idea that many associations in the social and behavioral sciences are more *complex* than the models previously considered. Complexity can mean many things, but researchers have discussed complexity in terms of the number of variables (e.g., Kendler, 2019), the nature of modeled associations (i.e., interactive and nonlinear effects; Van Doorn, Verhoef, & Bijmolt, 2007), heterogeneity (e.g., Ram & Grimm, 2009), or the existence of dynamic changes over time (e.g., Cole, Bendezu, Ram, & Chow, 2017). Each chapter in this book either lays the groundwork for assessing complex associations or directly addresses at least one of these ideas regarding complexity.

1.2.1 Machine Learning Thesis

We believe that part of the motivation for *machine learning* lies in the thesis that psychological phenomena are extremely complex, possibly infinitely complex (Lin, Tegmark, & Rolnick, 2017; Jolly & Chang, 2019), requiring large numbers of variables, each likely only producing small effects (Götz, Gosling, & Rentfrow, 2021). Thus, the thinking is that complex algorithms *must* improve our modeling of these data. While this has undoubtedly been the case in a large number of published articles, there has concurrently been a surprising number of studies that have found equal predictive performance for linear models relative to machine learning algorithms that search for nonlinear and interactive effects (see Christodoulou et al., 2019; Jacobucci et al., 2021). In contrast to the notion that these latter studies disprove our complexity thesis, we instead view these studies as informative for elucidating various limitations regarding study design. For example, the predictors and/or outcome may contain too much measurement error (Jacobucci & Grimm, 2020), be designed to represent latent variables and not to assess unique entities (the idea behind constitutive versus indexical; Kendler, 2017), have limitations regarding the number and which predictors were included, contain a sample size that was too small, have insufficient time elapsed between predictor and outcome assessment, among many others. Our point here is that this area of research is too new to jump to premature conclusions. Thus, instead of blaming the algorithm or the underlying thesis, we believe that much more work is needed to understand how study design contributes to predictive performance. Despite supporting the complexity thesis above, it is simultaneously necessary to prevent the proffering of what could be termed a naïve complexity — simply put, almost every study will be missing important components. For example, studies that assess various environment factors for understanding depression will likely not also assess important genetic contributors. This can be referred to as *integrative pluralism* (Mitchell, 2009) and requires assessing the rules for combining various causes across multiple ontological levels.

1.3 How Is This Book Different?

The three authors all have backgrounds in psychology and have worked with a wide variety of datasets coming from multiple areas of social and behavioral research. This means the following distinctions from most machine learning books:

- Less of a focus on datasets with more variables than sample size. In our research domains we rarely see datasets of this form.
- Greater focus on multivariate outcomes and specifically on imposing structure on the outcome variables. Each author is an expert in latent variable modeling and this expertise is infused into multiple book chapters.
- Greater focus on dealing with measurement error which is incorporated into multiple chapters. Simply put, most of the data that we analyze have non-negligible measurement error which can have a large effect on our ability to accurately model associations in the data.

- Additional detail on the replication, stability, and reporting of results to increase the chances that the findings are published. Our goal is that readers of the book can take what they learn and apply it to their own data with the aim of publishing their findings.

Additionally, instead of attempting to cover machine learning comprehensively, we take a narrower focus in primarily detailing *regularization*, *decision trees*, and *ensembles of decision trees*. We describe each of these in Chapters 4 through 6, and discuss how these algorithms have been combined with latent variable models in Chapters 8 through 10. By focusing on these algorithms, we omit other commonly used families of algorithms, most notably, support vector machines and deep learning. Support vector machines have a long history of being applied in neuroimaging data, whereas deep learning has become the state-of-the-art algorithm for image recognition and natural language processing. While we would expect future editions of this book to include deep learning, we opted to omit both deep learning and support vector machines due to their lack of interpretation and absence in being integrated with latent variable models. Readers are referred to James et al. (2013) for an accessible introduction to support vector machines and Chollet and Allaire (2018) for an introduction to deep learning. One may question why we primarily detail algorithms that have not changed, to a large extent, since the 1980s, but to put it simply, little progress has been made in prediction performance in more standard datasets (e.g., Hand, 2006). Similar things could be said in the context of variable selection (cf. Hastie, Tibshirani, & Tibshirani, 2020).

1.3.1 Prerequisites for the Book

Our goal in writing this book was to provide a background for understanding published machine learning papers or reference material for researchers to publish journal articles using machine learning. With this goal in mind, we wrote the book to be used as a standalone reference or to be used as a part of a graduate machine learning course. Thus, the first part of the book requires readers to have taken at least a graduate level course in regression or be familiar with that level of material. Chapter 4 specifically covers regression but does not provide a background on linear regression and only a small level of detail regarding the use of regression for alternative outcome types. Chapters 7 through 10 focus heavily on the use of latent variables. Chapter 7 provides a background on the use of factor analysis, the foundational technique behind the methods described in these chapters, but it is relatively brief in nature. If readers wish to supplement this material, we recommend Beaujean (2014). Further, a number of the methods detailed in these chapters focus on longitudinal data. For further detail on the use of latent growth curves or multilevel models we recommend Grimm, Ram, and Estabrook (2016). We do not expect most readers to have a background in either text mining (Chapter 11) or social network analysis (Chapter 12), so these chapters were written at a more introductory level and contain references to other relevant books for additional background.

1.4 Definitions

1.4.1 Model vs. Algorithm

One of the confusing pieces of terminology in the realm of machine learning is the use of *model* or *algorithm* when referring to specific aspects of the analysis. To put it simply, the term *algorithm* refers to the type of method (e.g., linear regression, random forest), whereas the term *model* refers to the results of fitting an algorithm to data. Thus, fitting an *algorithm* to data yields the *model*, and a model can take data as input and provide predictions as output. Linear regression is an algorithm. After fitting this algorithm to data, we get a model, such as: $\hat{y}_i = 12.3 + 0.3 \cdot x_{1i}$. The same thing occurs for more advanced algorithms as the resulting model can take data as input and generate a predicted value for each observation. The fitting process typically requires a higher computational burden, and the relationship between input and output is more complex, but the procedure across algorithms is similar.

1.4.2 Prediction

To define what we mean by *prediction*, we first define what we mean by the term *predictions*. In the simplest case, we can use a single sample and fit a linear regression model, $y = x\beta + e$, deriving estimates for each of the unknown coefficients, comprising the vector β. With this, we now have our estimates that can be used to create predictions for the observations in this sample, $\hat{y} = x\beta$, where $\hat{y}$ is a vector of predictions for our sample. Additionally, we follow Shmueli (2010) in assigning the term *predictive model* to the regression equation that produces β. More specifically, we can generally refer to the predictive model as $\hat{f}(x)$, differentiating this from $f(x)$, as $\hat{f}(x)$ is estimated from the data x and y, whereas $f(x)$ refers to a general function, such as a linear regression or a random forest. Because we are using the same sample to estimate β and $\hat{y}$, there will be some form of positive bias in our predictive performance, such as R^2. Instead, we can use separate datasets to estimate β as we do to test $\hat{y}$. In the simplest case (see Chapter 3 for additional strategies), we can split our sample into two partitions, 50% assigned to the *training* dataset, and 50% assigned to the *test* dataset. In the first step, we estimate β using the training dataset and then use these estimates to create predictions for the observations in the test data. With this, we can calculate the predictive performance solely in the test set by assessing the discrepancy between the observed and predicted values in the test dataset.

On a more nuanced level, we can differentiate *prediction* from *forecasting*, noting that *forecasting* involves the prediction of future data, whereas the term prediction refers to generating predicted values for existing observations. At times, prediction is defined in terms of creating predictions for *new* observations (observations not a part of the sample used to train the model), which emphasizes the need to separate the data used to generate the model's unknown values (i.e., parameters, hyperparameters) from the data used to evaluate the predictions from the model.

1.5 Software

The analyses for this book were all done in the `R` statistical environment (R Core Team, 2020). While the techniques covered in Chapters 3 through 6, as well as 11 and 12 can be done in many other software environments, particularly `Python` (Van Rossum, & Drake, 2009), many of the methods developed in the other chapters are only available in `R`. This book should not be viewed as providing an introduction or background on programming in `R`. Instead, we refer to the other books that solely focus on `R` programming. Of these, we recommend books that have a focus on using `R` for statistics, as many of the programming conventions are unnecessary for implementing the methods we describe. Of these, we highly recommend Zhang and Wang (2017) or Navarro (2013).

When referencing `R` code in each of the chapters, we follow the same convention as for referencing data by the use of the `Sans Serif and Monospaced font`. It should be clear by the context whether it is `R` code or data/variables. Additionally, we opted against directly including blocks of `R` code in the chapters or at the end of each chapter. We decided against this in favor of posting each of the programming scripts on the book's website as this better facilitates the updating of each script as conventions for any of the techniques or algorithms change over time. We hope to keep this code repository up to date with the inevitable changes to `R` statistical environment and required packages.

1.6 Datasets

We use a number of datasets in this book with some datasets detailed in multiple chapters. To reduce redundancy in detail across chapters, we detail most of the datasets here. We do not detail the datasets analyzed in Chapters 11 and 12 because they are data of a different type. We use the `Sans Serif and Monospaced font` when referencing datasets or variables from a dataset in the chapters.

1.6.1 Grit

Grit (Duckworth, Peterson, Matthews, & Kelly, 2007) is defined as perseverance and passion for long-term goals, and we attempt to predict this construct with items that measure the Big Five aspects of personality and demographic variables. The `Grit` data were downloaded from Open Psychometrics (https://openpsychometrics.org/_rawdata/), and include responses from 4,270 participants who completed the survey online. The Grit Scale is a 12-item survey that asks participants about the extent to which they have overcome obstacles and setbacks, and the focus they have to complete a task. There is a 1 to 5 response scale for these items with scale points: 1 — *Very much like me*, 2 — *Mostly like me*, 3 — *Somewhat like me*, 4 — *Not much like me*, and 5 — *Not like me at all*. The International Personality Item Pool (IPIP) Big-5 Personality Inventory contains 50 items with 10 items measuring each personality construct: *Openness*, *Conscientiousness*, *Extraversion*, *Agreeableness*, and *Neuroticism* (for more on the Big Five see Raad & Perugini, 2002). These items were rated on a 5-point scale with the following scale points: 1 – *Disagree*, 3 – *Neutral*, 5 – *Agree*.

1.6.2 National Survey on Drug Use and Health from 2014

The National Survey on Drug Use and Health from 2014 (NSDUH; Substance Abuse and Mental Health Services Administration, 2015). This survey focused on assessing the use of illicit drugs, alcohol, and tobacco among U.S. civilians 12 years or older. For the purpose of our analysis we focus on questions that assess mental health issues. The dataset detailed in the chapters is pared down from the original dataset to include 39 predictor variables with the aim of predicting suicidal ideation (last 12 months; `SUICTHINK`). Predictors included symptoms of depression and other mental health disorders, the impact of these symptoms on daily functioning, and four demographic variables (*gender*, *ethnicity*, *relationship status*, and *age*). The dataset can be freely downloaded from https://www.datafiles.samhsa.gov/study-dataset/national-survey-drug-use-and-health-2014-nsduh-2014-ds0001-nid16876.

1.6.3 Early Childhood Learning Study — Kindergarten Cohort

The Early Childhood Longitudinal Study — Kindergarten Cohort 1998/1999 (ECLS-K, National Center for Education Statistics, 2009) is a longitudinal study of over 21,000 children who were in kindergarten in the 1998/1999 school year. These children were measured from the beginning of kindergarten through eighth grade on a variety of assessments, which included tests of reading, mathematics, general knowledge, and science. Additionally, there were assessments of the child completed by the parents and teachers, demographic data collected by the parents, as well as classroom, teacher, and school-level data. For our illustration, we examine changes in reading ability measured during the first two years of school (four assessments — fall and spring of each year), and limit ourselves to children with complete demographic and parent rating variables. These data include the following variables: *gender*, *home language* (English vs. non-English), *disability status*, *mother's educational attainment*, *father's educational attainment*, *poverty status*, *amount of time spent in preschool* (0 = none, 1 = part time, 2 = full time), *number of preschool care arrangements*, *parent-rated health*, *attention skills* (approaches to learning), *self-control*, *social interaction*, *sad/lonely*, and *impulsive/overactive*.

1.6.4 Big Five Inventory

We use two different datasets from the `psych` package that contain personality items. The `bfi` dataset (Big Five Inventory) was collected from 2,800 subjects as a part of the Synthetic Aperture Personality Assessment (Revelle, Wilt, & Rosenthal, 2010). We only included those observations with no missingness, resulting in a final sample size of 2,236. In this dataset, our focus was on the use of the 25 personality items as predictors, which included five items to measure each of the five factors of the Big Five theory of personality. The item data were collected using a 6-point response scale: 1—*Very Inaccurate*, 2—*Moderately Inaccurate*, 3—*Slightly Inaccurate*, 4—*Slightly Accurate*, 5—*Moderately Accurate*, 6—*Very Accurate*. The `epi.bfi` dataset includes 231 observations and contains 13 scales from the Eysenck Personality Inventory and Big Five Inventory. In contrast to the `bfi` dataset, a number of the scales in the `epi.bfi` dataset are more clinical in nature, including anxiety (state and trait) and depression (Beck Depression Inventory).

1.6.5 Holzinger-Swineford

The `Holzinger-Swineford` (Holzinger & Swineford, 1939) dataset is a part of the `lavaan` package and is a classic dataset to illustrate the use of factor analysis and structural equation models. The dataset includes 301 observations. Our focus is on the nine cognitive scales (`X1-X9`), each of which was assessed on seventh- and eighth-grade children across two schools.

1.6.6 PHE Exposure

The data comes from the Maternal PKU Collaborative Study (Koch et al., 2003). The study started in 1984 with the aim of monitoring the pregnancies of women with phenylketonuria (PKU), which is a genetic metabolic defect that disrupts the metabolism of phenylalanine (PHE) into tyrosine. These data are only used for a simple demonstration in Chapter 3, which uses the variables full-scale IQ and PHE in milligrams per deciliter. For additional detail see Widaman and Grimm (2013).

1.6.7 Professor Ratings

The data set includes 27,939 teaching evaluations on a total of 999 professors that were scraped from an online website conforming to the site requirements. The dataset has five variables/columns. The first variable is the unique id of each evaluation. The second variable is the unique id of the professors. The third variable is the numerical rating of a professor with 1 to 5 indicating *worst* to *best* in response to a question "How would you rate this professor as an instructor?" The fourth variable is a response to the question "How hard did you have to work for this class?" with a score of 1 indicating *least hard* and 5 indicating *hardest*. The last variable is the response to an open-ended question prompting individuals to write about their overall experience in the class.

■ 2

The Principles of Machine Learning Research

Applying machine learning takes more than just understanding the methods and algorithms, particularly for social and behavioral research. In this chapter, we discuss our perspective on the philosophical foundation of applying machine learning in the current climate of science, addressing a number of competing notions and ideologies. Specifically, we detail how machine learning research is oriented with four principles that address the goals of machine learning, accurately labeling and describing machine learning research, and how to be transparent about what was done.

2.1 Key Terminology

- Explanation. Research with the aim of understanding the underlying mechanisms.
- Description. Research with the aim of describing relationships or distributions.
- Prediction. Research with the aim of maximally explaining variability in an outcome.
- Inductive. Moves from observation (data) to hypothesis to theory.
- Hypothetico-Deductive. Moves from general to more specific, from theory to observation (data) to confirmation.
- Abductive. Moves from observation (data) to deciding among competing theories to determine which best explain the observation.

- Exploratory Data Analysis. This has traditionally referred to the use of data visualization tools, while in more recent years has encompassed the use of machine learning as an exploratory analytic tool.

2.2 Overview

Increases in the application of machine learning have occurred simultaneously with an elevated emphasis on the use of exploratory research, best encapsulated in the term of *data mining*. Most conceptualizations eschew the use of hypotheses in favor of predictive modeling, or mining the data to see what golden nuggets are yet to be discovered. However, there is a concurrent rise in the re-emphasis of confirmatory modeling, mainly a result of the recent rise in research that has not been able to reproduce hallmark findings in social and behavioral research, termed the *replication crisis* (e.g., Maxwell, Lau, & Howard, 2015). Indeed, questions regarding replication have spanned scientific disciplines, along with an extension from experimental research to the application of highly complex models (e.g., Haibe-Kains et al., 2020). Therefore, the fundamental question that a book advocating for the use of machine learning has to answer is how can we reconcile a convergence of advocacy for both exploratory and confirmatory research? To address this, we first define and distinguish the concepts of confirmation and exploration, concluding with our perspective on how machine learning is paired with theory and fits into the current climate of science.

The use of machine learning in social and behavioral research is less a movement to replace traditional methods of analysis, and more a necessary addition given the increases in the size and kind of available data. But the rationale for machine learning goes beyond being a necessity and also reflects a change in mindset. In the past, scientific culture strongly advocated theoretical simplicity, which may be best captured in: "just as the ability to devise simple but evocative models is the signature of the great scientist so overelaboration and overparameterization is often the mark of mediocrity." (Box, 1976, p. 176). In contrast, more recent conceptions propose that truly understanding various phenomena may require infinite degrees of complexity (Lin, Tegmark, & Rolnick, 2017), which may be best encapsulated by the use of black box algorithms, where complexity is strongly favored over parsimony (e.g., Holm, 2019). These competing notions set up a fundamental tension between old and new, parsimony versus complexity, linear models versus black box algorithms. However, we do not see it in terms of a dichotomy. Instead, our fundamental goal in this book is to propose the use of methods that may add incremental prediction and/or understanding to the use of more traditional, linear models. Further, a subset of the algorithms we detail allows for the analysis of new types of data, such as in the use of social network or text data.

To explicate how machine learning fits into the current climate of science, we propose four principles that we believe will better orient and guide social and behavioral researchers in the application of machine learning:

- Principle #1: Machine Learning Is Not Just Lazy Induction
- Principle #2: Orienting Our Goals Relative to Prediction, Explanation, and Description
- Principle #3: Labeling a Study as Exploratory or Confirmatory Is Too Simplistic
- Principle #4: Report Everything

2.3 Principle #1: Machine Learning Is Not Just Lazy Induction

Machine learning has both benefitted and suffered from outlandish claims regarding the paradigm shift that will occur. An article much maligned, particularly from those with a more traditional scientific background, is the article by Anderson (2008) in *Wired*. This article provides a convenient bogey man for those espousing traditional forms of scientific reasoning, namely, hypothetic-deductive and abductive, in contrast to Anderson's inductive arguments. This debate detracts from a large degree of nuance inherent in applying machine learning algorithms, and maybe more importantly, in the integration of theory with machine learning. This latter piece is often neglected in favor of describing machine learning in simplistic, atheoretical terms, often using the monikers *black box* or some form of the term *predictive*. While the use of machine learning is often motivated by goals that do not take into account explanatory or descriptive aims, we view this as being a consequence of the majority of papers describing machine learning as eschewing theory. Thus, it is our goal to provide additional depth regarding the goals of machine learning, as well as to describe the potential for incorporating theory.

As stated previously, the application of machine learning is often dictated in large part by the data at hand, lending itself to scenarios where the data contain larger numbers of variables, thus larger numbers of competing

FIGURE 2.1. Simplistic depiction of how, particularly in large datasets, the goal of research is to identify those previously validated findings that are most pertinent to explaining phenomena of interest.

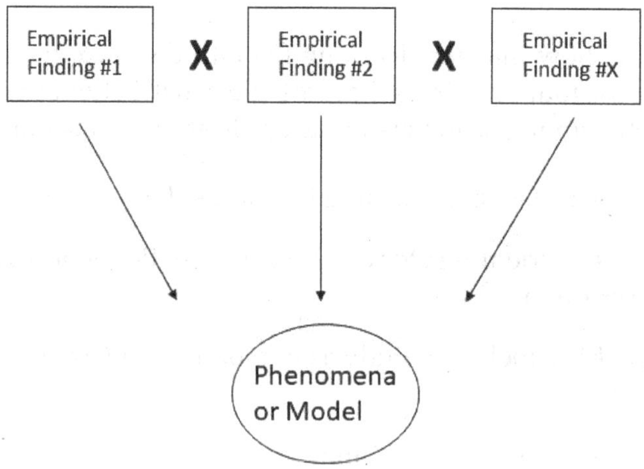

or complementary theoretical findings. This often manifests itself in data that contain variables that have previously been found to be individually related to an outcome or phenomena of interests. This concept is depicted in Figure 2.1. In this scenario, a specific dataset may lend itself to the assessment of which variables contribute to an explanation of the outcome after controlling for every other variable. Principles from machine learning lend themselves to this form of assessment as many algorithms can better handle collinearity issues than traditional linear regression models. The results of the application of a machine learning algorithm may be able to determine which of these many variables are necessary to predict the outcome of interest and may inform subsequent theory.

As an example of this form of *theory development*, or maybe better labelled as *theory expansion*, is Brandmaier, Ram, Wagner, and Gerstorf (2017). This paper used a quadratic growth model to track terminal decline in well-being, while modeling heterogeneity in these trajectories with a number of covariates. Each of the covariates was selected based on prior research findings, with the goal of identifying which covariates were most important, as well as identifying interactions among covariates. To link a number of observed variables to the quadratic growth curve model, the authors used two forms of machine learning: *structural equation model trees* (Brandmaier, von Oertzen, McArdle, & Lindenberger, 2013) and *structural equation modeling forests* (Brandmaier, Prindle, McArdle, & Lindenberger, 2016). The authors found that social participation and physical health factors were among the most important variables, and there was an interaction among these variables in the structural equation model tree. Specifically, the authors found that for those with low social participation, disability was the strongest correlate of differences in the well-being trajectories. In contrast, for those with high social participation, spending a considerable time in the hospital determined varying trajectories. Therefore, this study was able to identify that social participation, physical health factors, and hospital stays were the most important factors to explain well-being trajectories.

2.3.1 Complexity

Brandmaier et al. (2017) also highlight an additional question researchers utilizing machine learning must answer: What degree of complexity do I wish to interpret? Despite this, it is common for researchers to seek simple results. This may be best exemplified in the desire to identify a small number of large effects among many interrelated variables. Not only is this unlikely to occur in practice, particularly in social and behavioral data where the variables are often all related to one another to at least a small degree (e.g., the *crud* factor; Meehl, 1990), but forcing this structure upon the results comes at a price (detailed in Chapter 3). A second way that this manifests itself is in the desire to select a final model, treating the results as if they reflect the *true* model. Not only does this strategy negate the fact that other models evidence model fits that are only minutely worse, despite these models differing largely in functional form (and thus their explanations as to the underlying relationships), but it also bludgeons nuance in understanding the underlying relationships.

We borrow the term *explanatory pluralism* (e.g., Kendler, 2005) to describe the common phenomenon of observing multiple algorithms evidencing almost identical predictive performance along with very little differentiation in the importance of predictor variables. In fact for this latter piece, it is a common experience to remove the most important predictor from the model and not see an evident decrement in predictor performance. We use the term *explanatory pluralism* to point out that there are multiple explanations for the functional form between predictors and an outcome, as well as to which variables contribute to the prediction of the outcome. This is obviously not always the case, but is more common than not when predictors come from interrelated constructs. Observing such results makes answering the study's original questions and hypotheses exceedingly difficult.

In contrast to most other statistical texts that contain empirical examples that are, for the most part, relatively neat, we primarily use datasets that were collected as a part of large studies, containing many interrelated variables, thus muddying the simplicity to the modeling and interpretation.

Our goal in this is to better prepare researchers for the inevitable trials and tribulations that come in analyzing real data with machine learning algorithms, particularly so that researchers do not believe that their data are unique in the sense that the analysis results are less than perfectly clear.

2.3.2 Abduction

In a stark contrast to how machine learning was applied in Brandmaier et al. (2017), machine learning is often discussed and presented in a relatively mindless way, akin to the sole discussion of null hypothesis significance testing in introductory textbooks (Gigerenzer, 2004). While there is certainly a potential benefit to the mindless application of black box algorithms to maximize prediction, there is a much larger degree of nuance and integration with theory than is often discussed. A less discussed rationale is a shift in how social and behavioral science is performed, namely, decreasing support for hypothetico-deductive methods. This can be seen as a natural byproduct of a concurrent rise in the focus on complexity and the inability of researchers to explicitly state theories that can be directly translated to mathematical models. This, paired with criticisms of the hypothetico-deductive approach stemming from the replication crisis, has made the conditions ripe for the advent of a new modeling paradigm. While machine learning can be characterized as a set of algorithms, we see it more as an alternative method for conducting psychological science.

As previously mentioned, machine learning has often been described as inductive, which is in contrast to the most prominent account of scientific inference, abduction (e.g., see Haig, 2014). This also relates to whether machine learning can be used for explanation; however, before we discuss machine learning and explanation, we wish to show how machine learning can be used for abduction. Following Psillos (2002) and Cabrera (2020), abduction can be described as a four-step process:

1. F is some fact or collection of facts

2. Hypothesis H1, if true, would explain F.

3. H1 is a better explanation of F than its competitors

4. Therefore, probably, H1 is true

The important point here is Step 1, where Cabrera (2020) uses the term *facts*, whereas Psillos (2002) uses data (facts, observations, givens). This mimics what Cattell (1966) termed the *inductive-hypothetico-deductive* spiral, which is quite similar to most accounts of abduction (also see Box, 1976). However, most areas of social and behavioral research have at least some degree of research foundation, so purely inductive research is unlikely. Instead, most research combines some degree of theoretical backing and uncertainty. Our purpose in highlighting abduction is that a large portion of research is motivated by identifying conclusions that synthesize competing or previously disconnected theoretical findings or perspectives.

In social and behavioral research, data are very rarely the main unit subjected to explanation; instead, research tries to explain effects (van Rooij & Baggio, 2021), phenomena (e.g., Haig, 2014), or more broadly, empirical relations. Thus, there are really two steps in this process. First, there is an identification of facts, effects, phenomena, or relations, which is followed by the explanatory phase. Using Brandmaier et al. (2017) as an example, the phenomena could be identified as: quadratic growth in well-being trajectories. Building on this, it is up to machine learning to discern among multiple explanations for these well-being trajectories in the form of previously validated covariates. Assessing among these empirical relations to identify what is most pertinent allows researchers to derive more parsimonious explanations for phenomena, namely, by whittling away those factors that explain less in a conditional as opposed to unconditional sense.

A number of papers that attempt to place machine learning among scientific methods focus too much on the ultimate goal of aligning hypotheses with observations in an explanatory framework (Haig, 2019; Cabrera, 2020), to the detriment of understanding the aims of machine learning, which most often align with prediction or with the identification of what is termed observation or fact. To provide an example, we detail the application of machine learning to suicide research, which has seen a number of applications (see Burke, Ammerman, & Jacobucci, 2019) with varying degrees of predictive success (see Jacobucci, Littlefield, Millner, Kleiman, & Steinley, 2021). While prediction is ultimately the main goal in most papers, a tertiary goal of the majority of papers is to derive a better understanding of which theoretically informed predictors are most important, and among these, which demonstrate nonlinear relationships (see Burke et al., 2019 for examples). As most theories of suicide are relatively simplistic (e.g., only involving a handful of variables), establishing the relative importance of specific relationships and identifying their functional form can then be used to provide greater specificity to these theories. Further, while some research posits that there needs to be a causal-nomological connection between two variables in order to trust this relationship for prediction purposes (Cabrera, 2020), in most research scenarios this is obviated by the process in which the variables were selected, as most studies only collect theoretically relevant variables.

The Role of Data One motivation for the use of machine learning is that it is seen as a natural opposition to the traditional reductionist approach. Many areas of social and behavioral data have identified a host of potential risk factors, casual variables, mediators, etc. However, given that most of these factors are interrelated, it remains to be seen which of these factors were most important when studied in conjunction with others. Big data, and the use of machine learning, facilitated large-scale analyses that included well-validated independent variables, even when the independent variables correlated to a significant extent.

2.4 Principle #2: Orienting Our Goals Relative to Prediction, Explanation, and Description

What specifically are the goals of machine learning? At possibly the simplest level, our goals could either focus on (1) prediction, meaning we focus almost solely on Y, or (2) identifying relationships, with the goal of trying to shed light on how X associates with Y (see Figure 2.2; Breiman, 2001b). Breiman (2001b) uses these two goals to differentiate between the *algorithmic modeling* and *data modeling* cultures in statistics, with the data modeling group focusing on extracting information about the relationship between X and Y, while the algorithmic modeling group focuses on the prediction of Y.

We can go beyond just the distinction between prediction and extracting information as the goals of research. Shmueli (2010) differentiates *causal explanation, empirical prediction,* and *descriptive modeling*. Machine learning is often described in terms of giving favor to prediction rather than explanation (Breiman, 2001b; Shmueli, 2010; Yarkoni & Westfall, 2017). Although using machine learning for causal inference (explanation) is a more recent area of inquiry, our application will favor the application of machine learning for description and prediction. However, we view our aim of using

FIGURE 2.2. In *data modeling* culture, the primary concern is learning the relationship between X and Y (Nature), whereas the *algorithmic modeling* culture is solely focused on explaining Y. Note that this is adapted from Breiman (2001b).

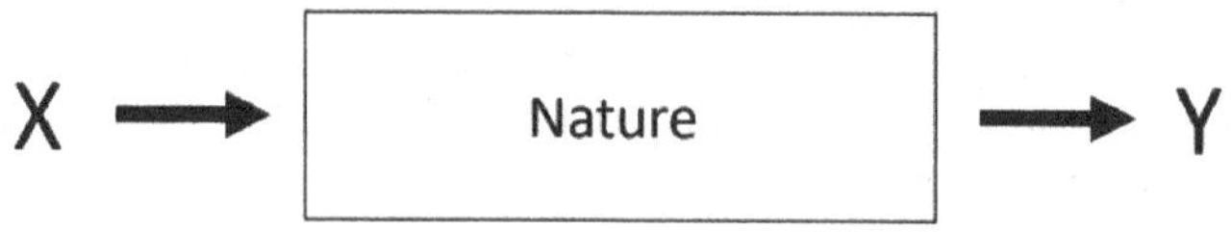

machine learning for descriptive modeling as a means to possibly inform later explanatory investigations.

Before providing additional description, we first need to explain what we mean by both prediction and description. Going back to our definition of prediction in Chapter 1, our goal in using machine learning for prediction is to minimize the distance from $\hat{Y}$and Y, with $\hat{Y}$ being our model predicted outcome and Y being the observed outcome. Importantly, Y needs to be from a dataset that was not used to train the model (see Chapter 3), thus we are able to derive a less biased assessment of the model's predictive performance. $\hat{Y}$ is generated from the same dataset of Y, however, this is based on a fixed model that was created on a different dataset. Once we have both Y and $\hat{Y}$, there are a number of performance metrics that we can calculate (see Chapter 3) that answer: "How well did we predict Y?"

In using machine learning for social and behavioral research, our aim is rarely just prediction, but encompasses some degree of balance between prediction and description. Importantly, we can view the goals of prediction, description, and explanation as existing in a three-dimensional space (Shmueli, 2010). Description in terms of modeling the relationship between a set of predictors and an outcome is most clearly captured by the generalized linear model, as each coefficient in the model can be interpreted. In contrast to description, pure prediction can be best depicted in the use of deep learning (Goodfellow, Bengio, & Courville, 2016), where the relationship between the predictors and outcome is a function of an extremely large number of parameters, each of which relates the predictor space to the outcome in a nonlinear fashion (see Figure 2.3).

Just as in regression, performance metrics can be calculated, however, understanding the relationships between predictors and the outcome is almost impossible. However, one of the primary algorithms that we detail, random forests, can capture extremely complex relationships, thus often demonstrating the best predictive performance relative to other algorithms, but also allows for some degree of interpretation. Individual relationships are not as clear as they are in linear models, however, variable importance metrics are calculated to ascertain which variables contribute the most to the prediction of the outcome variable.

While many methods can be usced to evaluate prediction, we take a perspective that focuses on whether the methods can be used to fix a set of model parameters, and thus generate individual predictions in settings where data are fed. We think of implementing a screening algorithm in a hospital, where a patient fills out a questionnaire, the answers are entered, and used to generate a predicted quantity (often a probability). Instead of saying that researchers should instead spend more time focusing on pre-

FIGURE 2.3. Note that in the neural network (right) we follow the convention of representing manifest predictors (X) and the outcome (Y) as circles instead of the typical psychometric convention of squares.

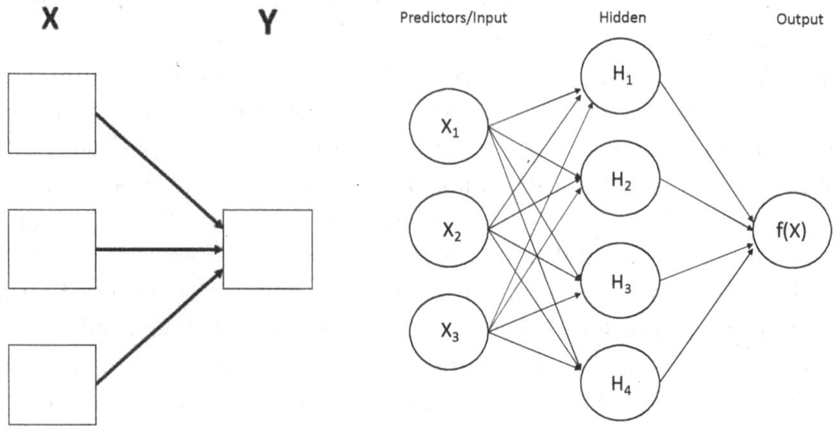

diction as opposed to explanation (Yarkoni & Westfall, 2017), it may be more productive to advocate for incorporating predictive aims and evaluation into studies that are primarily concerned with explanation (e.g., see Shmueli, 2010). In social and behavioral research, it is rarely the case that researchers may be solely interested in prediction, as descriptive or explanatory goals can almost always be seen as beneficial supplements. Further, it is rarely the case that something is not lost by only focusing on prediction in research studies. As an example of this, few machine learning studies in clinical research have found that algorithms that afford no interpretation of variable importance or functional form (e.g., neural networks or support vector machines), clearly outperform algorithms that allow for some interpretation (e.g., random forests or gradient boosting machines) or traditional statistical methods (regression). As such, focusing solely on prediction would result in a loss of information in the form of what variables contribute to modeling the outcome of interest. While incorporating prediction into explanatory studies sounds great, in practice, there are a number of challenges. First is what is meant by the term *predict*. In a large amount of psychological research, the term predict is used in various ways, from whether a theory can predict a numerical point value (Meehl, 1990), which can be differentiated from a predictive task (i.e., use of the Minnesota Multiphasic Personality Inventory to predict a clinical outcome; Meehl, 1990), predicting future behavior (forecasting), among others. The most common way the term *predict* is used in social and behavioral research is likely to denote the generation of expected values for an outcome of interest based on a set of predictor or independent variables. This relates to the assessment of between-person differences in a variable of interest, given a set of predictor variables. Further, there is often an effect size connotation added to predict, often in the form of assessing whether an outcome can be accurately predicted. As a consequence, two researchers could be conducting similar explanatory studies, wishing to incorporate predictive aims, and come away with quite different strategies for incorporating prediction.

Further, we do not have to identify a fixed point in this three-dimensional space, but can test multiple algorithms each of which gives varying weights to prediction and description. In most circumstances, we would advocate for testing multiple types of algorithms, each of which has varying strengths with respect to prediction and description. For instance, we almost always advocate for including a linear model, which if that model fits best, results in clearly interpretable results[1]. However, if random forests fits best, there will be some degree of limitation regarding interpretation, as individual relationships are difficult to assess. Thus, the researcher does not have to assign their preferences a priori, but can choose a range of weightings between prediction and description that directly informs which algorithms are tested. We believe that it is better to be more liberal in the algorithms that are included than the converse, as for instance in not including a linear model, researchers may falsely conclude that there are interactions or nonlinear effects present as a result of only using random forests.

An important component to both descriptive and predictive modeling is that each type of modeling can support the other. For instance, researchers are more likely to trust an algorithm that they can interpret, regardless of the predictive performance (Pearl, 2019). Further, while understanding individual relationships can be directly tied to theory, assessing predictive performance on unseen data can add incremental information on the magnitude of effect that is likely to be seen in future research. Lastly, just as extremely complex results can be difficult to assess, overly simple results also have drawbacks. For instance, we can see this in research regarding decision trees, one of the most used machine learning algorithms that also forms the basis for more complex algorithms such as random forests. Although small trees may be highly interpretable, they may not be trusted due to their overly simplistic interpretation of the functional relationship (Freitas, 2014).

---

[1]We note, however, that there are some scenarios where this is not the case, such as when the number of predictors is large relative to the sample size. See Chapter 4 for additional detail.

In some research scenarios there is little flexibility with regard to description. One example is the case of a single predictor—there are a limited number of options for modeling this single relationship. At the other extreme is when the number of predictors is extremely large. For example, if the predictors represent a large battery of depression scales, with each scale including 10 to 30 items, then there is likely to be a large number of small effects. If the sample size is large, a majority of these coefficients are likely to be significant and contribute to prediction. As an example, Mottus and Rozgonjuk (2019) found that increasing the number of personality items included to predict age improved out-of-sample predictive performance, such that 300 items predicted better than 120, which predicted better than 30, which improved upon just using Big Five domain scores. In an example such as this, though each of the 300 individual relationships can be examined, and interpreted, one must take into account the effects of the other items that contribute to the prediction of Y, making description in a linear model less clear. On the other hand, summed scores could be created for each scale, thus drastically simplifying the number of parameters in the linear model. However, just as in the above example, this almost always results in a decrement in performance, thus making it unlikely that both prediction and explanation can be maximized with one method. This highlights that there is often flexibility not only with the algorithms that are tested, but also in the predictors included, and whether summaries of the predictors are used (e.g., summed scores), with each choice having consequences for both prediction and description.

Oftentimes, the distinction between description and explanation is less than perfectly clear. A statistical method that exemplifies this is structural equation models (SEMs). Discussed further in Chapters 7 through 10, SEMs involve the specification of regression equations between both latent and observed variables, while often imposing a number of weak and strong constraints. While SEMs are seemingly equivalent to linear regression, the imposition of constraints imply causal relationships between variables (Bollen & Pearl, 2013). As a result, using SEMs means favoring explanation over description given the requirements of imposing specific constraints into the model.

The final point we make with respect to the second principle is that research often does not just involve a single study or paper, but a series of steps, with each step encompassing multiple goals. As an example, in relation to machine learning, this may involve first assessing which variables contribute to the prediction of Y (falling under both description and prediction), and then in follow-up studies, assessing these selected variables across multiple time points to ascertain causal relations with Y. Further, we can include prediction as a part of these follow-up studies to determine the magnitude of effect for *Y*. Notably, the neglect of incorporating aspects of prediction into explanatory research is one of the causes of the replication crisis (e.g., see Yarkoni & Westfall, 2017). The benefit of combining explanation and prediction is well described in Shmueli (2010): "The consequence of neglecting to include predictive modeling and testing alongside explanatory modeling is losing the ability to test the relevance of existing theories and to discover new causal mechanisms."

2.5 Principle #3: Labeling a Study as Exploratory or Confirmatory Is Too Simplistic

Often, the terms *exploratory* or *confirmatory* are used to provide a meta description of the research being conducted and to describe research that lies on the continuum between exploratory and confirmatory. Although this continuum is not difficult to understand, at the very least, most researchers could agree on the research that falls at the end points. Fully confirmatory research entails full theoretical justification for study design and the analyses performed (these studies are often experimental in nature), whereas exploratory research entails no theoretical justification and is often described as the "kitchen sink" approach. However, difficulties arise in assessing research that falls in between: theoretical justification for variable inclusion, but not what types of relationships are examined; partial inclusion of nontheoretically justified variables; transforming a variable-based sample distribution; and studies with little theoretical justification, to name a few. As described earlier, this becomes increasingly difficult as both the number of variables increase and as the algorithm options expand.

Machine learning is often described as the kitchen sink approach: just throw everything in and see what results come out. This is often depicted as the miner from the 1800s holding up a golden nugget, providing an unrealistic depiction of the process of using data *mining*. In practice, researchers often use theoretical justification for the the sample and variables analyzed, and even may hypothesize on the presence of specific interactions. However, there are no hypotheses for each variable included, which variables will be most important, and the degree of prediction error. Obviously, these characteristics do not justify a label of confirmatory research, and because there is some theoretical justification, it is not entirely exploratory research either. But how much more confirmatory (or less exploratory) is this than the kitchen sink approach?

If our goal was to label specific practices according to their level of accordance with confirmatory or exploratory research, what would this look like? We created Figure 2.4 along these lines, labeling points on this continuum with specific practices.

FIGURE 2.4. Exploratory—confirmatory continuum.

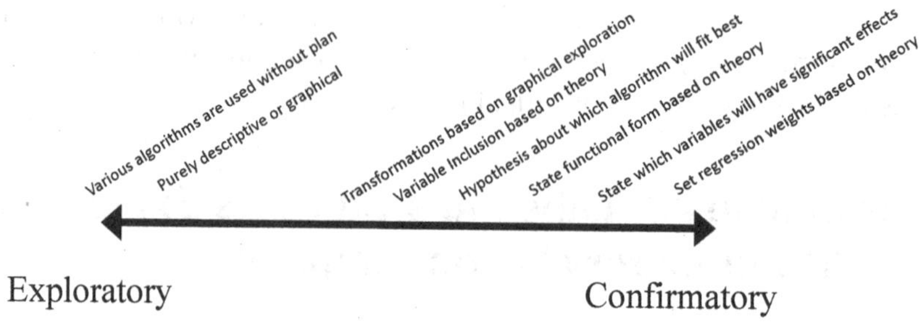

These labels and practices represent just a subset of possible characteristics to a data analysis. We have reached the logical conclusion in trying to describe the pairing of machine learning and social and behavioral research:

> What use is a continuum if you cannot reasonably ascribe a marker on that continuum?

Instead of labeling an analytical approach according to this continuum, we instead advocate for fully describing the theoretical justification for each aspect of the analysis and approach. As an example, are the predictors included based on theory? If a subset is, which ones? There are advantages and disadvantages to different degrees of theoretical specification. For instance, only including theoretically justified predictors can increase one's confidence in the generalizability of the results, whereas nontheoretically justified predictors offer an opportunity to discover unexpected associations. Additionally, we describe an approach to modeling that uses a comparison across differing degrees of complexity: *main effects* only versus *interactions* and *nonlinear effects*. This has important consequences for the resulting theoretical conclusions and subsequent interpretations, while not neatly fitting into a dichotomy between exploratory and confirmatory research.

This dichotomy is typically applied to algorithm use as well, with linear regression being a confirmatory (causal) modeling approach, and algorithms, such as random forests, purely exploratory. This becomes particularly difficult when attempting to describe models that are not supervised in nature, such as certain text mining algorithms.

2.5.1 Model Size

The question of assessing the degree of confirmation becomes more difficult in the case of complex models, such as SEMs, dynamical systems, and network models. *Simply put, the simplicity of stating and testing hypotheses in traditional experimental designs does not translate to complex models.* As the number of variables increases, and the models grow in size, it becomes increasingly difficult to specify hypotheses that account for every aspect of the model. Simply stating a one-line null hypothesis and one-line alternative hypothesis no longer holds. Additionally, with larger models comes more ways to be wrong, thus rejecting a hypothesis. As a result, *confirmatory* has come to mean something else in these situations, taken as almost a straw man argument. Instead, by saying *confirmatory* researchers really mean a minimal degree of specification—not completely exploratory. As models grow, this becomes a more and more tortuous practice, until the word *confirmatory* ceases to mean anything.

This difficulty may be a contributing factor to why there is a dearth of complex models in many social and behavioral publications. This leads to the specification of many simple relationships. For instance Lieberman and Cunningham (2009) found that a randomly selected issue of the *Journal of Personality and Social Psychology* had an average of 93 statistical tests performed per paper.

An additional contributing factor is an explicit bias against complexity—thus there is a preference for parsimony. One hallmark of this viewpoint comes from Box (1976):

> Since all models are wrong the scientist cannot obtain a "correct" one by excessive elaboration. On the contrary following William of Occam he should seek an economical description of natural phenomena. Just as the ability to devise simple but evocative models is the signature of the great scientist so over-elaboration and overparameterization is often the mark of mediocrity. (p. 792)

Selecting the correct model is indeed extremely difficult and there are a number of competing factors that influence the model selection (see Chapter 3); however, this idea is in stark contrast to more recent emphasis on embracing complexity (e.g., Fried & Robinaugh, 2020). If you think of brain functioning as an infinitely complex set of interactions (Brodmann, 1994), the question becomes, how can we understand various subaspects without the use of extremely complex algorithms or models? The traditional idea has been to test subcomponents of processes thought to be extremely complex, as this more narrow evaluation should generalize to an integration with the whole. However, in some cases this does not work. For instance, Saucier and Iurino (2020) derived a high-dimensional personality structure from a natural-language lexicon. From this high-dimensional structure they were able to identify the Big Five from within this structure, but the converse did not hold, as they were unable to zoom out and expand from the Big Five structure to the high-dimensional structure.

2.5.2 Level of Hypothesis

Most researchers describe a *hypothesis* as a specific, well-formulated statement. Part of the motivation for this stems from the philosophy of science's fixation on hard sciences, such as physics, where general laws take mathematical forms. In reality, particularly in social and behavioral research, a hypothesis is often "nothing but an ebullition of alternative ideas and a pure emotion — consuming speculative curiosity about a certain aspect of the world" (Cattell, 1966). A further problem with the term hypothesis is its generalization from an introduction to statistics formulation (i.e., H_0 = no effect) to complex theoretical formulations. A hypothesis taking the form of a single sentence necessarily denotes some form of reductionism from theory, whereas a hypothesis matching the degree of theoretical complexity would require at the very least a paragraph of formulation. Even with the more recent calls to match theory with mathematical structures in the areas of computational modeling (e.g., Fried & Robinaugh, 2020), the degree of complexity necessitates some degree of simplification (DeYoung & Krueger, 2020).

In more traditional social and behavioral research, stating hypotheses takes the form of whether or not an effect is zero. This effect typically refers to the influence of a singular variable, often a grouping resulting from an experimental manipulation. Other times, nonexperimental research may report hypotheses that refer to whether a regression coefficient is nonzero, which can become more complex in the presence of more than one predictor. In research settings such as these, where the number of variables is small, it is relatively straightforward to state and test hypotheses. Two factors inherent in more contemporary research make this process far more complex: larger numbers of variables and the ease of specifying models with complex relationships. Simply put, the more variables in an analysis, the more complicated it is to test a purely confirmatory model. This process is eased if the majority of the variables are included as *confounders;* however, controlling for these variables is often more complex than researchers assume (Westfall & Yarkoni, 2016).

Next, we discuss complications in the use of hypothesis testing with large numbers of variables. The most common way in which this occurs

FIGURE 2.5. Figures depicting two different mediation models.

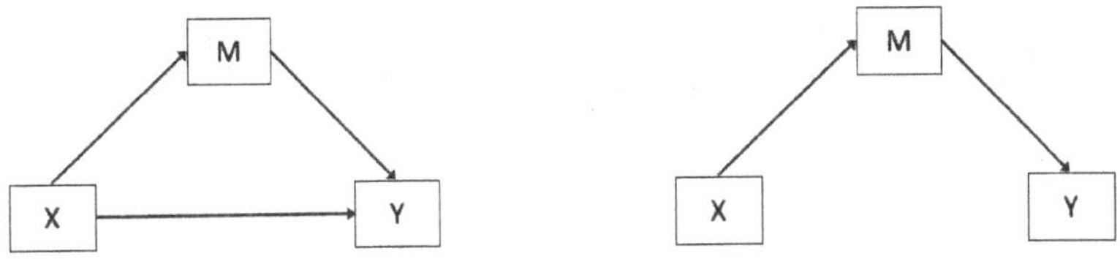

is with the specification of theoretically informed models, often through the use of a SEM. In contrast to a model that includes paths between all variables, thus fitting a covariance (correlation) matrix perfectly, this involves the placement of constraints in the model based on theory, often taking the form of removing paths between variables (i.e., setting these parameters to 0). One of the most common models is a mediation model, examples of which are displayed in Figure 2.5.

In this figure, the left panel depicts a full mediation model. More importantly, though, is that this is a *saturated* model — every variable has a relationship (don't worry about the direction of the arrows) with every other variable. Saturated models have no misfit. In contrast, the right pane has one arrow removed between X and Y, representing a constraint that the *direct* relationship between X and Y is 0. There can still be a relationship between X and Y, although in this model it is an *indirect* path through M. Our purpose in describing both models is that they represent different theoretical ideas, which can be generalized to models containing more variables, paths, and different forms of relationships (e.g., nonlinear).

This form of modeling requires a higher degree of specification because each path needs to have a justification, and the model as a whole must relate to a specific hypothesis. However, a large number of variables can be related to a specific hypothesis. This increased flexibility allows not only for the input of theory, but also for balancing the specification of theoretical relationships with uncertainty as to the types of relationships in other parts of the model. The default label ascribed to the statistical analysis of large numbers of variables is exploration, as inputting theory into the model is rarely done in practice. We discuss this in Chapter 8, but first demonstrate it with the model depicted in Figure 2.6.

2.5.3 Example

To make our perspective more clear as it relates to larger models, we work with the model depicted in Figure 2.6.

FIGURE 2.6. Example of a multiple indicator-multiple cause (MIMIC) model.

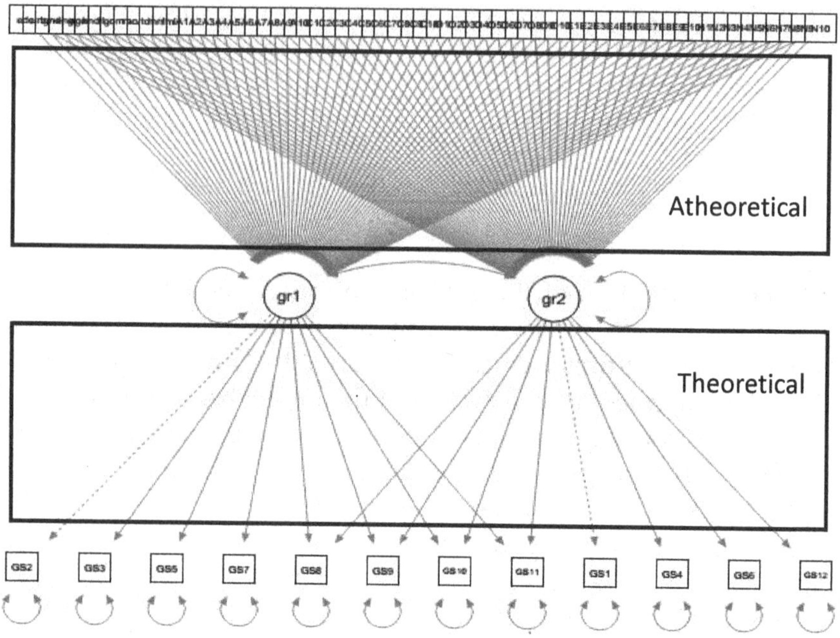

In this model, the formation of the latent variables has a large number of constraints included for identification. For instance, the observed variable *GS*2 does not have a directed path stemming from the latent variable *gr*2, meaning that there are a number of hidden constraints dictating that *GS*2 does not have a directive relationship with multiple other observed variables in the model. While this part of the model is specified based on theory, the regression coefficients from each of the predictors (other personality items) to both of the latent variables do not include any constraints, and in this sense we could search for which of these paths is nonzero, and therefore contributing to the prediction of a latent variable. Instead of labeling an analysis such as this as atheoretical (or exploratory), it is more appropriate to define what degree of theory is specified and with respect to what parts of the model. Our point here is that with complex models, the model can be comprised of varying degrees of theory, as in our example we constrained the makeup of the latent variables based on theory, while *searching* or *exploring* the predictor space to determine which variables explain some degree of variance in the latent variables.

Part of the issue is that recent papers and or books on the application of machine learning for social and behavioral research make little to no mention of the role of theory. For instance, Dwyer et al. (2018) only men-

FIGURE 2.7. Relatively simple example depicting two different models with uncertainty with respect to specific parameters.

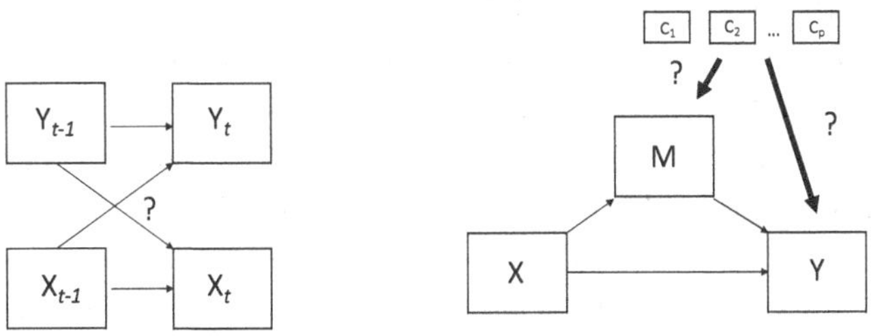

tions the role of theory in making decisions regarding outcomes. While a number of articles discuss the role of machine learning in theory building or refinement (e.g., Chapman, Weiss, & Duberstein, 2016), very little detail is given with regard to how this is accomplished. In fact, while a large amount of research acknowledges that theory generation, refinement, and any form of acceptance/confirmation is a long process, very little detail is given regarding the intermediate stages, and what types of methods are most appropriate for refining a nascent theory. This stage of theory refinement does not fit neatly into being described as inductive, hypothetico-deductive, or abductive, or to the concepts of exploration and confirmation. The closest parallel is that of Bayesian updating; however, most applications in this realm deal with relatively simple forms of modeling (for counters, see Gelman, 2004). To address this, some recent publications have characterized their proposed methods that do not fit into any of these neat boxes as *semi-confirmatory* (Huang, Chen, & Weng, 2017). The question is whether the term *semi-confirmatory* makes sense. To be confirmatory, one would be using hypothetico-deductive reasoning, to appraise a theoretical model. To translate from strict confirmatory to something that is not fully exploratory, there are two possible routes. The first is that the theoretical model evidences a significant level of misfit and therefore discounts the theory. Second, one could acknowledge uncertainty with respect to part of the model at the outset, and include this as part of the theoretical specification.

A more simplistic example than is depicted in Figure 2.6 is displayed in Figure 2.7.

The left panel depicts a simplistic two timepoint model, where each variable has an autoregressive relationship within, with uncertainty regarding the coupling relationship from X_{t-1} to Y_t, and from Y_{t-1} to X_t. However, this degree of uncertainty as manifested in two paths is something that relates directly to what a hypothesis would address, as in the simplest case regarding a nonrisky hypothesis one would state either the presence or nonpresence of a relationship for both paths. The left panel of Figure 2.7 is contrasted with the right panel, where a mediation model is specified, and there is uncertainty regarding the influence of a large number of covariates on both the mediator and Y variable. Modeling of this nature could progress in two ways, either as a one-step or two-step process, with the distinction relying on whether the fit of the mediation component needs to be assessed. In practice, it is likely that the mediation model already has support, and researchers wish to expand the theory to take potential confounding variables into account, or variables could possibly account for heterogeneity. However, just as we ran into problems in labeling the left panel as anything but confirmatory, the same can be ascribed to the right panel.

To specify this model, one would first have to posit the potential for heterogeneity or confounding, collect these variables as a part of the study design, and include these effects in the statistical model. As such, this example is better conceptualized as confirmatory, with a less specific hypothesis. This relates back to an acknowledgement of exploratory and confirmatory being a continuum, not dichotomy (e.g., Scheel, Tiokhin, Isager, & Lakens, 2021; Fife & Rodgers, 2022). An additional term that has been used is *theory-guided exploration* (Brandmaier et al., 2013). However, this phrase is somewhat redundant, as any exploration in a field with a theoretical basis as broad as psychology, sociology, etc., is guided at least somewhat by theory. This reminds one of the most biting criticisms of induction, namely, that observation is permeated by theory (e.g., see Chalmers, 2013). Thus, the phrase *theory-guided exploration* is really just a fuzzy reference to exploration, in a similar vein to how the phrase *semi-confirmatory* refers to a vague version of confirmation. Most attempts to label a statistical analysis as exploratory versus confirmatory, or based on deductive versus induction, negate the fact that the predominant stage of theory integration takes place in the study design, and thus is largely moot by the time an analysis takes place. The above attempts to define recently developed machine learning methods has, in our estimation, resulted in more confusion than clarity.

We view a more productive way to think about modeling in general, and more specifically, the role of machine learning in social and behavioral research is to eschew the labels of *exploratory* and *confirmatory*, and instead describe the goals of research as either following theory generation, development, or appraisal (see Haig, 2014). Further, these three phases of theory construction are clearly aligned with the goal of explanation, of which there is less of a clear footing for the underlying goals when using the labels *exploratory* or *confirmatory*. Namely, both the phrases *theory-guided exploration* and *semi-confirmatory* are aimed at theory generation and development, specifically addressing the drawbacks to strict adherence to hypothetico-deductive reasoning: "Explicit hypotheses tested with confirmatory research usually do not spring from an intellectual void but instead are gained through exploratory research" (Jaeger & Halliday, 1998, p. S64). While exploration is most often discussed in terms of theory generation, often using the moniker *fishing* to denote a search for effects, most new algorithm developments address theory development, which is aligned with the right pane of Figure 2.7. In this, the mediation model has theoretical support from prior studies, but can be expanded through the inclusion of important confounding variables or those that account for heterogeneity.

2.5.4 Types of Relationships

The second complication that has arisen more recently with respect to hypothesis testing is the type of relationship specified. Historically, social and behavioral research has almost solely considered linear relationships, either in the form of analysis of variance or regression models. This occurred for a number of reasons, partially due to difficulties in obtaining large sample sizes, thus power was a main concern, or due to the available computational machinery. Currently, researchers have access to larger sample sizes than in the past, and there are generally few limitations to the type of analyses that can be run (e.g., supercomputing infrastructures). This has opened up the door to a researcher's ability to specify interactions or various types of nonlinear relationships as a hypothesis. The difficulty in this lies in the higher degree of detail needed; is it a linear interaction and at what values of X, or what type of nonlinear relationships, quadratic, cubic, or alternative? Simply put, this increased complexity may not be in line with traditional hypothesis testing. Instead, softer forms of hypothesis testing may be more amenable. For example:

- It is hypothesized that interactions exist between a subset of X_1 through X_5.
- A model that allows for interactions between predictors will fit better than a main effects only model.
- Nonlinear relationships exist between X_1 through X_{10} and Y, thus a boosting model with stumps will fit better than linear regression.
- A model that allows for a higher degree of nonlinearity will be a better fit to a model with all possible interaction and quadratic effects.

Note that in these hypotheses, our focus is at the model level, not at specific relationships or variables. In most machine learning applications, there are too many variables and possible relationships to describe hypotheses at this level of granularity. Instead, we propose a more model-based approach, in line with common testing procedures in analysis of variance and SEM (Maxwell, Delaney, & Kelley, 2017), but applied to machine learning (Hong, Jacobucci, & Lubke, 2020)[2].

Even more general hypotheses (adapted from Chollet & Allaire, 2018):

- The outcome can be predicted with a specific set of predictors better than chance.

Or, given that it is typical in social and behavioral research to have at least marginally related variables in the dataset:

- The dataset at hand is sufficiently informative to model a relationship between the set of predictors and outcome.

Our goal in this is to not transfer the continuum of exploratory versus confirmatory to how specific a hypothesis is, but instead advocate for researchers to be more forthcoming for what degree of theoretical input is imparted into various aspects of a research study. As a simplistic template, we differentiate between theory-based and non-theory- (i.e., atheoretical) based decision on multiple aspects of a research study in Table 2.1.

[2]We discuss this procedure in more detail in Chapter 5 after providing an overview of ensemble techniques.

TABLE 2.1. Differentiation between Theory-Based and Non-Theory-Based Components of the Study. This is not meant to be comprehensive but to implore researchers to add additional detail to the degree of theory imparting into the many decisions that go into planning and executing an analysis.

	Theory Based	Non-Theory Based
Algorithm	Algorithm inclusion based on hypothesized relationships in data	Algorithm inclusion based on convenience or maximizing prediction
Hyperparameters	Set to be single values or a small set	Based on software defaults or test a wide range
Variable inclusion	Each predictor is justified	Variables are chosen based on convenience
Functional form	All or a subset of relationships are specified	Using ensembles to derive variable importance
Model choice for interpretation	Prefer parsimony	Prefer best fit

What we see in Table 2.1 is the multiple facets to the role of theory in an analysis plan. Perhaps the use of exploratory or confirmatory to describe each aspect is warranted; however, we chose to use the distinction of theory versus nontheory (atheoretical) to better remove ourselves from tradition. Our goal here is to not further complicate an already complex process. Instead, we hope for a culture change, one that doesn't require every paper that uses some form of machine learning to be labeled as exploratory.

2.5.5 Exploratory Data Analysis

Our goal in explaining Principle #3 is to be as specific and clear as possible when differentiating theoretical from atheoretical input. To accomplish this, we decided against providing history and background on the confirmatory versus exploratory research debate, along with describing the subcomponents to each, particularly exploratory (for a recent discussion of this, see Fife & Rodgers, 2012). Here, we want to briefly describe the role that exploratory data analysis as traditionally defined plays a role in machine learning. The seminal work on exploratory data analysis (EDA) is often considered to be Tukey (1977). Tukey (1977) almost exclusively focuses on the use of data visualization as a means to carry out EDA. However, as the tools available to researchers have changed, so has what falls under the umbrella of EDA, with most recent descriptions including machine learning as being under the EDA umbrella (e.g., Fife & Rodgers, 2012).

The one distinction between confirmatory and exploratory that we do find important is in what data are used for each. Most research recommends that EDA should be conducted on different data from which is used for confirmatory data analysis (Behrens, 1997). We almost completely agree with this (see Chapter 3 for detail on cross-validation), but note that one often should perform some form of cross-validation even in analyses that could be deemed confirmatory. For instance, if a researcher wished to test a SEM that was specified based on prior theory, but included a large number of variables, and a relatively small dataset, some degree of overfitting would likely occur. Given this, it may be beneficial to perform a type of cross-validation to derive more accurate model fit statistics, or use bootstrap sampling to derive p-values for the parameters. Again, just as the distinction between confirmatory and exploratory becomes less clear in the presence of a large number of variables, so too does multiple components thought to be important aspects of both exploration and confirmation.

The main reason why we do not advocate for differentiating confirmatory versus exploratory data analysis is not because we see this distinction as continuum, as others hold this same view (e.g., see Fife & Rodgers, 2022). Instead, it is because lumping things under a single term is far too simplistic for the degree of complexity facing researchers with large datasets and powerful statistical tools at their disposal. As described in Table 2.1, there are at least *five* possible dimensions to the theoretical versus atheoretical distinction, thus describing a study as exploratory or confirmatory lessenss a large degree of nuance to modern research. Of course there are exceptions to this, particularly in relatively simple experimental designs; however, this book advocates for more complex modeling, and we equally advocate for further high-dimensional theoretical modeling as atheoretical modeling.

2.6 Principle #4: Report Everything

Our main point is a reiteration of others' calls for being honest (McArdle, 2012): if you have hypotheses, state them, or better yet, preregister them before beginning your study (Nosek, Ebersole, DeHaven, & Mellor, 2018). If you don't have hypotheses, state this as well. The purpose of this book is not just to address this latter condition, when researchers don't have hypotheses, but also to discuss methods for incorporating weaker forms of hypotheses — when researchers have some theoretical formulation of a model or analysis, but uncertainty exists to some degree. Do not hide that one is exploring the data, and more pertinent to this book, don't explore using methods that were meant to be used in a confirmatory fashion. We aim to introduce researchers to newly developed methods that can increase the efficiency to search for relationships, all the while building in protection against spurious conclusions. Both confirmatory and exploratory research have there place, and it is not often the case that some form of research is solely confirmatory or exploratory.

Applying machine learning is often associated with larger *researcher degrees of freedom* (i.e., Simmons, Nelson, & Simonsohn, 2011), or to put it more plainly, researchers have to make an increased number of decisions regarding data manipulation, algorithm settings, and final model selection relative to more traditional statistical modeling. In the following chapters we detail many of these decisions, and how researchers can use best practices to avoid capitalizing on chance given the large number of choices and settings. However, the first step in avoiding confusion regarding what was done, affording transparency to engender greater degrees of trust in the veracity of one's results, is to report everything. Reporting what was done comes in many forms; it varies based on what aspect of the analysis is being detailed. The easiest step one can take is to make all programming scripts openly available. While traditionally this has been done by including scripts in the paper's appendix, ideally researchers not only detail the code for the model's run, but also the data analysis, and any follow-up analyses to summarize the results. If using `R`, this entails sharing the full `R` scripts, from start to finish, which often times may entail sharing multiple `R` scripts, as data manipulation, analysis, and summarization all took place in separate scripts. In our view, the easiest way to make these documents available to other researchers is to post them on the Open Science Framework (OSF; see Foster & Deardorff, 2017).

A further step that can be taken to aid in transparency is to openly share the data that were analyzed in the study. Data can also be posted to the OSF. However, in many cases, data contain confidential information, thus precluding open sharing. To get around this hurdle, researchers can create synthetic versions of their data that do not reveal confidential information. This entails creating fake versions of each variable, while preserving the same relationships between the fake variables as in the real dataset. Thus, when external researchers apply the algorithms detailed in the shared scripts to the synthetic data, the results should be nearly identical to those reported in the paper. In `R`, the `synthpop` package makes this relatively easy (Nowok, Raab, & Dibben, 2016).

The main point that we wish to emphasize is to report all of the steps taken during the analysis. This includes the following:

- What algorithms were used

- Tuning parameters tested for each algorithm
- Algorithm variants and which software package was used
- Combinations of variables entered
- Any transformations used
- Type of cross-validation or bootstrapping used for each algorithm (can vary)
- Degree of missing data and how this was handled in each algorithm

Comprehensive reporting guidelines have not yet been developed for machine learning in social and behavioral research applications, and, in all likelihood, would not be terribly useful, as each area of research has a number of unique characteristics. For the time being, we recommend that researchers report as much as possible, as the current reporting standards are relatively weak with respect to level of detail required.

2.7 Summary

This chapter focused on the application of machine learning algorithms. While a majority of the rest of the book focuses on the algorithms themselves, we view the *why* and *how* of machine learning to be just as important as the *what*. While each of the four principles we espoused could likely form the basis for books unto themselves, our goal was to provide a context for how to view machine learning, particularly in relation to the current climate in social and behavioral research. In summary, we advocate for including as much detail as possible in the manuscript, either in the *Methods* and/or *Results* sections, or as supplementary materials. When possible, code and documentation (and data when permitted) should be posted in repositories, such as the Open Science Framework. We specifically note that hypotheses can take nontraditional forms and focus on a large number of variables. For instance, by hypothesizing the existence of nonlinear or interaction effects between a subset of predictors to predict the outcome. The theoretical specification can involve the functional form, while other aspects of modeling are left atheoretical.

One limitation to our perspective on describing the theoretical input into the myriad of study decisions is the degree of flexibility afforded to researchers. This is particularly salient in light of the aforementioned replication crisis, a movement that engendered a renewed focus on purely confirmatory modeling through the use of registered reports to ensure that hypotheses are truly a priori. This begs the question of how can the rise of machine learning in social and behavioral research coexist with the replication crisis? We do not have a straightforward answer to this conundrum; instead, we focus on providing researchers with knowledge of the best practices in machine learning to foster both transparency of the analyses conducted and the reproducibility of the results. While the focus of this chapter was on the role of integrating theory into machine learning studies, thus providing further support for the validity of the conclusions, important complements are the focus of Chapter 3, such as cross-validation and the manipulation of the data and models.

2.7.1 Further Reading

- Replication Crisis. Concerns regarding replication have touched many areas of science, but particularly so in psychology. See Shrout and Rodgers (2018) for a recent review.

- For further reading on the scientific method, specifically applied to social and behavioral research, we recommend the book by Haig (2014). For a more general introduction to the philosophy of science, see Chalmers (2013).

- A number of recent papers discuss the distinction between explanation, description, and prediction. Hamaker, Mulder, and van Ijzendoorn (2020) discuss this from a developmental research perspective, while Mottus et al. (2020) discuss these three terms from a personality research lens. While Breiman (2001b) talks about the varying goals of statistics, Shmueli (2010) extends this to the terms prediction, explanation, and description.

- For more detail on the use of the Open Science Framework and the process of posting data, code, and manuscripts, see Foster and Deardorff (2017).

3 The Practices of Machine Learning

While Chapter 2 discussed the principles underlying machine learning, with a focus on the role of theory, Chapter 3 discusses the practices of machine learning, which takes tangible form in evaluating and programming the analysis and resultant statistics. This mainly concerns answering the question: How well did our model fit, with the important qualifier: Can I trust my assessment of model fit? To set the stage, we first discuss the concepts of bias and variance, and how these quantities play a part in evaluating whether our model overfit the data. This is followed by a lengthy exposition on model fit with continuous (regression) and categorical (classification) outcomes. While there are relatively few options for fit assessment with continuous outcomes, there are a host of metrics when the outcome is binary. We follow this with a discussion of best practices in using resampling to produce trustworthy assessments of fit, detailing multiple recommended forms of resampling, followed by a brief discussion on modeling imbalanced outcomes.

3.1 Key Terminology

- Classification. This can refer to using models to place observations into separate groups (cluster) or the modeling of a categorical, most often binary, outcome.
- Regression. In the simplest case, this refers to the modeling of a continuous outcome, which in parametric models, involves using the Gaussian distribution.
- Imbalance. This occurs when the outcome of interest has a smaller proportion of one class, which is also referred to as a skewed outcome. This most often occurs with clinical outcomes that have a low proportion of positive cases in the population, such as suicide attempts or cancer diagnosis.

- Resampling. This refers to the general process of selecting observations (rows) from a dataset, oftentimes repeated. In the simplest case, this involves splitting a dataset into two partitions, while more complicated methods repeat this process a large number of times, and may reuse observations for populating the newly partitioned datasets (bootstrap sampling). This is done so that the data used to train the model is not also used to produce fit metrics, thus deriving less biased assessments of prediction performance.
- Predicted probability. When the outcome is binary, most algorithms generate probabilities of belonging to the positive class (coded 1, as opposed to 0). This vector of probabilities (one for each observation) can be used to assess fit (using area under the receiver operating characteristic curve [AUC] or area under the precision recall curve [AUPRC]), or to generate predicted class labels based on a cutoff, and then further assessed with a host of fit metrics (i.e., accuracy, recall).

3.2 Comparing Algorithms and Models

In machine learning, there is generally no reason to have an a priori notion that one method will fit better than any other. This is colloquially known as the "No Free Lunch" theorem (Wolpert, 1996). In a more recent paper that tested a broad spectrum of data mining algorithms (179 in total) across 121 datasets, although a method such as random forests (covered in Chapter 6) did well across many types of datasets, there was a large degree of variability in which algorithms performed best on each dataset (Fernández-Delgado, Cernadas, Barro, & Amorim, 2014). Our point here is that in an individual application, there is no reason to necessarily believe that one method will outperform others. Instead, we recommend the use of multiple types of machine learning algorithms, preferably with varying degrees of nonlinearity and interpretation. In almost every application, it is worth including a linear model, either linear or logistic regression, with or without variable selection (i.e., lasso). Just because you may be able to run some highly nonlinear algorithm (often with a catchy name), does not mean that it will necessarily outperform the tried-and-true linear model. Particularly with smaller sample sizes or noisy predictors, highly nonlinear models may have too high of a propensity to overfit the data, limiting their performance when evaluating either with resampling or on a validation dataset.

Similar to the use of a nomological network for the testing of theories (Cronbach & Meehl, 1955), we believe that conclusions achieve stronger support when buoyed by the results from multiple algorithms. Part of this justification can be attributed to the assumptions underlying each type of algorithm, namely, what types of functional forms can be fit. As an example, if a random forests model (which can fit linear, nonlinear, and interactions) fits significantly better than a logistic regression model (no interactions included, only linear relationships), this points to the existence of either nonlinear or interactive effects inherent in our data. We detail this further in Chapter 6.

3.3 Model Fit

Central to every analysis is answering the question: "How well did we do?" or "How well does our model fit?" Both questions relate to the performance or fit of our analysis. With respect to the outcome, our analysis can either utilize a univariate (singular) or multivariate (multiple) outcome. Most analyses in machine learning are concerned with the case of modeling the relationship between multiple predictors and a univariate outcome. The first half of the book focuses on this case, while the second half focuses on the multivariate outcome case. This involves the use of one or many values or statistics. Different fit statistics or indices can be used when evaluating a model fit. In the case of a continuous outcome (regression), this is usually the *mean squared error* (MSE) or *R-squared* (R^2). When the univariate outcome is categorical (classification), either taking the form of two or more finite values, we can use a statistic such as accuracy, or what percentage of cases do we correctly assign the correct class or label. For categorical outcomes, there are a whole host of additional metrics.

3.3.1 Regression

To understand the concept of model fit, we will use linear regression with a continuous outcome as an example. For such a model, we can calculate the *mean squared error* (MSE) as

$$MSE = \frac{1}{n}\sum_{i=1}^{n}(y_i - \hat{f}(x_i))^2, \tag{3.1}$$

where y_i is the outcome and $\hat{f}(x_i)$ is the prediction of $f(x_i)$ for observation i. By taking the square root, we get the root mean squared error (RMSE). We can imagine the misfit (MSE) as small if the predicted and actual outcome for observation i are similar. As an extension, we can calculate the commonly used R^2, which gives us the proportion of variance explained in

FIGURE 3.1. Scatterplot of the PHE data.

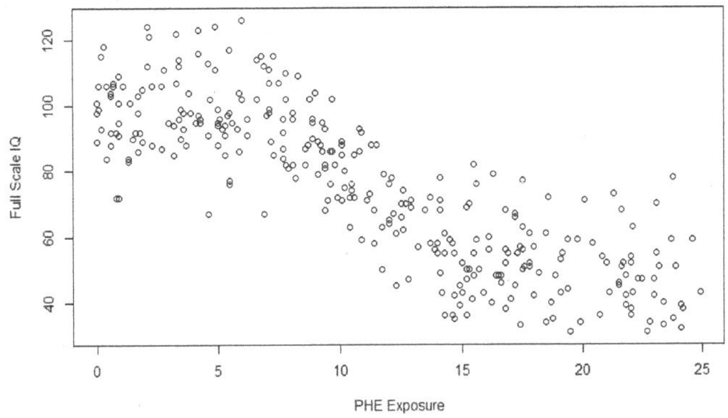

the outcome as predicted by the independent variable(s). We can calculate this coefficient a number of ways. In the ANOVA framework, we can first calculate the sum of squares of regression (SS_{reg}),

$$SS_{reg} = \sum_i (\hat{f}(x_i) - \bar{y})^2, \tag{3.2}$$

where $\bar{y}$ is the mean outcome of the observed data, and the total sum of squares (SS_{tot})

$$SS_{tot} = \sum_i (y_i - \bar{y})^2. \tag{3.3}$$

Given SS_{reg} and SS_{tot}, we can then calculate the R^2 as

$$R^2 = \frac{SS_{reg}}{SS_{tot}}. \tag{3.4}$$

However, we can also calculate the R^2 as the squared correlation between the vector of predicted responses and actual responses. This is more common in the regression, as opposed to ANOVA, framework, and can best be visualized in a plot. While both the RMSE and R^2 are reported in practice, there is some research that advocates using the RMSE, not R^2, for comparing predictions across models (see Alexander, Tropsha, & Winkler, 2015).

To demonstrate the fit of a continuous outcome, we will run a linear regression on the `PHE Exposure` data, using prenatal phenylaline exposure (PHE) by the fetus in utero as a predictor of childhood intelligence. Figure 3.1 depicts the bivariate relationship between `full scale IQ` on the *Y-axis* with `PHE exposure` on the *X-axis*.

FIGURE 3.2. Predicted line from the linear regression on the `PHE exposure` data.

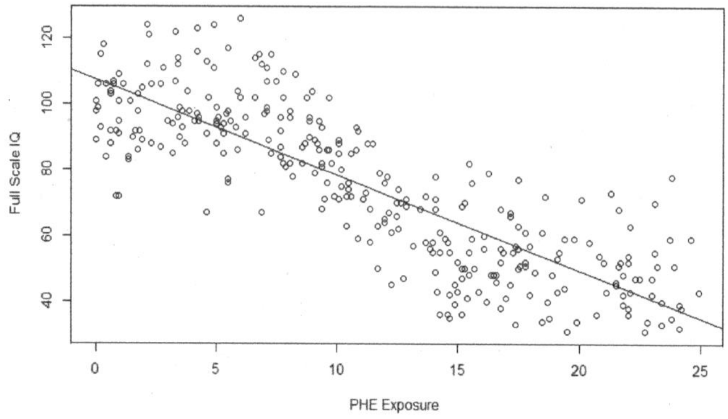

As PHE increases, we can see a general decline in full-scale IQ. However, this does not seem to be a monotonic decline, as there is a degree of nonlinearity to this bivariate relationship. Simply by examining the plot of the bivariate relationship signals to us that a linear model may not fit as well as a model that allows for some degree of nonlinearity, such as polynomial regression. Fitting a linear regression model to the data results in the prediction equation of

$$\hat{IQ}_i = 107.43 - 2.91 \cdot PHE_i. \tag{3.5}$$

The prediction equation as it relates to the values of both the X and Y values is displayed in Figure 3.2.

If we were to take the mean of the squared vertical distance from each data point to the regression line we would get an MSE of 174.487 and an R^2 of 0.699. Explaining approximately 70% of the variance seems like a pretty high number, particularly for social or behavioral datasets. However, as evidenced in the plots, assuming the linear relationship between PHE and full-scale IQ seems to miss the nonlinear trend in the data.

One option would be to test polynomial regression, where we could include $PHE^2, PHE^3, \ldots$ all the way up to say PHE^{20}. This would drastically improve the fit of our model, even if interpretation may become more difficult. Instead, in keeping with the aim of this book, we can apply one of the popular data mining methods, specifically decision trees. Although decision trees will be covered at length later, for the time being, we can think of them as tree structures that map a nonlinear relationship between the predictor(s) and the outcome. With the `PHE exposure` data, we can use decision trees to try and capture the nonlinear curve seen in Figure 3.1. In

FIGURE 3.3. The first decision tree applied to the `PHE exposure` data.

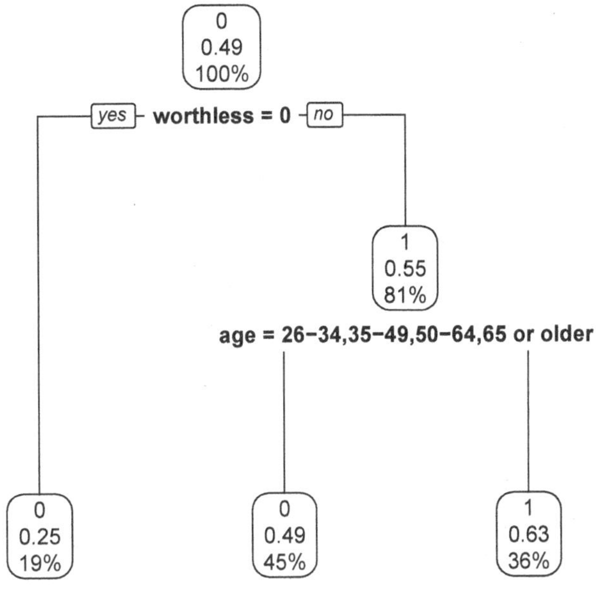

using decision trees, the question we have to ask ourselves is how big of a tree is necessary? For instance, the tree structure in Figure 3.3 has three splits, and corresponds to the predicted curve in Figure 3.4.

To see the mapping from the tree structure in Figure 3.3 to the predictions in Figure 3.4, we can read the structure of the tree like a set of `if/then` statements: if an observation has an `PHE exposure (apexpos)` value greater or equal to 14.15, then they have a predicted `full scale IQ` score of 50.41, if less than 14.15, then a predicted `full scale IQ` of 65.03, with the same process holding on the other side of the tree. However, although this predicted curve seems to match our data to a reasonable extent, according to MSE and R^2, a bigger tree, displayed in Figure 3.5, fits better. The MSE is 115.849, the R^2 is 0.800 for this tree, compared to a MSE of 130.348 and R^2 of 0.775 for the tree displayed in Figure 3.3. The predictions from the larger tree are displayed in Figure 3.6. Both trees fit the data better than the linear regression model, however choosing among them presents a challenge. Although the fit of the tree in Figure 3.5 is superior, it seems to fit "too closely" to the data, capitalizing on small numbers of observations to add additional curve to the predictions. This concept of fitting too closely to the data is known as *overfitting*. In a different light, overfitting pertains to generalizability, meaning our model fits our sample well, but will gen-

FIGURE 3.4. Relationship between the predictor and predictions from the first decision tree in Figure 3.3.

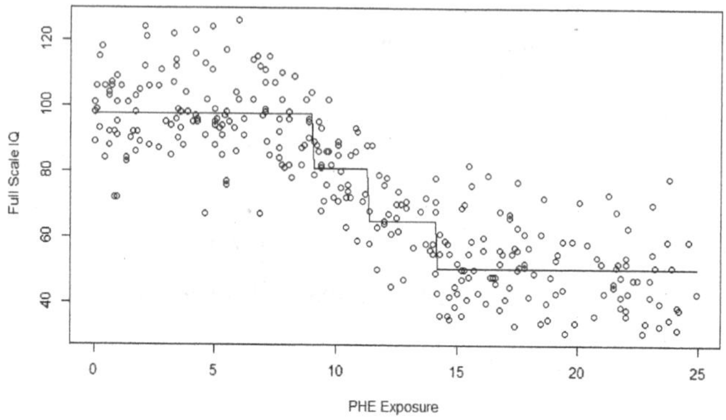

FIGURE 3.5. The second decision tree applied to the `PHE exposure` data.

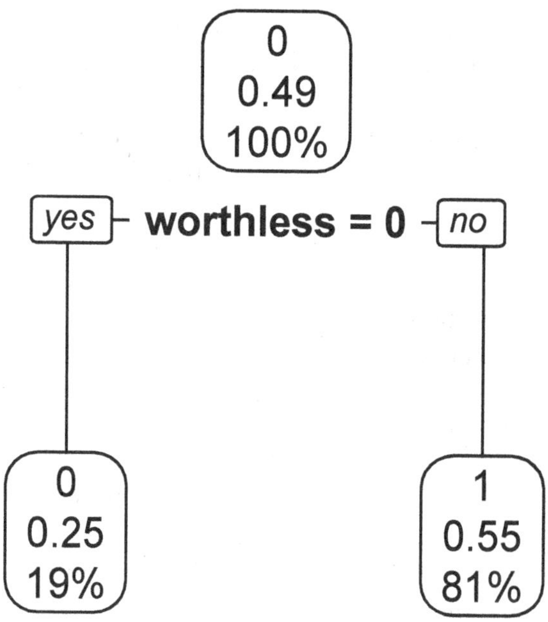

FIGURE 3.6. Relationship between the predictor and predictions from the second decision tree in Figure 3.5.

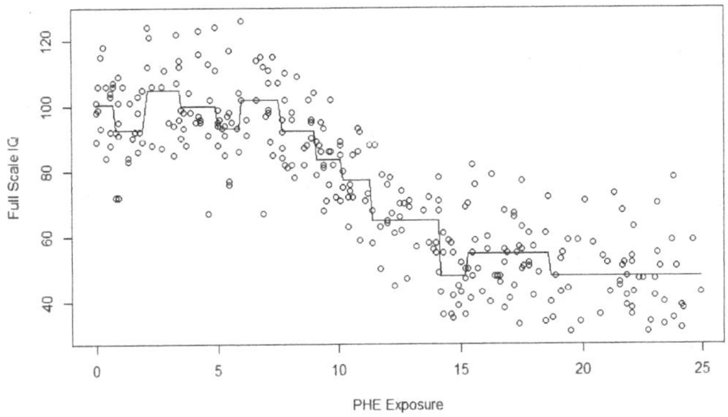

eralize poorly to alternate samples, which is important when assessing the validity of our model for new patients (Steyerberg, 2019). It is important to note that to fit is not to overfit (i.e., see Yarkoni & Westfall, 2017). That is, even in ideal circumstances, fit metrics such as R^2 will demonstrate some degree of upward bias. As such, it is important to see overfitting as a matter of degree, and less as an all-or-nothing concept. Finally, we can further break down the concept of overfitting, and discuss the trade-off between bias and variance in selecting a model for our data.

3.4 Bias–Variance Trade-Off

Every dataset has a finite amount of information that may be gleaned or extracted. The amount of information is related to many factors, most notably sample size (increasing the training set size was a large factor in improving the use of neural networks in areas such as object recognition; Goodfellow et al., 2016), as well as the number and quality of the predictors. The more information in a dataset, the more that can be extracted, in theory. This generally manifests itself as fitting more complex models. While taking model complexity into account, it helps to break down fit into three fundamental quantities: bias, variance, and error. The variance of error is easiest seen in the case of one predictor and outcome, where two observations have identical X values (e.g., same score on a reading test), but different scores on Y (e.g., learning disability classification). This overlap leaves no room for a prediction model to separate these cases, hence the rationale for calling the variance of error *irreducible error*.

What we do have some degree of control over in modeling an outcome is the bias and variance. *Bias* refers to whether our estimates and/or predictions are, on average (across many random draws from the population), equal to the true values in the population. *Variance*, on the other hand, refers to the variability or precision of these estimates (see Yarkoni & Westfall, 2017 for further discussion). Practically speaking, we want unbiasedness and low variance, however, both can be difficult to achieve in practice.

One practical way in which bias and variance can be demonstrated is with the use of linear regression. If the true function is linear, a linear regression model will be unbiased. However, there are many types of relationships that do not follow a strictly linear function—in these cases linear regression will be biased as it is not flexible enough to model the underlying relationships. Given this, it would be necessary to test more complex models, such as polynomial regression. In polynomial regression, the amount of flexibility is controlled by the degree or order of the polynomial term, thus making it necessary to test multiple values to determine which is most appropriate for the data. This concept of varying a parameter that controls the behavior of an algorithm is referred to as a *tuning parameter* (also known as a hyperparameter).

Tuning Parameters Tuning parameters refer to the "settings" of each algorithm that control the behavior (flexibility) of each algorithm. As maybe the easiest example, we can view polynomial regression as an overarching algorithm, with various options for controlling the degree of power. For instance, using the PHE data, we could test a linear model, a quadratic model, cubic, all the way up to a 20th degree. The degree of model is referred to as the tuning parameter for this type of algorithm. Typically, these tuning parameters are placed in a vector and then tested either in sequence or in parallel to determine a model fit for each value, often assessed with cross validation (CV). As with our prior discussion of model selection, this can refer to selection both within one type of algorithm (e.g., which degree of polynomial fits best), or across different types of algorithms (e.g., linear regression versus decision trees).

We demonstrate this with the `APE Exposure` data, subsampling (50 observations) the original training set and fitting algorithms, one that is not flexible enough (linear regression), and one that is too flexible (polynomial regression with up to an eighth degree). We can assess variance by how much the parameter estimates vary across 100 subsamples, which indicates how much the underlying functional form varies. This is displayed in Figure 3.7.

FIGURE 3.7. Plots depicting the mean and variance MSE values across different degrees of power in polynomial regression.

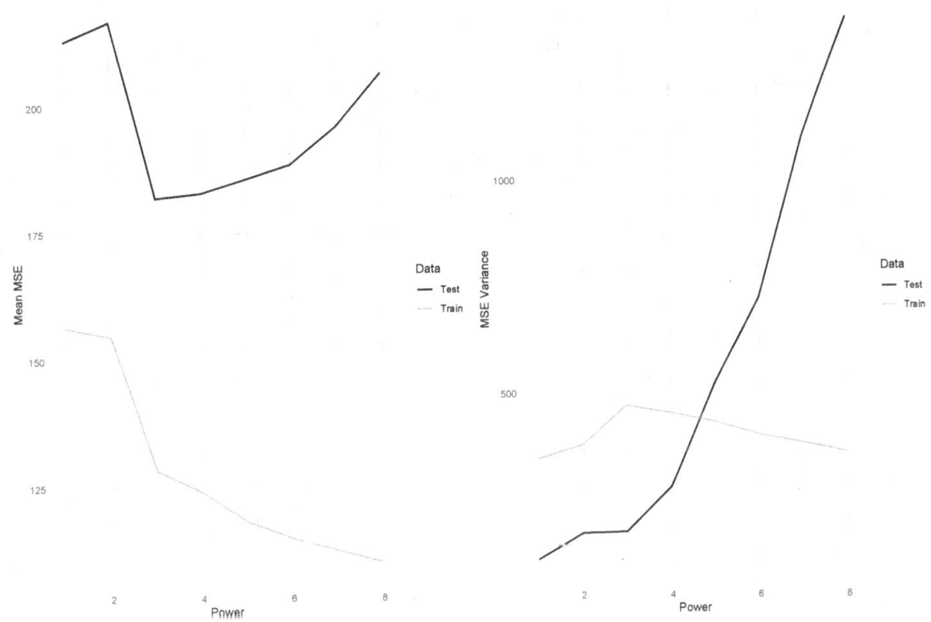

The first result to highlight is a visual depiction of overfitting in the mean MSE values. We see that as the power increases, the training MSE monotonically decreases. This is typical behavior in using flexible algorithms. In contrast, the mean MSE as evaluated on the test set first decreases to a low at a power of 3, and then increases with each subsequent increase in power. The right pane tells a similar story. While the bias typically decreases with the use of increasing degrees of flexibility, we often see a corresponding increase in the variance of fit of the model. This is most clear in the MSE variance as evaluated on the test side (right pane). Increasing degrees of flexibility often afford better fit on some samples, but at the expense of increased uncertainty with respect to fit. Similar behavior would have been seen if we tested the decision trees from Section 3.2 in the same way, with larger trees decreasing mean MSE on the training sample, at the expense of higher mean and variance MSE on the test sample.

There are a few takeaways from this example. The first is the importance of including some form of data splitting or resampling in order to derive a less optimistic or more realistic assessment of the model bias. We will discuss this further below in the Resampling section. Additionally, our concern should be with minimizing *both* bias and variance in selecting models. High degrees of variance can be especially problematic with small sample sizes, further necessitating the use of less flexible algorithms. The method of regularization, which we cover in detail in Chapter 4, is very important for minimizing variance. Finally, in assessing bias and variance, our aim is not necessarily to select a "true" model, but instead to choose a model that is appropriately flexible given the limitations in our data. Again, this becomes particularly evident when modeling data with small sample sizes; everything else being equal, the larger the dataset, the more flexible the model we can validly conclude is the best fitting model. This is further demonstrated in Chapter 4, where forms of regularization keep more variables in the model with increasing sample sizes.

In most settings, the number of predictors will be greater than one, making the visual inspection of how well our model's predictions fit our data difficult. This necessitates the use of various metrics that shed light on how well our model fits, but instead of answering: "How well does my model fit within this sample?", we hope to answer "How well will my model fit on a holdout sample?" There are numerous methods for accomplishing this, most of which involve splitting up the sample in various ways, known as *resampling*, to obtain additional information about the performance of our models.

3.5 Resampling

To answer the question "How well will my model fit on a holdout sample?", there are a number of methods that were developed to provide answers without the need for a second dataset. before detailing these methods, it is important to note that this question reflects model *assessment*, which is distinct from model *selection*. Both concepts can be roughly defined as (Hastie, Tibshirani, & Friedman, 2009):

Model assessment: In estimating a single model, or after choosing a final model, determining the most unbiased assessment of model fit, either on new data or what it would be on new data.

Model selection: Estimating the performance of multiple algorithms/models and choosing a final model among these.

Model assessment can involve the use of only one machine learning algorithm or traditional statistical method, whereas model selection involves choosing among methods. In the prior example, we may use model assessment to determine how well a quadratic regression model fits. Particularly in small sample sizes, assessing the model on the entire sample may result in an overly optimistic assessment of fit, whereas the use of resampling, notably testing the model on a partition not seen by the model, could result in a more realistic assessment of fit. Further, more complex machine learning algorithms such as ensembles (e.g., random forests) have a high propensity to overfit the data when safeguards for both model assessment and selection are not used.

To try to determine how well our model's predictions will generalize and to select among competing models, there are three general strategies: cross-validation (CV; e.g., Browne, 2000), bootstrap sampling (Efron & Tibshirani, 1986), and the use of different forms of fit indices that penalize for model complexity. The goal of both resampling methods (CV and bootstrapping) is to try and estimate how well our method will perform on independent data with the same characteristics as our original sample. There are multiple variants of both cross-validation and bootstrapping, but we focus on two approaches. The first is what is referred to as the validation set approach (see Table 3.1; e.g. Harrell, 2015; James, Witten, Hastie, & Tibshirani, 2013), also referred to as the *Learn then Test* paradigm (McArdle, 2012), while the second is on variants of *k*-fold CV. The validation set approach is a strategy not unique to machine learning, but has been advocated for by social and behavioral scientists for decades. The issue with this approach is the loss in power by splitting the sample into two. A further variant on this approach involves splitting the data into three partitions, train, validation, and test (e.g., Hastie et al., 2009).

TABLE 3.1. General Scheme for Train–Validation–Test Paradigm

50% of Sample	25% of Sample	25% of Sample
Train	Validation	Test
"Train" the models to derive model parameters.	Model Selection	Model Assessment

FIGURE 3.8. Example of a partitioning strategy for the 5-fold cross-validation. For each step, the blocks in dark grey are used to train the model, while the light grey block is used to create holdout predictions.

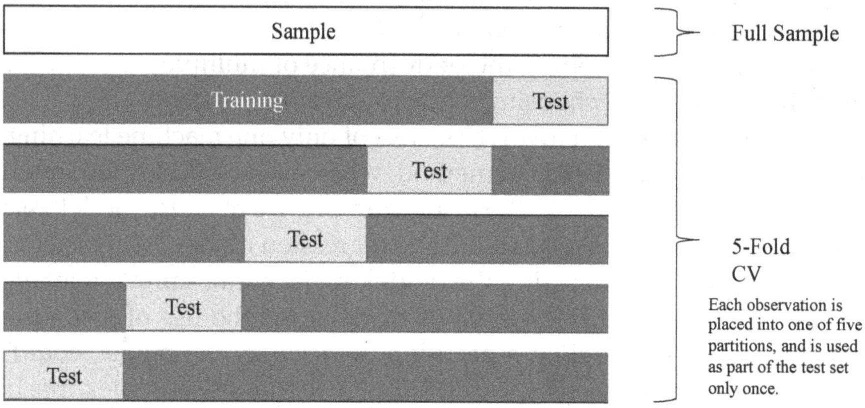

In general, this strategy can only be advocated for if the starting sample size is large (e.g., $N > 5000$), but it also depends on other characteristics of the data. Therefore, we do not recommend using the validation set approach, or further splitting into three partitions as there are very few data environments in social and behavioral research that can afford such a loss of data for training the models. Instead, we discuss other strategies for both model assessment and selection, namely, variants on repeated resampling methods.

3.5.1 *k*-Fold CV

By keeping the original sample intact, one can perform numerous variants of CV, with the most common being k-fold CV. This involves repeatedly splitting the sample into k partitions (i.e., 5 or 10), running the model on k-1 combined partitions of the data, and then testing the model on the single partition that is held out. To make this more concrete, the general strategy is displayed in Figure 3.8 using the 5-fold CV as an example. Before starting, we randomly partition the dataset into 5 subsets. In the first step of 5-fold CV, we run the model on 4 randomly selected and combined subsets (dark grey blocks), take this model and then create predictions on the 1 holdout subset (light grey block). This gives us a first estimate of holdout performance, using a group of observations the model "did not see." In the second step, this procedure is repeated by selecting an additional 4 subsets to run the model on and then creating predictions using the holdout subset (each holdout subset can only be used once). This is then repeated 3 more times, resulting in 5 estimates of model performance. These 5 metrics are then aggregated to create a 5-fold CV metric. One point in this procedure that is worth reiterating, and is common to other forms of CV (and bootstrapping), is that while the model is run on the k-1 partitions of the dataset, it is not rerun on the holdout partition. *Instead the model is kept fixed and used to create predicted responses for the observations.* Using the MSE as an example, this formally manifests itself as:

$$MSE_{holdout} = \frac{1}{n}\sum_{i=1}^{n}(y_{i,holdout} - \hat{f}_{training}(x_{i,holdout}))^2, \tag{3.6}$$

where now n is the number of observations in the holdout partition, x and y are the values for observation i in the holdout sample, and $\hat{f}_{training}$ is the prediction from the model already trained on the training sample (e.g. k-1 partitions). Once we have this estimate for each of the k holdout samples, we can then compute the k-fold MSE,

$$MSE_{k-fold} = \frac{1}{k}\sum_{i=1}^{k}(MSE_k). \tag{3.7}$$

One common practice when using k-fold CV is to repeat the process, as repeating the partitioning process can remove the potential for aberrant results due to chance. Specifically, repeated (i.e., 100) 10-fold cross-validation is often recommended (Borra & Di Ciaccio, 2010; Krstajic, Buturovic, Leahy, & Thomas, 2014; Kuhn & Johnson, 2013). However, one clear drawback of this approach is the increase in run times, as even 10 repeats increases the amount of time by 10×.

3.5.2 Nested CV

Often, in using resampling for comparing algorithms the same process is used for both model selection and assessment, with practitioners reporting the resampling based fit metric for the final model. Conflating both sets of assessment can lead to overoptimistic estimates of model assessment (Boulesteix & Strobl, 2009; Varma & Simon, 2006). Particularly when examining a larger number of models, there is insufficient randomness imparted into our model selection procedures. By selecting a best model, we are more likely to select a model that has an upwardly biased assessment of model fit, purely as a result of performing model selection. The idea behind nested CV is to separate model selection and assessment.

To demonstrate this, we provide a simple simulation where we simulated 30,000 samples that have a moderately strong relationship between two predictors and one continuous outcome. The R^2 in this sample was 0.33. From this, we repeatedly sampled (repeated 200 times) two datasets, each with 100 samples. For both of these new datasets, we ran a linear regression models, using 10-fold CV to assess the R^2 of each model. Across these 200 replications, the first set of models had a mean R^2 of 0.37 (SD = 0.07), while the second set of models had a mean R^2 of 0.35 (SD = 0.07). Even though no model selection was performed, there was still a bias to the estimates using 10-fold CV, which can mainly be attributed to the much smaller training sample size.

To elucidate the effect of conflating model selection and assessment, we instead chose the highest R^2 value across the 200 repetitions, averaged these values, and treated this as our result. This process resulted in a mean R^2 of 0.41, much higher than the mean of both sets of models. However, if we separate the process of model assessment and selection with nested CV, pairing 5-fold CV for the outer loop with 10-fold CV for the inner loop, and repeating this process 200 times (done only for demonstration purposes), we get an a mean R^2 estimate of 0.34, which was much closer to the estimate from the full sample of 0.33 than any of the other estimates. This highlights the importance of separating the process of model selection and assessment to come up with more realistic estimates of model performance.

Nested CV works by creating two sets of loops, one loop for model selection, and one loop for model assessment, and can be seen as a repeated extension of the training–validation–test paradigm displayed in Table 3.1. This general process is displayed in Figure 3.9.

To give an example of how nested CV would work, we used polynomial regression as an example, using the tuning parameter of degree, with values of 2 and 3. For outer loop number 1 (using 80% of the sample), we run the inner loop, 5-fold CV to test both polynomial models. For instance, we could get a 5-fold estimate of R^2 of 0.57 for degree 2 and 0.49 for degree 3. Given that the degree 2 model fit best, we can then test this model (with the model being rerun on the training partition of the outer loop) on the test set from the outer loop, thus deriving a better estimate of the true R^2. This process is then repeated four more times (outer loop), each time coming up with an estimate of model fit (5 total). One thing to note is that the optimal tuning parameter values can vary across the five partitions,

FIGURE 3.9. The general strategy for nested cross-validation, which splits the process into two loops, separating model assessment and selection.

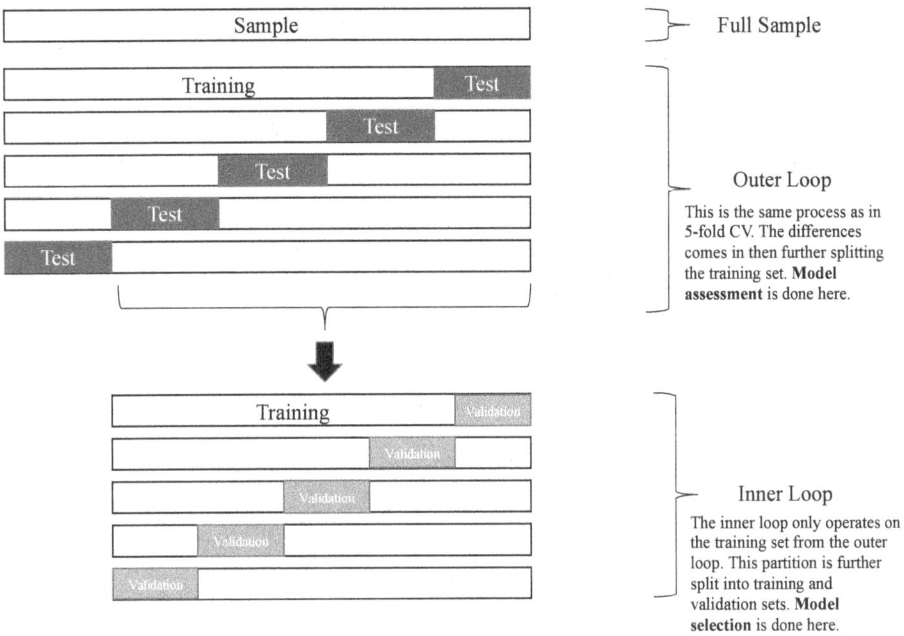

particularly when the tuning parameter vector is large. Typically, this is done for each algorithm, then using the mean fit estimates for comparison across algorithms, while allowing the tuning parameters to vary within the nested CV loops.

One large drawback of this approach is the computational complexity. Using 5-fold CV for both the inner and outer loops will take approximately 5× as long to run than just using 5-fold CV. The amount of time it takes to run this procedure can be drastically cut if using parallel processing, however, there exist few helper functions that pair both nested CV and parallelization in R.

3.5.3 Bootstrap Sampling

In comparison to *k*-fold CV, we dedicate much less space to the use of bootstrap sampling as a method of resampling to derive less biased model assessment. This is not because bootstrap sampling is not considered a recommended approach but because the process is quite similar, which we detail shortly, and it can be used in the same way as the above approaches. For instance, bootstrap sampling can be used as a part of either the inner or outer loops, or both, in nested CV. In fact, the main R package we use for

FIGURE 3.10. The general process for using bootstrap sampling for model assessment. Note that in practice it is recommended to use more than 5 repeats.

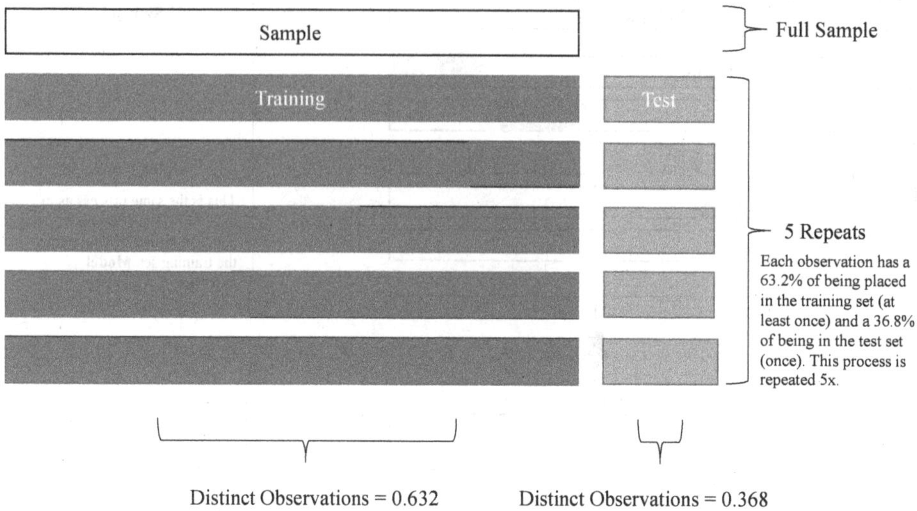

running resampling and testing various algorithms, `caret`, defaults to the use of 20 bootstrap samples for model assessment. The general process of using bootstrap sampling for model assessment is displayed in Figure 3.10.

The main distinction between the bootstrap and *k*-fold CV is that where *k*-fold CV uses sampling *without* replacement, the bootstrap uses sampling *with* replacement. Thus, each of the dark grey boxes representing the training sets in the bootstrap process contains a set of cases with an equal number compared to the original sample, with the caveat that approximately 0.632 of the distinct observations are represented in this training set, with a subset of cases being represented multiple times. In contrast, the test set contains approximately 0.368 of the observations, with no cases being included more than once. Given that a subset of cases is represented more than once in each training set, it is common to use a larger number of repeats (at least 20) than in *k*-fold CV.

3.5.4 Recommendations

The first thing to note is that there are a number of variants of both CV and the bootstrap that we do not cover. While methods such as leave-one-out CV have performed well in small sample sizes, other methods have demonstrated poor performance. Further, a number of resampling methods were developed prior to the development of many machine learning algorithms, and haven't been tested in conjunction with flexible algorithms with a high propensity to overfit. This was seen recently in a paper by Jacobucci, Littlefield, Millner, Kleiman, & Steinley (2021), where extreme amounts of bias were found when the random forests algorithm was paired with the optimism corrected bootstrap.

There have been a number of studies that have compared the bias and variance (detailed below) of CV and bootstrapping, but it has generally been difficult to evaluate the results given the differences in which algorithms were used, types of data (simulation or benchmark datasets), and which methods of resampling were tested. Across studies, a general recommendation has been to use repeated k-fold CV when the sample size is not small (a few hundred), and the bootstrap when the sample size is small. Just as in the no-free-lunch theorem, no method has performed universally best across various conditions of study, as shown in a recent study by Xu and Goodacre (2018). Further, this study concluded that when using the bootstrap, the number of repeats should be large (> 100).

While the use of repeated k-fold CV or bootstrap sampling is recommended for model assessment, nested CV should be used when conducting *both* model selection and assessment. In nested CV, it does not seem to matter whether k-fold CV or bootstrap sampling is used for the outer and inner loops. The main drawback to this approach is a lack of easy implementation in R. As of this writing, users need to program their own nested CV script.

Regardless of the resampling method used, it is extremely important to use the same resampling method when comparing results across models or algorithms. Depending on dataset characteristics, each resampling method is likely to be at least slightly biased. Thus, when performing model selection it is important to use the same resampling method so that the bias is consistent across models or algorithms.

3.6 Classification

In modeling binary outcomes (classification), the methods and recommendations detailed above apply equally well as they do to continuous outcomes. The one caveat is in the presence of imbalanced (skewed) binary outcomes. We cover this further in the Imbalanced Outcomes section. In this section, our focus is on detailing the many prediction performance metrics that are different with binary outcomes.

To demonstrate predicting a binary[1] outcome as opposed to one that is continuous, we use a simple example that is predicting whether a case is labeled as having depression or not (using a cut score on the Beck Depression Inventory) with the Big Five personality scale scores (agreeableness, conscientiousness, extraversion, neuroticism, and openness; taken from the `epi.bfi` dataset in the `psych` package). With this data, we ran a logistic regression, first making sure that the outcome classes are labeled with 1 = "dep", and 0 = "no". Designating the class label of most interest as "1" makes inference into the various metrics easier down the line. To assess model performance, the most straightforward metric is accuracy, or the percentage of correct predictions:

$$Accuracy = \frac{1}{n}\sum_{i=1}^{n} I(y_i = \hat{y}_i), \tag{3.8}$$

where $\hat{y}_i$ is the predicted response for observation i, and I is an indicator of 1 if there is agreement in class label and 0 if the labels do not agree. The most important thing to note here is that calculating accuracy involves creating a predicted class label for each observation. Most machine learning algorithms (including logistic regression) create predicted class probabilities, then require the user to either use the default probability of 0.5 (those with predicted probabilities > 0.5 are assigned to class one) or use a different cutoff that better reflects the cost for misclassifying both classes.

Before examining the accuracy from our logistic model, we first examine the predicted probabilities from the model. In Figure 3.11 we display a histogram and a density plot for each class of the predicted probabilities. The first thing to note here is the large degree of skew in the histogram. Note that this is not what we hope to see. In a well-calibrated model we would hope to see somewhat of a symmetric, or bimodal distribution, as we are hoping to generally model both classes about equally well. However, in modeling hard to predict outcomes, such as attempting suicide or who has a diagnosis of psychopathology, this is rarely what we see. In general, it is easier to model the nonpositive cases (generally those without a diagnosis or disease), while we are rarely able to generate confident predictions in those with positive values of the outcome. This can further be seen in the two-class density plot, with little separation between the predicted probabilities for each class, and a small number of predicted probabilities > 0.75.

[1]Our focus in the book is generally on continuous (regression) versus binary (classification) outcomes, but we discuss other types such as count or other types of categorical outcomes within each of the chapters.

FIGURE 3.11. Histogram (left) of predicted probabilities and density (right) from logistic regression model.

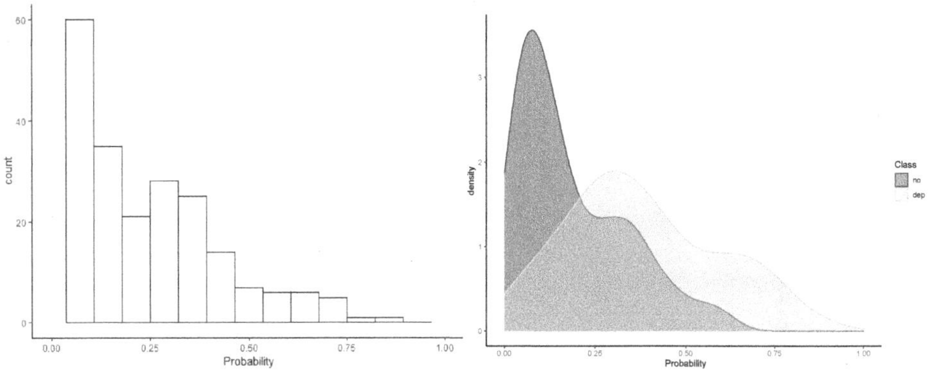

An additional way to assess the performance of our model through the predicted probabilities, particularly if we want to compare performance across models, is to use a calibration plot. In addition to the predicted probabilities from logistic regression, we also used random forests for comparison. This is shown in Figure 3.12.

In this plot, the probabilities are binned (by decile), with those having similar predicted probabilities being grouped together. This is then compared to their actual response values (What is the percentage of depression diagnoses for those binned together?). For example, of those observations with the lowest 10% of predicted probabilities, what is the observed percentage of occurrence of 1s (depression diagnoses). This process is repeated through each decile of predicted probabilities to determine the concordance between actual and predicted outcomes.

We would expect that in a well-calibrated model there is a monotonic increase in the relationship between predicted probabilities and actual outcome values (hence the 45 degree line). From this we can see two different things that indicate poor performance. First off, both models had difficulties in generating high predicted probabilities, easily seen in the sharp drop-off in the line at high values of the *x–axis* stemming from a lack of predicted probabilities > 0.80. Secondly, there are visual signs of overfitting in the random forests model. Notably, cases were assigned either extremely low or high probabilities, which does not reflect the actual degree of uncertainty in the model and a false sense of confidence in our predictions. Although this will be covered in greater depth in Chapter 5, this performance is not surprising given that the random forests model was only evaluated on the full sample and there were a relatively small number of observations. If

FIGURE 3.12. Calibration plot for both logistic regression (black) and random forests (grey).

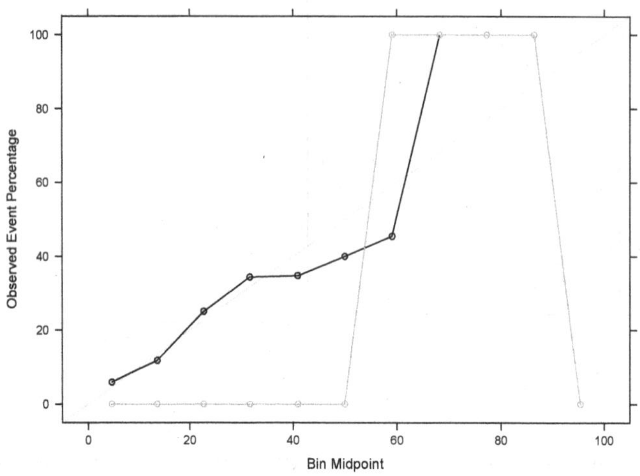

we had a test set, we could generate a second calibration plot which would likely depict vastly different performance.

After creating a logistic regression model, we output the predicted probabilities and then converted these to predicted labels (using 0.5). To visualize our performance, we first create a comparison table between actual and predicted class labels, or better known as a "confusion matrix."

		Actual Outcome		
		Positive	Negative	Total
Predicted Outcome	Positive	*TP*	*FP* (α)	*PPV*
	Negative	*FN* (β)	*TN*	*NPV*
	Total	*Sens*	*Spe*	*N*

From the table, we can calculate the following metrics:

$$Sensitivity\,(Sens),\, Recall = \frac{TP}{TP + FN}$$

$$Specificity\,(Spe) = \frac{TN}{TN + FP}$$

$$Precision, PPV = \frac{TP}{TP + FP}$$

$$Negative\,Predictive\,Value\,(NPV) = \frac{TN}{TN + FN}$$

The cells in the table can be broken into four different terms: true positives (TP), true negatives (TN), false positives (FP), and false negatives

FIGURE 3.13. Confusion matrix from the depression example.

```
Confusion Matrix and Statistics

          Reference
Prediction dep  no
       dep  14   8
       no   39 170

               Accuracy : 0.7965
                 95% CI : (0.7388, 0.8465)
    No Information Rate : 0.7706
    P-Value [Acc > NIR] : 0.1957

                  Kappa : 0.2759

 Mcnemar's Test P-Value : 1.209e-05

            Sensitivity : 0.26415
            Specificity : 0.95506
         Pos Pred Value : 0.63636
         Neg Pred Value : 0.81340
             Prevalence : 0.22944
         Detection Rate : 0.06061
   Detection Prevalence : 0.09524
      Balanced Accuracy : 0.60960

       'Positive' Class : dep
```

(FN). From these values, a host of additional metrics can be calculated. Sensitivity (Sens or true positive rate) and Recall refer to the rate of correct classification for positive cases, or in our example, of those diagnosed with depression, how many do we correctly classify. Specificity (or true negative rate) is typically used to characterize the flip side of sensitivity, which calculates that rate of correct classification for negative cases. Both specificity and negative predictive value (NPV) measure the rate of classification for negative cases, with NPV using false negatives in the the denominator (instead of FP) to characterize classification rate in relation to those predicted to be negative cases (not have depression; TN + FN). Finally, precision and positive predictive value (PPV) assesses the prediction of positive cases in a slightly different manner than sensitivity and recall, by using those predicted to be positive in the denominator instead (TP + FP). If one solely wants to focus on assessing how well a model predicts positive cases, it would be most appropriate to use both recall (sensitivity) and precision.

There are a host of additional metrics that characterize different aspects of the classification of positive and negative classes. One of the best ways to assess these metrics is with the `confusionMatrix` function from the `caret` package in `R`. From our logistic regression model, and the resulting predicted classes, we created the confusion matrix displayed in Figure 3.13.

The first thing to note in Figure 3.13 is the small number of cases that had a diagnosis of depression (14 + 39). This is reflected in both the prevalence (0.229; TP + FN/total), as well as the no information rate (NIR; 1-Prevalence).

The NIR is used as a comparison to accuracy to determine whether our prediction model improves our classification above and beyond classifying every case as negative. In our example this would mean an accuracy of 0.77, which was slightly lower than our actual accuracy of 0.80. To look specifically at our classification of positive cases, we achieved a sensitivity of 0.26 and PPV (precision) of 0.64. The precision (PPV) is much higher than recall (sensitivity) because so few cases were predicted to have depression, while a large number of cases that actually had a diagnosis of depression were misclassified (FN). With almost all of the metrics detailed in Figure 3.13 we hope to achieve values > 0.70, preferably closer to 0.90. Given this, we can see that our model does not predict positive cases well, despite our accuracy being in a range we would hope to see. One metric missing from the table is the F1 score (also termed F score), which is the harmonic mean of precision and recall, creating an overall summary metric for classifying positive cases.

Class imbalance can skew some metrics (detailed further below), which has led to alternative ways to quantify prediction. This highlights the importance of quantifying the base rate, as accuracy values below this indicate worse prediction than classifying every case as a zero. One metric that accounts for this is balanced accuracy, which takes the mean of sensitivity and specificity, giving equal weight to both, whereas accuracy is weighted based on the class distribution. An additional metric is kappa, which was originally created to measure agreement between raters, but can also be used to characterize prediction, specifically comparing observed accuracy to what would be expected based on the marginal totals. For kappa, we are looking for values greater than 0, with values between 0.30 and 0.50 indicating reasonable agreement (Kuhn & Johnson, 2013). One criticism of Kappa is that it is dependent on the prevalence of positive cases and has resulted in an alternative metric prevalence and bias adjusted kappa (PABAK; Byrt, Bishop, & Carlin, 1993), which is recommended for use to complement kappa (Sim & Wright, 2005), particularly to highlight the effects of class imbalance on the value. In our example, the PABAK value was 0.59, showcasing the attenuation of the kappa statistic due to class imbalance.

The one thing to note in our discussion of the prior performance metrics is that they all required converting predicted probabilities to predicted class membership. This can be problematic for at least two reasons: 1) researchers may not have a previously determined cutoff, or the typical value of 0.50 may not be appropriate, and 2) converting probabilities to class engenders a loss of information, namely, the nuance to the probabilities within each predicted class (see Figure 3.11 on probability distributions).

FIGURE 3.14. Relationship between cutoff values and accuracy (left) and F1 (F measure; right).

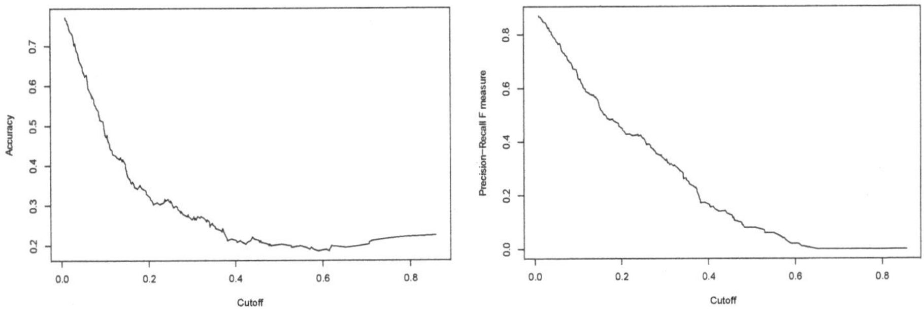

For these reasons it is often more informative to examine metrics that solely use predicted probabilities, with the most common being the receiver operating characteristic (ROC) curve (e.g., Fawcett, 2006).

Using Cutoffs ≠ 0.5

Prior to a discussion of ways to evaluate models with the predicted probabilities, we first cover how to alter the cutoff used to turn predicted probabilities into predicted classes. While there are a number of R packages that can calculate optimal cutoffs, the important thing to consider is what metric is most important to maximize. For instance, we can identify the optimal cutoff that maximizes accuracy, thus taking into account prediction of both positive and negative classes, or we can solely maximize our prediction of the positive class, using a metric such as sensitivity, or the F1 score. We used the logistic model from above, and assessed the cutoffs and their effect on both accuracy and F1, with the results displayed in Figure 3.14.

In Figure 3.14, we see a clear decrease in both F1 and accuracy as the cutoff becomes closer to 1. Further, we can see that using the default cutoff of 0.5 results in far worse performance in both metrics than if we use a cutoff closer to 1. To select an optimal value, we chose to maximize the F1 score, of which a cutoff of 0.008 was chosen as optimal. Note that this was the smallest tested cutoff value, signaling the lack of class separation in the predictions from our logistic regression model. To detail a scenario in which our modeling of a binary outcome results in a clearer separation of classes, thus leading to the selection of a less extreme cutoff, we used the same predictors as before but changed the outcome using the Eysenck

FIGURE 3.15. The relationship between F scores and cutoff values in the new example using neuroticism as an outcome.

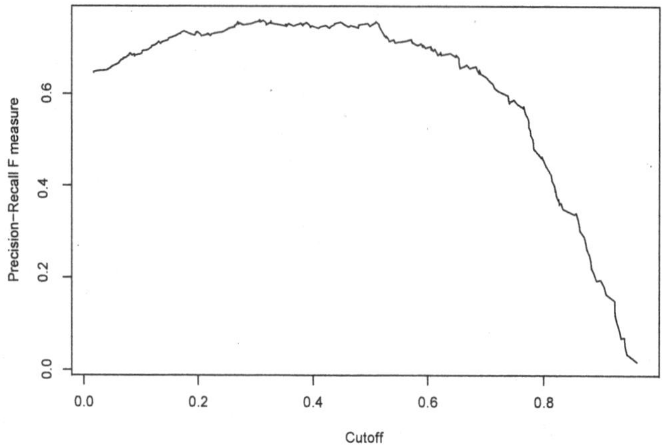

Personality Inventory neuroticism scores, dichotomized based on the mean. The relationship between cutoffs and F scores is displayed in Figure 3.15.

Here, we see that the optimal cutoff is not at the boundaries of cutoff values. By selecting the cutoff that maximizes the F score, we get a value of 0.31. From here, we could reproduce the confusion matrix, calculating new values of the host of metrics based on cutoffs. While this may be desirable in many scenarios, there are often times in which a cutoff is not needed, and performance can be calculated solely based on the predicted probabilities. We detail the receiver operating characteristic (ROC) curve next for this situation.

3.6.1 Receiver Operating Characteristic (ROC) Curves

The ROC curve was designed to use a collection of continuous data to derive a cutoff (threshold) that maximizes a balance between two continuous metrics. In the context of classification, this involves plotting both sensitivity and specificity (using the false positive rate or 1 – specificity in practice) across the range of possible cutoffs (e.g., what is the sensitivity and specificity for a cutoff of 0.1, 0.5, and all the way to 0.99). It is important to note that in our above discussion of deriving optimal cutoffs, these plots only display one fit metric, while the ROC curve denotes the impact of cutoffs on two metrics, sensitivity and specificity. Just as above, the ROC curve can be used to derive an optimal cutoff. Back to our example predicting depression: using the ROC curve to identify an optimal cutpoint involves

FIGURE 3.16. ROC curve from the depression prediction example. Note that the black dot refers to the optimal cutpoint for maximizing the sum of sensitivity and specificity.

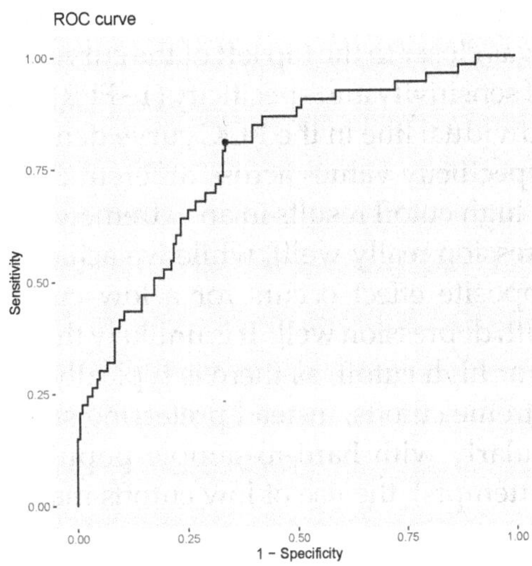

maximizing the sum of sensitivity and specificity, as we display in Figure 3.16.

Here, we can see the point in the line that is closest to the top left of the plot, denoting the cutpoint with the highest sum of specificity and sensitivity. This cutpoint is 0.21, and could be used as before to calculate new classification metrics.

To further elaborate on the information provided in an ROC curve, as an example to describe the values displayed in Figure 3.16, we can calculate the sensitivity and FPR (1 − specificity) for a cutoff of 0.2, 0.5, and 0.8. For a cutoff of 0.5: sensitivity = 0.26, FPR = .05; for 0.2, sensitivity = 0.98, FPR = 1; for 0.8, sensitivity = 0.19, FPR = 0.64. Following the figure, we can trace approximately where each of the cutoffs correspond to on the curve, denoting the sensitivity and FPR for each cutoff. Note the truncation at high cutoffs, which is due to a small number of cases receiving a high (> 0.8) predicted probability.

An additional use of this curve is to calculate the area under the curve (AUC), which gives us a threshold-free metric for characterizing our prediction performance. The AUC can be characterized as the probability that a randomly drawn positive case has a higher probability than a randomly drawn negative case (Fawcett, 2006). Values close to 1 indicate thresholds exist that result in a near 1 value for sensitivity and specificity, meaning that on balance, we are predicting both classes well. Similar to the previous characterization of alternative performance metrics, it is desirable to achieve values greater than 0.8.

In our example, we achieve a value of 0.78, below what we would hope to achieve. If our model better separated outcome classes we would expect to see a curve that was closer to the top left of the curve pane, indicating that both a high value of sensitivity and specificity (1−FPR) can be achieved with this model. The individual line in the ROC curve denotes the actual values of sensitivity and specificity values across different cutoffs. In our results, we see that using a high cutoff results in an extremely low FPR (we classify those without depression really well), while we achieve an extremely low sensitivity. An opposite effect occurs for a low cutoff with our model classifying those with depression well. It is unlikely that a researcher wishes to use either a low or high cutoff, as there is typically a large performance decrement with extreme cutoffs, instead preferring something near 0.5. In some cases, particularly with hard-to-sample populations (those with a history of suicide attempts), the use of low cutoffs may be justified.

3.7 Imbalanced Outcomes

With binary outcomes, it is common to have some degree of imbalance, and in some settings, particularly in clinical research, the level of imbalance (i.e., < 10% positive cases) can cause a host of problems. With imbalanced outcomes we will detail changes that can be made to *k*-fold CV, whether sampling-based methods can improve our prediction, and alternative performance metrics are more attune to assessing specifically the positive cases.

The first strategy developed that we will discuss for imbalanced outcomes is the stratified *k*-fold CV. As an example, we can think of attempting to predict whether participants have a history of attempting suicide. Since this is typically a rare event, less than 10% of the sample is likely to have a "Yes" response. Given this, splitting the sample into 5 or 10 different partitions could lead to partitions with far less than 10% just by chance. Stratification involves prearranging the distribution of the outcome in each partition of the data to ensure roughly equal distribution of the outcome. Results have been mixed in the assessment of the efficacy of stratified *k*-fold CV, with some research indicating positive effects in classification settings (Kohavi, 1995), as well as no improvements in the regression setting (Breiman & Spector, 1992).

3.7.1 Sampling

A number of strategies have been developed that sample from either the positive or negative class, or both, to create new distributions that are more balanced. The two simplest are random oversampling (ROS) and random undersampling (RUS). While ROS randomly samples from the minority case to produce an equal distribution of positive and negative cases, RUS randomly removes majority cases to produce an equal distribution. A more sophisticated approach that has a large degree of study is the synthetic minority oversampling technique (SMOTE; Chawla, Bowyer, Hall, & Kegelmeyer, 2002). SMOTE is similar to ROS, but instead of just duplicating positive cases, SMOTE creates artificial minority class cases by using the *k*-nearest neighbors for a given minority case. More specifically, for a particular minority case *i*, the SMOTE algorithm finds *k* similar minority cases to case *i* and generates synthetic cases with predictor values that represent a blend of the *k*-nearest neighbors.

Among the simple sampling strategies, ROS is typically preferred over RUS (e.g., Batista, Prati, & Monard, 2004; Buda, Maki, & Mazurowski, 2018). Further, SMOTE has been generalized into a large number of variants, while additional strategies have also been developed that generate synthetic cases. A recent comprehensive study of these strategies found that any form of oversampling generally performs better than no sampling, with the best performance attributed to more recent generalizations of SMOTE. However, the majority of the studies that have evaluated sampling methods have used benchmark datasets from computer science, making the generalizability of the findings to social and behavioral research questionable. Two recent papers focused on evaluating these strategies in simulated data that are more in line with social and behavioral research (Goorbergh et al., 2022; Jacobucci & Li, 2022). While Goorbergh et al. (2022) found detrimental effects of sampling strategies with respect to calibration (defined below) and did not lead to better AUC values than no sampling. Jacobucci and Li (2022) found only slight benefits to the use of sampling strategies for both the AUC and AUPRC, and of the sampling strategies, ROS performed just as well if not better across conditions than SMOTE. Of note in Jacobucci and Li (2022) is that they also tested the random over sampling examples (ROSE; Menardi & Torelli, 2014) which is implemented in the `caret` package along with SMOTE. Notably, they found that ROSE performs poorly in some conditions and is not a recommended approach.

Based on the large number of studies that have evaluated the use of sampling in other domains, and the two recent papers that are more relevant to social and behavioral research, we recommend the use of ROS when dealing with imbalanced outcomes. The use of oversampling nullifies the

FIGURE 3.17. Left: The densities for the first set of simulated cases. Right: The resultant ROC plot.

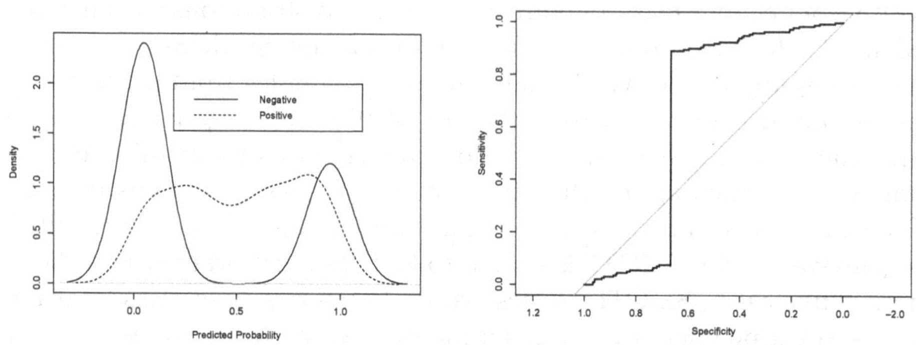

concerns addressed by stratified *k*-fold CV, and is easy to test when using the `caret` package.

Is the AUC Biased with Imbalanced Outcomes?

Some have questioned the use of the AUC when outcomes are imbalanced (Lobo, Jiménez-Valverde, & Real, 2008; Saito & Rehmsmeier, 2015). Particularly, problems can occur when examining specific areas of the ROC plot. To demonstrate this, we simulated data according to different levels of class imbalance. We started with a relatively balanced dataset of 200 positive cases and 400 negative cases. The true positive cases were simulated to have uniform 0–1 probabilities of belonging to the positive case: 200 true negative cases were simulated with zero probability of belonging to the positive class, while the additional 200 true negatives were simulated to have uniform .9–1 probabilities of belonging to the positive case. In this condition, the AUC was 0.64. In a second condition, we added 1600 true negatives, all with simulated to have uniform 0–.1 probabilities. In this condition, the AUC was 0.84.

To understand why we get higher AUC values by adding cases, recall the underlying definition of the AUC: The probability that a randomly selected positive sample has a higher predicted probability than a randomly selected negative sample. Namely, in looking at the right panel of Figure 3.17, we can see that at higher thresholds (> .7), our sensitivity plummets, without much of an effect on the specificity. This occurs due to the structure of the simulated data, with 200 negative cases having extremely high predicted probabilities and the positive cases having few high predicted probabilities.

The important thing to note is that while this example highlights a flaw in the use of the AUC with imbalanced outcomes, it is an extreme simulated example. In more realistic scenarios of imbalance, the AUC has not been found to be problematic for use in model assessment (Jacobucci & Li, 2022). However, the ROC plot and AUC still focus equally on positive and negative cases, which in the case of imbalanced outcomes, we likely care far more about the prediction of the positive cases. While a number of metrics and visualizations have been developed to help focus on positive cases, the most commonly used is the area under the precision recall curve (AUPRC; Davis & Goadrich, 2006).

Area under the Precision Recall Curve

In comparison to the AUC, the AUPRC is more sensitive and provides more information particularly when classes are imbalanced (Saito & Rehmsmeier, 2015). AUPRC does not take into account true negatives, instead focusing on the classification of positives (those with a diagnosis of depression). In fact, going back to the simulated examples in the prior section, the AUPRC stays approximately the same (0.29) when adding a large number of negative cases, which is what we would want to see in a metric.

With the AUC, a value of 0.50 denotes chance level prediction. However, with the AUPRC, chance depends on the distribution of the outcome, with minimum values calculated as the ratio of positives (P) and negatives (N) as $y = P/(P+N)$ (Saito & Rehmsmeier, 2015). This plot is depicted in Figure 3.18, and tells a different story than the AUC. We see that across the range of cutoffs, there is no "ideal" value that results in both a high precision and recall. Our AUPRC value of 0.57 is difficult to interpret but can hold more value when comparing different models.

FIGURE 3.18. The precision recall curve and AUPRC value from the logistic regression model.

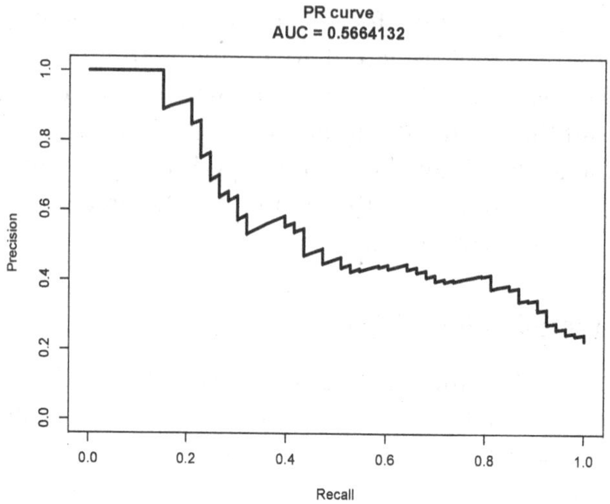

3.8 Conclusion

Beyond Continuous or Binary Outcomes This chapter has discussed the common fit functions and model fit metrics for continuous (Gaussian) and binary outcomes. The outcome type influences two primary aspects of modeling: 1) the fit function paired with each algorithm, and 2) the model fit metric used to evaluate the model. For point #1, the main limitation occurs at the software level, as most machine learning algorithm software packages only include fit functions specific to continuous and binary outcomes. Note that in R, this is generally referred to as the argument `family`. Some packages and functions, such as `glmnet`, allow for the specification of count, multinomial, and survival (cox) outcomes. Oftentimes there are additional packages that implement algorithms for a specific type of outcome, such as the `ordinalForest` package (Hornung, 2021). For aspect #2, it is often less straightforward, and fewer specific methods have been developed for interpreting the relationship between the outcome and predictions outcome types outside of continuous or binary. For instance, for multinomial or ordinal outcomes, one can use the AUC for a single class versus single or multiple other classes, but this results in multiple AUC values. Additionally, while some methods have been developed, for instance to create a single AUC for ordinal outcomes (DeCastro, 2019), they often aren't implemented as `R` packages.

Summary The substance of this chapter was focused on model assessment, with a shorter discussion of model selection. As discussed in the nested CV section, it is important to separate these two aspects of evaluation when using resampling to overcome the propensity of machine learning algorithms to overfit data. A primary takeaway is that when applying machine learning, an equal amount of thought and time needs to be put into model assessment as is put into choosing or selecting which algorithms to apply. With easy-to-use software such as the `caret` package, it has become increasingly easy to fit a wide variety of algorithms, whereas it is often less straightforward to assess and select which of these algorithms/models is most appropriate to interpret or report. Thus, while the following chapters detail a number of machine learning algorithms, it is important to follow the guidelines covered in this chapter for both assessing and selecting among these algorithms.

3.8.1 Further Reading

- With imbalanced outcomes, there are a host of other techniques outside of the use of sampling, such as using different misclassification costs for each class or additional types of resampling (i.e., stratified k-fold). See Haixang et al. (2017) for a general overview of the various methods.

- We only reviewed what we see as the most commonly applied forms of resampling, namely k-fold (and a few variants) and bootstrap sampling. Further, we neglected possible modifications if the datasets have some form of nested structure. A host of techniques have been developed and evaluated for longitudinal data, which we detail further in Chapter 9 (but see Bulteel et al., 2018 for a recent discussion in the context of autoregressive models).

- Our coverage of calibration and further steps in the decision-making process of using a model was relatively brief. We recommend Steyerberg (2019) for further detail in this area.

- The bias–variance tradeoff is a fundamental concept in machine learning. For alternative perspectives or examples, see Hastie et al. (2009) or James et al. (2013).

3.8.2 Computational Time and Resources

While the process of partitioning the data is, in and of itself, computationally simple, the number of partitions, and its effect on the number of models run, can have a significant impact on analysis runtime. Particularly when using nested cross-validation, the runtimes can easily double. This has been mentioned as a key drawback of this approach, and in some situations minimal improvements in bias over *k*-fold is overshadowed by the increase in computational time (Wainer & Cawley, 2021). The easiest way to speed this up is to run this process in parallel, which `caret` makes relatively easy, as it defaults to using parallel processing as long as the user has set up the `R` environment with a specific number of cores allocated (see the `caret` manual dedicated to this topic: https://topepo.github.io/caret/parallel-processing.html). While the `caret` package facilitates the use of *k*-fold, repeated *k*-fold, and bootstrap sampling, one has to write their own routine for nested CV. An example script is provided in the supplemental material. Finally, when the outcome of interest is not continuous, it is necessary to alter the default code or change the class of variable to invoke the use of loss function unique to the outcome type. There are a number of ways to do this, and many `R` packages (`caret` included) will try and guess the outcome type based on the class assigned in R. By default, integer and numeric classes invoke regression, while nominal or factor variables default to classification. This is particularly important when assessing fit metrics with `confusionMatrix`, and can often require the specification of named levels to the factor variable. However, this behavior differs by package, and a more straightforward way (in most `R` packages) to change the loss function is to specify the `family=`, which is further discussed in Chapter 4.

Part II

ALGORITHMS FOR UNIVARIATE OUTCOMES

4

Regularized Regression

This chapter is the first to focus on the algorithm side of machine learning, with the prior two chapters detailing and discussing the philosophy and practice of machine learning. An important piece to remember is that while our discussion may focus on the algorithm in this and the following chapters, the aspects to model evaluation detailed in Chapter 3 are an integral component to the application of each algorithm. The topic of this chapter centers on the integration of regularization with regression models, spurred by a change in motivation from inference in relatively small data (both sample size and predictors) with linear regression (using ordinary least squares), to more of a focus on prediction in larger data, necessitating the use of various forms of regularization. We begin with a thorough overview of regularization in standard regression models, while covering a number of extensions that take into account varying predictor structures.

4.1 Key Terminology

- Link function. A mathematical function that allows the linear model to be applied to outcome variables with varying distributions (e.g., binary, count).
- Logit. A function, also referred to as the log-odds, that maps probability values to real numbers. This forms the basis for logisitic regression, where predicted probabilities are generated with the linear model.
- Probit. Similar to the logit function, the probit is based on using the standard normal distribution (as opposed to logistic distribution with logit). While sometimes used for binary outcomes, it is more commonly used with ordinal outcomes.
- Multinomial. A type of regression used with categorical outcome variables that are assumed to be nominal.

- Ordinary least squares (OLS). The most common form of estimation in linear regression, OLS involves minimizing the sum of squared residuals.

- Regularization, shrinkage, or penalized likelihood. An alternative form of estimation often used in regression to reduce the propensity to overfit or perform variable selection.

- Variable selection. A common goal in statistics where some alternative type of regression (regularization or stepwise) is used to remove predictor variables from the model.

- Standardization. An important step when applying regularization, standardization involves transforming predictor variables so they have a mean of 0 (centering) and standard deviation (scaling) of 1. This does not alter the relationship between variables but can have a number of benefits for estimation.

- Interaction. Testing for interactions (also referred to as moderation) in regression involves adding additional terms to the linear model, often of a form $b_{x_1x_2}X_1X_2$ to determine if the effect of X_1 varies across the values of X_2.

4.2 Linear Regression

Ordinary least squares (OLS) regression has been, both historically and currently, the estimation method of choice for linear regression in the social and behavioral sciences. Particularly when the sample size is small and the number of predictors is not large, OLS will have the smallest standard errors and be unbiased, if the assumptions are met. However, it is becoming increasingly common for researchers to have a larger number of predictors, along with the desire to make inferences into more than just a handful of predictors. In these cases, OLS no longer is the best suited tool.

With respect to the assumptions of OLS and how best to test these, we refer readers to one of the many exceptional regression textbooks (e.g. Cohen, Cohen, West, & Aiken, 2003; Darlington & Hayes, 2017). In many respects, the methods that we discuss have many of the same assumptions. In the rest of this chapter, we discuss various applications of regularization, and how this addresses a change from the desire to make inferences with respect to only a small number of initial variables to scenarios with a larger number of variables.

Switching from the context of a single continuous dependent variable, to an analysis with a binary, count, or multinomial requires a switch in the type of model we use. Falling under the umbrella of the generalized linear model, we can change the type of link function to be used based on the distribution of the outcome. Most packages in `R` require the specification in the form of a distribution. Common distributions based on the `glm()` function or the `glmnet` package are listed in Table 4.1.

TABLE 4.1. Common Link or Distribution Specifications. Note that we specifically do not include both ordinal and survival outcomes.

Outcome Class	Link	Distribution
Continuous	Identity	Gaussian
Binary	Logit	Binomial
Count	Log	Poisson
Multinomial	Logit	Multinomial

Changes in the interpretation of coefficients and model fit can be tricky to understand when switching from one type of outcome to another. We do not provide an extensive coverage of this and instead focus on both continuous and categorical (dichotomous) outcomes. In most applied textbooks, logistic regression receives considerably less coverage than linear regression. However, in machine learning, categorical outcomes are very common, in forms such as who completed treatment or diagnosis status. Below, we provide a brief overview of logistic regression, followed by multiple examples that use a continuous outcome, and we end the chapter with an example categorical analysis.

4.3 Logistic Regression

4.3.1 Motivating Examplc

As a motivating example, we analyzed data from the National Survey on Drug Use and Health from 2014. Thirty-nine variables were included in order to predict suicidal ideation (binary; whether experienced in last 12 months; SUICTHINK). Predictors included symptoms of depression and other mental health disorders, the impact of these symptoms on daily functioning, and four demographic variables (gender, ethnicity, relationship status, age; all were dummy coded).

4.3.2 The Logistic Model

Using categorical outcomes in a traditional linear regression models leads to a number of problems, thus logistic regression uses a logit link function to model the probability of belonging to a class. With just one predictor, X_1, we can model the probability of Y by

$$P(Y) = \frac{e^{-b_0+b_1X_1}}{1+e^{-b_0+b_1X_1}}, \tag{4.1}$$

or, equivalently

$$logit(Y) = b_0 + b_1X_1, \tag{4.2}$$

where $logit(Y_i) = ln(\frac{P(Y_i)}{1-P(Y_i)})$. Now, we are predicting the *log odds* of Y, despite the inclusion of the same formula as in linear regression. We map the linear regression equation to a logistic curve, with an example depicted in Figure 4.1.

In Figure 4.1, we simulated data that had a larger degree of separation between 0s and 1s. This manifests itself in a larger slope (b_1, or the slope at the inflection point). In social and behavioral data, this degree of class separation is unlikely, as it is generally difficult to accurately predict the outcome of interest. A more realistic representation is depicted in Figure 4.2, where we modeled the probability of having a 1 on SUICTHNK with a predictor that measures depression symptomology. Here, the greater overlap of both outcome levels with respect to the X variable leads to a less steep slope, indicating worse prediction accuracy. Here, to better model the outcome we would need to drastically improve our model to better understand how people who have a history of suicidal thoughts differ from those without a history.

For interpreting the coefficients, we start with an intercept-only model. With this model, we get an estimated intercept of −0.02. To interpret this, we take the exponent of the parameter, or $e^{-.02}$, equaling 0.98, which is in odds format. This equals $log(\frac{P(Y_i=1)}{P(Y_i=0)})$, which in our sample is close to 50–50. The value of 0.98 is the odds ratio between class 1 and class 0. Going forward with the addition of predictors, the intercept is interpreted as the odds ratio between observations with an outcome of 1 and 0, with 0s on the X variables. By adding a predictor, we interpret the coefficient as e^{b_1}, or what is the expected change in odds with a 1-point increase in X_1. In using a sum score of depression items as a single predictor, we get a slope of 0.94, or $e^{0.94} = 2.57$, and an intercept of 0.06, or $e^{.06} =$ 1.06. Because our predictor was standardized before the analysis, we can interpret the intercept as the odds ratio of having a history of suicidal deviation for those at the mean of the depression score. For b_1, those that are 1 standard deviation higher in depression, we expect to see a 157% increase in the odds of endorsing a history of suicidal ideation. We can see that similar to linear regression, the interpretation of logistic regression

FIGURE 4.1. Simulated example of clear class separation.

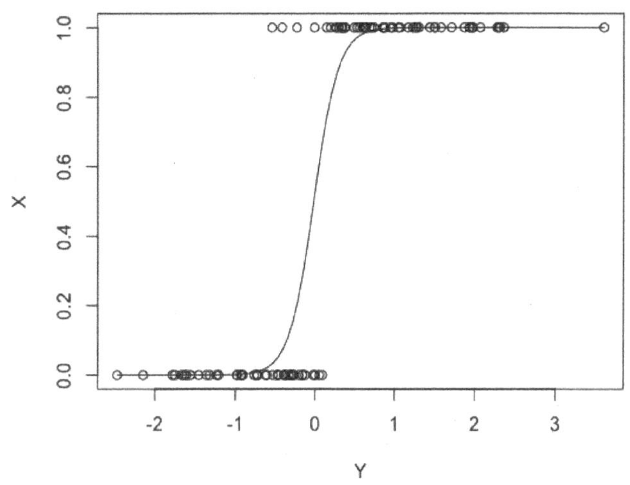

is greatly aided by standardizing the predictors. Below in our discussion of regularization, this also becomes a mathematical necessity. As we have already assessed model fit in Chapter 3, we do not reiterate comparisons of using accuracy, area under the curve, or precision recall curves. In our example, because we have a balanced outcome, it is more reasonable to interpret the accuracy. Using this one depression predictor led to an accuracy of 0.66. This can be attributed to the large amount of class overlap in Figure 4.2, and the resultant small slope to the logistic curve. In many cases in social and behavioral data it will be highly unlikely to achieve a high degree of accuracy (e.g., > 0.9). Instead of using this as an absolute metric, it may be more informative to use it in a model comparison framework, evaluating the fit of the model in comparison to a more restrictive model. In our example, the addition of the depression predictor increased our accuracy from 0.5 in the intercept-only model, to 0.66. Although not a "good" absolute model fit, we can at the very least conclude that depression is somewhat informative to understanding who does and does not endorse having a history of suicidal ideation. In summary, interpretation in logistic regression may be less intuitive, however the process for model testing the selection of variables is very similar, as detailed below.

FIGURE 4.2. Using depression symptoms as a predictor of suicidal thoughts in the last 12 months. Note that random noise was added to the predictor to jitter the X values.

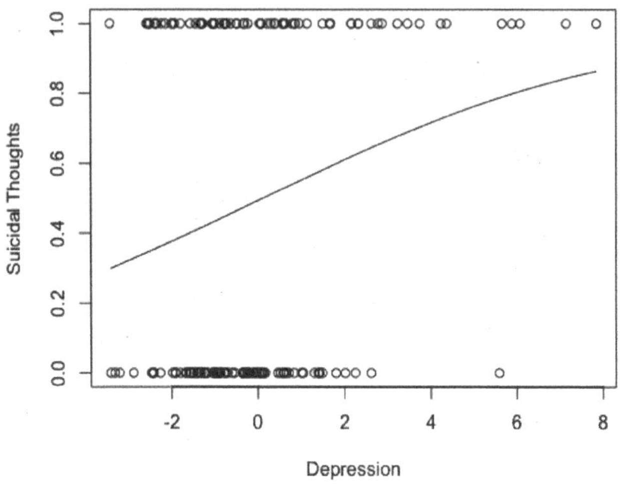

4.4 Regularization

There exist a multitude of reasons to perform variable selection in regression. As we discuss later in the chapter, one is that a subset of variables may have lower model error when evaluated on a holdout (alternative) sample. Alternatively, we may have more predictors than we are willing to interpret, thus we use variable selection for a more parsimonious representation. At its extreme, common in neuroscience or genetics research, we may have more predictors than we do observations. In this scenario we must perform some form of dimensionality reduction. Finally, our purpose for variable selection may be more practical. If we wish to develop a screening measure to be used in contexts outside of research, time is often of the essence so the smaller the number of variables to measure, the better.

Given our desire to perform variable selection, we must choose among a myriad of methods available that were developed for this purpose. In the tradition in the social and behavioral science, some form of stepwise selection is often used. Built as a computationally simpler approach than best subsets, either backward elimination or forward selection only requires p models run, where p is the number of predictors. Best subsets on the other hand require 2^p number of models run to find the "best" model. For 5 predictors, this is a manageable 32 models. However, for 20 this requires running 1,048,576 models, and 100 predictors requires over a quintillion models ($> 1e^{30}$). This is simply not possible, or advisable, to attempt unless the number of variables is more manageable. Heuristic algorithms, such as genetic algorithms, tabu search, or simulated annealing, have been proposed to overcome this limitation of best subsets, however, these methods are often quite computationally intensive as well.

Although computationally less burdensome, stepwise selection methods have a long history of use and abuse in the social and behavioral sciences. Most notably, the adaptive nature of the algorithms has a tendency to capitalize on chance, particularly if researchers try and interpret the p-values from the best fitting model. Used correctly, both backward and forward stepwise selection methods often perform well in selecting close to the optimal number of predictors. However, confusion over proper use of this method (particularly that it is an atheoretical technique), and the recent development of a host of more flexible techniques, cause us to not recommend its use. Instead, we discuss the use of *regularization* and how it can be applied in a number of ways to perform variable selection.

4.4.1 Regularization Formulation

Estimating coefficients in a regression model that are shrunken toward 0, relative to that of ordinary least squares, is called many names including shrinkage, regularization, or penalized estimation. This involves placing constraints (penalties) on the coefficients in a regression model. The two most common forms of penalized regression are the *ridge* (Hoerl & Kennard, 1970) and the least absolute shrinkage and selection operator (*lasso*; Tibshirani, 1996, 2011). Both methods add a penalty term to the ordinary least squares fit function. Given an outcome y and a matrix of predictors X, ordinary least squares estimation can be defined as minimizing the residual sum of squares (RSS),

$$RSS = argmin\Big\{\sum_{i=1}^{N}(y_i - \beta_0 - \sum_{j=1}^{p} x_{ij}\beta_j)^2\Big\}, \tag{4.3}$$

where b_0 is the intercept, and β_j is the regression coefficient for x_j. In this, our aim is to minimize the discrepancy between our actual outcome (y_i) and the predicted outcome ($\hat{y}_i$). Given that certain assumptions are met, the estimated coefficients β_0 and β_1 will be unbiased estimates of their population parameter counterparts. To perform regularization, we add a penalty term to the equation for the RSS that will bias the parameter coefficients toward 0. For ridge regularization, this is defined as

$$ridge = \underbrace{RSS}_{OLS} + \underbrace{\lambda \sum_{j=1}^{p} \beta_j^2}_{ridge}, \tag{4.4}$$

where λ is the penalty that controls the amount of shrinkage. Note that when $\lambda = 0$, Equation 4.3 reduces to ordinary least squares regression. As λ increases, the β_j parameters are shrunken toward 0. The counterpart to ridge, lasso regression, is defined as

$$lasso = \underbrace{RSS}_{OLS} + \underbrace{\lambda \sum_{j=1}^{p} |\beta_j|}_{lasso}. \tag{4.5}$$

In Equation 4.5 the sum of the absolute value of each β_j coefficient is multiplied by a parameter, λ. λ quantifies the influence of the lasso penalty on the overall model fit—as λ increases, a steeper penalty is incurred for each parameter, which results in greater shrinkage of the coefficient sizes. It is common to test a range of λ values, combined with cross-validation, to examine what the most appropriate degree of regularization is for a given dataset.

In contrast to the lasso, the ridge penalty takes the sum of the squared coefficients. Whereas the lasso will push the betas all the way to 0 (as any non zero beta will contribute to the penalty term), the ridge penalty will instead shrink coefficients, but not necessarily all the way to 0, as the squaring operation means that small betas incur negligible penalties. Both methods have benefits and drawbacks (see James et al., 2013), and can be seen as reflecting diverging views on the nature of the underlying association (i.e., whether the coefficients are sparse). One benefit of ridge regularization is that it better handles multicollinearity among predictors.

In an effort to combine the variable selection aspects of the lasso along with the ability to handle collinearity from ridge regularization, Zou and Hastie (2005) proposed the *elastic net* (enet) regularization. Through the use of a mixing parameter, α, the elastic net combines both ridge and lasso regularization

$$enet = \underbrace{RSS}_{OLS} + \underbrace{(1-\alpha)\lambda \sum_{j=1}^{p} \beta_j^2}_{ridge} + \underbrace{\alpha\lambda \sum_{j=1}^{p} |\beta_j|}_{lasso}, \tag{4.6}$$

FIGURE 4.3. Comparison of ridge and lasso estimates for the ECLS-K. L1 norm refers to the summation of the parameter estimates, with higher values denoting less penalty.

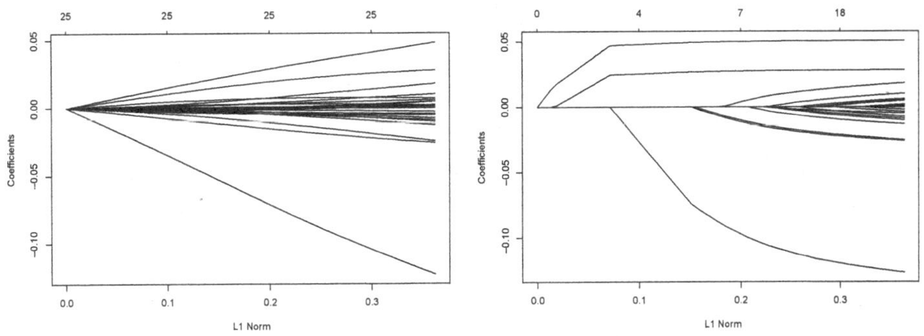

where α controls the degree of mixing between ridge and lasso penalties. When $\alpha = 1$, Equation 4.6 reduces to the lasso, while the opposite occurs when $\alpha = 0$. Just as it is common to test a sequence of λ values, the same can be done for α. However, little is to be lost if α is fixed to a value such as 0.5 to have an equal amount of mixing. In using the elastic net for variable selection, note that the solutions are often less sparse than the lasso, due to the influence of the ridge penalties. However, it often produces improved prediction performance when predictors are correlated.

To ensure that the amount of penalty is uniform across predictors, each predictor needs to be standardized prior to the analysis. As it is less common to penalize the intercept, centering each variable removes the need for estimating β_0 in many cases. Leaving the predictors in the original scale would result in the use of disproportionately larger penalties for those predictors with larger scales. Standardizing variables prior to analysis removes the influence of scale on the results. For categorical predictors, this requires first dummy coding the variables and then standardizing (Tibshirani, 1997). Note that some software for regularization internally standardizes the variables, does the analysis, and then returns parameter estimates in the original metric.

To understand how these different forms of regularization result in differing effects on β_j, we used the `glmnet` package to penalize predictors from the ECLS-K dataset. In the analysis of predicting eighth-grade science scores, we included five "real" predictors: eighth-grade general knowledge, eighth-grade math, gender, income, and BMI. Additionally, we created 20 "noise" predictors (simulated as standard normal) which had no relationship with the outcome.

In Figure 4.3, both the ridge and lasso estimates are displayed with the amount of penalty decreasing from left to right on the X-axis. Starting from the far right in each figure, with the OLS estimates ($\lambda = 0$), as the penalty increases (moving left), each of the parameter estimates is gradually shrunken toward 0. In comparing lasso estimates to ridge estimates, note that the lasso sets parameters to 0 at differing rates, with some parameters set to 0 almost immediately (small penalties). In the right panel of Figure 4.3, three parameters exhibit differing behavior and aren't set to 0 until the penalty becomes much larger. With the ridge parameter trajectories, none of the parameters reaches 0 until they all do at the largest penalty (most programs stop increasing λ once all parameters are set to 0).

Note that in this example, a couple of the parameters are not shrunken toward 0 until larger penalties are used. Additionally, in some cases with regularization, penalized parameters will actually increase with larger penalties. In both of these scenarios, this occurs when there are some parameters that have a more influential effect on the outcome. As the less influential effects are shrunken, these more influential effects are actually increased. The point of this is that there is not always a uniform effect of increasing the penalty on all of the parameters.

To better understand why the use of ridge and lasso regularization results in different effects on the parameters as the penalties are increased, it is helpful to display the equivalent configurations of both Equations 4.4 and 4.5. For ridge regression, this is $\beta_1^2 + \beta_2^2 + ...\beta_j^2 \leq s$ and for the lasso, $|\beta_1|+|\beta_2|+...|\beta_j| \leq s$, where s is a constraint. As a result, in contrast to thinking of either the ridge or lasso as ways of penalizing coefficients, we can think of them as placing constraints on the summation of either the squared (ridge) or absolute value (lasso) of the regression coefficients. Thinking of it in this way, as we decrease s, the sum of all coefficients is required to become smaller, thus pulling each parameter towards 0 at differing rates, depending on each predictor's relationship with other predictors as well as the outcome. To visualize this, Figure 4.4 depicts the constraint forms of Equations 4.4 and 4.5 using two predictors.

The left side of Figure 4.4 contains the constraints of ridge regularization, where the squaring of both parameter estimates results in a circular constraint region. In the right side, summing the absolute value of each parameter in lasso regularization results in a diamond-shaped constraint region. Additionally, $\hat{\beta}$ represents the OLS parameter estimates, while the ellipses centered around $\hat{\beta}$ are regions of constant residual sum of squares. In both of these figures, we can imagine constraining the parameters to be less than 1. Decreasing the value of s results in smaller constraint regions, and thus parameters closer to 0. Increasing the value of s moves each pa-

FIGURE 4.4. Parameter and constraint space for ridge (left) and lasso (right).

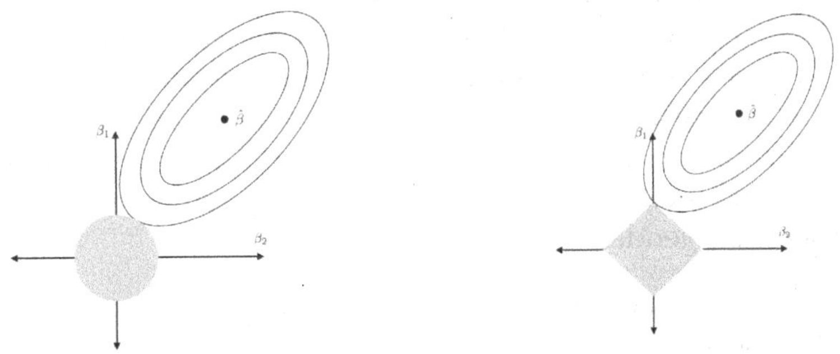

rameter closer to the the OLS solution. Additionally, as s decreases, the bias of the solution also increases, pulling the parameter estimates farther and farther away from $\hat{\beta}$, thus increasing the residual sum of squares. Finally, the diamond constraint regions of lasso regularization contain edges, edges that correspond to estimates of 0 for either regression coefficient. In contrast, the circle constraint region for ridge regularization has such a smooth surface around both axes that it tends to not pull parameters directly to one axis, thus resulting in estimates around 0, but not necessarily *at* 0.

4.4.2 Choosing a Final Model

Although these methods for regularization are intuitively appealing, to get final parameter estimates, one needs to choose a single λ, and thus a final model. The most common way to accomplish this is through the use of cross-validation. In this method, a large number of prespecified λ values can be utilized (e.g., 100). Instead of choosing the model with the lowest mean squared error averaged across the CV folds, one can choose the model with the fewest number of predictors (most sparse) within one standard error of the best fitting model (Hastie et al., 2009; for recent evaluation, see Chen & Yang, 2021). Despite using CV, choosing a simpler model than the best fitting further reduces our propensity to overfit, and provides a more parsimonious model that is virtually indistinguishable in model fit from the best fitting model.

We demonstrate the use of the one standard error rule using the same ECLS-K example. The fit across each value of λ for the lasso model is displayed in Figure 4.5. In this, each value of λ (log value) is on the X-axis, while the mean squared error assessed across 10-fold cross-validation is on the Y-axis. As the penalty is increased, there is a slight improvement in the average fit of the model. The best fitting model is denoted by the first (furthest left) vertical dashed line, while the second line displays the maximum value of λ that has an average model fit no worse than one standard error of the best fitting model. After this model, increasing values of penalty result in drastically worse MSE values. We chose one standard error metric as a basis for a final model, which had 4 nonzero regression coefficients. All of the noise parameters were set to 0, as well as the coefficients for gender and BMI.

FIGURE 4.5. Cross-validated MSE for each λ value. The left-most vertical line indicates the model with the lowest MSE, while the rightmost line indicates the most parsimonious model within one standard error of the lowest MSE model.

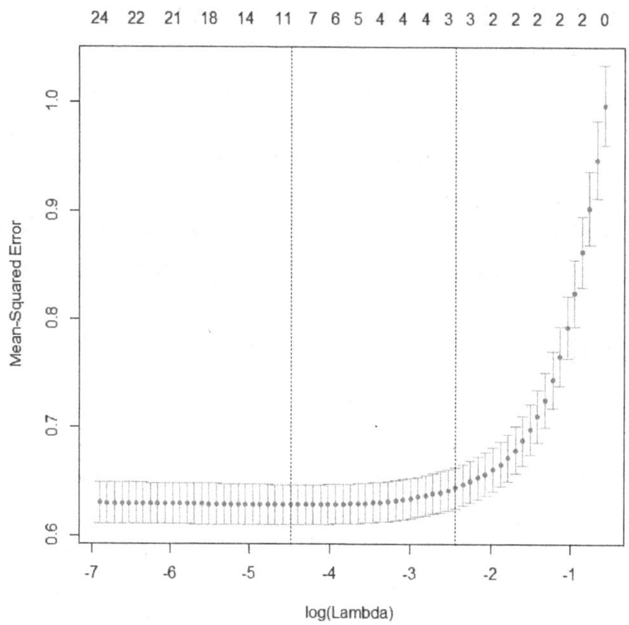

One drawback to the use of lasso regression is that it tends to over-penalize those parameters that were not set to 0 (Fan & Li, 2001; Hastie et al., 2009). A number of additional types of regularization have been proposed to overcome this problem, however, one simpler solution is to use a two-stage fitting process. In the first step, the lasso is paired with cross-validation to identify which variables are estimated with non zero coefficients. In the second step, a linear (or other type depending on the outcome) regression model is fit with only those variables not screened out in the first step. This process is known as the *relaxed* lasso (Meinshausen, 2007). One thing to note is to *not* use the p-values from this second model as they do not take into account the adaptive nature of the algorithm. For the three nonzero parameters in our example, running a second model increased the estimates from the lasso model in the following way: math score increased from 0.023 to 0.378, general knowledge increased from 0.045 to 0.263, and income from 0.001 to 0.083.

4.4.3 Rationale for Regularization

Bet on Sparsity

Underlying the use of the lasso, or sparser extensions, is this concept of a "bet on sparsity" (Hastie, Tibshirani, & Friedman, 2001). By this, there is an assumption that the underlying model is sparse, or that there are few prominent or meaningful effects (nonzero coefficients). In the case of regression, this means that removing predictors outside of a handful will not appreciably reduce the model fit. The opposite of a sparse underlying model is that of a dense model, or one where there are many effects, of which most may be small, but most importantly few are truly zero. In social and behavioral research, an underlying "true" sparse model is unlikely to exist. Instead most variables in a dataset probably have small correlations among themselves (e.g., the "crud" factor; Meehl, 1990). As a result, the use of regularization in applied research will impart some degree of bias to the results. Although this seems an undesirable side effect, we explain two aspects that support this rationale.

Functional Sparsity

The first and foremost is that even though there may be a confluence of small effects in our dataset, their inclusion into our model makes interpretation quite difficult (e.g., parsimony), or we wish to screen variables to increase our efficiency in future studies. In this case we care more about what could be termed *functional* sparsity, where we specifically aim to estimate a parsimonious model for these various reasons. In situations with larger sample sizes and a confluence of variables that contribute small effects, inference can be difficult due to this level of complexity in understanding what variables are important contributors. The idea behind functional sparsity is in contrast to data contingent sparsity, where the ratio between sample size and number of variables precludes an accurate estimate. Despite having a strong theoretical rationale for including variables in our model, we may have to use regularization to accurately estimate the model coefficients.

As an example of this, we used all of the complete cases from `bfi` dataset, resulting in a sample size of 2,236. In this dataset, we used age as

FIGURE 4.6. OLS and lasso regression coefficients in the `bfi` dataset.

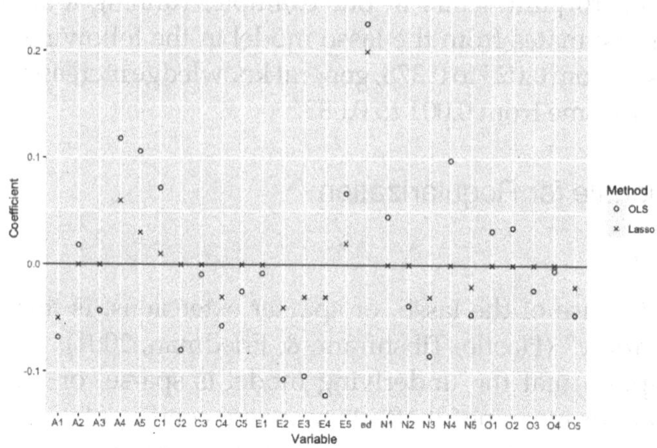

an outcome, with 25 personality items, and education as predictors. The 25 personality items include 5 items to measure each of the 5 factors of the Big Five theory of personality. These 5 factors include neuroticism, extraversion, conscientiousness, openness, and agreeableness. The coefficients from a linear regression using these 26 predictors are displayed in Figure 4.6.

Of the 26 predictors, 14 of them were significant. The resulting standardized OLS regression coefficients are displayed in Figure 4.6. In OLS regression, the inclusion of predictors that have overlap (correlation) with many other variables inflates the standard errors, making this number of significant predictors somewhat surprising. If the sample size was not as large as in this example (2,236), this would be unlikely to happen. However, none of these standardized coefficients was above 0.12. Despite this, we could describe this model as dense in that most effects are small.

One method for reducing the dimensionality and increasing the interpretability is structural equation modeling. The Big Five items were originally created with this method in mind. We discuss the integration of machine learning in structural equation modeling in Chapters 7 and 8. Instead of moving to the use of latent variables, researchers may instead be interested in knowing which items are predictive, and ideally this entails using only a subset of the available items. This form of selection will inevitably incur some bias given the dense structure of the predictors, however, this may be more in line with a researcher's aims.

We used lasso regression on the same `bfi` dataset and the results are displayed in Figure 4.6. Of the 26 predictors, half were estimated as 0. The first thing to note is the bias toward 0 uniformly applied to each of

FIGURE 4.7. Parameter estimates across the 1,000 repetitions. Asterisks denote the simulated estimates, dots are the mean estimates, with standard error bars representing 1 standard deviation. Predictor 1 – 5 refers to $x1 - x5$.

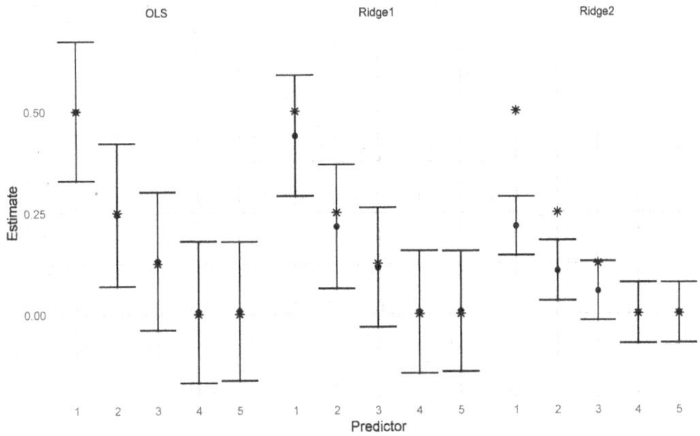

the coefficients. Given the large sample size, this is not a sparse model, representing somewhat of a mixture between a purely sparse model (only a couple of nonzero parameters) and a dense structure (the OLS results). However, our results may be more interpretable than that from OLS, and a researcher may have a better basis for removing predictors than that of the p-values.

4.4.4 Bias and Variance

The second benefit of applying regularization to create a sparser model is a reduction in the variance, which comes at the expense of bias. To demonstrate this, we simulated data according to the following linear model:

$$y = 0 + 0.5 * x1 + 0.25 * x2 + 0.125 * x3 + 0 * x4 + 0 * x5 + N(0, 1) \tag{4.7}$$

From a simulated sample size of 1,000, we randomly selected 40 cases to test three different models, OLS regression, ridge regression with a penalty of 10 (Ridge1), and ridge regression with a penalty of 50. We repeated this sequence 1,000 times, with the mean and the standard deviation of the parameter estimates displayed in Figure 4.7

In this, we can see both the reduction in variance, and systematic biasing of parameter estimates toward 0 in ridge regression. OLS is unbiased, at the expense of higher variance. In contrast to the discussion of the bias–variance tradeoff in Chapter 3, which focused on the resulting fit, the same process holds for parameter estimates. Shrinking parameter estimates towards 0 results in a corresponding shrinkage of model predictions toward the mean. While this systematic biasing results in worse within-sample fit, it oftentimes results in better out-of-sample fit, particularly when competing models are too flexible for the data (e.g., small sample sizes).

Sample Size

One of the main motivations behind the development of regularization methods is for datasets that have a larger number of variables than total observations. In this case, OLS regression can't be used. Most social and behavioral datasets do not take this form, however, small sample sizes are often an issue. To achieve adequate power to detect a given parameter, a suitably larger sample size (depending on the magnitude of the effect) is required. The larger the effect, the smaller the sample size required. This is why rules of thumb for a minimum sample size given a specific number of predictors (Green, 1991) are difficult to operationalize.

When multiple effects are considered, this sample size requirement is inflated. If collecting additional data is not possible for practical purposes, one strategy for testing complex models in the presence of a small sample is to reduce the dimensionality of the model. Traditionally, this meant using a method such as stepwise regression to reduce the number of coefficients in a regression model. However, regularization can be used for the same purposes. Additionally, the number of predictors selected as nonzero in lasso regression is a function of both the effect size and sample size, thus almost automatically creating a rule of thumb for selection. We demonstrate this in a simple simulation, where we simulated data with 100 predictors, varying the sample size (50, 100, 200, 1,000) and the value of all 100 regression coefficients (0.1, 0.4, 0.7). Across 100 replications, we investigated how both of these simulation conditions would influence the number of predictors lasso regression (using the one standard error rule to select a final model) would identify as nonzero.

As is evident in both sides of Figure 4.8, as the coefficient size and sample size increased, fewer predictors were selected as 0. Although we could go into more detail about each condition and the results, the point we wish to make is that not only does the magnitude of the effects matter for variable selection, but also that sample size can have an equally strong effect on the number of variables selected.

Also using the `bfi` dataset, we can demonstrate the effect of regularization on improving the generalizability of the results, particularly when the ratio of sample size to number of predictors is low. To do this, we varied the size of training set we created from the 2,236 observations, using this training set to run 26 predictors, and then tested this model on the remain-

FIGURE 4.8. The effect of coefficient value (left pane) and sample size (right pane) on the number of parameters selection as nonzero.

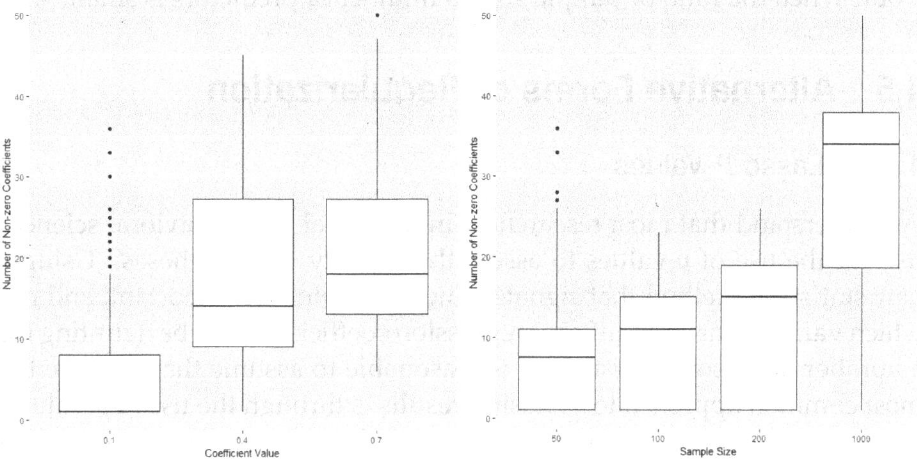

ing sample (2,236—training set size). For each training set, we compared both OLS and ridge regression to select a model of coefficients, repeating this 500 times across each sample size. The results are displayed in Figure 4.9.

FIGURE 4.9. Performance of OLS and ridge on the test set while varying the sample size of the training set.

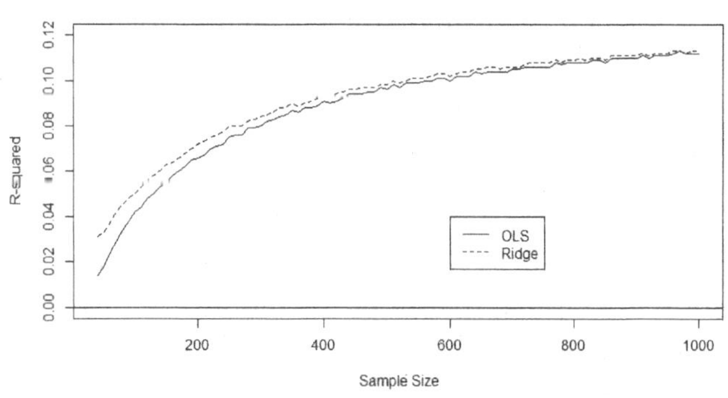

We see in this figure that model performance increases as the size of the training set increases. A larger training set size contains more information, thus increasing the generalizability of results. Additionally, we can see that shrinking the parameters toward 0 with ridge regression also increases our model performance on an alternative sample. The gap in model performance between OLS and ridge decreases as the number of training observations increases, which can mostly be attributed to OLS performing worse when the ratio of sample size to number of predictors is small.

4.5 Alternative Forms of Regularization

4.5.1 Lasso P-Values

We understand that most researchers in the social and behavioral sciences rely on the use of p-values to assess the validity of hypotheses. Using a new statistical method that signals which variables are important, and not which variables have significant regression coefficients, can be daunting for a number of reasons. First off, it is reasonable to assume that because the most common approach to assessing results is through the use of p-values, that other researchers, and maybe most notably journal reviewers, may find the changing of frameworks and terminology unconvincing. As a result, we now discuss a recently developed method that computes p-values for coefficients in lasso regression, taking into account the adaptive nature of the algorithm. This procedure is based on work by Lockhart, Taylor, Tibshirani, and Tibshirani (2014) that builds on one method for computing the entire lasso path, across all penalty values. This computational procedure is called *least angle regression* (LARS; Efron, Hastie, Johnstone, & Tibshirani, 2004), of which the lasso is a subset. LARS is actually computationally very similar to stepwise regression. Stepwise regression and LARS each enter predictors one at a time based on their correlation with the residuals; however in LARS, when each predictor is entered, the beta coefficient is restricted (penalized) to some degree. Along the path of the computation, once a predictor enters the model, the beta coefficient is gradually increased until an additional predictor has an equal magnitude of correlation with the residual. This procedure has been found to be a computationally simple approach to computing the entire lasso regression solution.

One of the main challenges in computing p-values for the lasso is taking into account the adaptive nature of the algorithm. To overcome this, Lockhart et al. (2014) developed a new distribution for the test statistic that takes into account the adaptive nature of the algorithm. We tested this method as implemented in the `covTest` package (Lockhart et al., 2014) with our example in the ECLS-K data. All three variables that were chosen with the lasso using the one standard error rule were also chosen on the basis of p-values. Additionally, gender also had a p-value less than 0.001. Going back to pairing lasso regresison with cross-validation, if we had chosen a final model on the basis of the best fit (not largest penalty within 1 standard error), gender would also have been chosen. Here we highlight one of the biggest issues with variable selection—it is inherently unstable on the basis of making dichotomous decisions on whether variables are included or not. In the next section we discuss a method that was developed specifically to address this drawback in the use of the lasso for variable selection.

4.5.2 Stability of Selection

In any statistical method that performs some form of variable selection, the stability of the final model will always be somewhat in question. By *stability*, we refer to the influence of taking random subsamples (or bootstrap samples) of the data and the resulting variability to the variable selection. With OLS regression, this means that the regression coefficients might be slightly different across each subsample. In contrast, variable selection methods might select completely different variables across each subsample, inducing uncertainty into what the best subset of variables is. Practically speaking, this is less of a concern with the current dataset and more of a problem of confidence in how this model might generalize to alternative samples.

Stability is particularly a problem with stepwise regression methods (Flack & Chang, 1987; Austin & Tu, 2004; Austin, 2008). As an example, in the Holzinger–Swineford (1939) study, we split up the sample in two ways. Of the 301 cases, both the first 100 cases and second 100 cases were split into separate datasets. We ran backward elimination with both of these datasets, as well as on the full sample. In the first sample, variables $x4$ and $x5$ were chosen, while $x3$, $x4$, and $x6$ were chosen in the second sample, and $x2$ and $x4$ in the full sample. The only variable common across all three datasets was $x4$. As a result, we have some uncertainty regarding whether $x2$, $x3$, $x5$, and $x6$ are important variables to include in a subsequent analysis.

The idea behind stability selection is to repeatedly split a sample to create a subsample, run an algorithm for variable selection on each sub sample, and and then choose the variables that are selected in a majority of subsamples (Meinshausen & Buhlmann, 2010). In the context of regularized regression, Meinshausen and Buhlmann (2010) argue that instead of just focusing on *regularization paths*, which is the path for each parameter across all penalty values, you can also look at the *stability paths*, which refer to the probability of each variable to be selected when random resampling the data. Variables are now chosen that exhibit a high probability of being selected after using multiple iterations of subsampling.

Using the `bfi` dataset, with 24 predictors of the agreeableness sum score, we used the `stabs` package (Hofner & Hothorn, 2017) to test the stability of lasso regression across 1,000 subsamples. On each of the selected

FIGURE 4.10. Stability selection results using the *bfi* dataset. We set the selection probability at 0.9 (vertical line), resulting in five predictors being selected. The *X*-axis refers to the selection probability.

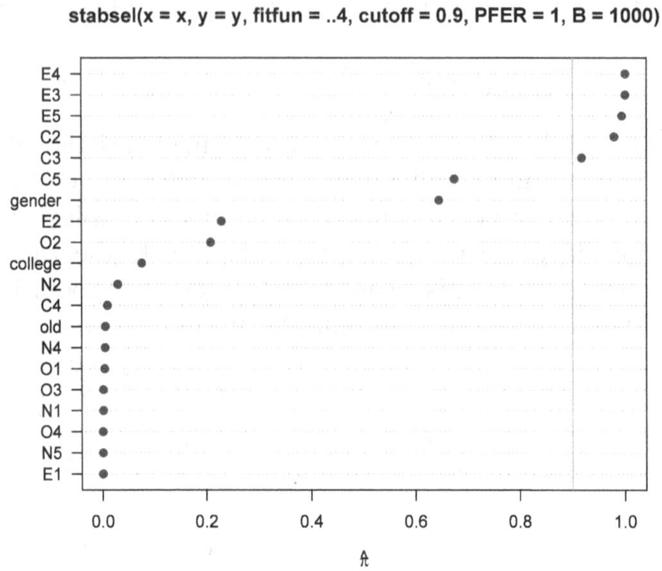

subsamples, we set lasso regression to select seven variables in each model, opening the possibility for multiple variables to be selected and reduce the possible influence of suppression among predictors with a high degree of correlation. The selection probabilities across the 1,000 subsamples are displayed in Figure 4.10.

In this figure, using a cutoff of 0.9, we would select *C2*, *C3*, *E3*, *E4*, and *E5*. To compare these results to what we would conclude using just one run of lasso regression, we ran the model using `glmnet` with 10-fold cross-validation, using the one standard error rule to select a final model. In this one lasso model, the five variables selected by stability selection were selected, but the one lasso model also selected *C5*, *O2*, and gender. Using a different seed, we ran lasso regression again, and this time the model selected the college age variable. What we see here is the effect of randomly selecting observations for each cross-validation partition. Even this degree of random variability can influence which variables are selected. It is for this reason that we recommend evaluating the stability of the lasso regression results. Additionally, if the lasso regression results select too many variables in one run, using stability selection allows researchers the ability to also set a threshold for the degree of stability desired, very likely resulting in a sparser final model. We set our threshold at 0.9, but this is a user-controlled tuning parameter, and should be set based on both practical and theoretical considerations. For more detail regarding stability selection in regression models, see Hofner, Boccuto, and Göker (2015).

4.5.3 Interactions

In the social and behavioral sciences, one of the most important topics of statistical analysis is that of identifying and understanding interactions in regression models. Formally, we follow Darlington and Hayes (2017) in defining an interaction as a change in one regressor's relationship with Y when another regressor changes. This can alternatively be called *moderation*, where we attempt to identify variables that moderate the effect of another X variable on Y. In contrast to main or simple effects, where the effect of X_1 on Y remains constant across the values of X_2, interactions denote a change in the slope. These represent effects of particular importance given the difficulty in identification and theoretical consequences.

The identification of interactions is an extremely important topic in machine learning. Methods such as decision trees and extensions (see Chapters 5 and 6) *automatically* try to identify important interactions between the predictors and outcome. Other methods, such as multivariate adaptive regression splines, have options for testing different levels of interactions (e.g., no interactions, two-way, three-way). Linear regression typically requires the manual specification of interactions. For large numbers of variables, this can be extremely tedious. To overcome this limitation, a number of different methods have been proposed for the identification of high-dimensional interactions in linear regression. These can be seen as extensions of regularized regression methods, where they not only perform variable selection of main effects, but also selection of interactions as well (Bien, Taylor, & Tibshirani, 2013; Choi, Li, & Zhu, 2010; Haris, Witten, & Simon, 2016).

To use regularization to *search* for interactions, we first specify a linear regression model with all possible interactions, following Bien et al. (2013), as

$$Y = \beta_0 + \sum_{j} \beta_j X_j + .5 \sum_{j \neq k} \Theta_{jk} X_j X_k + \epsilon \tag{4.8}$$

where the goal is to estimate the main effects, β_j, and all two-way interactions, Θ_{jk}. Θ_{jk} is a symmetric matrix of interactions, with a diagonal of 0s. With a large number of predictors, it would be difficult computationally and from an interpretation perspective to estimate all possible interactions.

Instead, the hierarchical lasso penalizes both the regression and two-way interaction coefficients, producing a sparse model at both levels. The decision to include interactions or not can follow two types of restrictions. Strong hierarchy estimates an interaction between variables X_j and X_k only if β_j and β_k are both nonzero. Weak hierarchy requires only one of β_j or β_k to be nonzero. There are both statistical and practical considerations in choosing which type of hierarchy to impose. Given that two-way interactions represent a quadratic relationship between X_j and X_k, if either of these main effects is small, it is unlikely that the interaction between variables will be of an appreciable magnitude. In social and behavioral science research, this is more likely the case than not, with a preponderance of small effects among variables. Given this, we advocate for its use and only discuss the application of the strong hierarchy restriction.

We do not further examine the formulaic implementation of the lasso applied to Equation 4.8. Instead, we demonstrate an application of the method to data from the ECLS-K with noise variables added. To apply the hierarchical lasso, a number of packages in R exist to implement these methods, including the `hierNet` (Bien & Tibshirani, 2014) and `FAMILY` (Haris et al., 2016) packages. In this application, we implement a two-step approach similar to the relaxed lasso. In the first step use the `hierNet` package with the strong hierarchy assumption and cross-validation to select main, interaction, and quadratic effects (default in package is to include quadratic effects, or diagonal of Θ_{jk}), and then rerun a linear regression model including the selected parameters from step 1. In order to accomplish this, because the ECLS-K is a large dataset ($N = 4{,}556$), we used the validation set approach, by running the hierarchical lasso on one half of the dataset, and then using the selected parameters in a linear regression run on the other half of the dataset.

Using the hierarchical lasso with cross-validation and 20 values of λ, the best fitting model within one standard error of the minimum fit selected the main effects for math, general knowledge, income, and gender; quadratic effects for math, knowledge, income, and BMI; and along with interactions between math and general knowledge, and between general knowledge and income. We also tested the method with only the weak hierarchy restriction, which resulted in the same results. In the second step, the selected parameters in a linear regression results are displayed in Table 4.2.

To interpret the coefficients in Table 4.2, one important thing to note is that the variables were standardized beforehand. Not only is this an important step to take when using regularization, but it also simplifies the interpretation of regression coefficients with interactions. For instance, two cases that have values of 0 on the other X variables, but differ by 1 on math

TABLE 4.2. Parameter Coefficients That Include the Selected Quadratic and Interaction Effects as Applied on the Holdout ECLS-K Sample

	Dependent variable:
	science
math	0.376*** (0.025)
knowledge	0.287*** (0.021)
income	0.191*** (0.026)
bmi	0.016 (0.021)
gender	−0.079*** (0.016)
I(math^2)	−0.038*** (0.013)
I(knowledge^2)	−0.009 (0.021)
I(income^2)	−0.021*** (0.005)
I(bmi^2)	0.00005 (0.008)
math:knowledge	−0.098*** (0.028)
knowledge:income	−0.036* (0.021)
constant	0.149*** (0.024)
Observations	2,278
R^2	0.403
Adjusted R^2	0.400
Residual Std. Error	0.770 (df = 2,266)
F Statistic	138.877*** (df = 11; 2,266)

Note: *p <0.1; **p <0.05; ***p <0.01

are predicted to differ by 0.38 standard deviations in science. Note that this is due to science also being standardized before the analysis. Standardizing the X variables particularly makes the interpretation of simple effects easier, as we interpret the effect conditional upon the values of every other predictor being at 0, or when standardized, the mean.

For interpreting the two-way interactions in the model, we use the general knowledge variable as the reference as it is present in both interactions. Going from the mean of knowledge to 1 standard deviation above the mean, the effect of both math and income decrease, and vice versa if we flipped the variables. What we may be observing is, in fact, nonlinearity, a commonly confouding influence on interactions. However, this is why we included the specification of quadratic effects as well, since it is common for the relationship between cognitive variables and various outcomes of interest to decrease at higher values (e.g., at high IQs, small gains have little effect in comparison to lower values), thus producing a form of nonlinearity. We highlight this to caution readers against only searching for interactions with a blind eye toward possible nonlinearity. In the following chapter we discuss methods that are both nonlinear and search for interactions.

4.5.4 Group Regularization

Oftentimes in social and behavioral research our predictors are not completely independent from one another. Instead, there are groups of variables, for example, five items purported to measure one facet of personality, a set of demographic variables, etc. In this case, we may not only want to select individual predictors, but instead select *groups* of predictors. The use of the group lasso could be portrayed as a less theoretical counterpart to hierarchical regression. This refers to hierarchical *entry* of single or sets of predictors. This is distinguished from what has been termed *hierarchical, multilevel,* or *mixed effects models*. This latter form of modeling is about the inclusion of random, as opposed to solely fixed, effects to account for variability due to clustering or time. Hierarchical regression is a more theoretical form of modeling where sets of predictors are entered based on an a priori specified sequence. For a scenario where the numbers of variables preclude strong theoretical specification, Yuan and Lin (2007) proposed the group lasso

$$grplasso = argmin\Big\{\sum_{i=1}^{N}(y_i - \beta_0 - \sum_{j=1}^{p} x_{ij}\beta_j)^2 + \lambda \sum_{g=1}^{G} \sqrt{p_g}||\beta_g||_2\Big\}, \tag{4.9}$$

where p_g accounts for the varying sizes of groups and β_g is the vector of all β coefficients in group g. In the group lasso, the lasso penalty acts at the group level, where instead of individual parameters being set to 0, entire groups of parameters can be pushed to 0. This does not lead to sparsity *within* group, just *across* groups of predictors. An alternative form of group regularization is for scenarios where researchers are not only interested in selecting groups, but also selecting variables within those groups. This is termed *bi-level* variable selection (Breheny & Huang, 2009). When they only wish to penalize at the group level, researchers have the option to use the group lasso, along with some sparser extensions (see Huang, Breheny, & Ma, 2012). One, termed the *sparse group lasso* (sgrplasso; Friedman, Hastie, & Tibshirani, 2010), has the same group lasso as in Equation 4.5, but adds a penalty for each individual parameter,

$$sgrplasso = argmin\Big\{\sum_{i=1}^{N}(y_i - \beta_0 - \sum_{j=1}^{p} x_{ij}\beta_j)^2 + \lambda_1 \sum_{g=1}^{G} \sqrt{p_g}||\beta_g||_2 + \lambda_2||\beta_j||_1\Big\}, \tag{4.10}$$

where λ_1 represents the group penalization and λ_2 is for the individual β_j coefficients. This model produces sparsity at two levels, ideal for incorporating group information into variable selection.

To make this form of modeling more concrete, we include a simple example using 150 observations from the *bfi* dataset. Across 20 variables, there are four groups of variables: demographics, and items measuring conscientiousness, openness, and neuroticism. We could specify a hierarchical sequence of five models:

$$\begin{aligned}
&Model_0 : agree = b_0 \\
&Model_1 : agree = b_0 + A * demo \\
&Model_2 : agree = b_0 + A * demo + B * consc \\
&Model_3 : agree = b_0 + A * demo + B * consc + C * open \\
&Model_4 : agree = b_0 + A * demo + B * consc + C * open + D * neur
\end{aligned}$$

where *agree* is a summed score of agreeableness items, *demo* refers to a set of gender (0 male; 1 female) and three dummy variables for age, *consc* are five items measuring conscientiousness, *open* are five items measuring openness, and *neur* are five items measuring neuroticism. Each predictor set addition is based on a specific theoretical relationship. For instance, in the first model, we test whether the addition of demographic variables contributes a significant degree to the prediction of agreeableness over and above a null model. In the second model, we similarly test the addition of conscientiousness items over and above demographic variables. In this model sequence, we can estimate the increase in ΔR^2 solely due to the addition of a set of variables, resulting in

$$R^2(Model_4) = \Delta R^2(Model_4) + \Delta R^2(Model_3) + \Delta R^2(Model_2) + \Delta R^2(Model_1). \tag{4.11}$$

Results from testing this sequence of models is displayed in Table 4.3.

TABLE 4.3. Hierarchical Regression Results. Note that *Res.df* refers to the residual degrees of freedom, *Df* the degrees of freedom, and *Sum of Sq* is the sum of squares due to the regression model.

	Res.df	RSS	Df	Sum of Sq	F	Pr(>F)	ΔR^2
$Model_0$	149	2190.83					
$Model_1$	145	2036.00	4	154.83	3.18	0.0158	0.07
$Model_2$	140	1908.60	5	127.40	2.09	0.0704	0.06
$Model_3$	135	1708.12	5	200.48	3.29	0.0078	0.09
$Model_4$	130	1583.23	5	124.89	2.05	0.0757	0.06

In Table 4.3, we see that a subset of predictors increases the R^2 by a significant ($p < 0.05$) amount. Given this prespecified sequence of models, we could either conclude that $Model_1$ or $Model_3$ resulted in the best model fit, as the addition of conscientiousness and neuroticism items did not significantly increase the value the R^2. However, this would be based on a rather arbitrary cutoff given that the ΔR^2 values were comparable. Ultimately, when performing a statistical analysis within a hypothesis-driven framework, theoretical considerations influence the model selection to a large extent.

In an alternative research scenario, we may not have any hypotheses regarding the ordering of variable sets. In this, we may wish to explore and identify which sets of variables contribute to the prediction of *agree*. Using a regularization method such as the lasso, we would select predictors without reference to what set or group of variables they belong. If instead we wished to select *groups* of variables, we could use the abovementioned group lasso to apply the group lasso to the same data example we used in the `grpreg` package (Breheny & Huang, 2015). Within this package there is an option to pair the group lasso with cross-validation, using the lowest cross-validated model fit to select a final model. The results from the best fitting model are displayed in Table 4.4.

TABLE 4.4. Group Regularization Results.

Set	Group Lasso Selected	Bi-Level Number Selected
Demographics	Y	2
Conscientiousness	Y	1
Openness	Y	3
Neuroticism	N	2

Additionally, we applied a variant of the sparse group lasso, the composite MCP, an even sparser form of bi-level penalization. In Table 4.4, we can see that this resulted in a different number of variables being selected in each group, shedding a different light on which variables may be important. For instance, the group lasso selected the set of conscientiousness items, while the composite MCP only selected one item. This was the second item, "continue until everything is perfect," answering from "very inaccurate" to "very accurate" with four options in between. Of the conscientiousness items, the second item had the highest correlation with agreeableness (0.26), as well as the highest correlations with other conscientiousness items. As a whole group, conscientiousness predicted agreeableness, but the intercorrelation among items might have made it less clear which variable or variables predicted agreeableness to the greatest degree until the use of variable selection (it was also the only conscientiousness item that was significant in the linear regression).

4.6 Bayesian Regression

The use of Bayesian estimation is becoming increasingly popular in the social and behavioral sciences. As such, researchers often wonder whether the same types of methods that they have utilized in Frequentist estimation also exist in the Bayesian framework. A full description of Bayesian estimation is well beyond the scope of this book. Instead we present a simple applied example of how lasso regression can be applied in a similar manner using Bayesian estimation.

In Bayesian estimation, results similar to ordinary least squares regression can be achieved by using a noninformative (diffuse) normal distribution priors on the regression coefficients. Extending this to both ridge and lasso regularization, the ridge has been shown to be equivalent to the use of a more restrictive normal distribution prior, while the lasso is equivalent to a Laplace distribution prior (Tibshirani, 1996). The lasso estimate is the mode of the posterior while the ridge is the mean. To actually perform variable selection, it is generally preferable to use sparse extensions of these two methods. In contrast to the common practice of testing 100 values of λ in ridge or lasso regression, in Bayesian regularization it is preferable to use a hierarchical representation of a sparse prior, which only requires running one model that implicitly selects an ideal degree of prior variance. Hierarchical Bayesian regularization currently includes methods such as the Bayesian adaptive lasso, the spike and slab prior, and the horseshoe. We provide a brief application of the horseshoe prior. For more detail, see Van Erp, Oberski, and Mulder (2018).

As a simple application with a subset of 150 observations from the ECLS-K dataset, we applied the horseshoe prior with the `rstanarm` package, using the specification of Piironen and Vehtari (2016). This was assessed across four chains, with the posterior distributions displayed in Figure 4.11.

In Figure 4.11, only the regression coefficients for math and knowledge have evident posterior distributions away from 0. These are the only two parameters that have median estimates away from 0 (rounded to the nearest decimal). Using 95% credible intervals (the Bayesian counterpart to confidence intervals) to select which parameters are nonzero induces more uncertainty into which estimates are nonzero, as additional noise parameters have intervals that do not include 0. In contrast to Frequentist regularization, Bayesian regularization paints a richer picture of the results, giving the user a posterior distribution for each estimate, instead of a single point estimate. This allows for more subjectivity and theoretical input into which variables are *selected* in terms of performing variable selection, through placing different types of priors on each of the regression

FIGURE 4.11. Posterior distributions from the ECLS-K Bayesian linear regression using horseshoe priors.

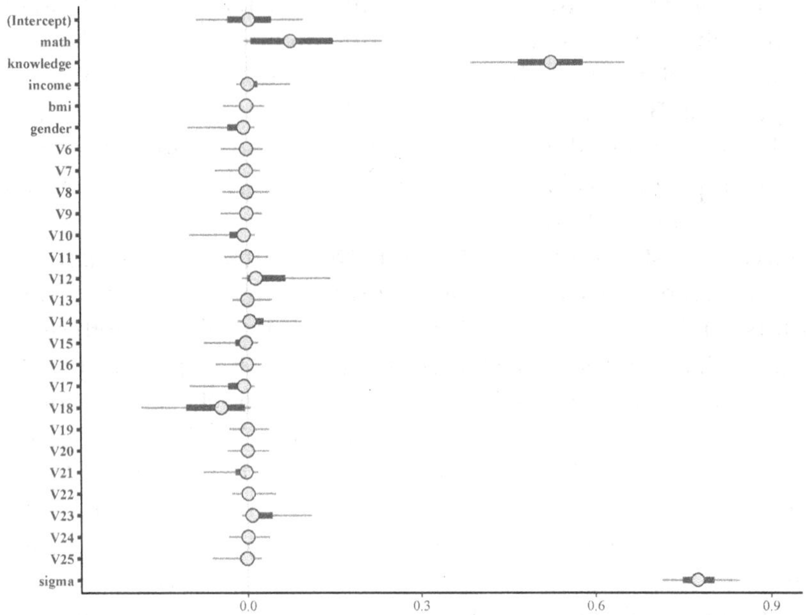

coefficients. Bayesian regularization can also be used in scenarios where uncertainty exists as to whether a parameter should be included, allowing the user to fit a more complex model, placing regularization priors on parameters that are not of interest, resulting in a more holistic modeling procedure that does not necessarily have to proceed in a series of several steps, removing or adding variables based on the previous model's results.

Although we get results similar to the use of the lasso in Frequentist estimation, because we created a smaller subset of the data to speed the computational time (Bayesian estimation typically takes longer with increasing sample sizes), it is necessary to remember that variable selection can depend heavily on the sample size. Larger sample sizes generally result in larger numbers of selected variables.

One of the main benefits of the Bayesian framework is the flexibility it gives users to specify models that reflect not only their theoretical ideas, but also a combination of different aims. For instance, the different forms of regularization discussed earlier, such as the lasso, group lasso, and the lasso for interactions, can also be specified using Bayesian regularization. This requires manual specification, however, the principles described in applying Bayesian regularization to linear regression scale to more complex modeling scenarios such as multilevel or structural equation modeling. Our main point in detailing Bayesian regularization is that the use of Bayesian estimation in statistics and machine learning is becoming more popular and an awareness of the similarities and distinctions of approaches (regularization) across estimation frameworks will be increasingly important.

4.7 Summary

In this chapter we detailed the application of regularization to regression models, with variable selection as a primary focus. The most commonly applied forms of regularized regression include both the ridge and lasso, which serve different purposes in their application. We explained a number of extensions, including the elastic net, the group lasso, hierarchical lasso, and Bayesian forms of regularization. The most important component of applying regularization is for researchers to be clear in their research aims and limitations to their data, as each form of regularization applies to specific facets of these two considerations. While our focus in this chapter was on the application of regularization to univariate outcomes, we discuss the extension of regularization to multivariate outcomes in Chapter 8, with modeling measurement error (Chapter 7) as a specific consideration.

4.7.1 Further Reading

- For background or further detail on linear regression, we recommend either Cohen et al. (2003) or Darlington and Hayes (2017). Notably, they provide much more extensive detail regarding assumptions, diagnosing assumption violations, and interpretation. However, neither book provides a great deal of information on logistic or other outcome types. For this, we recommend the book by Fox (2015).

- This book details Bayesian estimation and regularization in this chapter and Chapter 8. We thought it important to introduce these concepts given that they are being increasingly used in practice. Unfortunately, space constraints limited the amount of background we could provide. Fortunately, the past 10 years has seen the publication of a number of great resources on Bayesian statistics. We recommend Gelman et al. (2013) for a more technical background, Kruschke (2014) for a more introductory text, or McElreath (2020) for more of a focus on hierarchical models.

- We did not discuss how to handle missingness with regularization models. This was little discussed until recently, where Gunn, Hayati

Rezvan, Fernandez, and Comulada (2022) detail how to integrate regularization methods with multiple imputation.

- For further reading on regularization in regression, the following papers have been written as introductory overviews: McNeish (2015) and Helwig (2017).

- Oftentimes in social and behavioral research, when researchers are considering whether interactions exist in their data they are also interested in mediators. Much has been written about both interactions and mediation, and for introductory articles, see MacKinnon and Luecken (2008) or for a general textbook, Hayes (2017).

4.7.2 Computational Time and Resources

The runtime for the algorithms detailed in this chapter vary greatly. On the quick end, the application of regularized regression with the `glmnet` package often takes only a matter of seconds, even with testing the default of 100 penalties. This amount of time can increase as the number of predictors increases, but it rarely takes longer than a few minutes. On the slow end is the hierarchical lasso, with models often taking on the order of hours to fit a small number of penalties (i.e., 10). The authors have tested this method (as implemented in multiple packages) across a variety of empirical problems, and have on more than one occasion been unable to get models to finish, as the runtimes were on the order of days. In between regularized regression and the hierarchical lasso lie stability selection and the forms of the group lasso, with both methods being closer to regularized regression in run times. Bayesian estimation almost always takes longer, but there are a number of front-end packages that have been developed that require less programming and model specification, have built-in functions to implement shrinkage priors, and drastically cut the runtimes. See both the `brms` (Bürkner, 2017) and `rstanarm` (Goodrich, Gabry, Ali, & Brilleman, 2022) packages for implementing Bayesian regression. Both packages recommend the use of the horseshoe prior for regularization.

5 Decision Trees

Decision trees are one of the core algorithms of machine learning, both as an individual algorithm, as well as forming the basis for many more complex algorithms (Chapter 6). Their primary benefit is the level of interpretability afforded by the visually depicted tree structure along with propensity to identify interaction effects without manual specification. We spend the majority of this chapter focused on describing the tree creation process and how to interpret the tree structure, while ending with details on the specific implementations and nuances in application.

5.1 Key Terminology

- Decision tree. Also commonly referred to as classification and regression trees, decision trees refer to an algorithm that recursively partitions the predictor space to create a nonlinear mapping from predictors to an outcome. The resultant mapping is then depicted as an interpretable tree structure.
- Partition. The process of dividing the dataset into subgroups based on predictor cutoff values.
- Heterogeneity. In contrast to homogeneity, heterogeneity refers to the existence of between-person variability, namely, that assuming that an entire sample represents a singular population is untenable.
- Node. A group of cases in a tree structure. The root node refers to the entire sample that has yet to be partitioned, while the terminal node is the final subgroup at the end of the partitioning process.
- Surrogate split. A split in the decision tree that does not show up in the final tree as it did not produce as much of an improvement in fit as the chosen split, but is used for cases with missingness on the predictor used in the chosen split.

- Pruning. The process of creating a large decision tree, followed by pruning or removing splits to create a smaller, more generalizable tree.

- Variable importance. A summary statistic for how much an individual predictor contributes to explaining variability in the outcome. This is used primarily as a way to understand which predictors are important in algorithms (trees and ensembles; see Chapter 6) that are not as interpretable as linear regression.

5.2 Introduction

Decision trees were first introduced in the 1960s by Morgan and Sonquist (1963). However, the use of the method did not capture the attention of the statistics community until 20 years later with the work of Breiman, Friedman, Olshen, and Stone (1984). First termed *automatic interaction detection*, the purpose of the algorithm was to efficiently identify interaction effects when the number of predictors was large. In large datasets, the sequential testing of a large number of models and possible combinations of variables quickly depreciates the statistical properties of the models (i.e., false positives; Morgan, 2005).

As there are a number of variants to decision tree algorithms, we refer to decision trees as the *umbrella methodology*, and refer to specific algorithms that fall under this umbrella terminology as such. For instance, the most popular variant of decision trees is *classification and regression trees* (CART; Breiman et al., 1984). Note that classification and regression trees is also commonly used to refer to decision trees, while CART refers to a specific algorithm.

Decision trees' popularity can be attributed to their easy-to-understand tree structure, a structure that mimics the way that humans make decisions. We elaborate on this further below. To create a tree structure, the algorithm proceeds as follows: First, divide the predictor space into all possible unique values. Across these unique predictor values, the algorithm iteratively partitions the dataset to determine an improvement in model fit. This involves placing each observation into one of two groups, of which each group member receives the same predicted response. The actual partitioning of the dataset functions differently based on the type of each predictor variable. For quantitative variables, each unique value is tested in order: For example, if predictor values range from 50 to 100, the process is as follows: Everyone with a predictor value equal to 50 versus everyone with a predictor value greater than 50, then everyone with a predictor value equal to 50–51 versus everyone with greater than 51, until every possible successive value is tested in this manner. Given m unique sorted values, this involves testing $m - 1$ unique splits. For nominal variables, as there is no ordering to the values, all possible groupings are tested. If there are m categories, this involves testing $2^{m-1} - 1$ dichotomous splits. Particularly for predictors with large numbers categories, this can quickly become computationally burdensome.

Predictions derived from the tree structure are then compared to each observation's actual response to calculate error (model misfit). For continuous outcomes, this is generally mean squared error, for categorical it can be accuracy or two alternatives, such as entropy or the gini index. After every possible partition has been tested, and an error is calculated and assigned to this specific partitioning, the split that results in the largest reduction in error is chosen. Effectively, the algorithm has created two new datasets: dataset A contains every observation that adheres to one side of the best splitting rule and dataset B contains all other observations.

At its core, decision trees are an atheoretical method for creating subgroups. This assumes that identifying heterogeneity (creating subgroups) with respect to the observations in the sample will explain some portion of the outcome.

5.2.1 Example 1

To make the process of creating a tree structure more concrete, we use data from the National Survey on Drug Use and Health, as was detailed in the previous chapter. This dataset was split into a subset to have equal proportions of the suicidal ideation (last 12 months; `SUICTHINK`) outcome, as well as selecting cases that received questions about depression. Predictors included variables that measure feelings of worthlessness (`worthless`; 1 for Yes), whether depression problems interfered with work or personal life (`interfere`; 1-5, 5 = extremely), whether symptoms of depression are felt everyday (`dep`; 1 = Yes), `sex` (1 = Female), `age`, and `race`. Note that in contrast to the logistic regression analyses, it is not recommended to dummy code categorical predictors. Instead, these should be treated as nominal, as it is worthwhile to test a one-versus-all scheme for group differences (as opposed to just a comparison to the reference group).

Decision trees first start with a root node, as displayed in Figure 5.1.

FIGURE 5.1. The root node from the NSDUH dataset. No splits have occurred, as every observation is treated as a homogenous sample. "0" refers to the predicted response for each case in the node, 0.49 is the mean of the outcome, and 100% denotes that the entire sample is contained in this node.

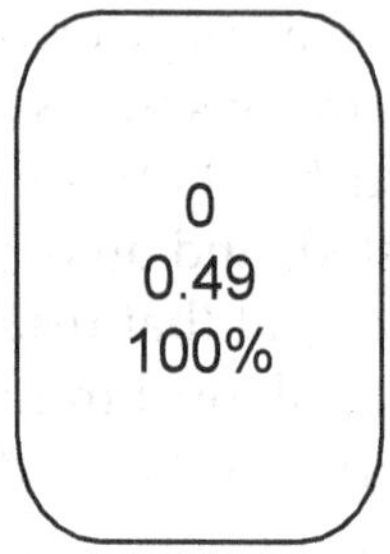

For classification trees, the prediction for each observation reflects the distribution of both classes, which in our example is 0.49, or 49% 0s. In regression trees, this would be the mean of the outcome. In our example, those with a history of suicide attempts (1) and those without a history (0) are roughly distributed 50–50.

To create a first split, the algorithm tests all possible splits, according to the rules dictated by the predictor variable types (which is important to check the class of the predictors before creating the tree). This resulted in the following split depicted in Figure 5.2.

FIGURE 5.2. First split in the NSDUH dataset. The split occurs between the values of 0 and 1 on `worthless`.

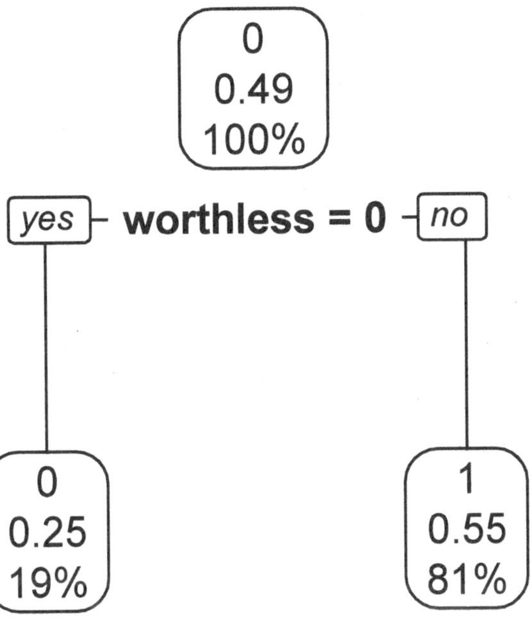

This split occurred between 0 and 1 on `worthless`, with those having a value of 0 (19% of sample) receiving a predicted probability of suicide attempt of 0.25. Note that this predicted probability is simply the class proportion in each node (e.g., 25% of the sample in this node have 1s). Similar to logistic regression, decision trees output predicted probabilities, with class assignment dependent on the probability cutoff (generally 0.5). Cases with a `worthless` value of 1 received a predicted probability of 0.55 (81%) of the sample. Now that we effectively have two subgroups of cases based on `worthless`, the algorithm proceeds by trying to partition each subgroup further. This results in the next set of splits is given in Figure 5.3.

FIGURE 5.3. Second split in the NSDUH dataset. Cases with values of 1 on `worthless` are further split between ages of 18–25 and older.

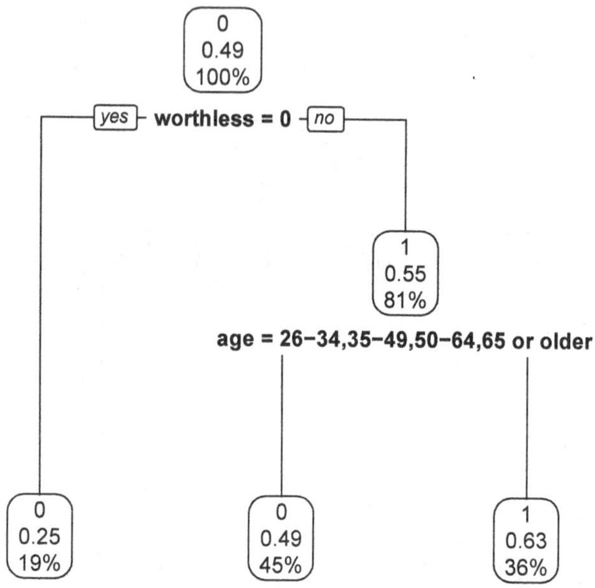

The next split occurs among the 81% of the sample with a value of 1 on `worthless`. The split, on `age`, partitions those whose `age` falls in the category of 18–25 into one node, and those in the older `age` categories into the other node. These nodes then receive different class predictions based on their predicted probabilities. Note that those that were partitioned with a response of 1 on `worthless` did not receive a further split. Although this could be attributed to a number of aspects, the smaller sample size (19% or 190) could be partially accountable.

The next step of splitting occurred among those with `worthless` values of 1 and in the older `age` categories, as displayed in Figure 5.4. This split occurred between values of 1–3 and 4–5 on `interfere`. Those with values of 1–3 mostly had outcome values of 0 (0.36), whereas the partition of cases with values of 4 or 5 were approximately evenly split (0.53).

FIGURE 5.4. Example tree with four terminal nodes. The third split occurred among those cases that are older than 18–25, between the values of 3 and 4 on `interfere`.

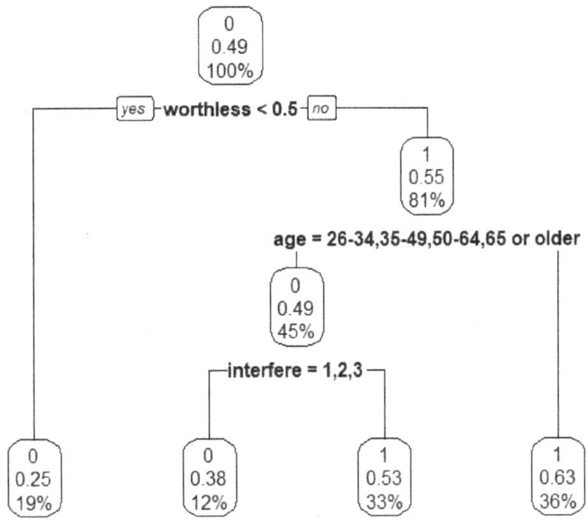

In this final tree (we set the maximum depth to four), displayed in Figure 5.5, a split occurs among cases that we just placed in the node with `interfere` values of 4 or 5. Cases with `age` values of 50–64 or 65 or older were partitioned from those that had age values of 26–49. Note that this is the second split on `age`, with cases having an age of 18–25 already placed in a terminal node. For the current split, it results in slightly different predicted probabilities of a suicide attempt, with older individuals having slightly lower probabilities (0.46 versus 0.55).

FIGURE 5.5. Final tree model. The final split occurred among cases with `interfere` values of 4 or 5, occurring between the ages of 25–49 and 50 or older.

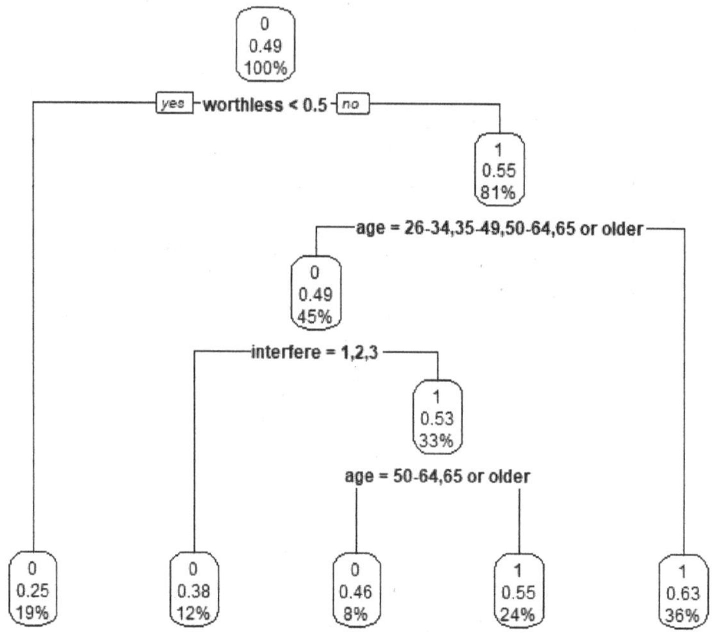

5.3 Describing the Tree

The steps taken to interpret the resulting subgroups can be described as a set of rules, summarized in Table 5.1.

TABLE 5.1. Example Splitting Rules. Note that we could have alternatively included their predicted probabilities, as this is closer to what decision trees attempt to optimize.

Splitting Rule	Prediction	Probability
`worthless` = 0	0	0.25
`worthless` = 1 & `age` > 25 & `interfere` = 1-3	0	0.36
`worthless` = 1 & `age` > 25 & `interfere` = 4-5 & `age` > 49	0	0.46
`worthless` = 1 & `age` > 25 & `interfere` = 4-5 & `age` < 50	1	0.55
`worthless` = 1 & `age` =18-25 & `age` = 18-25	1	0.63

Now that we have a final decision trees model displayed as the rules in Table 5.1 and Figure 5.5, we can be more explicit about the terminology used to describe the tree. This is depicted in Figure 5.6.

FIGURE 5.6. Terminology for each node.

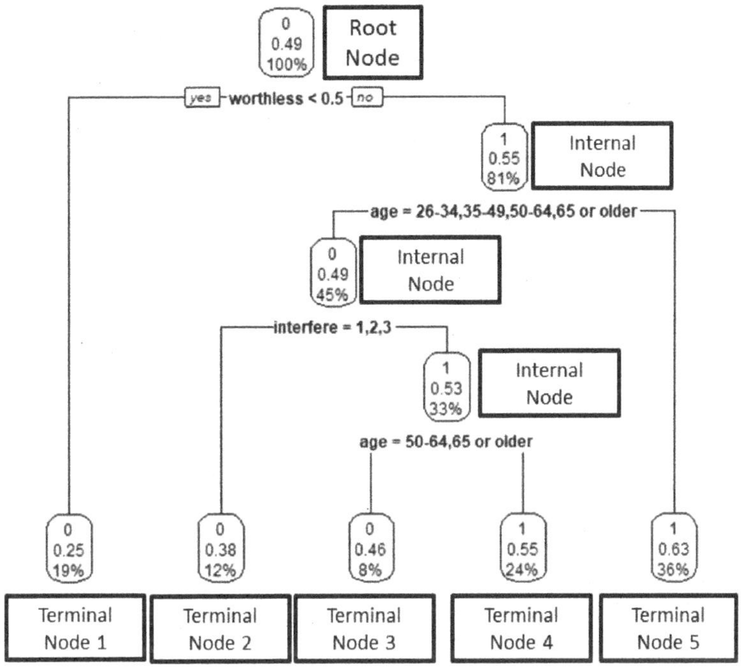

In this figure, the first (topmost) node is termed the *root* node, while each additional node that is then further split is referred to as an *internal* node. Finally, those nodes that are not further split (bottommost) are referred to as *terminal* nodes. We have already described the splitting functions (rules) that dictate where people are placed. Note that there are alternative terminologies used to describe the parts of the tree. One alternative is the use of *parent* and *child* nodes, used in a relative way to describe splitting the cases in the parent node that results in two child nodes. Lastly, the terminal nodes care also referred to as the *leaves* of the tree

5.3.1 Example 2

The same process that can be used for decision trees and categorical outcomes (classification trees) applies to continuous outcomes (regression trees). To portray this and take it a step further in understanding the mapping between predictor and response, we will use data from the ECLS-K. For this example, we will use math and general knowledge scores to predict science scores in the eighth grade. To get a better sense of the relationships between variables, Figure 5.7 is a scatterplot between math and knowledge, where each point is colored by the science score.

FIGURE 5.7. Three variable scatterplot.

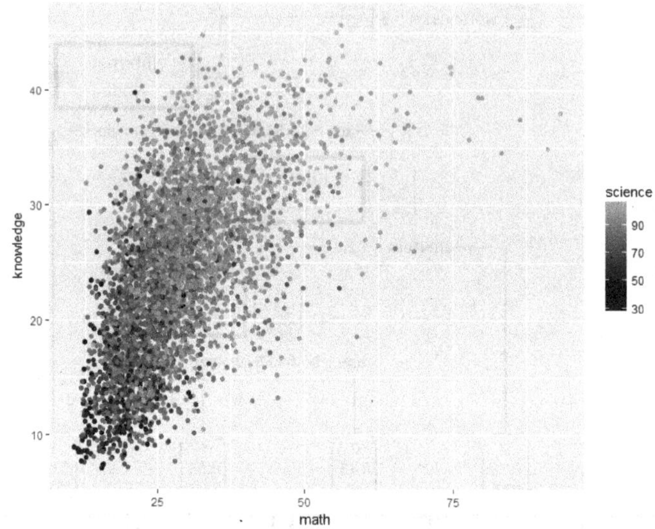

We can see that, in general, as both `math` and `knowledge` increase, so does science. Although the relationship between `knowledge` and `math` looks linear, we would have to plot the marginal relationships between both math and knowledge with science to understand how a linear model would work. Eschewing the linearity assumption using decision trees, with `math` and `knowledge` as predictors of science scores, results in the structure displayed in Figure 5.8.

FIGURE 5.8. ECLS-K decision tree.

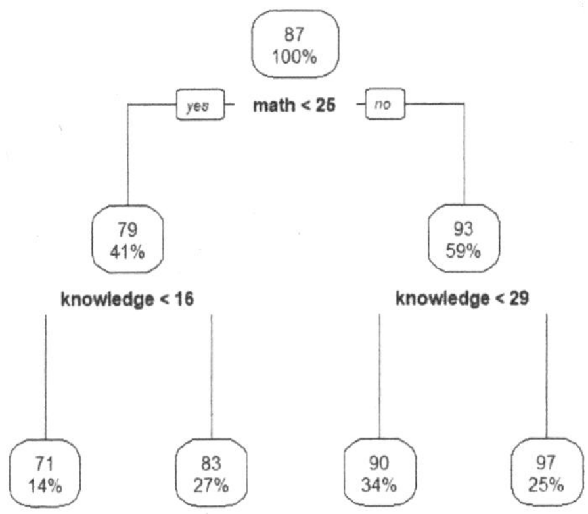

The next step in understanding what a tree structure depicts is to see the binning as applied to the scatterplot in Figure 5.9. This is displayed in Figure 5.7.

FIGURE 5.9. Decision boundaries.

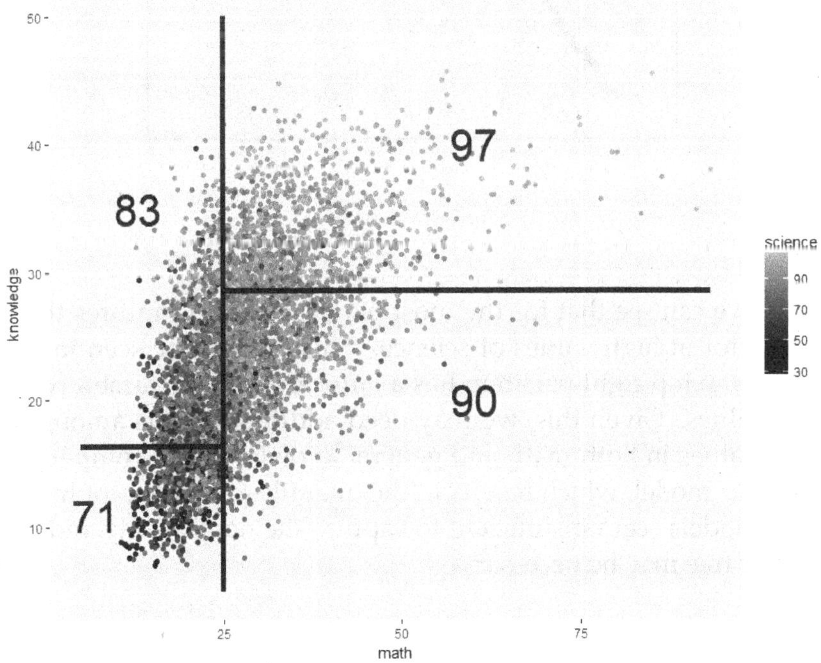

In this, we can directly map the binning of observations by their predictor values and predicted responses. For instance, the group with cut points of less than 25 on math and less than 16 on knowledge falls into Terminal 1, which occupies the lower left corner of Figure 5.9 and has a predicted science score of 71.

To better understand how well this model fits the data, we also can examine the residuals. The quantile–quantile plot of the standardized residuals is displayed in Figure 5.10.

FIGURE 5.10. Decision tree Q–Q plot.

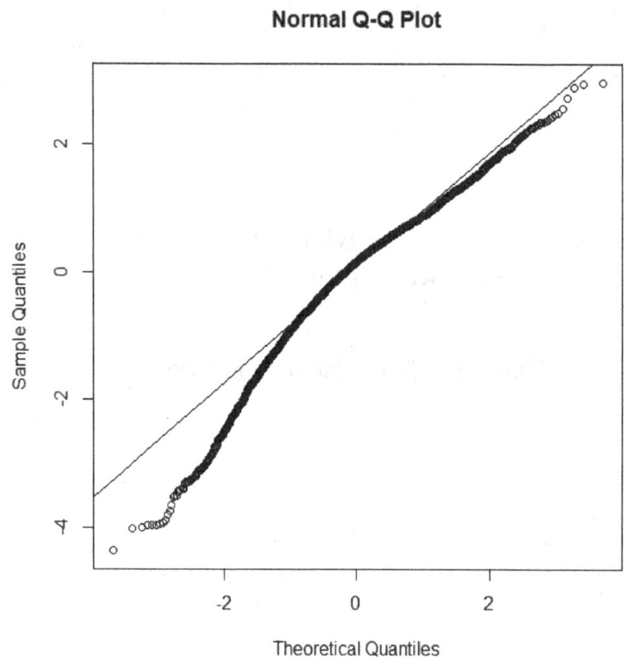

In this, we can see that for the most part, the model captures the data well except for at high values of science. This can also be seen in Figure 5.10, where the top right partition has a large amount of variability to the predictor values. Given this, we may need additional splits among those with high values in both math and general knowledge. In comparison to using a linear model, which results in the quantile–quantile plot in Figure 5.11, both models seem insufficient to capture the nonlinearity, indicating that a larger tree may be necessary.

FIGURE 5.11. Linear regression Q–Q plot

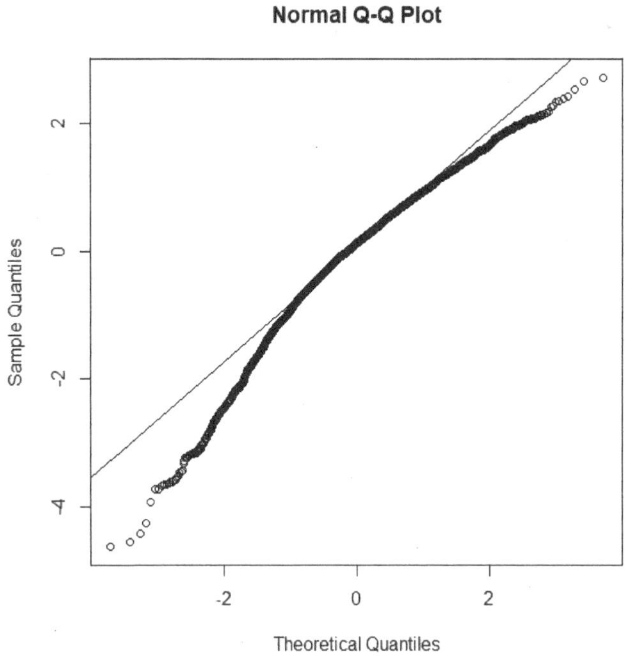

The linear model has difficulty in capturing observations at both the high and low end of science responses. In examining the R^2 for both the linear model and decision trees, the decision trees model performs only slightly worse, explaining 32.6% of the variance in comparison to 36.4% for the linear model. To better understand how decision trees capture nonlinear relationships, we first reran the analyses only using knowledge as a predictor of science. The resultant tree, depicted in Figure 5.12, can then be translated to the nonlinear function in Figure 5.13.

FIGURE 5.12. Decision trees result only using knowledge.

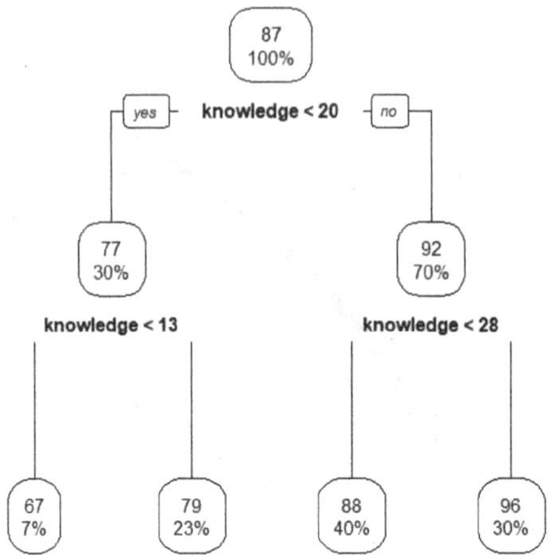

FIGURE 5.13. Nonlinear decision trees prediction line.

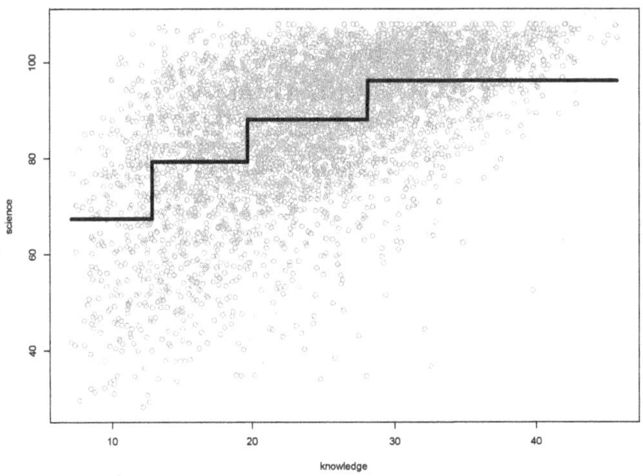

In this figure, we see that the group with the lowest predictions for science act as a form of intercept for the model. From here, as knowledge increases, predicted science scores increase according to a step function, with steps located at the cutoffs in the actual tree structure. With more than one predictor, it becomes more difficult to visualize this relationship. Going back to our original tree, using both knowledge and math as predictors, we can view this step function in three dimensions, as displayed in Figure 5.14.

FIGURE 5.14. Three-dimensional decision surface.

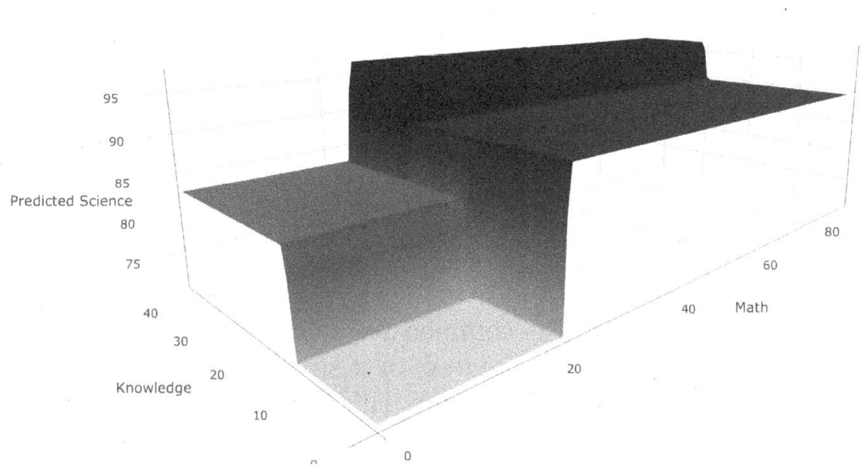

For this predicted surface, we see abrupt changes at coordinates that correspond to the cutoffs in the tree structure. If we grew an even larger tree with both of these predictors, we could image a much more uneven surface.

5.4 Decision Tree Algorithms

Under the umbrella of decision trees fall a number of different algorithms that create tree structures, albeit in different fashions. Although this could in and of itself, be a book, we only provide a general introduction of two algorithms that are available in R.

5.4.1 CART

The term decision trees often refers to the use of classification and regression trees, denoted as the overarching methodology, classification and regression trees (CART; Breiman et al., 1984), and refers to a specific algorithm that falls under the umbrella of decision trees. CART creates binary splits between ordered or unordered predictor categories in order to reduce impurity (heterogeneity). This creates more homogenous groups of observations with respect to the predicted classes. The CART algorithm creates trees in a greedy fashion, where at each level of the tree, the split that reduces impurity the most is chosen, with no consideration to splits occuring farther down the tree. After the first split (root node), the covariate space is recursively split further until there is no longer an improvement greater than some threshold in the model fit.

Oftentimes this tree structure fits the data too well (overfit), meaning that parts of the tree structure are unlikely to generalize well to alternative samples. One strategy to overcome this propensity is to *prune* the initial tree back to a smaller size. CART is one of the most popular implementations and inspired a host of future implementations that were variants of the original methodology. One of these is the `rpart` package (Therneau, Atkinson, & Ripley, 2015).

5.4.2 Pruning

In choosing a final model, it is common to build a large tree, and then prune back the tree to select a subtree, or a smaller version of the tree that minimizes the cross-validation error. This is done in order to prevent "missing" an important additional split (see Breiman et al., 1984) Note that the largest tree will always have the lowest within-sample error. However, we generally want to choose the tree structure that will generalize the best. This can be accomplished by choosing the model with the lowest average error using k-fold cross-validation (or bootstrapping).

Oftentimes when creating a tree, the tree structure can be larger than is practically interpretable, that is, the size of the tree compromises the generalizability. To test this, we first create a tree without attempting to control the size of it, then proceed to *prune* back the leaves to create a series of submodels (subtree). In pruning, the initial tree is pruned back based on the performance of a complexity parameter (α) that controls the size of the tree. The cost-complexity measure is

$$R_{\alpha}(T_p) = R(T_p) + \alpha s_p, \tag{5.1}$$

where $R(T_p)$ is the error, and s_p is the number of leaves (terminal nodes) for tree T_p (Breiman et al., 1984). When $\alpha = 0$, then we have the original tree structure. In testing a sequence of increasing values of α, the models incur larger and larger penalties, thus creating successively smaller subtrees. Although the fit of each of the subtrees will be worse on the training data in comparison to the original tree T_0, we would expect better fit according to cross-validation, or with assessing the fit on a test set.

Going back to Example 1 and running the CART algorithm separate from the process described, we get the following tree sizes and errors according to different metrics depicted in Table 5.2.

TABLE 5.2. Table of Complexity Parameters and Fit From Example 1

	CP	Splits	Sample Error	Avg. CV Error	CV Error Std.
1	0.17	0.00	1.00	1.00	0.03
2	0.03	1.00	0.83	0.83	0.03
3	0.02	3.00	0.77	0.84	0.03
4	0.01	5.00	0.74	0.82	0.03
5	0.01	6.00	0.73	0.83	0.03

Although the Sample Error decreases with increasingly larger trees, the Average CV Error decreases dramatically, at first going from a tree with no splits to one split, but then remains consistently in the range of 0.82–0.84 with additional splits. An additional mechanism for understanding cross-validation and the effect of pruning trees is to examine the performance on a separate holdout sample. To demonstrate this process we used the ECLS-K data, this time predicting reading achievement in grade 8. The sample was split into both a train and test set. For each tree, we recorded the fit on the train set, the average fit across the 10 CV folds, and on the test set. This is displayed in Figure 5.15.

FIGURE 5.15. Comparing three forms of assessing fit.

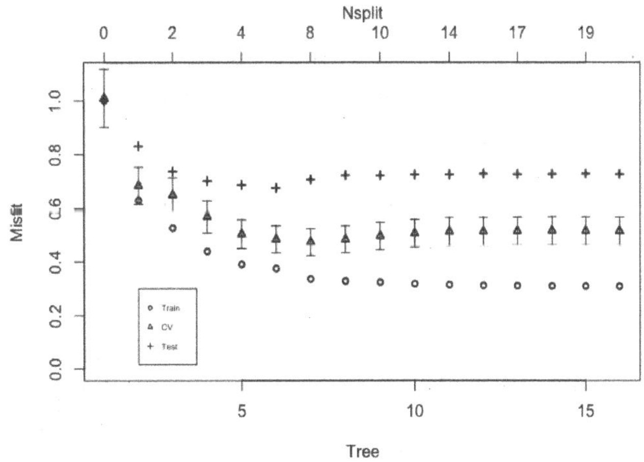

First we examine the fit on the training sample, and we see that as the tree gets larger (Nsplit), the amount of misfit declines monotonically. In contrast, assessing misfit with CV and on the test sample results in a different conclusion. For both, the misfit declines until a tree size of three splits, and then either only increases in the case of CV or finds another low point at six splits for the test sample, before increasing at larger tree sizes. Using CV we get additional information in the form of the standard deviation of the calculated misfit across the 10 folds. We can use this information to examine *how much* improvement in fit occurs by comparing trees. For instance, although the lowest misfit was achieved at three splits, we can see considerable overlap of the error bars between the two adjacent tree sizes. Similar to the use of the standard deviation of fit using CV in regularized regression, we could also choose the smallest tree within one standard deviation (standard error) of the minimum misfit. This would lead us to choosing the tree with only one split.

5.4.3 Conditional Inference Trees

Conditional inference trees (CTree; Hothorn, Hornik, & Zeileis, 2006) are based on a general theory of permutation tests, by performing a hypothesis test at each node resulting in a *p*-value criterion to help determine whether the tree should stop or keep growing. Using a permutation test to calculate a *p*-value entails comparing a split on the original sample to one using that same split on randomly shuffled response values (e.g. swapping observation 1s and 2s responses). Once completed many times, a *p*-value for the conditional distribution of tests statistics is calculated. This allows for unbiased variable selection as each *p*-value was calculated based on a partial hypothesis. This in effect controls for the scale of each covariate, overcoming the propensity for CART to select variables with larger numbers of response options. As an additional feature that is different than CART, by using a *p*-value to test each split, it negates the use of pruning, as it attempts to control for false positives (splits on noise variables) during the tree construction process.

This algorithm is implemented as the `ctree()` function in the `partykit` package (Hothorn & Zeileis, 2015). The default for the *p*-value criterion is 0.05 (expressed as 0.95, or 1-*p*), although this can manually be altered or tested as a tuning parameter using the `train` function in the `caret` package (Kuhn, 2008). In practice, the trees created by CTree tend to be overly large, making interpretation difficult. Although one could change the *p*-value threshold to something smaller (e.g., 0.01), a new algorithm was proposed that attempts to control the size of the tree without missing important effects, particularly interactions. This algorithm, termed CTreePrune (Alvarez-Iglesias, Hinde, Ferguson, & Newell, 2016), proceeds by first growing a large, saturated tree using CTree by setting a large (0.999) *p*-value criterion. Once a saturated tree is created, the algorithm proceeds bottom up, recalculating each p-value based on a false discovery rate procedure (Benjamini & Hochberg, 1995), an alternative method for controlling familywise error rate. This newly proposed algorithm is implemented in the `dtree` package (Jacobucci, 2017).

5.5 Miscellaneous Topics

5.5.1 Interactions

In linear regression (or other types of regression), it is common to manually enter two-way interactions if it is hypothesized that the effect of one variable may depend on the values of another variable. In Chapter 4, we discussed atheoretical approaches to identify linear interactions in the presence of no a priori hypotheses. As already mentioned, decision trees *automatically* searches for and includes interactions into the resultant tree structure. Despite this, some confusion exists as to what exactly constitutes both a main effect and interaction in a tree structure (see Strobl, Malley, & Tutz, 2009).

An example that uses two variables for splitting and represents two main effects is displayed in Figure 5.16. In the left-hand panel, the first split occurs between males and females. Then within each gender, the same split occurs on depression, resulting in the same predicted increase in the terminal nodes. Examining each internal and terminal node shows that each split results in a four-point increase in the resulting subgroup in comparison to the combined observations. In contrast to this, the right hand side of Figure 5.16 represents an interaction between gender and depression. Notably, the split on depression *depends* on the value of gender.

We can visualize this further with three-dimensional plots of the relationship between both predictors and anxiety. In the left panel of Figure 5.17, the slope of the prediction surface stays constant across values of depression and gender. In contrast, the right side of Figure 5.17 represents an interaction, denoting different effects across the values of both depression and gender. Notably, there is less slope at moderate values of depression, with stronger slopes at both lower and higher values.

In most applications of decision trees, the resulting tree structure will reflect interactions between variables. Particularly with continuous predictors, it is highly unlikely in real data to see the exact same cut-point reflected multiple times in a tree. Additionally, as compared to linear regression, where researchers must manually enter interaction effects, decision trees place no constraints on the interaction effect, while automatically including

FIGURE 5.16. Comparison of tree structures with main effects and an interaction.

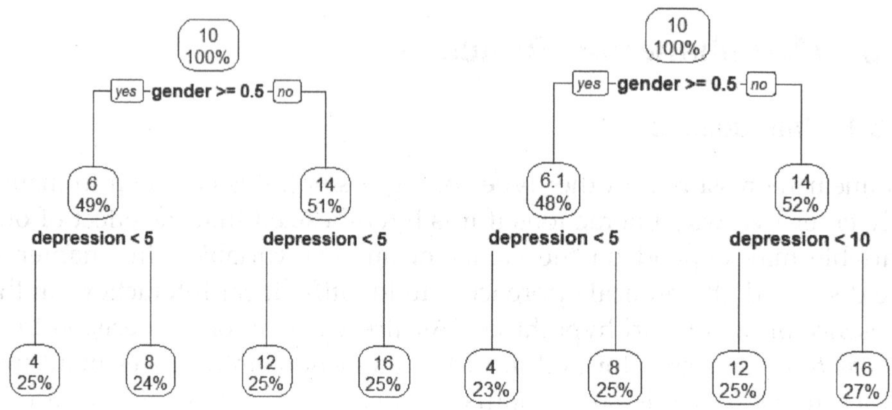

FIGURE 5.17. Comparison of tree structures with main effects (left pane) and an interaction (right pane).

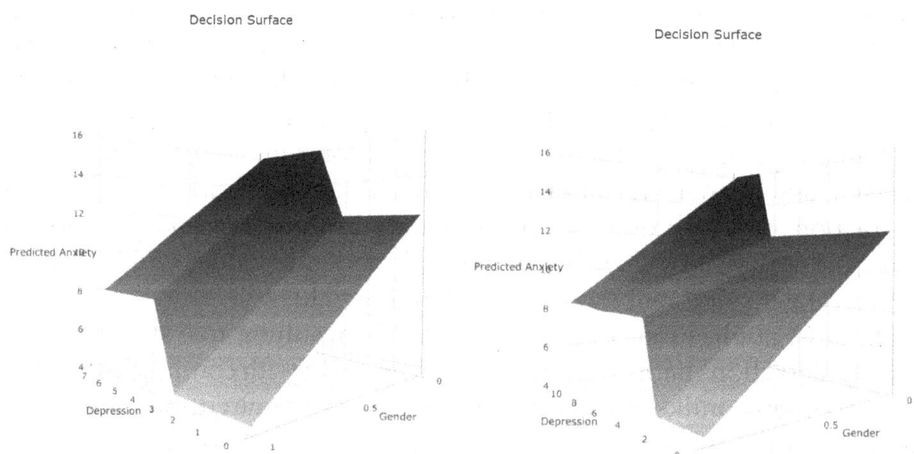

the possibility of interacting effects among predictors. Thus, in line with Berk (2008) most splits represent interactions in decision trees.

5.5.2 Pathways

Beyond just identifying main and interaction effects present in the trees, trees have also been used to describe the various pathways that cases can take to end up receiving similar predictions. More formally, we can describe this as *equifinality* and *multifinality*, following Scott, Whitehead, Bergeman, and Pitzer (2013). In the context of data analysis and tree models, *equifinality* refers to cases having different responses on predictor variables, but similar values on the outcome. On the other hand, *multifinality* refers to cases having similar values on predictor variables, but different outcome values.

As an example of how both of these concepts can be represented in a tree structure, see the tree displayed in Figure 5.18.

FIGURE 5.18. A tree structure demonstrating equifinality. Notice that the interaction between `math` and `knowledge` results in Nodes 4 and 6 with similar distributions on the outcome, despite different pathways.

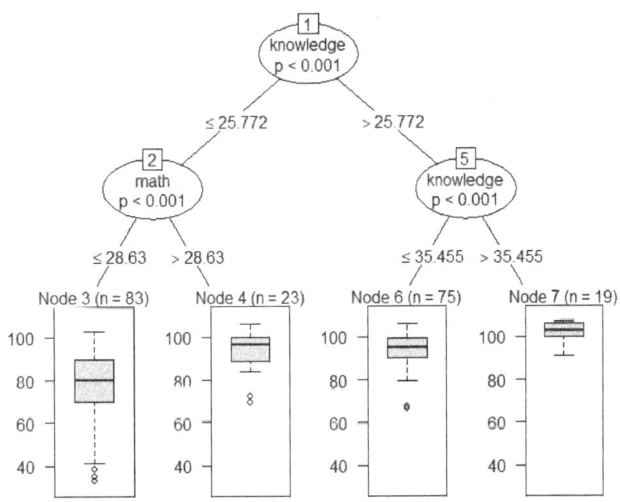

Note that for this we used the CTree algorithm, which results in a different form of output. In this example, we used a subset of the ECLS-K data, with `math` and `knowledge` scores as predictors of `science` scores. In this, examine Node 4 and 6. Node 4 contains cases that had lower `knowledge` scores (< 25.7), but higher `math` scores (> 28.63) relative to those that ended up in Node 3. Node 6 contains cases that had higher `knowledge`

scores, but not the highest (≤ 35.5). Even though the observations that ended up in Nodes 4 and 6 had different *paths*, as in splits on both `math` and `knowledge`, both groups had very similar expected `science` scores as evidenced by the boxplot in each node. This could be attributed to a higher math score having a compensatory effect that makes up for slightly lower knowledge scores.

Multifinality is more difficult to define in terms of a tree structure. Decision tree algorithms explicitly attempt to identify group differences on the outcome, with respect to the predictors in the model. Instead, one can identify subgroups that have very similar values on multiple predictors, but a split on an additional variable results in a discrepancy in outcome predictions. An example of this can also be seen in Figure 5.18, through examining Node 3. Notice the variability within this subgroup of cases, where the whiskers of the boxplot reach above values of 100 and down to values of 40. Part of this could be attributed to the fact that the splits on both knowledge and math do not fully determine, or cause, science values, hence the degree of uncertainty or variability in each terminal node.

One caveat with regard to describing the tree as resulting in *pathways* of observations is what we discuss later in the section on stability. Use of this level of description of the tree structure should be accompanied by a healthy dose of skepticism regarding this structure as "optimal." Additionally, just because a decision trees algorithm results in splits does not denote a magnitude of effect. To understand this more broadly, one needs to pair explanation with prediction, or describing model performance. This will be touched on in more depth later in the chapter, however, with the tree in Figure 5.18, the predictions from the four resultant subgroups explained 37% of the variability in science. Although far from explaining most of the variance, this might represent an important contribution, depending on performance relative to other methods (linear or lasso regression) or based on results reported in the research area of application.

5.5.3 Stability

The principle criticism of decision trees is that they are unstable (Breiman, 1996b). This instability occurs when small changes in the dataset produce large changes in the fit of the model (Breiman, 1996b). Instability makes the choice of the final model more difficult, while also imparting doubt into the generalizability of the results, particularly in comparison to a method that produces more stable results. Much of the cause for concern for the instability of decision trees can be attributed to their reliance on binary splits. Problems caused by binary classification is not unique to decision trees. For instance, in mental illness diagnosis, low reliability in rater disagreement on whether an individual has a disorder or not can be mostly attributed to difficulties in applying categorical cutoffs to disorders that are dimensional in nature (e.g., Brown, Di Nardo, Lehman, & Campbell, 2001). In contrast to comparing whether an individual is diagnosed with a form of schizophrenia or not, low stability (reliability) with decision trees manifests itself as disagreement in the tree structure across datasets that use the same variables.

Example

To make the concept of (in)stability more concrete, we will use the `Holzinger-Swineford` dataset from the `lavaan` package (Rosseel, 2012). With this dataset, we created three trees using the `rpart` package, one on the first 100 respondents, one on the second 100 respondents, and finally on the entire sample (N=301). The resulting tree structures are displayed in Figures 5.19 to 5.21.

FIGURE 5.19. Tree created using first 100 HS observations.

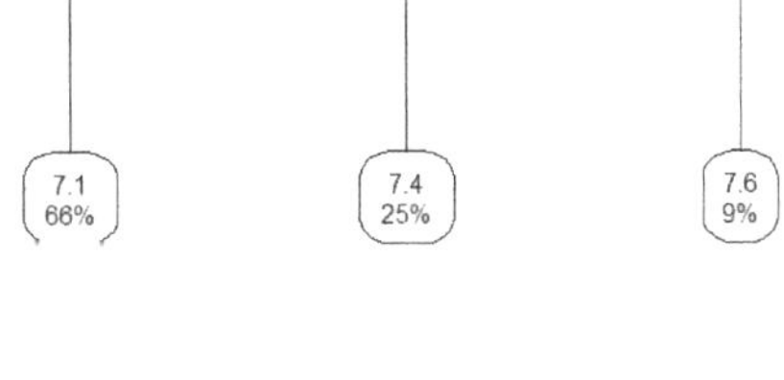

In Figures 5.19 to 5.21, we capture vastly different ideas about what predictors are most important, as well as the functional relationships between the selected predictors and the outcome. The first tree used two variables, $x5$ and $x2$, while the second tree also used two variables, $x2$ and $x3$, and split twice on $x3$. Finally, in the tree created on the entire sample, a new variable was used, $x4$, along with $x2$ and $x3$. Note that although $x2$ was used in each of the three trees, each time was a different cutoff (5.875, 6.125, 7.375). Part of this problem can be attributed to the use of continuous variables as

FIGURE 5.20. Tree created using second 100 HS observations.

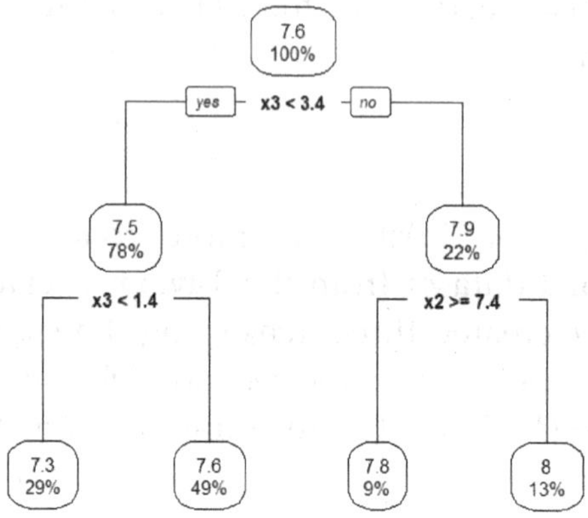

FIGURE 5.21. Tree created using the entire HS sample (N=301).

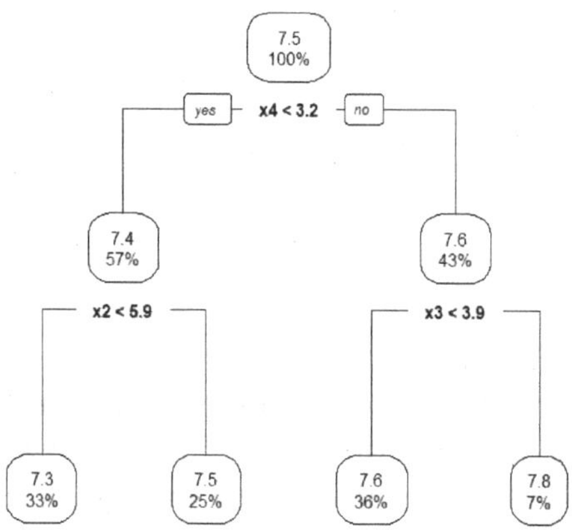

predictors, as there are more possible splits in comparison to an ordinal or nominal variable in most cases.

It is important to note that variability in model estimates is not unique to decision trees, as a similar process can occur with linear regression, although not to the same extent. In Table 5.3 are the results from applying linear regression to the same three datasets.

TABLE 5.3. Linear Regression Coefficients across the Subsamples of the Holzinger-Swineford Dataset

	First 100		Second 100		Full Sample	
Variable	β	p	β	p	β	p
(Intercept)	7.15	.001	7.27	.001	6.83	.001
$x1$	0.01	.83	.02	.74	.03	.36
$x2$	0.02	.53	-.03	.48	.03	.22
$x3$	-0.02	.60	.19	.001	.03	.31
$x4$	0.09	.15	.09	.12	.06	.11
$x5$	-0.09	.09	-.02	.75	.02	.50
$x6$	0.04	.61	-.11	.09	-.02	.63

Although there is some variability to the parameter estimates across the three models, notably with $x4$ denoted as a significant predictor only in the second sample of 100, for the most part, our conclusions stay the same. However, when we add variable selection to the process, our conclusions can vary greatly. Adding backward selection to choose which variables should be in the model (using the Akaike information criterion to choose a final model), we get additional uncertainty. In the first sample, variables $x4$ and $x5$ are chosen, in the second sample $x3$, $x4$, and $x6$, while in the full sample $x2$ and $x4$. As we can see here, it is the act of variable selection and dichotomous cutpoints that induce instability into the resulting models, not just the use of binary splits for decision trees.

Although there have been many suggestions for overcoming the instability of decision trees, the method that has generated the most research is that of bootstrap aggregating (bagging; Breiman, 1996a). The general idea is that instead of creating one tree, many (hundreds or thousands) are created on bootstrapped samples taken from the original dataset. This topic will be the focus of the following chapter, along with extensions of this concept. The main drawback is that although the creation of a host of trees makes the results more stable, we no longer have a single tree structure to interpret. Because the goal of many research projects is the creation of a single, interpretable tree structure, our focus for the rest of the chapter is only on methods that address stability, while resulting in a single tree.

As a more practical solution, when entering variables as predictors in decision trees, researchers should first determine the level of granularity of interest in splitting these variables. In some research domains, creating a cutoff between values of 7.345 and 7.346 may be of interest, in others, much less so. If three decimal places is not of interest, then rounding the predictor values will increase the potential for creating stable trees, along with the benefit of decreasing computational time.

To understand the degree of (in)stability to a tree structure, we recommend the use of repeated bootstrap or subsample sampling to determine possible structures. This has been implemented in the `dtree` package with the `stable()` function. Additionally, we recommend pairing decision trees analyses with those from either boosting or random forests, methods that will be covered in the following chapter. Both of these methods create hundreds or thousands of trees, allowing researchers to further examine whether variables used in a singular tree structure are also consistently used when this process is repeated.

As an example of repeatedly creating tree structures, we used the `stable` function on the ECLS-K example with both `math` and `knowledge` as predictors of science scores. In this, we compared the use of linear regression to the CART and CTree algorithms. Linear regression was used to compare performance using CV, while both CART and CTree can be compared with respect to stability and other metrics.

TABLE 5.4. Stability Results from the ECLS-K Example

	nodes	nvar	nsplits	RMSE CV	R^2 CV
lm	-	-	-	11.75	0.37
rpart	15.42 (4.4)	2.00	14.42	11.51	0.39
ctree	22.67 (9.4)	2.00	21.67	11.48	0.40

Some of these results are displayed in Table 5.4. Using 100 bootstrap samples, and 10-fold cross-validation to assess performance on each bootstrap sample, we can see that both decision trees algorithms outperformed linear regression. This gives us some degree of confidence in the utility of nonlinear relationships in examining this set of predictors and outcome. Next, each tree structure was compared to every other across both algorithms to assess stability. Even with rounding cutpoints to the nearest decimal place, each tree structure was unique. This can partly be attributed to the large trees, with an average number of nodes equal to 15.4 and 22.7 for CART and CTree, respectively.

The fact that both predictors are continuous makes the uniqueness of each tree structure more likely. Going back to Figure 5.13 and examining the predictions for just the `knowledge` variable, one can imagine why this level of instability occurs. With random sampling fluctuations, the predictions for each decision trees structure will vary slightly based on how the bootstrap sample varies.

The purpose of this demonstration is not necessarily to dissuade researchers from the use of decision trees, but instead to impart a degree of skepticism with regards to the optimality of a single tree. Instability is not necessarily problematic for inferences within the sample, but instead for the assumption that a tree structure derived on this sample is likely to be the same or highly similar to a tree structure created on an alternative sample. Instead, each tree structure should be interpreted with some apprehension, as alternative structures exist that may represent the data just as well.

5.5.4 Missing Data

Significant research exists that evaluates various strategies for handling missing data in decision trees (e.g., Ding & Simonoff, 2010; He, 2006). Some decision tree methods have options for using surrogate splits in the presence of missing data. Surrogate splits work in the following way. After a primary split is found for a given node, surrogate splits can be found by reapplying the partitioning algorithm to predict the binary primary split. For example, if the primary split on education is between ≤ 12 and > 12 years and greater than 12, then this new binary variable becomes the outcome, with the remaining variables used as predictors. Those variables that perform best in predicting the primary split are retained (default is five in `rpart`) and used for those cases that had missing values on the primary split variable. In the example detailed earlier, if cognitive score is the first surrogate variable, with splits between high (predicted > 12 years of education) and low values (< 12 years of education), then those with high values on cognitive score (and missing on education) would be given predicted values of > 12 years of education in the tree.

The use of surrogate splits is implemented in both the `rpart` and `partykit` packages, however, in `partykit`, surrogate splits is only implemented for cases when both variables are ordered. If researchers wish to use the CART algorithm, then we recommend the use of surrogate splits. However, with other decision trees algorithms, multiple imputation may be the only option for handling missingness. Unfortunately this does not result in a single tree structure, however the *K* trees, where *K* is the number of imputations, could be used for high-level inferences, such as which variables were split on and where, as well as the stability of the results.

5.5.5 Variable Importance

Similar to linear regression, high correlations among covariates presents problems for decision trees. In the tree building algorithm, at a given split two collinear variables may produce almost identical improvements in fit, but only one can be chosen for a given split. This is analogous to the idea of masking, but in the case of decision trees, it results in one of the variables either not being split on at all, or lower in the tree. To quantify how influential a variable is in predicting the outcome variable, one can also calculate the *variable importance* metric for a given tree. These alternative splits can be used to calculate how much improvement in fit would have occurred for a given variable if the split was chosen. This allows us to quantify the importance of a variable even if it was not split on in the tree. Although there are various ways to calculate this, which is not limited to decision trees, the `rpart` package creates an overall measure of variable importance that is the sum of the fit improvement for all splits of which it was the primary variablc (i.e., in the tree), plus for the improvement in fit (adjusted for improvement above baseline) for all splits in which it was a surrogate (Therneau & Atkinson, 1997).

As an example, we used the ECLS-K dataset to create an additional tree. Using both general knowledge and math as predictors of eighth-grade science, we added a third variable, which we created by duplicating each observation's math score and adding a small amount of noise. This simulated math score had a correlation of 0.95 with the original math score. We expected that this would result in only one of the math variables being selected in the tree, but that the variable importance should show roughly similar values for each math score. The resultant tree is displayed in Figure 5.22.

As expected, one of the math scores was not used in the tree (the simulated math score). However, the variable importance metrics were as follows: 39 for math, 33 for knowledge, and 28 for the simulated math score. Note that the variable importance metric is scaled to add up to 100. Despite not showing up in Figure 5.22, the simulated math score receives an importance score that is nonzero. This metric should not be interpreted to too high of precision, as there are only so many splits in a tree, making it difficult to fully account for each variable's importance. In general, only the relative ranking of variables should be interpreted with respect to importance metrics (Strobl, Malley, & Tutz, 2009). In the next chapter, we will build variable importance metrics that are much more robust, as we are using hundreds, if not thousands, of trees to average each variable's effect.

FIGURE 5.22. Tree structure with collinear variables.

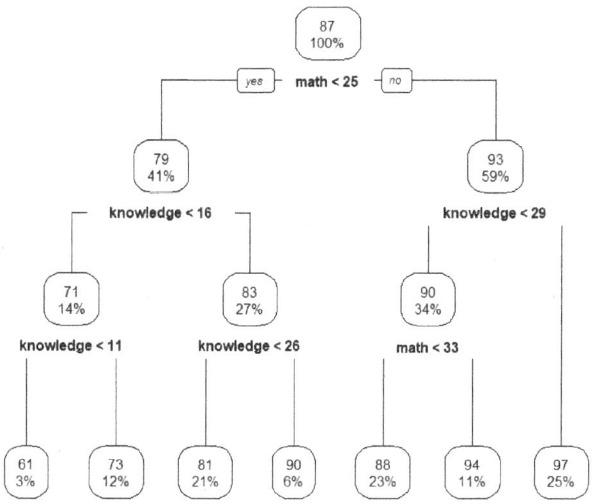

5.6 Summary

Decision trees require researchers to make a fundamental shift in the way they interpret results, namely, in that the mapping between predictors and an outcome can be visualized and not reliant on understanding slope coefficients in regression models. Instead, interactions are automatically tested and can be visualized in a number of ways. Although decision trees can in many cases produce more theoretically informative results in comparison to generalized linear models, there are a number of drawbacks to decision trees. Below we detail some of the main points that characterize the advantages and disadvantages of decision trees.

Advantages:

- Are robust to outliers—single misclassifications don't greatly influence the splitting.
- Perform variable selection.
- Generally result in easy-to-interpret tree structures.
- Automatically include interaction effects.

Disadvantages:

- Instability.
- Collinearity presents problems.
- Relatively lower predictive performance.

Just as researchers need to understand the assumptions of linear models, and in what situations these models may not be appropriate, we urge them to not just turn a blind eye and believe that decision trees represent a panacea. As we have noted, there are some research contexts for which tree structures are not appropriate, and there are underlying assumptions that can be violated. Decision trees should instead be viewed as complementary to the use of linear models, and in most cases we recommend using both methods to compare and contrast the different theoretical conclusions that the results represent.

5.6.1 Further Reading

- For further discussion on the instability of decision trees and how to assess them, see Philipp, Rusch, Hornik, and Strobl (2018).
- A number of tutorials have been written on the use of decision trees for various disciplines. Two that we recommend include King and Resick (2014) and McArdle (2012).
- One topic that was not discussed was the use of decision trees in a number of applications as a model for imputing data and for creating propensity scores. See Lee, Lessler, and Stuart (2010) for an evaluation of the use of trees for creating propensity scores, and Carrig et al. (2015) for imputing when datasets are to be integrated.

5.6.2 Computational Time and Resources

Relative to the algorithms that comprise the following chapter, decision trees are relatively quick to fit, even when paired with cross-validation or the assessment of stability. Similarly to regularized regression, decision trees often take on the order of seconds or a few minutes to fit. The runtime is mainly influenced by the number of predictors, and number of possible cutpoints on each predictor. Predictors that are continuous and contain a large number of unique values, along with predictors coded as nominal (requiring one vs. all comparisons), can drastically increase the runtime.

In this chapter, we covered two of the most commonly used R packages for decision trees: rpart and partykit. Many additional packages are available, either ones that implement quite similar algorithms, such as the tree package (Ripley, 2023), or ones that were developed with novel splitting procedures, such as the evtree package (Grubinger, Zeileis, & Pfeiffer, 2014). Further, while the rpart package is restricted to binary or continuous outcomes, a number of packages have been developed to extend the fundamental tree algorithms to cover alternative outcome types, such as the rpartOrdinal package (Archer, 2010). Finally, while most packages also contain functions for plotting the resultant trees, a number of additional packages were built specifically to improve the visualization of trees. The partykit package allows for plotting rpart trees in the same manner as ctree() trees, while rpart.plot package (Milborrow, 2022) drastically improves the quality of plots from rpart trees.

6 Ensembles

Decision trees can make flexible, powerful, and interpretable prediction models; however, they are not without their limitations. Chief criticisms of decision trees include bias in variable selection, parameter instability, and poorer prediction in future samples (e.g. Berk, 2008; Hastie et al., 2009). Ensemble methods, where multiple prediction models are estimated, were developed to overcome these limitations of decision trees. For many ensemble methods, their underlying rationale comes from sampling theory. For example, say we're trying to estimate a population parameter (e.g., mean, regression coefficient). Holding all else constant, our estimate of the population parameter improves (and the standard error shrinks) when sample size increases. The decision tree estimated in our sample represents a single prediction model. Ideally, we would draw multiple samples from the population and estimate a decision tree for each sample. Then, the predictions from the ensemble of decision trees could be combined to create the final prediction for each individual. Since obtaining multiple samples from the population is not often feasible, many ensemble methods rely on the bootstrap. That is, the data are bootstrapped, a decision tree is fit to each bootstrapped sample, and the predictions are averaged to create the final prediction model. In this chapter, we review several ensemble methods that differ in their approach, but all methods create an ensemble of prediction models to create the final prediction model.

6.1 Key Terminology

- Ensemble. A combination of individual models. In this chapter we discuss ensemble methods that create a large number of individual decision trees and aggregate the predictions.
- Bagging. Creating an ensemble of individual decision trees on independently generated bootstrap samples.
- Boosting. Creating an ensemble of individual trees in a sequential process using the residuals from the previously created set of trees.

- Permutation. A form of resampling where case outcome values are shuffled (permuted) to be used in statistical tests. In more traditional statistical use, permutation tests are used to create a null distribution to calculate significance.

- Node purity. In a terminal node, the percentage of cases that have the same observed outcome value.

- Conditional inference forests. An alternative form of random forests that uses different statistical tests to calculate variable importance.

- Gradient. This term is often used to refer to the partial derivatives in optimization, but in this chapter, the gradient refers to the residuals for each case and how these are used to create the new tree.

- Learning rate. In gradient boosting, the learning rate refers to how fast or slow the residuals (gradient) are updated based on the predictions for each new tree.

- Partial dependence plot. An approximation of the relationship between a predictor and outcome while controlling for all other predictors. This is often used for ensemble methods given that interpretable "effects" are not generated for individual predictors.

6.2 Bagging

One of the first proposed ensemble methods was *bootstrap aggregation*, or *bagging* (Breiman, 1996a). The algorithm proceeds in two steps. First, a bootstrap sample is taken. To create a bootstrap sample, the data are resampled with replacement and each bootstrap sample has a sample size that is equal to the sample size of the original sample. Then for each bootstrap sample, a decision tree is fit using all predictor variables as potential splitting variables. Given that each bootstrap sample is different, each tree will have a unique structure manifested in the variables used, splitting values chosen, and tree size given the instability of decision trees. Once a series of decision trees are estimated, the predicted values for each person from each of the trees are output and then averaged to create the final prediction. More formally, predictions from a bagging model are created by

$$\hat{f}_{bag}(x) = \frac{1}{B} \sum_{b=1}^{B} \hat{f}^{*b}(x)$$

where $\hat{f}_{bag}(x)$ are the final predicted values, $\hat{f}^{*b}(x)$ are the predicted values from the decision tree fitted to bootstrap sample b, and B is the number of trees.

As an example of how averaging the predictions from multiple decision trees is implemented, we analyzed data that examines prenatal phenylaline exposure (PHE) by the fetus in utero as a predictor of childhood intelligence in a sample of children of mothers with phenylketonuria (PKU; see Widaman & Grimm, 2013). Figure 6.1 is a bivariate scatterplot of the observed data between the child's full-scale intelligence score (Full Scale IQ) on the Y-axis with PHE exposure on the X-axis.

FIGURE 6.1. Scatterplot from the PHE data.

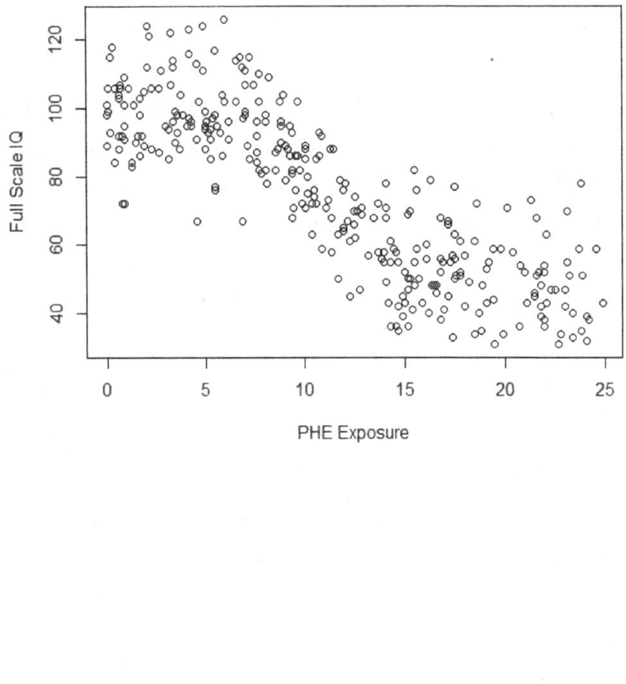

FIGURE 6.2. Scatterplot from the PHE data with predicted step functions from decision trees with a tree depth of 1, 2, and 3.

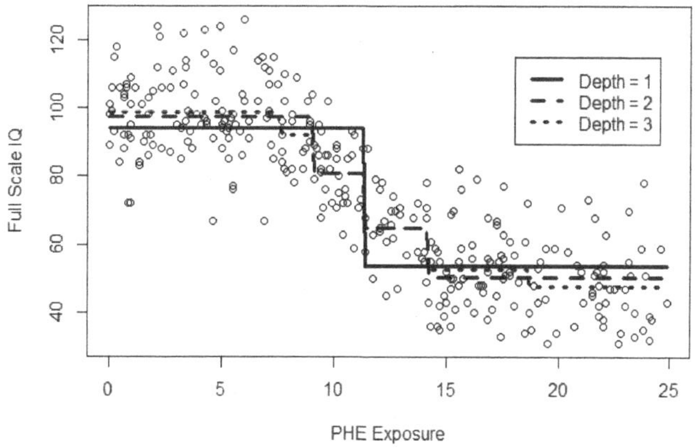

First, as a comparison, we fit decision trees of different depths to these data and plotted the predicted full-scale IQ values given the level of PHE exposure from each model. These predictions are overlaid on top of the scatterplot in Figure 6.2. As is evident in this plot, as the tree incurs more splits, the prediction line is more nuanced. This is why the propensity to overfit the data increases with the size of the tree. That is, the likelihood that the tree learns aspects of the training sample that are unlikely to generalize to alternative samples increases with each split. A second aspect of the predictions to note in Figure 6.2 is that the prediction line only changes at 90 degree angles, given how the decision tree algorithm partitions the data, even though the data suggest a smoother functional form. As we will see, a smoother prediction function can be obtained when averaging predictions from many decision trees.

The bagging algorithm was then applied to the illustrative data with predictions averaged over five decision trees and then averaged over 2,000 decision trees. The prediction functions created from a single tree with three splits, the bagging model with five decision trees, and the bagging model with 2,000 decision trees are plotted in the three panels of Figure 6.3, respectively. These prediction functions highlight how the predictions from bagging can be more flexible than those from single decision trees. In Figure 6.3, we see an increasing amount of smoothing as the number of trees increases. Even though each tree can only produce step functions, averaging across *many* step functions results in an almost smooth curve. This is most evident in the middle values of PHE exposure variable (8 <

FIGURE 6.3. Prediction from 1 tree, 5 bagged trees, and 2,000 bagged trees. Note how the prediction line becomes smoother as the number of trees increases.

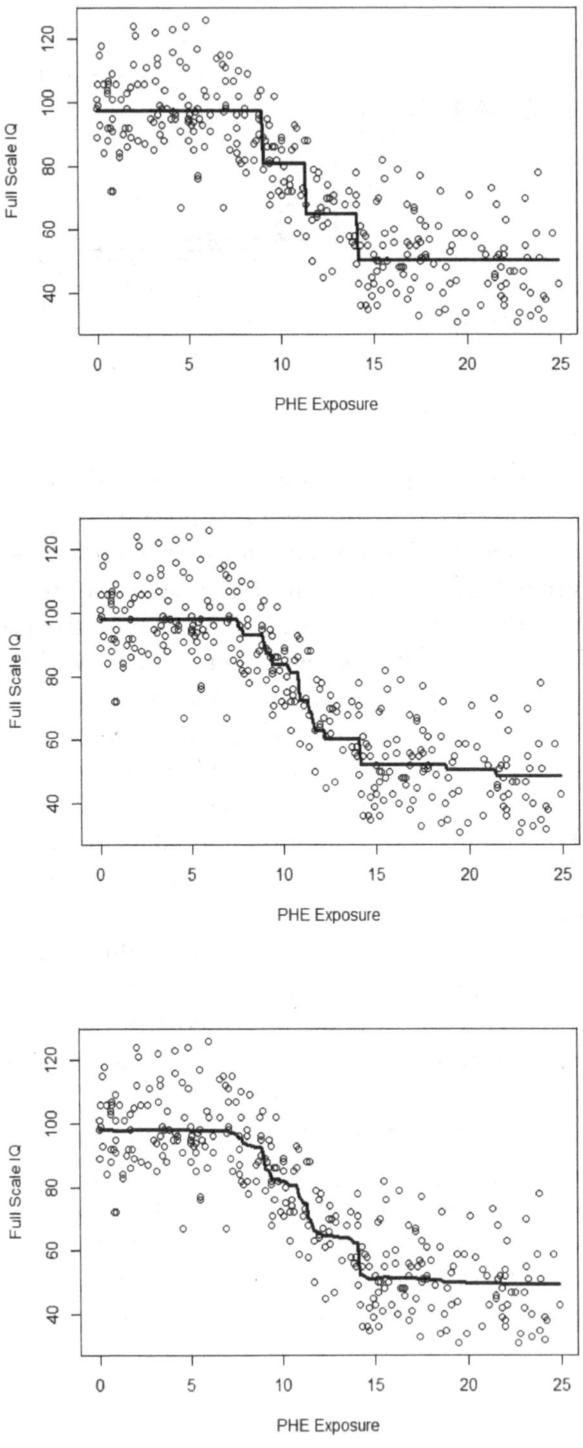

FIGURE 6.4. Comparison of performance as the number of trees increases. RPart is the use of the `rpart` package for decision trees. Only every 20th result is displayed.

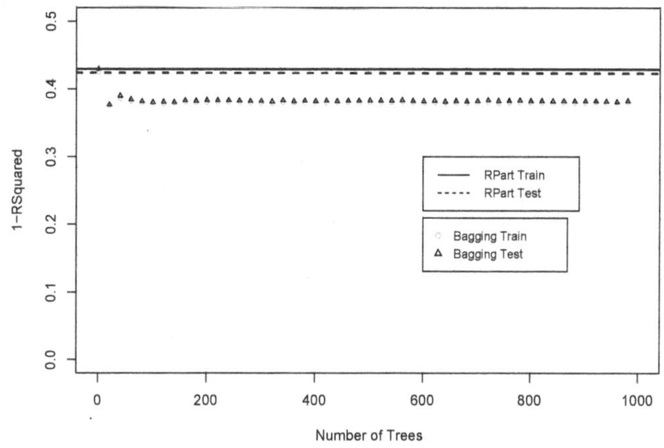

PHE exposure < 15) with 2,000 decision trees as the prediction function follows a smooth transition from higher IQ values to lower IQ values. We note that the step function in the top panel of Figure 6.3 captures this decrease; however, the almost smooth transition in the bottom panel is a much closer approximation to the data.

As the number of trees increases in bagging, so does the fit of the resulting predictions to the training dataset. To demonstrate this, we used the ECLS-K data, predicting science scores using reading, math, and knowledge scale scores, as well as socioeconomic status, weight, height, and income. The results are displayed in Figure 6.4, where we plotted the fit of the predictions when increasing the number of trees. From this figure, we can see that it only takes a small number of bagged trees to improve the fit of decision trees on both the training and test datasets, with the performance leveling off at approximately 100 trees. Selecting the number of trees is the main tuning parameter in bagging. Selecting too few trees can result in underfitting, while there is typically less consequence for using too many trees. Typically, 500 trees works relatively well, while more trees may be required in the presence of many predictors.

Bagging tends to produce prediction models that are a notable improvement over a single decision tree; however, bagging does have some inherent limitations. A main limitation of bagging, as well as with all ensemble methods, is a loss of interpretability of the resulting prediction model. While it is clear how the prediction model is determined (i.e., averaged predictions from the ensemble of decision trees), it is less clear how each variable is associated with the outcome. To reduce the effect of this limitation of bagging, researchers have developed variable importance metrics. As noted, one of the largest drawbacks to ensemble methods, such as bagging, is uncertainty as to the relationship between the predictors and the outcome. Simply put, there is no single tree structure or set of parameter coefficients to interpret. To overcome this limitation of ensemble methods, relative variable importance[1] metrics have been proposed to determine how much each variable contributes to the prediction of the outcome. Following Breiman et al. (1984), variable importance for a decision tree is calculated as

$$I_l(T) = \sum_{t=1}^{J-1} \Delta I(\delta_l, t) \tag{6.1}$$

for each predictor x_l, where there are $J - 1$ internal nodes, each node t, δ_l is the surrogate split for x_l, and ΔI_l is a measure of error improvement for node t (e.g., decrease in impurity or other measure of misfit). This variable importance metric is referred to as the *increase in node purity*. Note that by using surrogate splits, as opposed to just the actual split that was selected, it allows variables that were not included in the derived tree to have importance values greater than zero. This is particularly important in the presence of correlated predictors. It then becomes relatively straightforward to extend this variable importance metric to an aggregation across trees. That is, variable importance for an ensemble of decision trees is

$$I_l = \frac{1}{M} \sum_{m=1}^{M} I_l(T_m) \tag{6.2}$$

where M is the number of trees. These values for each predictor are rarely interpreted in this metric, but typically transformed so that the sum equals 100 or the most important predictor is given a value of 100. An alternative method for calculating variable importance is through the use of permutation tests. From Strobl, Boulesteix, Kneib, Augustin, and Zeileis (2008): "that a random permutation of the values of the predictor variable is supposed to mimic the absence of the variable from the model." This form of variable importance was proposed in Breiman (2001a) using the out-of-bag (OOB) samples. Specifically, for the Mth tree grown, prediction performance (e.g., RMSE) is recorded for the OOB sample. Next, for the lth

[1]Note that we subsequently drop the term *relative* and just refer to *variable importance*.

variable, permute the values in the OOB data and record the prediction performance in this OOB sample with permuted variable. Variable importance is then calculated as the difference between the prediction performance in the nonpermuted and permuted OOB samples (averaging over the trees).

Using the same ECLS-K data, the variable importance values from a bagging model with 500 trees are displayed in Table 6.1. In this analysis, we used the `randomForest` package, which by default uses the permutation test for assessing percent increase in MSE due to permuting the variable. This metric is displayed in the left column of Table 6.1, whereas increase in node purity is displayed in the right column. Both metrics paint a similar picture with reading scores highlighted as the most important variable.

TABLE 6.1. Variable Importance for Bagging Using the ECLS-K Data

	Percent Increase in MSE	Increase in Node Purity
math	6.87	7815.79
knowledge	7.32	6551.93
weight	3.86	4240.14
height	-0.13	3775.70
income	6.41	5207.22
SES	4.58	4576.67
read	80.76	71669.52

Note there is inherent randomness to the variable importance values, which is why setting a seed and using a sufficiently large number of trees is recommended (e.g., using 2,000 trees even when 500 achieves the same prediction performance). The actual number of necessary trees varies by application and number of predictors used. Irrelevant variables will evidence importance values randomly around zero, sometimes producing negative estimates. We note, however, that the ranking of the variable importance values is more important than the values themselves. This is outside of importance values close to zero, as they can be interpreted as this variable contributing little to the prediction of the outcome.

A second limitation of bagging is that the decision trees created in the bootstrap samples are somewhat related. More specifically, imagine two strongly correlated variables, x_1 and x_2, with x_1 having a slightly stronger association with the outcome y. Across bootstrap samples, x_1 is going to be selected into the decision tree at a much higher frequency than x_2 even though x_1 and x_2 are highly correlated. This can lead to decision trees that are more similar to one another because of their overreliance on x_1 and disregard for x_2. To overcome this issue, Breiman (2001a) proposed random forests, discussed subsequently, which randomly samples predictor variables when partitioning the data.

6.3 Random Forests

Random forests is an extension of bagging that attempts to reduce the similarity between the decision trees estimated on each bootstrap sample. Simply stated, random forests proceeds in the same way as bagging by bootstrapping the data and fitting a decision tree to each bootstrapped dataset. However, decision tree construction does not proceed as usual. In random forests, a subset of the predictors, as opposed to all predictors as in bagging, are considered when partitioning the data. This added level of randomness encourages the decision trees to differ more from one another, which allows for a more diverse predictor space. That is, the decision trees are less likely to rely on the same few variables, which can pigeonhole the prediction space. Once the decision trees are fit to each bootstrapped sampled, predictions are made by averaging predictions from the decision trees.

Selecting a random subset of predictors allows for variables that have high correlations with other variables to be included in the tree, along with allowing weaker variables to exert an influence. This accounts for the main distinction with bagging, and typically results in superior performance. More formally, the random forests algorithm is explicated in Algorithm 1.

Algorithm 1 Random Forests Algorithm

1. Set B, the number of trees
2. Set m, the number of variables to consider when making a partition
3. For $b = 1$ to B repeat
   (a) Draw a bootstrap sample of size N from the data
   (b) Grow a decision tree T_b on the bootstrap sample using a random set of m variables for each partition
   (c) Use the out-of-bag samples to create predictions from the decision tree
4. Output the ensemble of trees $\{T_b\}_1^B$
5. Calculate the final predicted values for each individual following

$$\hat{f}_{rf}^{B}(x) = \frac{1}{B}\sum_{b=1}^{B} T_b(x)$$

For random forests, there are two tuning parameters, the number of trees B (as in bagging) and m the variable subset size when making a partition of the data. Typically B is fairly large (i.e., 500 to 2,000) and larger than the number of trees needed when using bagging because the prediction from each decision tree is somewhat poorer with random forests. Oftentimes, the variable subset size m, often referred to as *mtry*, is a fairly small number (e.g., $\sqrt{p}$, where p is the number of predictor variable). When predictor variables are highly correlated, a smaller value of m typically leads to superior performance.

The optimal value of m can be determined using a grid search, whereas the optimal value of B is often examined using the out-of-bag (OOB) prediction error. OOB observations are the observations that are left out of the bootstrap sample. Recall that bootstrapping is resampling with replacement. Thus, a single observation can appear multiple times in a bootstrap sample, whereas another observation can be left out of a bootstrap sample entirely. These left-out observations are the OOB observations and the prediction error on these OOB observations is a decent approximation of the out-of-sample prediction error (Breiman, 1996a). Although the number of trees and variable subset size are treated as tuning parameters, the size of each decision tree is typically not controlled or varied. Although there is some research on this topic (e.g., Segal, 2004), most software programs utilize defaults for the decision tree size, mainly specifying the minimum number of cases in a terminal node.

In comparison to bagging, random forests is often able to model more nuanced relationships in the data, resulting in improved fit. This increased degree of flexibility can lead to a propensity to overfit the training dataset, while resulting in less dramatic improvements in fit in the test set. Random forests was also applied to the same ECLS-K data as demonstrated in section 6.2, with a sequence of trees and their corresponding training and test dataset fits displayed in Figure 6.5. Relative to both decision trees and bagging, random forests demonstrated striking improvements in the training dataset, while only incremental improvements are seen in the test dataset. Additionally, we can see that random forests required a larger number of trees to achieve a minimum misfit in test dataset, which can be attributed to the random selection of predictors when partitioning the data.

FIGURE 6.5. Comparison of performance as the number of trees increases. RF refers to random forests and RPart is the use of the `rpart` package for decision trees. Only every 20th result is displayed.

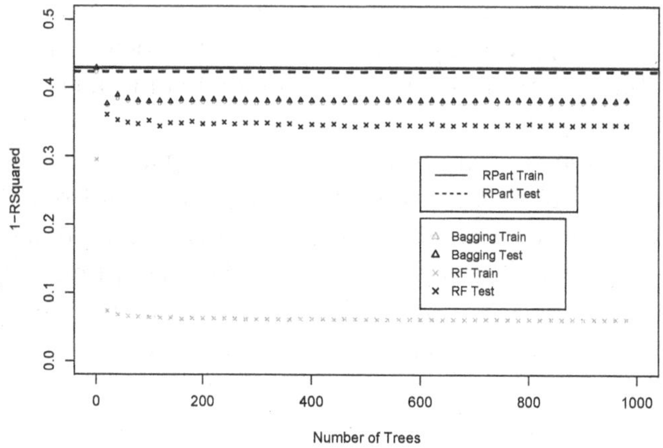

The main limitation of bagging is shared with random forests. Specifically, random forests lack interpretability because a single decision tree is no longer available. Variable importance measures discussed for bagging are also available for random forests and used to highlight which variables appeared to contribute more to the prediction of the outcome. The permutation approach to variable importance discussed earlier is the most common approach to documenting variable importance; however, the `partykit` package offers an alternative approach based on permuting the data, which has been found to reduce bias. The way of permuting x values discussed above is referred to as a *marginal* approach and is used in the `randomForest` package by default. The marginal approach to evaluating variable importance has been found to bias variable importance values in favor of predictors that are correlated (Strobl et al., 2008). As a result, Strobl et al. (2008) developed a *conditional* approach. In discussing the conditional approach, we refer to the set of predictors that do not include the variable x as Z. For each tree, we calculate the importance for x by extracting the cutpoints for all Z variables used in the tree and setting up a grid corresponding to these cutpoints. Then, for each subset of the bootstrap (subsample) sample created by the cutpoints on Z, we permute the values of x and the prediction performance is calculated after each permutation. This approach to variable importance is available in the `partykit` package when estimating random forests using conditional inference trees (`cforest` function).

To provide an example of interpreting variable importance, we used the ECLS-K data and 100 trees with the **randomForest** and **partykit** packages. As noted, the **randomForest** package uses the marginal approach to calculating variable importance, whereas the **partykit** package uses the conditional approach to variable importance. Note that conditional variable importance is not the default in the **partykit** package (`varimp(conditional=TRUE)`) because it is computationally intense and therefore only recommended when using a small number of variables.

We report the variable importance values from **randomForest** and **partykit** packages (both the marginal and conditional) in Table 6.2 and contrast these values with those from a decision tree created with **rpart**.

TABLE 6.2. Variable Importance Metrics across Four Different Methods

	randomForest	rpart	partykit conditional	partykit marginal
math	17.29	13	2.50	13.91
knowledge	28.14	13	1.23	15.6
weight	1.37	0	0.18	0.61
height	0.00	0	-0.37	-0.01
income	10.95	6	-0.10	3.28
SES	10.94	8	0.28	4.89
read	100.00	61	44.61	108.6

In assessing the values in Table 6.2, the first thing to note is the different scales of the values, with the values from **rpart** summing to 100, **randomForest** setting the importance of the most important variable to 100, and **partykit** is the mean decrease in accuracy which is on a different scale across the marginal and conditional metrics. Also note that these values are only unbiased when subsampling is used (the default in **partykit**). In comparing the marginal and conditional results from **cforest**, we note the much lower values for all variables other than reading in the conditional results. This is due to the correlations between reading and the other variables, with the conditional approach controlling for this correlation and the marginal approach not controlling for it. This colors our picture specifically of the math and knowledge scales, as the marginal approach points to these variable contributing in a non-neglible way (VI values > 0), while the conditional approach results in values of nearly zero. Lastly, all three of the random forest methods result in negligible values for height, income, SES, and weight, leading to the conclusion that their inclusion changes little regarding the predictions of the outcome. See Grömping (2009) or Fisher, Rudin, and Dominici (2019) for more general discussions of variable importance.

6.4 Gradient Boosting

Similar to random forests, *gradient boosting* (also known as *gradient boosting machines* or *gradient boosting trees*) is a method that combines the use of hundreds or thousands of individual decision trees in an attempt to overcome the problems with a single decision tree. However, in contrast to bagging and random forests, where each decision tree is created independently on a bootstrapped sample, boosting creates a sequence of trees based on reweighted forms of the data. Developed originally for classification in the form of the AdaBoost algorithm (Freund & Schapire, 1995; 1996; 1997), the idea behind the boosting algorithm has been extended to many other statistical problems (see Buhlmann & Hothorn, 2007 for more detail). Most notably, Friedman, Hastie, and Tibshirani (2000), as well as Friedman (2001), developed highly adaptable algorithms that can be applied to a host of different loss functions. This algorithm has also been extended to multivariate outcomes (Miller, Lubke, McArtor, & Bergeman, 2016). The basic idea of this algorithmic framework, originally termed *gradient boosting machines* by Friedman (2001), now more frequently referred to as simply *boosting*, is to fit an additive combination of *weak learner* (weak in the sense that its predictive performance is usually substandard) models, most often a decision tree with few (potentially one) partitions of the data, to the gradient (residuals) of the prior combination of weak learners. More formally, the algorithm is described as

Algorithm 2 Boosting Algorithm Overview

1. Set tree depth, D for each decision tree
2. Set learning rate or shrinkage parameter λ
3. Set the number of trees B
4. Initialize the residuals r_b with initial predictions p_0 of 0 for each y
5. For $b = 1, 2, ..., B$, repeat
   (a) Fit a tree t_b of depth D to the current residuals of the response, r_b
   (b) Create new predictions p_b for each case using t_b
   (c) Update the residuals using a shrunken version of the prediction, $r_b = r_b - \lambda p_b$

This algorithm creates a sequence of trees by continually fitting trees to the current vector of residuals. Shrinking the influence of each tree,

FIGURE 6.6. Plotting training set RMSE as a function of the number of trees across three different values of shrinkage.

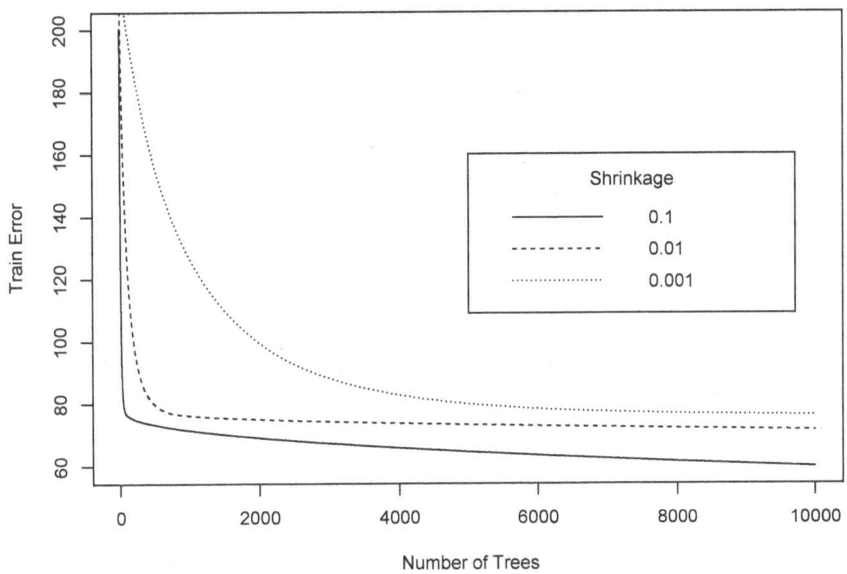

better known as the process of *learning slowly*, can prevent overfitting. The rate of learning or the amount of shrinkage is determined by λ, which is usually treated as a tuning parameter, with values typically ranging from 0.001 to 0.1. The smaller the value of λ, the more trees that are needed to adequately fit the data. To illustrate this point, we fit three boosting models with different values of λ to the ECLS-K data with the students' eighth-grade science scores as the outcome and the same seven predictors used earlier. After fitting the three boosting models, we plotted the training RMSE as a function of the number of trees in Figure 6.6. Here, we see how the shrinkage rate influences the training RMSE as a function of the number of trees. Across the shrinkage rates, increasing the number of trees reduces misfit (lower RMSE) because we are evaluating this on the training dataset. Most notably, however, is how shrinkage controls the rate at which each curve reaches its minimum, with higher shrinkage resulting in faster learning (reaching the minimum earlier).

To objectively examine the performance of these three boosting models, we plotted the average RMSE across different folds of the data in Figure 6.7. In contrast to Figure 6.6, Figure 6.7 shows a best fitting model is reached relatively early. With a shrinkage rate of 0.1 the best fit comes with less than

FIGURE 6.7. Plotting RMSE assessed with CV as a function of the number of trees across three different values of shrinkage.

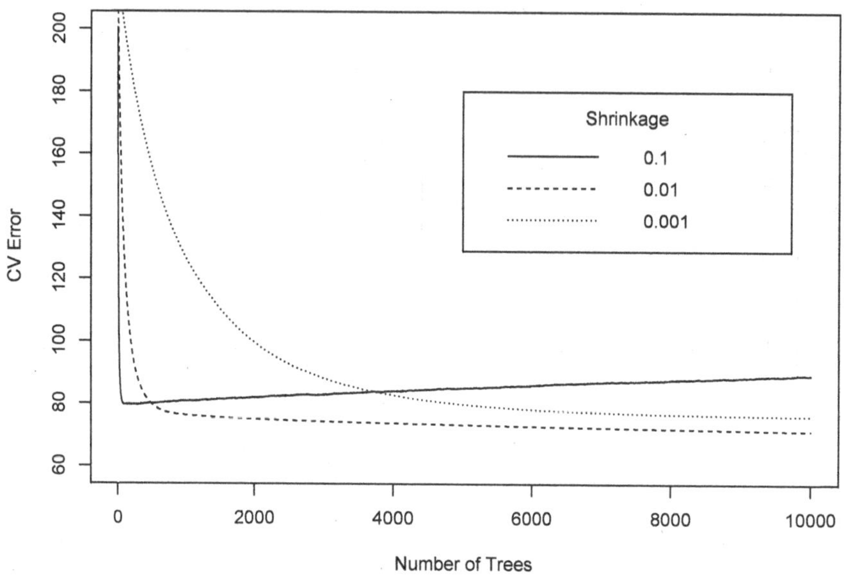

100 trees. However, the lowest fit is achieved with a learning rate of 0.01, and misfit continues to decrease when the number of trees is increased. Given that the improvement is not substantial after 1,000 trees, we could choose to stop after 1,000 trees as a further attempt to prevent overfitting. Despite the slow learning through the inclusion of a shrinkage parameter, choosing a final model with too many trees can result in overfitting.

To interpret the results of boosting, the same process of examining variable importance is conducted. It is worth assessing the procedure that the boosting software program of choice uses for calculating variable importance, as the same drawbacks, with respect to marginal versus conditional importance, pertain to boosting.

6.4.1 Variants on Boosting

Although most boosting algorithms follow the general structure in Algorithm 2, a number of alternative versions of boosting are available. A more recently developed algorithm that has demonstrated superior performance to gradient boosting in several applications is *extreme gradient boosting* (XGBoost; Chen & Guestrin, 2016), implemented in the `xgboost` package (Chen et al., 2015) in R. XGBoost alters the objective function of gradient boosting so it includes a regularization component, which smoothes the contribution from each of the individual trees. In XGBoost, the objective function is

$$L^{(t)} = \sum_{i=1}^{n} l(y_i, \hat{y}^{(t-1)} + f_t(x_t)) + \Omega(f_t), \tag{6.3}$$

for tree t in the sequence of trees, with $\Omega(f_t)$ being the regularization term for tree t. This regularization term helps to prevent overfitting in the creation of each tree, and is combined with the shrinkage component of gradient boosting to further reduce the influence of each tree. Moreover, XGBoost implements a number of additional components, including features that take advantage of parallel learning, sparse data structures, and utilizing approximations to the loss function and optimal tree structure to reduce computational complexity. Note that there are two variations on XGBoost implemented in the `caret` package, *xgbLinear* and *xgbTree*, with the difference being boosting based on linear models (e.g., regression) versus decision trees as base learners, respectively.

6.5 Interpretation

A number of different methods have been developed for investigating the relationships between variables when using ensemble algorithms. These can broadly be broken up into methods that assess global interpretation or local interpretation. In contrast to global interpretation methods, which aggregate effects across individuals (rows), local interpretation hones in on individual cases. We devote more space to global interpretation methods, and only briefly cover local interpretation. For additional detail on these approaches, see Molnar (2019).

6.5.1 Global Interpretation

After testing an ensemble method, such as random forests or gradient boosting, researchers may want to dive deeper into the results to determine what types of relationships were modeled by the algorithms. Although the totality of a variable's effect can be captured in variable importance, the actual relationship is not clear. One approach to probing modeled relationships is using *partial dependence plots* (Friedman, 2001). The idea behind partial dependence plots is to visualize the effect of a variable in a "black box" type algorithm. Broadly speaking, this involves examining the effect of x_1 on y, after accounting for the average effects of x_C, where x_C represents all other predictors. Note that this is not the relationship

FIGURE 6.8. Relationship between reading scores and predicted values of science in the left panel, between math and science scores in right panel.

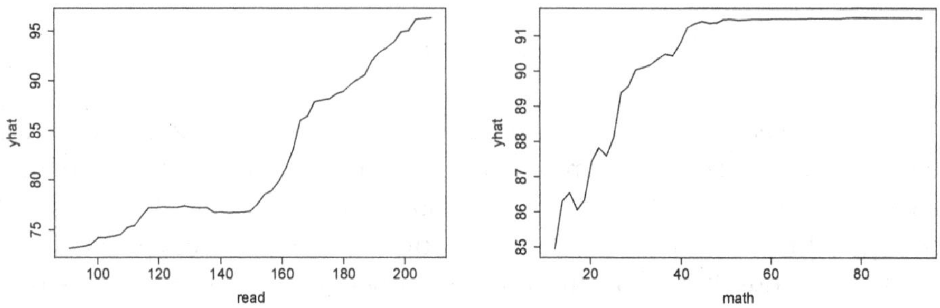

between x_1 on y ignoring the effects of x_C, but the effect of x_1 on y after taking into account the average effect of x_C. This means that interactions between x_1 and x_C are included in the partial dependence plot.

This approach allows for the visualization of interactions and nonlinear effects. However, these are descriptive approximations, not "true" derived relationships. To give an example, we continue with the application of random forests to the ECLS-K data, examining the relationships between the predictor variables reading and math scores and the outcome science score. The pdp package interfaces with `caret` to create partial dependence plots. One thing to note is that when using a categorical outcome, make sure your class ordering is correct. By default `caret` treats the first level of a factor variable as the positive class, which is used to denote more positive predictive values on the y axis in the partial dependence plot. Moreover, multiple partial dependence plots can be created when analyzing a categorical outcome with more than two classes.The relationship between Reading scores and predicted science scores ("yhat") is displayed in Figure 6.8. Here, we see an almost linear relationship between reading and predicted science scores. This is in contrast to the relationship between math and predicted science scores, displayed in Figure 6.8. In Figure 6.8, there is evidence of a nonlinear effect of the math scores—once a child reaches a certain level on math, there is no longer a corresponding expected increase in predicted science with an increase in math. This is commonly seen when using cognitive or achievement scales that are "too easy" for some respondents, with less variability in higher scores as opposed to lower scores.

We can visualize the relationship between all three variables, allowing for the inspection of interaction effects. The three-dimensional partial dependence plot is displayed in Figure 6.9. In Figure 6.9, we can again see the nonlinear effect for math, the linear effect for reading, with little variation

FIGURE 6.9. Three-dimensional relationship between math and reading in predicting science.

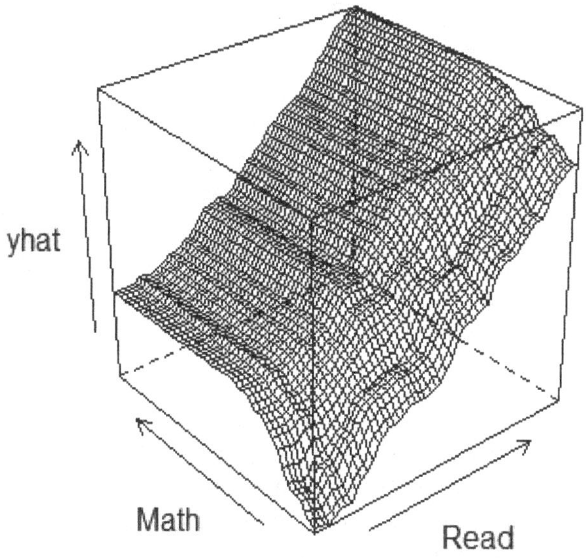

in the contour at different levels of each predictor, indicating the absence of an interactive effect.

One of the drawbacks of partial dependence plots is extrapolation of the expected curve to parts of x with few or no data points. The addition of rug marks help indicate where the majority of data points are for the x variable, and what points may have little support by actual data. This is demonstrated in Figure 6.10, where the majority of the math scores range from 20 to 40, and the nonlinear component at higher levels of math is partially due to few actual data points.

FIGURE 6.10. Partial dependence plot for math with rug marks.

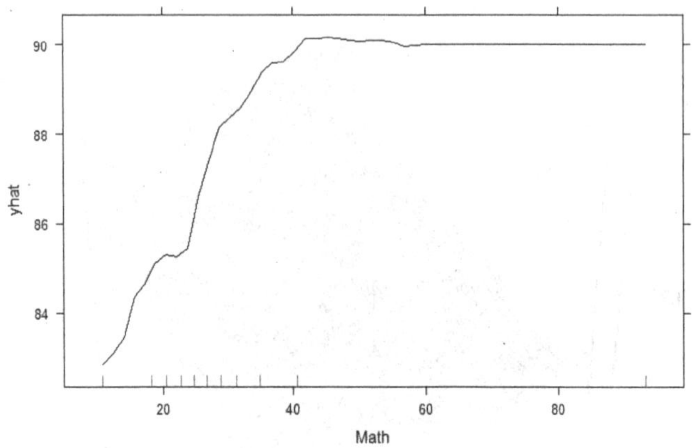

An additional drawback of partial dependence plots is that when predictors are correlated, the average across other predictors can bias the visualized relationship between x and expected y. A method developed to overcome this is issue and demonstrate unbiased function approximation in the presence of correlations among predictors is the *accumulated local effects plot* (ALE; Apley, 2016). In some data analysis scenarios, partial dependence and ALE plots can demonstrate discrepancies. To illustrate these differences, we simulated data where two predictors have a correlation of 0.88 and have effects on a continuous y variable. In this simulation, x_1 was simulated to have a linear effect on y, while x_2 was simulated to have a nonlinear relationship following a sine curve. Both the partial dependence and ALE plots are displayed in Figure 6.11.

FIGURE 6.11. Partial dependence plot in the left pane, while the accumulated local effects plot is displayed in the right pane for the simulated data.

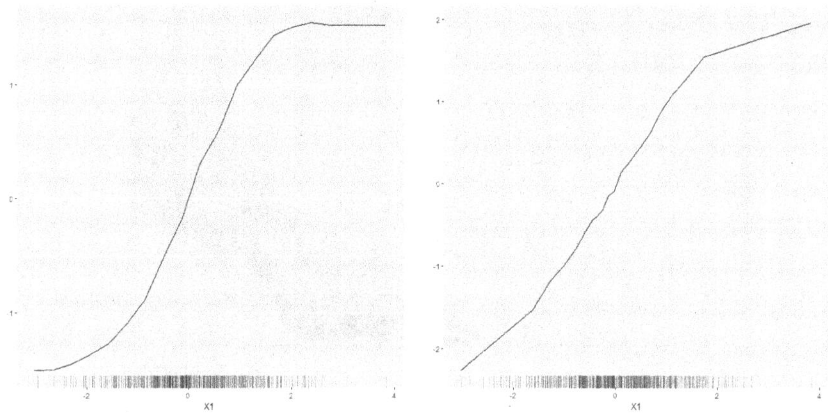

Despite x_1 having a linear relationship, the nonlinear effect of x_2 is essentially absorbed into the partial dependence plot in the left panel. In contrast, the ALE plot depicts a linear relationship within the highest density values of x_1. Given that many predictors are correlated in social and behavioral datasets, we would expect to see small biases to partial dependence plots in many analysis scenarios.

6.5.2 Local Interpretation

To visualize how an individual's prediction of the outcome can change when aspects of a predictor change, one can examine the *individual conditional expectation* (ICE) plot (Goldstein, Kapelner, Bleich, & Pitkin, 2015). In contrast to the partial dependence plot, which depicts the average relationship between a predictor and the outcome, ICE plots identify heterogenous relationships by plotting the expected relationship between a predictor and outcome for each observation. This involves replacing an individual's value on x with a grid of potential values while retaining the individual's values on the other predictors, and generating predictions of the outcome based on the grid of x values.

An ICE plot was generated for the ECLS-K analysis for the reading variable and depicted in Figure 6.12. In this plot, we see little evidence for heterogeneity, as most lines follow the general form of the aggregate (grey) line. However, based on our initial testing with simulated data, it seems as though this approach has difficulty picking up on heterogeneous effects, thus we urge caution in their use.

A second method for examining the relationship between variables at the individual level is to use *local interpretable model-agnostic explanations*

FIGURE 6.12. Individual conditional expectation plot for reading scores.

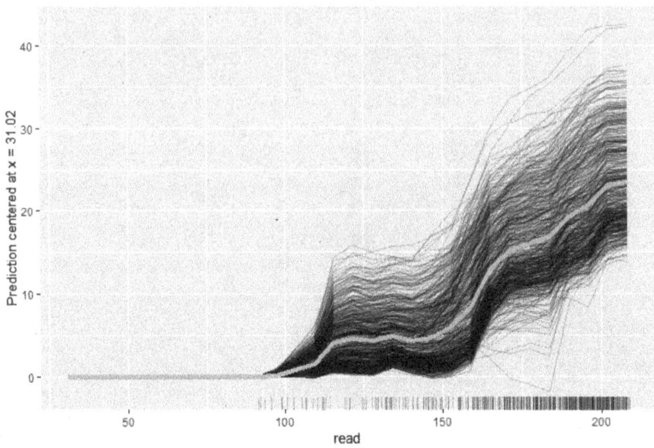

(LIME; Ribeiro, Singh, & Guestrin, 2016). The general idea behind LIME is that although complex algorithms may be necessary to adequately model a dataset, at the local level (individual case), linear relationships abound, allowing one to better understand the predictions from a complex algorithm. Using the global surrogate model approach as a basis, a complex algorithm (e.g., random forests) is used to generate predictions and repeated a large number of times based on permuted values of the predictors. Although there are a series of additional steps to this process, it results in a metric such as R^2 for how well the simpler model is able to capture the relationship for each individual, along with a feature importance weight for a subset of the most important predictors. This is implemented in the `lime` package, and we outputted the values for the first two observations from using random forests on the ECLS-K data in Table 6.3. From the values in this table, we examine how well a linear regression model with five features can explain the predictions from random forests. For the first two cases, 87% of the variance was explained with a much simpler model, along with the weights for each predictor used in explaining the predictions. Across all of the observations, there was very little variation to the amount of variance explained, with R^2 values ranging from 0.86 to 0.89.

TABLE 6.3. Results from Using LIME to Explain the Predictions from Random Forests with Linear Regression. Only the first two cases, using a maximum of five predictors are given.

case	feature	model_r2	model_intercept	model_prediction	feature_value	feature_weight
1	read	0.87	32.98	102.97	206.63	0.25
1	knowledge	0.87	32.98	102.97	38.15	0.27
1	math	0.87	32.98	102.97	44.44	0.12
1	SES	0.87	32.98	102.97	1.56	1.01
1	income	0.87	32.98	102.97	120000.00	0.00
2	read	0.87	32.15	82.36	163.26	0.26
2	knowledge	0.87	32.15	82.36	18.73	0.27
2	math	0.87	32.15	82.36	19.65	0.12
2	SES	0.87	32.15	82.36	0.62	1.02
2	income	0.87	32.15	82.36	55000.00	0.00

6.6 Empirical Example

To further explain the use of bagging, random forests, and boosting, we apply all three algorithms to the NSDUH dataset, with all 43 predictors to predict suicidal thoughts (SUICTHNK). From the original sample of 55,271, we subset the dataset into a training dataset with 1,000 observations, and a test dataset with 1,000 observations. These two new datasets were created so they have equal proportions of yes and no responses on suicidal thoughts, with the original sample being highly skewed in favor of no responses. We covered the application of machine learning to imbalanced datasets in Chapter 3, however, our focus here is solely on the application of ensemble algorithms. Nominal predictors were recoded to dummy coded variables to facilitate the use of logistic regression (used as a comparison).

We assessed the use of five different methods: logistic regression, bagging, random forests, gradient boosting, and extreme gradient boosting. Logistic regression serves as a baseline approach for comparison to quantify the addition of nonlinearity and interaction effects when creating a prediction model.[2] For all of the methods, we used 20 bootstrap samples to calculate AUC, facilitated through the use of the `caret` package. For both bagging and random forests, we used the `randomForest` package (`method="rf"` in the `caret` package). Bagging involved setting m to the number of predictors (53 with dummy codes). For random forests, we tested values of 3, 10, 20, and 35 for m, the number of variables available for partitioning. For each, we used 500 trees. In gradient boosting, we tested the following tuning parameters with the `gbm` package (`method="gbm"` in

[2] It would work just as well to use a form of regularized logistic regression in this example.

caret): tree depths of 1, 2, 3, and 5; 100, 500, and 2,000 trees; and shrinkage values of 0.001, 0.01, and 0.1. For extreme gradient boosting, we used the default three values for the five tuning parameters (method="xgbTree" in caret).

TABLE 6.4. AUC as Assessed Using Bootstrapping and Evaluation on the Test Sample.

	Bootstrapping	Test
GLM	0.78	0.79
Bagging	0.76	0.78
RF	0.79	0.79
GBM	0.81	0.80
XGBoost	0.81	0.80

Given the number of tuning parameters for each algorithm, we only present the results based on the highest AUC value for each approach. These are displayed in Table 6.4, as assessed using bootstrap samples and assessed on the test dataset. The AUC values are highly similar across algorithms, particularly on the test sample. However, both boosting algorithms evidenced slightly higher performance with both evaluations.

FIGURE 6.13. ROC plots for NSDUH example across the five algorithms as evaluated on the test dataset.

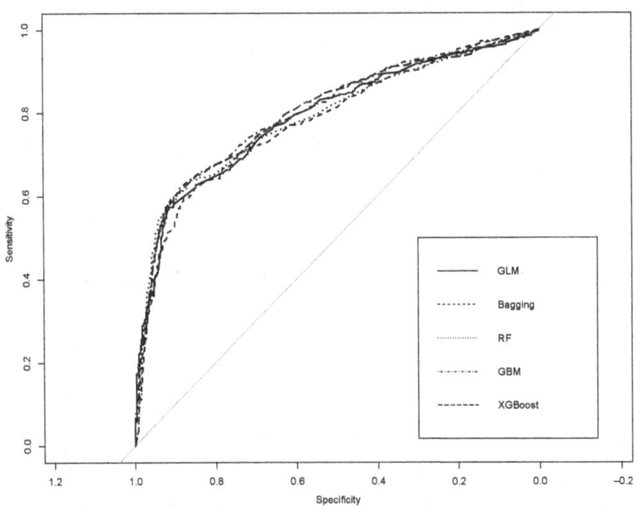

The comparison of AUC can be facilitated through the use of ROC plots, which are depicted in Figure 6.13. To create this figure, we used the model developed on the training sample to create predicted probabilities

FIGURE 6.14. Performance across the tuning parameters of gradient boosting.

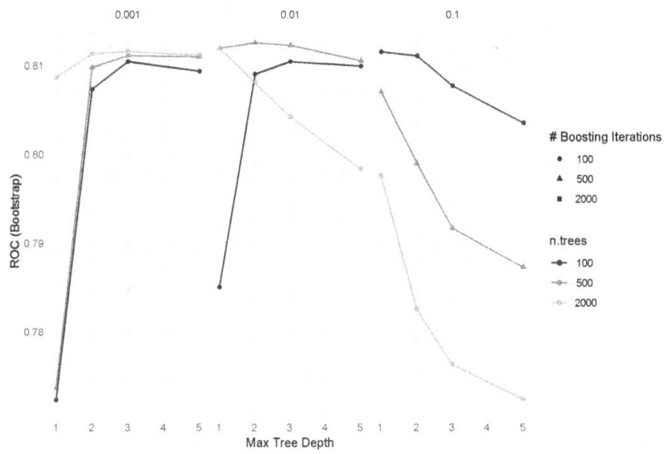

on the test sample. Again, we see similar performance across the five algorithms. We note that this is a visual depiction of the AUC as assessed on the test dataset. If researchers do not have access to a test dataset, we recommend against creating these plots with the training data because they will show overoptimistic results. Instead, researchers should use the predicted probabilities created on the OOB samples with algorithms such as random forests.

Given these results, we have two potential courses of action. The first would be to conclude that the machine learning algorithms did not produce results that were a significant enough improvement over those from logistic regression to warrant further interpretation into the results. The second would be to dive deeper into the results of the best performing model, producing variable importance and possibly partial dependence plots. We opt for this second option both for pedagogical purposes and because an improvement in prediction of 0.01 or 0.02 could represent an important improvement, particularly in research areas with hard to model outcomes.

To interpret the results, we chose the gradient boosting model, but note that we could just have easily opted for the results from extreme gradient boosting. For gradient boosting, there was some differentiation in performance across the tuning parameters, which can be seen in Figure 6.14. The thing to note in Figure 6.14 is the effect of maximum tree depth, with greater performance for depths greater than one. Additionally, lower shrinkage values (0.01 and 0.001) produced slightly higher AUC values. From this, we chose to interpret the gradient boosting model with 2,000 trees, a maximum tree depth of 2, and a shrinkage of 0.001. Then, we produced a variable importance plot, displayed in Figure 6.15. In the

FIGURE 6.15. Variable importance from the selected gradient boosting model.

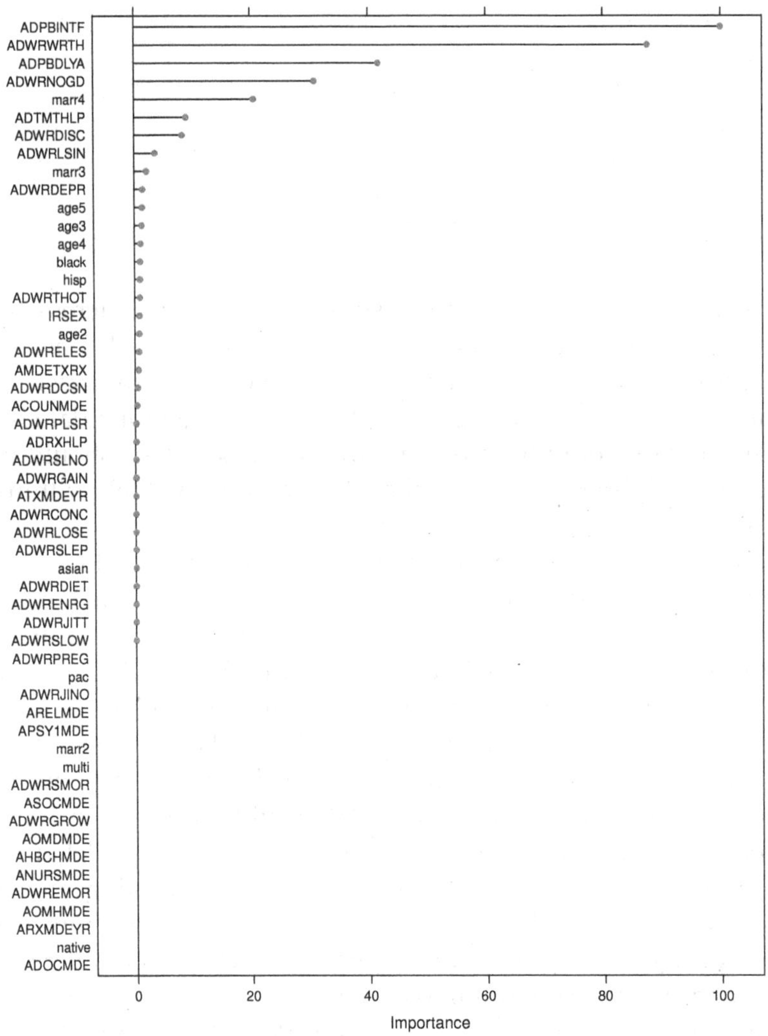

variable importance plot, two variables emerge with the highest relative importance values. These variables are ADPBINTF, which assesses how often depression symptoms interfere with work or personal life (higher values more interference) and ADWRWRTH, which assesses feelings of worthlessness nearly every day when depressions symptoms are at their worst (0 = Yes).

FIGURE 6.16. Partial dependence plots for ADPBINTF (left) and ADWRWRTH (right).

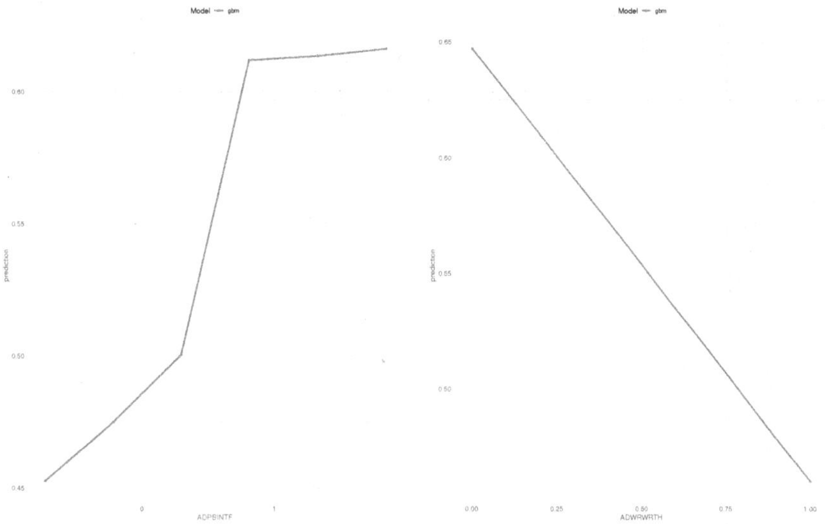

To further investigate the nature of the associations with suicidal thoughts, we present the partial dependence plots for both of these variables in Figure 6.16. In the right panel, we see the limitations of partial dependence plots for binary predictors. We are limited to assessing whether it is a positive or negative relationship between the predictor and outcome. In our example, indicating no on ADWRWRTH is associated with a drop in the probability of indicating yes on suicidal thoughts, which is in line with what we would expect theoretically. In the left panel of Figure 6.16 we see a nonlinear relationship between ADPBINTF and suicidal thoughts, indicating that the transitions between the first four response options are associated with increases in the probability of endorsing suicidal thoughts, while there is little differentiation between the two highest response options (*a lot* and *extremely*). The largest increase occurs for the transition between *some* (the third response option) and *a lot* (the fourth response option), which, given the wording of the response options, makes sense.

To examine the interaction between these two predictors, we have to create a three-dimensional partial dependence plot. Given that both the outcome and one predictor are binary, this is more difficult to assess, however, we display this plot in Figure 6.17. In this figure, each panel (*no* and *yes*) are essentially mirror images, thus we only interpret the right panel. Here, when ADWRWRTH is *yes*, it doesn't matter what the value of ADPBINTF is, because all but the lowest response option on ADPBINTF is associated with a high predicted probability of endorsing suicidal ideation. We see discrepant results when ADWRWRTH is *no*. Each increase in the ADPBINTF response option is associated with an increase in predicted outcome probability (outside of the top two response options). This constitutes a relatively clear interactive effect. If we suspected interaction effects (or nonlinear effects) among additional predictors, we could create these plots for several predictor variables.

FIGURE 6.17. Three-dimensional partial dependence plot for ADPBINTF and ADWRWRTH.

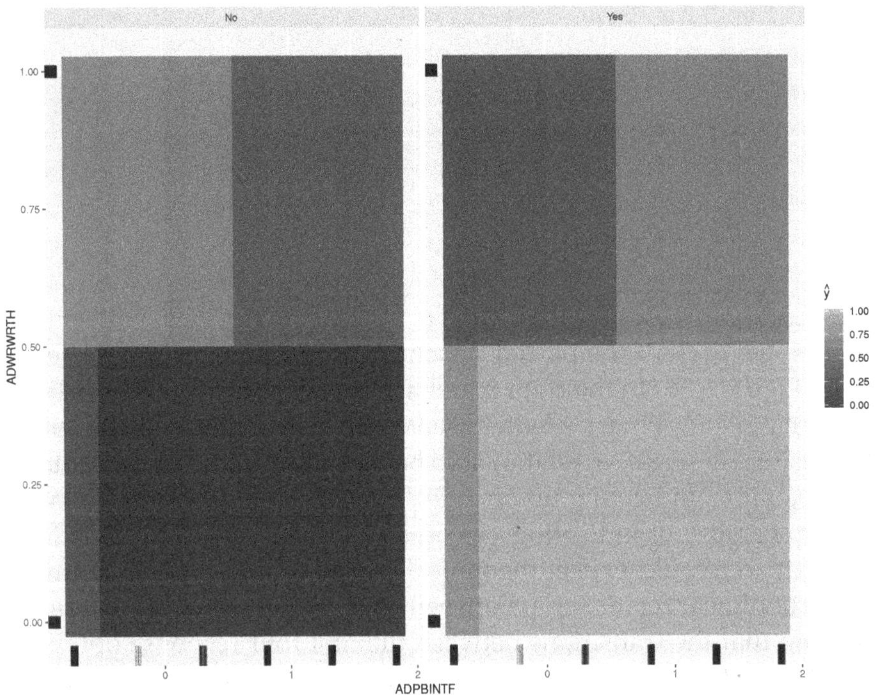

6.7 Important Notes

6.7.1 Interactions

Given the importance of interactions in social and behavioral science (Aiken, West, & Reno, 1991), identifying interactions with ensemble methods is of utmost importance. Although the complexity of these methods limits the interpretability of the main and interaction effects, previous research with boosting, in particular, has aimed at identifying which interactions are important (Elith, Leathwick, & Hastie, 2008). As discussed previously with random forests, the effect of each variable in tree-based ensembles can be quantified through the use of relative importance plots. However, the values of importance confound main and interaction effects, preventing a deeper level of interpretation into each effect. In the context of boosting, previous research has focused on quantifying linear interactions between each predictor (Elith, Leathwick, & Hastie, 2008). In this study, the strength of each possible interaction in the boosting model is tested, producing an additional relative importance metric. Finally, important interactions can be visualized through the use of joint partial dependence plots (Friedman, 2001).

In gradient boosting, the tree depth (complexity) reflects the order of possible interaction in the data. In social and behavioral research, it may be doubtful to have interactions greater than a three-way interaction. However, given that trees can include main effects as well as interactions, it may be worth testing up to a depth of five. Taken together, this means testing different tree depths, including 1 (stump; just main effects; nonlinear effects), 2 (can capture interactions), 3 (higher-order interactions), as well as 5 (higher-order interactions and other effects).

6.7.2 Other Types of Ensembles

Ensembles are a general procedure for combining functions of either the same type (e.g., boosting or random forests) or of varying forms (e.g., lasso regression and random forests).

Combining different forms of algorithms has become a popular approach recently, evidencing superior performance in some applications. One approach that has been applied in the context of clinical psychology (Bernecker, et al., 2019) is super learner (Van der Laan, Polley, & Hubbard, 2007). The general concept is to test various learners (algorithms such as trees and polynomial regression) because the true data generating process is unknown, weighting the contribution of each individual learning according to its effectiveness. As a simple illustration of how this form of ensemble learning works, we selected three different algorithms to combine: lasso regression, decision trees, and random forests. Using each of these, we created a prediction. We then combined the three sets of predictions into a single dataset, appending the actual outcome. Our data are organized and the first few lines are displayed in Table 6.5. From here, we entered these data into a linear regression (typically a different algorithm, particularly due to collinearity), predicting the actual outcome from the three sets of predictions. The regression weights from this regression analysis are then used as a way to determine the contribution of each individual learner to create a final set of predictions. In practice, it is necessary to estimate the weighting scheme using cross-validation (see Figure 1 in Van der Laan et al., 2007), however, the general strategy holds. This form of ensemble learning has been implemented in the `SuperLearner` package .

TABLE 6.5. Example Dataset That Combines Predictions from Three Learners.

Y	$\hat{Y}_{Lasso}$	$\hat{Y}_{DT}$	$\hat{Y}_{RF}$
1.2	1.0	0.8	1.5
-0.3	-1.2	-0.2	0.4
1.1	2.1	1.0	1.3
0.2	-0.6	0.2	0.2

To demonstrate the use of Super Learner, we used the ECLS-K dataset as above, along with the elastic net algorithm, extreme gradient boosting (i.e., XGBoost), and random forests. The Super Learner algorithm can be applied in a number of ways. One is to just estimate each individual learner, then enter the predictions into a secondary algorithm to estimate the weights from each prediction. By default, the `SuperLearner` package uses non-negative least squares to estimate the weight for each learner as assessed using cross-validation. In our example, the risk (MSE) was estimated as 107.6 for extreme gradient boosting, 84.7 for random forests, and 79.1 for the elastic net. These predictions were combined with the coefficients of 0.05 for extreme gradient boosting, 0.19 for random forests, and 0.76 for the elastic net, demonstrating a clear preference for a linear model. This combined model had an estimated risk of 79.3, approximately equivalent to the elastic net. Within the R package there are additional functions that combine the estimation of each learners contribution with nested cross-validation among other options.

6.7.3 Algorithm Comparison More Broadly

As discussed previously, it is highly recommended to test a sequence of algorithms, with each indicating a different level of complexity within the data. The degree of complexity one can model in the data is contingent upon a number of factors, but given this, one can then compare the prediction performance after to assess which model fit best. There are both informal and formal ways to accomplish this. Informally, one can examine the R^2 or AUC (or others) as assessed with some form of resampling, choosing the best fit. If the fit values are relatively close, or there is no clear winner, then it is often best to choose the most parsimonious model among the best fitting models.

A more formal way to assess the correspondence between results is to examine the correlation between the predictions with a global surrogate model (see Molnar, 2019). First, use a less interpretable algorithm to predict an outcome, such as random forests. From this, create predictions for each observation. These predictions are then used in a second step, when a more interpretable algorithm (e.g., linear regression or decision trees) is used to predict the predictions from step one, using the same predictors. Then, the prediction performance can be used to determine how much is lost by using a simpler algorithm. In using the ECLS-K, we used a linear regression to model the predictions from random forests, producing an R^2 of 0.83. Although a linear regression approximates the random forests model well, it is far from perfect, meaning that we are probably missing some degree of nonlinearity or interactions in the linear regression model. We will detail this approach using the ECLS-K data.

Although measures of fit should only be reported either using resampling or on a validation set, it can sometimes be useful to assess fit on the original sample. For instance, if pairing random forests with a small sample size, it can be common to fit the data perfectly (i.e., AUC or R^2 of 1). When this occurs, it would probably be beneficial to consider a less flexible model, as the random forests model is overfitting the data to such a degree that the conclusion and predictions will be unlikely to generalize. Again, in cases such as this, if random forests is too flexible for the size of the data, it will be common to see similar performance using both a linear model and random forests with the resampled metrics. In this case, although a linear model limits the amount that can be gleaned from the data, the dataset is not of sufficient size to allow for more complex conclusions regarding interactions and nonlinear relationships.

6.8 Summary

The use of ensembles marks the end of the transition from just assessing linear relationships in generalized linear models to automatically identifying interactions and nonlinear effects. Specifically, ensemble methods overcome many of the problems with decision trees, often evidencing superior predictive performance than less complex algorithms. In our discussion of ensembles, we mainly focused on boosting and random forests, as these are two of the most commonly used algorithms. We also noted a number of drawbacks to ensembles, such as loss of interpretability. For social and behavioral research, it is important to keep in mind the quality of the data, as this can have a large impact on whether the use of ensembles can adequately capture more complex relationships. We demonstrated that measurement error can have a larger impact on ensembles as opposed to linear regression. For these reasons, we almost always recommend pairing the use of ensembles with simpler methods, such as linear (logistic regression).

6.8.1 Further Reading

- For interpreting the results from ensembles and other "black box" algorithms, see the book by Molnar (2019). This text further discusses the use and application of partial dependence plots, local interpretation, and other methods.

- One additional algorithm that can be considered a form of ensemble is support vector machines (SVM; Cortes & Vapnik, 1995), as they perform L2 regularized model fitting in a high-dimensional representation of the predictors (Hastie et al., 2009). Interested readers should consult either Hastie et al. (2009) or James et al. (2013) for overviews.

- Similarly to SVM, deep learning can be seen as a type of ensemble method, or perhaps more importantly, it is often used as a comparison technique to random forests and boosting in prediction applications. However, the most important advantages of deep learning are evidenced with alternative data types, such as images, video, text, and others. For a more technical overview, see Goodfellow et al. (2016). For a more accessible overview with a focus on `R`, see Chollet and Allaire (2018).

- We highly recommend the `caret` package for implementing all of the methods discussed in this chapter. See Kuhn and Johnson (2013) for further detail on the use of this package and many of the implemented methods.

6.8.2 Computational Time and Resources

Relative to the algorithms discussed in Chapters 4 and 5, unsurprisingly, ensembles take much longer to fit. With a dataset containing 1,000 cases and a small number of predictors (e.g., 10), both random forests and boosting often take on the order of a few minutes. While random forests takes longer to fit a single sequence of trees relative to boosting, the number of tuning parameters is much smaller (often only mtry is tested) compared to boosting, which means that fitting boosting models can often take longer. However, boosting is more amenable to parallelization, which is extremely important when fitting ensembles on large datasets. Finally, while the conditional approach to calculating variable importance better captures a variables contribution to prediction in the presence of correlated predictors, this can often be infeasible to fit as the runtime is drastically greater than the marginal approach.

Both the `randomForest` and `gbm` packages are by far the most commonly used for random forests and boosting, respectively, in `R`. Further, we detailed the alternative forms of each type of ensemble as implemented in the `xgboost` and `partykit` packages. Finally, we wish to note that like in other chapters, a large number of add-on or alternative packages have been developed that extend the algorithms to alternative outcome types, algorithm variants, or to facilitate additional types of interpretation. Applying many of these packages is facilitated by the `caret` package, of which we highly recommend for testing each algorithm.

Part III

ALGORITHMS FOR MULTIVARIATE OUTCOMES

7 Machine Learning and Measurement

In social and behavioral research, most variables of interest are measured with error. While this has a number of consequences, one primary result is that researchers often provide some form of dimension reduction or summary to create new, higher-level representations of the variables. In this chapter, we detail the scenarios where this this may be the most appropriate strategy, and when dimension reduction may result in worse performance. We focus primarily on factor analysis, and detail the use of exploratory factor analysis in this chapter, while extending our discussion to confirmatory factor analysis in Chapter 8.
Measurement error can come in many forms, but it can have important consequences for prediction and inference. While this chapter focuses on the measurement of error in predictor variables, starting with a definition, discussing its impact, the following chapter discusses handling error in the outcome of interest. Further, the concepts and methods discussed will form the foundation for the following three chapters, where we focus on methods that directly model error, structural equation modeling (Chapters 8 and 10) and mixed-effects models (Chapter 9).

7.1 Key Terminology

- Latent variable. In a more restrictive sense, this is unique to factor analysis methods, and refers to a variable that is created, thus is not observed in the dataset. In fields such as sociology and psychology, there is a long history of defining the philosophical and statistical foundations to a latent variable (see Borsboom, Mellenbergh, & Van Heerden, 2003).

- Weighting. The use of some method to assign a numeric value to generate a composite (i.e., in factor scores) or predictions (in regression). In the simplest case, one can use unit weighting, where the contribution of each variable to the creation of a composite score is equally weighted (i.e., sum score).

- Factor loading. The regression relationship from a latent variable to an observed variable. The magnitude of the loading indicates how representative the observed variable is of the latent variable.
- Residual or unique variance. While the term residual is more often used in regression to denote the variance in Y not accounted for by the X's, the term *unique variance* refers to the variance in an observed variable not accounted for (or related to) the latent variable. This is often thought to comprise both error and specific variance.
- Factor score. A score derived to represent a latent variable in an SEM. Since there is not a unique way to assign scores at the individual level for a latent variable, a number of methods have been developed to generate factor scores. These scores can then be used in follow-up analyses.
- Node. In variable network models, each node represents an observed variable, with the edges denoting the strength of partial correlation.
- Item response theory (IRT). A methodology closely related to factor analysis in that it focuses on the specification of latent variables. While the methods have a large degree of overlap, the primary distinctions are that IRT is more often used to model categorical items and in the administration of scales for educational or psychological testing.
- Precision matrix. The precision matrix is the inverse of the covariance matrix, with each entry denoting the partial correlation. This is used as the basis of variable network models.

7.2 Defining Measurement Error

The concept of measurement error can be defined in both broad and narrow contexts, and is usually dictated by the type of errors usually encountered in that specific discipline. More generally, following classical test theory (see Kroc & Zumbo, 2020 for alternative formulations), we can define observed scores on a variable as a summation of both a true score and some degree of error,

$$\mathbf{X} = \mathbf{T} + \mathbf{E}, \tag{7.1}$$

where $\mathbf{X}$ is the *observed score*, $\mathbf{T}$ is the *true score*, and $\mathbf{E}$ is the *error score* with a mean of zero, meaning that $\mathbf{X}$ does not differ systematically from $\mathbf{T}$[1]. A

[1] A number of more complex models for measurement error that do not make this assumption are available.

second assumption is that covariance between **E** and **T** is zero, and this is termed *nondifferential error*. Differential error, or the concept that the degree of error is conditional upon ones true value of **T**, is more commonly studied outside of psychometrics.

This formulation is based on classical test theory, with **T** typically thought to represent an unobserved latent score. In a large part of social and behavioral research, the necessity of assessing measurement error is a result of the inability to measure constructs directly. For instance, neither depression nor intelligence is directly observable, thus they are considered latent variables. We infer someone's score on each of these latent variables through the use of multiple indicators (in the form of a scale), with each item created to directly assess the latent construct of interest (e.g., the Beck Depression Inventory). To understand the degree of precision in X,[2] we can decompose the variances of each component of Equation 7.1 to get at the concept of reliability,

$$reliability = \frac{\sigma_T^2}{\sigma_X^2} = \frac{\sigma_T^2}{\sigma_T^2 + \sigma_E^2} = \rho_{X,T}^2. \qquad (7.2)$$

From this, we can see that the closer the scores on **X** are to **T**, the higher the reliability coefficient, $\rho_{X,T}^2$. Conversely, we can discuss reliability in terms of variance, with **X** having higher reliability when the majority of its variance is due to **T**, not **E**.

7.3 Impact of Measurement Error

To understand the impact of measurement error, we focus on modeling the relationship between an outcome Y, and a set of error-prone predictors X_j.

7.3.1 Attenuation

In the simplest case of examining the correlation between Y and X_1, measurement error attenuates the association between X_1 and Y by the degree of error, or $1 -$ reliability, of X_1. For example, if the true correlation between X_1 and Y was 0.5, and the variance of X_1 was 1, the expected regression coefficient between X_1 and Y would be $0.5 \times \sqrt{\rho_{X_1}^2}$. Attenuation of regression coefficients due to measurement error in predictors in linear regression modeling has been well understood by methodologists in the social and

[2]The idea of reliability in the social sciences is analogous to precision in physical sciences.

behavioral sciences since the beginning of the 20th century (see Carroll, Ruppert, Stefanski, & Crainiceanu, 2006; Fuller, 1987).

7.3.2 Stability

As mentioned in Chapter 5, one of the chief criticisms of decision trees is instability, namely, that creating decision trees on slightly altered samples (bootstrap samples) can result in vastly differing tree structures. To better understand the influence of measurement error on the stability of the tree results, we created simple relationships between one or two predictors and a single outcome. This allows us to isolate the influence of specific factors. Of primary interest was an examination of the influence of predictor reliability and the strength of relationship between predictor and outcome. Correspondence between the machine learning algorithm and the data-generating process has been cited as a key influence of stability (Phillip et al., 2018).

We expect that both the signal inherent in the predictor and the strength of relationship between predictor and outcome will influence the degree of stability. To examine this, we simulated data according to a one-split tree model, with a base model of a normally distributed predictor (X_{Lat}), and a deterministic prediction of the outcome (Y): if $X_{Lat} \geq 0.5$, then $Y = 1$; if $X_{Lat} < 0.5$, then $Y = -1$. Based on this relationship between Y and X_{Lat}, we then followed a latent variable formulation for defining observed variables that represent X_{Lat}. Here, we created a single manifest indicator, X_{Obs},

$$X_{Obs} = \rho \times X_{Lat} + \sqrt{1 - \rho^2} \times e,$$

where e is a vector of normally (standard) distributed errors. The standardized version of ρ can be termed the reliability index, where ρ^2 represents the reliability.

To keep things relatively simple, we only varied the reliability index of X_{Obs} (values of 0.8 and 0.5) and sample size (300 and 2,000). We would expect that as reliability is decreased, the tree algorithm is more likely to use different splits on X_{Obs} , resulting in reduced stability. Note that we only used the CART algorithm for the simulation. For stability, we used a conservative metric that assesses agreement in exact tree structure across a set of bootstrapped trees. This manifests itself as:

$$stability = 1 - (\frac{unique\ patterns}{Total\ trees}) \tag{7.3}$$

A unique pattern is defined as two trees having the same number of splits, using the same variables and cutoffs for each. The results, averaged across 100 replications are displayed in Table 7.1.

TABLE 7.1. Stability Values across Different Simulation Conditions

Condition	$N = 300$	$N = 2000$
X_{Lat}	1	1
X_{Obs} $\rho = 0.8$	0.58	0.75
X_{Obs} $\rho = 0.5$	0.33	0.62

The first point of emphasis in Table 7.1 is that stability was perfect when the data conformed to the simulated tree structure. Secondly, reliability had a clear influence on stability, which was more pronounced at a sample size of 300. Finally, a point of emphasis is that there was only the correct variable in the model, as the stability would be further reduced by the presence of additional possible splitting variables. Given that most variables (non-demographic variables) in social and behavioral research are measured imperfectly, we can expect this to be an additional contributing factor to instability. In line with mapping the functional form assumption inherent in decision trees to that which is present in the data, we could also have simulated data according to a regression model, either correlated continuous variables in the case of linear regression, or a sigmoidal relationship between a continuous predictor and dichotomous outcome. This has already been explored in Phillip et al. (2018) with the conclusion of drastically reduced stability when using trees to model data that conforms to a regression model.

7.3.3 Predictive Performance

One of the things worth taking into account when deciding to use a method such as random forests or boosting that automatically includes interactions and higher degrees of nonlinearity is the quality of predictor. In later chapters we will consider directly modeling the measurement error, however, in the case of nonlinear methods, measurement quality can have a large influence. Jacobucci and Grimm (2020) demonstrated that poor measurement of predictors can mask underlying nonlinear effects, even resulting in the conclusion that linear models fit better than ensemble methods such as boosting.

To demonstrate this, we follow the simulation design of Jacobucci and Grimm (2020), creating two simulated nonlinear variables with the following equation

$$y = cosine(x1) + sine(x2) + tan(0.1 * x1 * x2) + normal(0, .1). \quad (7.4)$$

Additionally, we also simulated data according to linear relationships with no interaction. For each $x1$ and $x2$, we simulated four imperfect indicators,

FIGURE 7.1. Simulation results across different values of reliability for data simulated according to linear relationships.

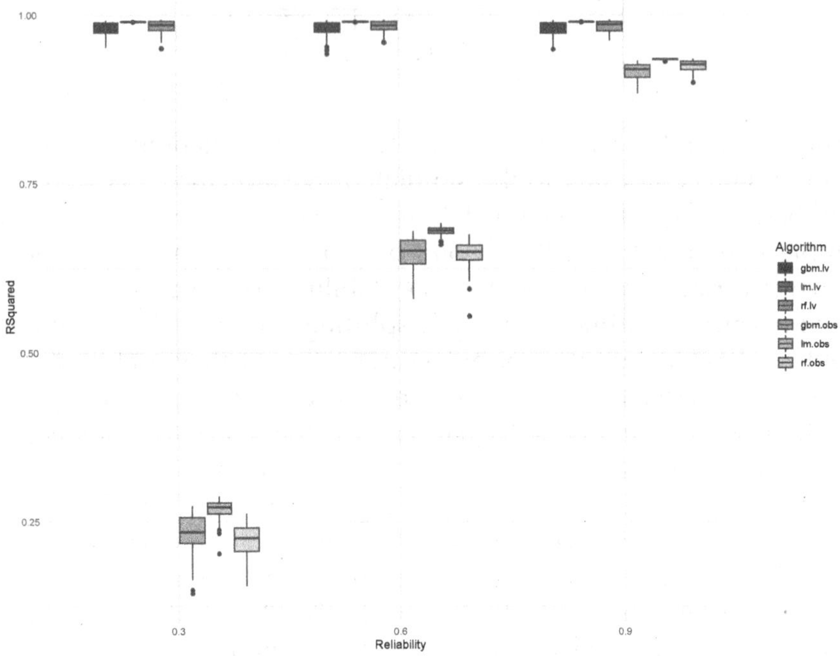

varying the reliability of 0.3, 0.6, or 0.9. Additionally, we varied the sample size to be 200, 500, 1,000, or 2,000. We do not display the results for each sample size condition as it had little effect (in line with Jacobucci & Grimm, 2020). We assessed performance across linear regression ("lm"), gradient boosting ("gbm"), and random forests ("rf"). Replicating each condition 200 times, the results are displayed in Figures 7.1 and 7.2.

In Figure 7.1, we can see a predictable decline in R^2 when the predictors are measured with lower reliability values. The thing to note is that when data are simulated according to a linear relationship, linear regression will demonstrate superior fit relative to more complex ensemble methods, with this improvement in fit becoming larger as reliability decreases. This can be attributed to the degree of noise in the data, with larger noise preventing complex algorithms from finding signal. Relative to the ensemble algorithms, linear regression can almost be seen as a type of shrinkage or regularization, which as demonstrated in Chapter 4, can be a beneficial attribute when there is a lack of information in the dataset, typically ascribed to small sample size. Our emphasis here is that measurement can be seen in a similar fashion, lowering the amount of information in the data, giving preference to simpler models.

This is further demonstrated in Figure 7.2.

FIGURE 7.2. Simulation results across different values of reliability for data simulated according to nonlinear relationships.

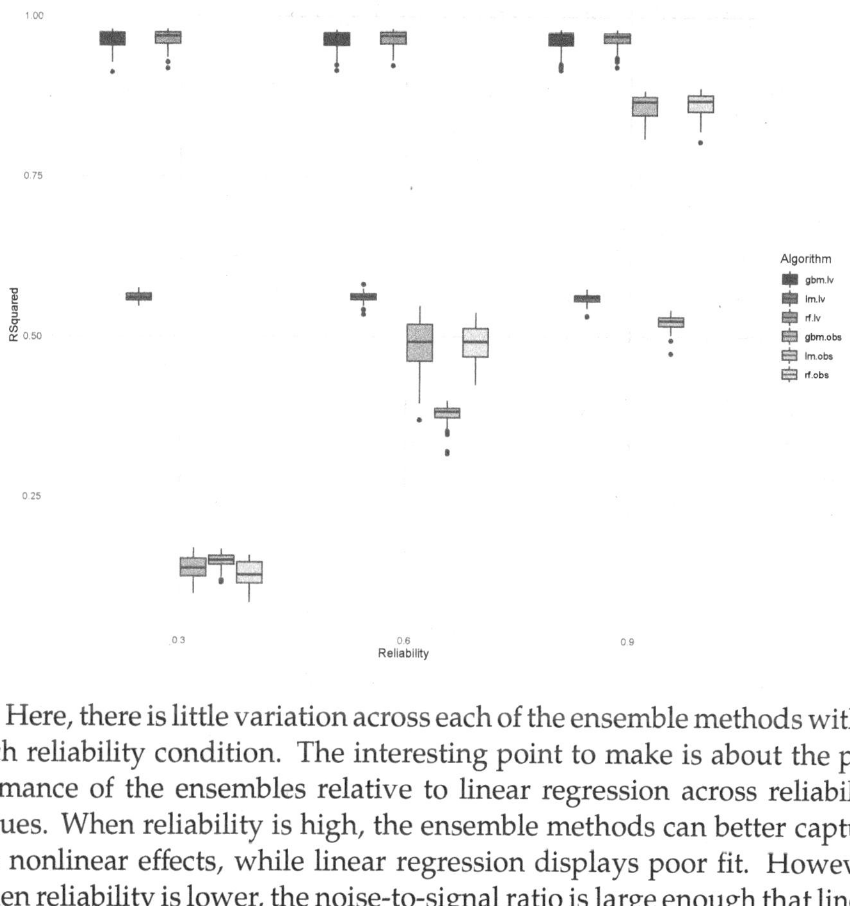

Here, there is little variation across each of the ensemble methods within each reliability condition. The interesting point to make is about the performance of the ensembles relative to linear regression across reliability values. When reliability is high, the ensemble methods can better capture the nonlinear effects, while linear regression displays poor fit. However, when reliability is lower, the noise-to-signal ratio is large enough that linear regression demonstrates comparable, if not superior, values of R^2, despite the mismatch between the expected functional relationship (linear) and the simulated relationship between variables. Again, we can attribute this to the idea of shrinkage or regularization, with the simplicity of linear regression being a positive attribute when there is a large degree of noise in the data.

Our point in this example is two-fold: 1) to highlight that using machine learning algorithms does not negate the necessity of quality measurement, and 2) in performing model comparison, our results are *conditional* not only on what variables are included in the model, but the quality of variables as well. Just because we use more powerful methods does not negate the term "garbage in, garbage out." In the following chapters we will discuss strategies for incorporating measurement error into our model, but for the time being we advocate for assessing the inclusion of variables and how measurement quality may be contributing to the results of the analysis.

7.4 Assessing Measurement Error

To demonstrate the concept of assessing measurement error we use the `Grit` data. From this initial sample, we created two separate datasets: a sample of 1,000 training cases and a separate test set of 1,000 observations.

7.4.1 Indexes of Reliability

We only provide a brief overview of indexes of reliability. For a more detailed coverage, see McNeish (2018). As displayed in Equation 7.2, the definition of reliability is rather intuitive. In practice, however, we do not have access to **T**, therefore we must estimate reliability solely with **X**. In psychological research, Cronbach's alpha (Cronbach, 1951) is by far the most commonly method for calculating reliability based on a single administration.[3] Cronbach's alpha can be defined as

$$\alpha = \frac{k}{k-1}\left(1 - \frac{\sum s_i^2}{s_X^2}\right)$$

where k is the number of items, s_i^2 is the variance of each item i, and s_X^2 is the sum of all variances and covariances for all the items. In line with Equation 7.2, we can characterize Cronbach's alpha as the proportion of variance in a scale attributable to a common source. In calculating Cronbach's alpha for the 12 Grit items, we get a value of 0.84 (95% CI = 0.82, 0.85). This represents a good reliability estimate,[4] however, it is worth delving into some of the assumptions and limitations regarding the use of Cronbach's alpha. Two of the most important limitations of Cronbach's alpha are the assumption of tau equivalence and unidimensionality (among others, see McNeish, 2018). Essentially this means that there is only a single latent variable that underlies the scale, and that each item is equally representative of that single latent variable. In practice these assumptions are unlikely to hold. To provide alternatives to Cronbach's alpha, we first need to provide background on the use of factor analysis.

---

[3]Compared to methods that are based on assessing **X** at two different times

[4]We do not report a more specific characterization of this value as we view cutoffs as arbitrary regarding reliability and we do not advocate for the use of Cronbach's alpha with this data.

7.4.2 Factor Analysis

The basis for methods such as exploratory factor analysis, confirmatory factor analysis, and structural equation modeling is the assumption of the existence of latent factors. In essence, what we are doing is saying that some "construct" underlies a set of observed variables. The simplest case is that of intelligence. Every (valid) IQ test is the result of some form of factor analysis. By measuring a host of scales, such as picture completion, vocabulary, arithmetic, and others, we are saying that the correlation between these variables is not a result of chance occurrence, but the overlap between scales can be attributed to a "common factor." The use of factor analysis "tests" to see whether there are latent factors underlying a correlation matrix (set of variables). The general model can be posed as such, decomposing a set of variables, x, into two components

$$\mathbf{x} = \mathbf{\Lambda f} + \mathbf{e}, \tag{7.5}$$

where the Λ matrix of factor loadings acts as a set of weights for the contribution of a single or multiple latent factors, $\mathbf{f}$, on the amount of variability in each observed variable. $\mathbf{e}$ is the part of $\mathbf{x}$ that is not directly attributable to $\mathbf{e}$. There is a direct relationship between the decomposition of $\mathbf{x}$ in Equations 7.1 and 7.5 in that $\mathbf{T} = \mathbf{f}$ and $\mathbf{E} = \mathbf{e}$. Equation 7.5 just adds a weighting component to $\mathbf{f}$ which can be equivalently done for $\mathbf{T}$ (e.g., see Bollen, 1989). Instead of working directly with the casewise scores for each observed variable, it is common in factor analysis to model the covariance between each $\mathbf{x}$, Σ. In this, we can translate Equation 7.5 into

$$\mathbf{\Sigma} = \mathbf{\Lambda \Phi \Lambda'} + \mathbf{\Psi}^2, \tag{7.6}$$

where there factor loading matrix stays the same, $\mathbf{\Phi}$ represents the variance-covariance matrix of the latent factors, and $\mathbf{\Psi}^2$ is the residual covariance matrix. Graphically speaking, we can represent this model in Figure 7.3 using our empirical example.

In Equation 7.6, there are a number of further constraints that we place on the matrices in order to make the model identifiable. Most of these identification constraints are beyond the scope of the chapter. Interested readers should consult Bollen (1989) on the specification and estimation of measurement models. The main constraint that we will focus on here is the specification of $\mathbf{\Lambda}$, as this represents one of the easiest to identify distinctions between exploratory factor analysis (EFA) and confirmatory factor analysis (CFA; see Chapter 8). In EFA, the only hypothesis we are making regarding our model is the number of factors, generally allowing

FIGURE 7.3. Two factor model. Note that the factor loading (Λ) labels are not displayed for each of the directed paths from the two latent variables, f_1 and f_2, to the 12 observed variables, $x_1 - x_{12}$. The parameters $\Phi^2_{11}$and Φ^2_{22} represent the latent variable variances, while Φ_{12} is the covariance between latent variables. Finally, Ψ^2_1–Ψ^2_{12} represent the residual (unique) variances for each of the observed variables.

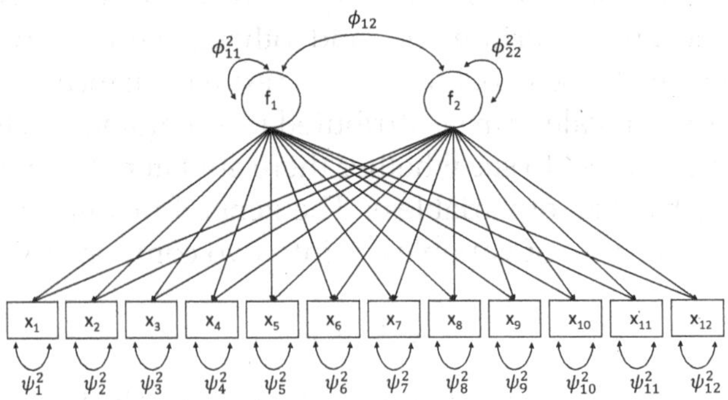

Λ to be freely estimated, meaning that each manifest (observed) variable loads on to each latent factor.

Our first step in this analysis to determine how many latent variables underlie the 12 Grit items. For this, we ran a parallel analysis, which attempts to determine the number of latent factors above and beyond what would be expected from running factor analysis on randomly generated correlation matrices (Horn, 1965). Using the `psych` package to perform this, we get the following result, as displayed in Figure 7.4.

From this, it is clear that two latent factors can be extracted, with the eigenvalues for two being above what would be expected from randomly generated data. With these two latent factors, we then ran an exploratory factor analysis to determine which items load onto which factor. While there are a number of different estimation methods for EFA, the methods that are common in most `R` packages typically result in very similar solutions. The main choice in running EFA is the type of rotation used. Solutions from EFA are not unique and can be "rotated" an infinite number of ways, resulting in different factor loadings but the same model fit. As such, a number of rotation methods have been developed to simplify this process (see Figure 7.5), generally with the aim of simplifying the factor loading matrix as much as possible. Within rotation methods that are two classes, orthogonal constrains the latent factors to be uncorrelated, while oblique, allow them to correlate. In social and behavioral data it is almost always most appropriate to use an oblique rotation as it is rather unlikely that the

FIGURE 7.4. Parallel analysis scree plot for the Grit data. FA refers to factor analysis, whereas PC refers to principle components. We are mainly concerned with the FA results in relation to the red line.

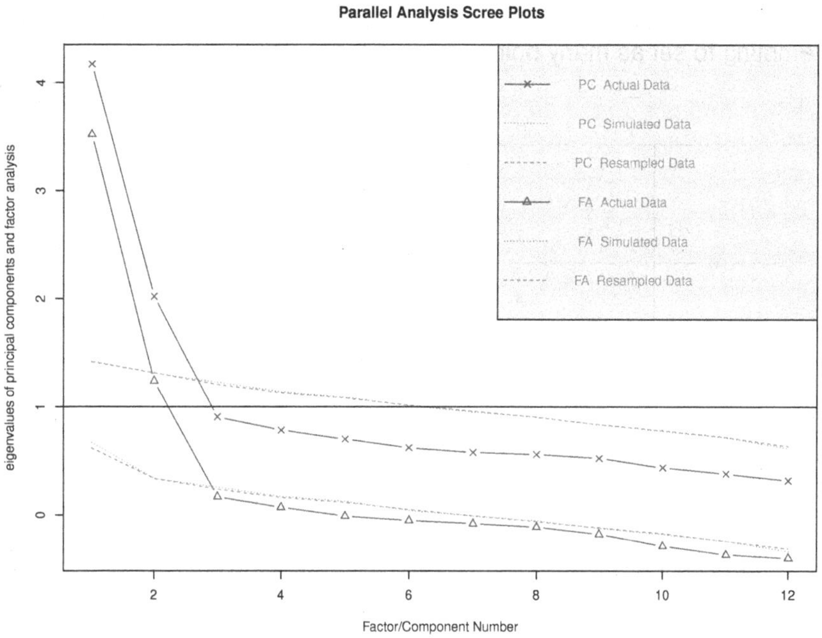

latent factors would be uncorrelated. For our example, we used oblimin rotation, a form of oblique rotation, that resulted in the factor loading matrix displayed in Table 7.2.

A standard practice at this point is to use the results from EFA to inform a CFA model. The use of CFA allows researchers to better incorporate the measurement model into more complex forms of SEM, with the added benefit of simplifying the factor loading matrix by not estimating a subset of parameters. Practically speaking, the use of CFA entails the placement of 0s into Table 7.2, which incurs some degree of model misfit, but often is negligible when the factor loadings from EFA are small (i.e., < .2). From this, we ran a CFA to determine the fit of the restricted model (removing small factor loadings from the EFA step). Note that in actual research, this model should be then tested on the test sample to avoid overfitting. This resulted in the following model displayed in Figure 7.6. In examining the loadings, it seems as the the first factor measures "persistence," while the second factor is better characterized as "hard work."

An additional layer of evaluation that is more commonly applied in CFA as opposed to EFA is assessing the fit of the model through a multitude

FIGURE 7.5. Example factor loadings on two latent factors from the `Holzinger Swineford` dataset. The top left panel depicts no rotation, top right panel varimax (orthogonal) rotation, and the bottom panel oblimin (oblique) rotation. Varimax rotation keeps the spacing between the points while trying to set as many loadings as possible to zero. Oblimin allows the distance between points to change while also attempting to set as many points as possible to zero.

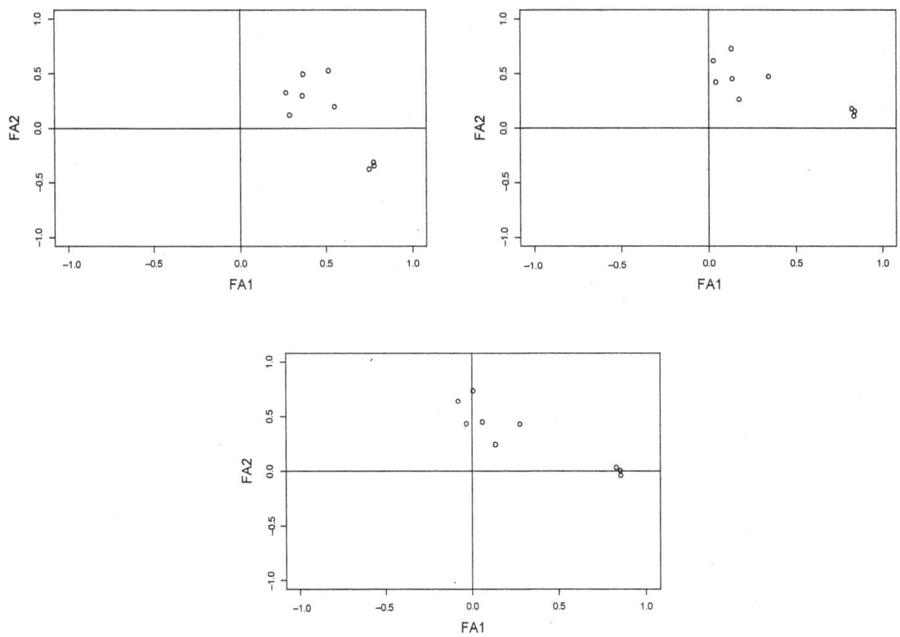

TABLE 7.2. 2-Factor EFA Solution with Oblique Rotation

	f_1	f_2
GS1	-.15	.66
GS2	.58	.08
GS3	.69	-.12
GS4	-.08	.52
GS5	.67	.09
GS6	.02	.67
GS7	.70	.10
GS8	.56	.29
GS9	.30	.53
GS10	.17	.55
GS11	.61	-.25
GS12	.10	.58

FIGURE 7.6. Two-factor Grit CFA model.

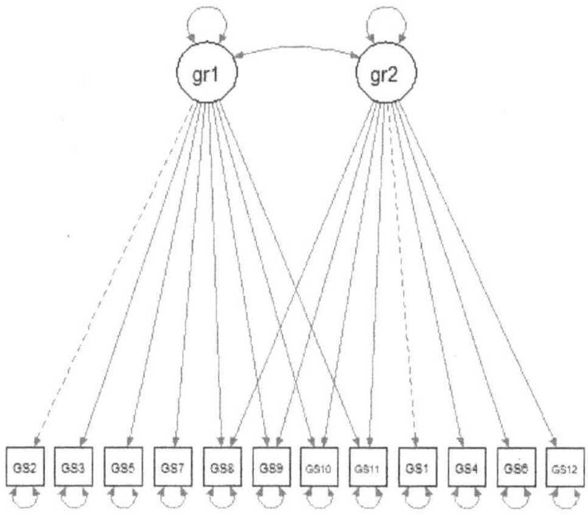

of fit indices. We do not aim to be comprehensive in our overfit of fit indices; instead, researchers should consult McNeish and Wolf (2020) and the references therein for the history of cutoffs for determining acceptable fit. For this chapter, we only use and detail three of the most commonly used fit indices, the root mean square error of approximation (RMSEA), Tucker–Lewis Index (TLI), and comparative fit index (CFI). For the RMSEA, lower values indicate better fit, while a cutoff of 0.1 is often used for determining poor fitting models, while 0.05 is often used for assigning good fit. For the CFI and TLI, higher values indicate better fit, with a cutoff of 0.90 being commonly used for poor fit, while > 0.95 indicates good fit. This model evidenced acceptable fit, with an RMSEA of 0.059 (90% CI 0.036, 0.081), CFI of 0.94, TLI of 0.93, and the following factor loadings as displayed in Table 7.3.

From here, we have a multitude of possible options for adding variables to the model. This CFA model represents the "measurement model" portion of a SEM, where we could add a number of structural relations through covariates that predict both latent variables and distal outcomes, along with other latent variables that have direct relationships either to or from the Grit latent variables. For the time being, we created factor scores (using the regression model; one for each latent variable) and are going to assess the validity and reliability of each.

TABLE 7.3. Standardized Factor Loadings for the Two-Factor Model

	Grit1	Grit2
GS2	0.59	-
GS3	0.55	-
GS5	0.70	-
GS7	0.75	-
GS8	0.61	0.19
GS9	0.33	0.49
GS10	0.43	0.41
GS11	0.65	0.33
GS1	-	0.60
GS4	-	0.45
GS6	-	0.76
GS12	-	0.64

7.4.3 Factor Analysis-Based Reliability

A common recommendation is to assess the factor structure of a scale prior to calculating reliability (e.g., Schmitt, 1996). Using a factor model, we can calculate omega total by constraining the factor variance to 1, as well as not imparting any residual covariances

$$\omega_{Total} = \frac{\left(\sum_{i=1}^{k} \lambda_i\right)^2}{\left(\sum_{i=1}^{k} \lambda_i\right)^2 + \sum_{i=1}^{k} \theta_{ii}},$$

where λ_i is the factor loading for item i, and θ_{ii} is the residual variance for item i. More colloquially, this index of reliability can be seen as assessing the amount of variability across items attributable to the latent variable divided by the total variability to the items. In contrast to Cronbach's alpha, omega total does not constrain the contribution of each item to be equal (hence λ_i not λ). In our 12 Grit items, we get an omega estimate of 0.84 (95% CI = 0.83, 0.86).[5]

One of the main limitations of omega total, and Cronbach's alpha, is their assumption that a one-factor model has reasonable fit. Extensions of these methods for dealing with alternative factor structures are beyond the scope of this chapter. Interested readers should consult Reise, Bonifay, and Haviland (2013). Both Cronbach's alpha and omega total are most appropriate if researchers aim to create a scale based on summing each of the items (referred to as *unit weighting*). In practice, however, items often contribute unequally to the representation of a latent construct, which can then be taken into account in the creation of scale scores. Before describing

[5]For interested readers, we achieved almost exactly the same estimates of hierarchical omega.

the assessment of reliability in terms of factor scores, we first provide a brief overview of factor score estimation.

7.4.4 Factor Scores

Within the general latent variable modeling framework, a common goal is often to use a model with one or more latent variables to estimate factor scores for each observation, and then use this variable either as a predictor or outcome, depending on the model. This is in contrast to using summed scores, which makes the fundamental assumption that each indicator is equally representative of the latent variable of interest.

Particularly if the model is large, this would be a computationally efficient strategy. However, the important unknown is what is lost by estimating a factor score and not keeping the model intact. This has been the subject of much past (e.g., Grice, 2001; Skrondal, & Laake, 2001) and recent (Devlieger, Mayer, & Rosseel, 2016; Devlieger & Rosseel, 2017; Mai, Zhang, & Wen, 2018) research. One of the consistent findings is that it can be more efficient to compute factor scores when a complex SEM model has an insufficient sample size.

There are many proposed methods for factor score estimates. We just cover one, the ordinary least squares (also referred to as Thomson's or Thurstone's regression method). This involves the use of SEM matrices, as well as the data matrix (x_i)

$$\hat{f}_{regression} = (\mathbf{I} + \mathbf{\Lambda}'\mathbf{\Phi}^{-1}\mathbf{\Lambda})^{-1}\mathbf{\Lambda}'\mathbf{\Phi}^{-1}x_i,$$

where $\mathbf{\Lambda}$ is the full factor loading matrix and $\mathbf{\Phi}$ is the variance-covariance matrix of the latent variables.[6] Alternative factor score estimation methods, such as the Bartlett's, have similar forms and typically result in factor scores that are highly correlated with one another. One caveat in the use of factor scores is that using two-step procedures, such as creating factor scores in a first step and then entering these scores into a SEM, can result in inaccurate parameter estimates and standard errors (e.g., Devlieger & Rosseel, 2017).

7.4.5 Factor Score Validity and Reliability

The validity of factor scores points to a larger issue underlying the use of factor scores, namely, that there are an infinite number of ways to compute factor scores, all consistent with the actual factor model (e.g., Grice, 2001). This is referred to as *factor indeterminacy* (Mulaik, 1972), and is diminished when the relationship between the observed indicators and latent factor is

[6] I is the identity matrix, $'$ is the transpose operator, and $^{-1}$ is the inverse operator.

strong or the number of indicators is large (Acito & Anderson, 1980). One way to assess the degree of indeterminacy is by calculating the coefficient of determination (Grice, 2001), which can be conceptualized as assessing the validity of the resultant factor scores. The coefficient of determination assesses the correlation between the factor score estimator and the factor itself. In our 12-item Grit example, the correlation between the factor scores and each individual factor was 0.98 and 0.70, respectively. For reliability, it wasn't until recently that reliability estimates for factor scores have been proposed (Beauducel, Harms, & Hilger, 2016). In Beauducel et al. (2016) reliability estimators are proposed for three of the most common factor score estimators. Using the regression (Bartlett) method with the 12-Grit items, we get reliability estimates of 0.96 and 0.88 for each of the latent variables, respectively.

At this point, a natural question to ask is what is the distinction between the reliability and validity of factor scores? In fact, there is a direct relationship between the estimates in specific models (see Beauducel et al., 2016), thus both assess the degree of similarity between the actual factor score estimates and the latent variables they represent. Of note, the exact relationship between reliability and validity estimates requires squaring the coefficient of determination scores (turning a correlation into a squared correlation), which results in estimates of 0.96 and 0.49 in our example, respectively. While the estimates for the first latent factor are almost identical, there are markedly lower estimates for the second latent variable. As this is a new area of research, further work is required to evaluate this comparison. For the purposes of this chapter, and for any investigation that uses factor scores, the main takeaway is that the first factor score estimate (persistence) is extremely reliable/valid, while some degree of uncertainty exists regarding the second latent variable (hard work). We will examine the downstream effects later in the chapter when using these factor score estimates in a predictive model.

7.5 Weighting

Most statistical applications are investigations into the optimal way to weight the contributions of variables. In linear regression this involves creating a single weight for each predictor. In nonlinear forms of supervised machine learning, weighting takes much more complex forms, but can often be assessed through metrics such as variable importance for boosting and random forests. A separate application of weighting involves the creation of composite scores from items on a scale. For instance, for the Grit scale, one way to summarize each respondent's score would be to sum each of their responses on the 12 items (after reverse-scoring negatively keyed items). This represents the simplest form of weighting, often termed *unit-weighting*, as each item contributes equally to the composite score. As discussed above, performing factor analysis opens up a wide array of additional ways to weight composite scores, often manifested as some variant on weighting based on the factor loadings.

Instead of weighting items to create a composite score, researchers can bypass this step and assess each item in terms of its relationship to a criterion of interest. This is often done for criterion-keyed scales and involves selecting only items that contribute beyond some threshold in predicting the criterion (outcome) of interest. This approach points to a fundamental question: Is it better to use items or composites as predictors? Prior to answering this, we define reliability at the item level.

7.5.1 Item Reliability

We just detailed the assessment of reliability with respect to a scale, not individual items. Item reliability can be assessed in factor models by inspecting all direct paths that point to x_i, namely, in factor models, factor loadings. Thus, we can define the reliability of an item as the squared multiple correlation coefficient, or $R^2_{x_i}$, which can be calculated in a number of ways using the direct relations, or just in using the unique variance, $\Psi^2_{x_i}$, and the variance of x_i, $s^2_{x_i}$

$$R^2_{x_i} = 1 - \frac{\Psi^2_{x_i}}{s^2_{x_i}}.$$

This is also referred to as *(item) communality* (h^2) in the EFA literature as it reflects the proportion of variance in item scores attributable to the common factor. Alternatively, if we are using a one-factor model, we can easily calculate $R^2_{x_i}$ by squaring the standardized factor loadings ($\lambda^2_{x_i}$). For example, see Table 7.4 for the item reliabilities using the 12 Grit items.

An important thing to note is that formulation of reliability excludes any aspect of x that could be explained by a variable, latent or observed, not in the model. Given that this is almost always likely to be the case, not the exception, we can further decompose each variable into three components,

$$\mathbf{x} = \Lambda\xi + \mathbf{s} + \mathbf{e},$$

where ξ are the latent variables in the model. In comparing this equation back to Equation 7.1, we can conceptualize $\mathbf{T} = \Lambda\xi + \mathbf{s}$, with the error components remaining the same. Conceptually, $\mathbf{s}$ refers to the specific component of each variable that is both not attributable to a latent variable

TABLE 7.4. Item Reliabilities from the 12 Grit Items. Note that those with cross loadings tended to have higher R^2

	R^2
GS1	0.31
GS2	0.39
GS3	0.36
GS4	0.21
GS5	0.51
GS6	0.50
GS7	0.57
GS8	0.54
GS9	0.51
GS10	0.39
GS11	0.28
GS12	0.43

and not random error. The difficulty with **s** is that it is often not possible to directly model, thus resulting in its conflation with **e**. This is why it is often more appropriate to term the residual variances as unique, not error, variances, as the estimates contain both **s** and **e**. An additional way to conceptualize **s** is that it is any systematic variance in item scores not attributable to the common factor.

7.5.2 Items versus Scales

A question that machine learning practitioners are often faced with is: Do I include items or scale scores as predictors? In this, we use the term *weighted aggregate* to refer to either summed or factor scores. Given that higher reliability should relate to higher predictive performance, it would seem logical then to advocate for the use of scale scores, not items scores, in prediction models. This is corroborated by the simulation results detailed above. However, this conclusion rests on the assumption that the specific score to each item does not have a relationship with the outcome. This is discussed and derived in McClure, Jacobucci, and Ammerman (2021). As a result, while s cannot be specifically assessed for each item, it can be somewhat inferred based on how the scale was developed. Briefly, while some scales are created to include items that are exchangeable and equally representative of the latent construct, other scales are created with the assumption that each item can assess a specific component. Kendler (2017) refers to these approaches to scale and item development as *indexical* and *constitutive*, respectively. With respect to prediction, using summed or factor scores from indexical scales should predict outcomes equally as

TABLE 7.5. Prediction Results Using Summed, Factor, and Item Scores from the Grit Data in Predicting Conscientiousness.

Algorithm	Variables	Bootstrap RMSE	Holdout RMSE
Regression	Sum	3.76 (0.18)	3.94
Boosting	Sum	3.77 (0.18)	3.94
Regression	Item	3.62 (0.11)	3.83
Boosting	Item	3.62 (0.11)	3.82
Regression	Factor Scores	3.61 (0.10)	3.85
Boosting	Factor Scores	3.71 (0.13)	3.86
Ridge Regression	Item + Factor Scores	3.61 (0.13)	3.83
Boosting	Item + Factor Scores	3.63 (0.14)	3.82

well as using items, whereas in constitutive scales, the use of items should outperform aggregate scores.

To demonstrate this in the same running example, it is first worth assessing how the items were created for the 12-item Grit scale. In Duckworth et al. (2007), items were selected based on item-total correlations, internal reliability coefficients, and redundancy. Notably missing from this was a discussion of individual item meaning. From this, we would conclude that scale scores should perform comparably to the use of items. To test this, we used factor scores, summed scores, and 12 variables as predictors, pairing each set of predictors with either linear regression models or gradient boosting. Additionally, we assessed the prediction with the RMSE evaluated across bootstrap samples, or on the holdout sample of 1,000 cases. These results are displayed in Table 7.5.

Our main conclusion from this is that while there was a large degree of variability across the bootstrap samples, summed scores fit the worst, with approximately equal performance in pairing factor scores with regression as both of the item models. This is in line with what we would expect given how the items were selected. For conclusions where items outperform scales, see McClure et al. (2021).

Additionally, given that scale scores are often preferable to items for interpretation purposes, but worse for prediction performance, we tested models with the items and factor scores included. Note that there is a strong degree of redundancy among the predictor set, given that the factor scores are derived from the items. To overcome this, we used ridge regression because of its ability to offset collinearity, while keeping with the use of boosting given that the use of small trees and shrinkage should overcome issues with collinearity. Both of these models fit comparably to the item models, and we display the variable importance values from the boosting model in Table 7.6.

TABLE 7.6. Variable Importance Values from the Best Fitting Boosting Model That Contained Both Items and Factor Scores. f_1 and f_2 are the factor scores

	Importance
f_2	100
GS6	45.0
GS12	22.9
f_1	20.1
GS4	16.6
GS9	15.0
GS5	11.5
GS11	11.0
GS2	9.4
GS8	7.1
GS10	2.2
GS7	1.4
GS3	1.2
GS1	0

Note that while f_1 had higher reliability and validity coefficients, f_2 was theoretically much more similar to the conscientiousness outcome score. By including the factor scores in this manner, it allows us to better summarize the contribution of the individual items (i.e., GS6 and GS12 both loaded on the 2nd factor). However, given the high correlations among the predictors, it would be best to use the conditional random forests method to calculate variable importance (see Chapter 6).

7.6 Alternative Methods

7.6.1 Principal Components

Principal components analysis (PCA) is often given ample coverage in many machine learning books. Like factor analysis (FA), PCA is a dimension reduction technique, simplifying what is often a high-dimensional dataset (number of variables or columns) into a much smaller number of components. To demonstrate the contrast between FA and PCA, we will work with the covariance among a set of variables, which we denote as C. As detailed above, FA decomposes C into two new matrices, the factor loadings matrix and unique variance matrix.

$$\mathbf{C} \cong \mathbf{\Lambda \Phi \Lambda}' + \mathbf{\Psi}^2.$$

In contrast, PCA does not model unique forms of variance to each variable

$$\mathbf{C} \cong \mathbf{\Lambda}\mathbf{\Phi}\mathbf{\Lambda}'.$$

Thus, whereas factor analysis models only the shared variance among a set of variables, PCA models the total variance among the variables. A closely related approach to PCA is singular value decomposition (SVD). SVD is a general matrix decomposition algorithm and is used widely given its efficiency in transforming a data matrix into a set of three new matrices

$$\mathbf{x} = \mathbf{USV}'.$$

From this, we can see that we are decomposing our data matrix **x** into the three matrices. Understanding the meaning of each matrix is beyond the scope of this chapter.[7] Given that the decomposition of SVD is in relation to **x**, we can relate these results back to **C** in that

$$\mathbf{C} = \mathbf{V}\frac{\mathbf{S}^2}{n-1}\mathbf{V}'$$

where n is the sample size. Given this translation of results between PCA and SVD, it is often more efficient to compute the results from PCA by decomposing the data matrix with SVD, as opposed to first calculating **C**. In fact, the built-in function for PCA in `R` uses SVD by default to compute $\mathbf{\Lambda}$ and $\mathbf{\Phi}$.

A great deal of literature exists in psychometrics that has examined and debated when it is best to use factors and when components are most appropriate (for instance, see Velicer & Jackson, 1990 and the responses). In general, if the aim is to simplify a set of predictors that are extremely large or contain redundancy (collinear predictors), then PCA may be most appropriate. However, if the goal is to extract scores that are thought to reflect latent dimensions that underlie the variables of interest, with corresponding psychological interpretation, then factor analysis is most appropriate (Widaman, 1993).

A common practice in machine learning is to use PCA on the predictor set to reduce the number of dimensions, using a rule of thumb for retaining the number of components that explain 95% or 99% of the variance. We note that this should only be conducted when the number of predictors is truly large (thousands), or the sample size is relatively small relative to the number of predictors (e.g., 200 people and 500 predictors). In social and behavioral research, it is unlikely that the predictors can be reduced efficiently given that the predictors often come from a variety of sources.

[7]Interested readers should see Hastie et al., 2009.

In contrast, if the predictors represent something like blood-oxygen-level-dependent (BOLD) signals from magnetic resonance imaging (MRI), using rules of thumb like this for PCA may work much better.

7.6.2 Variable Network Models

Developed on a separate track than that of factor analysis, graphical models, or Bayesian networks (in the directed case) have obvious similarities because of their graphical nature. Their development originated in computer science (Pearl, 1988), and have been more focused on explicating the "causal" relationship between variables without having to resort to longitudinal designs (Pearl, 2000; for causality in SEM, see Bollen & Pearl, 2013). The similarities between methodologies has spawned hybrid models (Duarte, Klimentidis, Harris, Cardel, & Fernandez, 2011) that capitalize on each framework's strengths, as well as models that build upon their equivalence with Gaussian variables (Buhlmann, Peters, & Ernest, 2014; Shimizu, Hoyer, Hyvärinen, & Kerminen, 2006).

Here, we focus specifically on the undirected graphical models, which have seen an upsurge in application in psychological research, specifically in personality research (e.g., Constantini et al., 2015) and in the study of psychopathology (e.g., Borsboom, Cramer, Schmittmann, Epskamp, & Waldorp, 2011). The differences between both graphical models and SEM arise in the presence of latent variables. Graphical models capitalize on the conditional distributions between variables in the model, reducing what could be a large network to only estimating what is termed *cliques*, or smaller networks that are conditionally independent from the rest of the network. These conditional distributions also hold in path analysis (SEM without latent variables), but when latent variables are present in the model it is no longer the case. Estimation with latent variables becomes more complicated, and may be the reason for less of a focus on using latent variables for dimension reduction (also can be termed *hidden variables* and used to represent unmeasured confounders especially in assigning causality, see Pearl, 2000) in graphical models (although see Glymour, Scheines, Spirtes, & Kelley, 1987), and subsequent books and articles from the same group).

In graphical models, when the models are not specified a priori, it is common to use some form of "search" to find the optimal model given the dataset. Although greedy, stochastic search algorithms were common at the outset (Chickering, 2003), more recently regularization has seen a wide variety of applications with graphical models (Friedman, Hastie, & Tibshirani, 2007; Meinshausen & Buhlmann, 2006; Yuan, & Lin, 2007). Although these proposed methods are similar in many senses, the method that has potentially seen the most application is that of the graphical lasso

(Friedman, Hastie, & Tibshirani, 2007, 2010; Mazumder & Hastie, 2012). In contrast to SEM, where the expected covariance $\mathbf{\Sigma}$ matrix is used for estimation, in graphical models it is generally the precision matrix $\mathbf{\Theta}$, or the inverse of the expected covariance matrix $\mathbf{\Sigma}^{-1} = \mathbf{\Theta}$. Assuming the observations follow a gaussian distribution indicates that all of the conditional distributions also are gaussian (Hastie et al., 2009). Given this, the precision matrix then contains the partial covariances between variables. Specifically, if the ijth component of $\mathbf{\Theta}$ is zero, then the variables i and j are conditionally independent given all of the other variables, meaning the path (either undirected or directed) between variables in the model is also zero. Using this, a penalty on the $\mathbf{\Theta}$ matrix can be introduced which leads directly to a form of constraint on the model. In the graphical lasso, this penalty takes the form of

$$f(\mathbf{\Theta}) = log(|\mathbf{\Theta}|) - tr(\mathbf{C\Theta}) - \lambda||\mathbf{\Theta}||_1, \tag{7.7}$$

where λ is the shrinkage parameter, similar to in regression context, $\mathbf{C}$ is the empirical covariance matrix, tr denotes the trace, and $||\mathbf{\Theta}||_1$ is the L_1 norm (Friedman et al., 2007).

The Gaussian graphical model is a model for continuous variables. For categorical variables (or mixed), one can use Ising network models, which has been similarly shown to be equivalent to different forms of latent variable models, specifically item response theory (Marsmann et al., 2018). As in other forms of regularization, one needs to use some criterion to choose a singular value of λ. One of the most commonly applied criterion is the expected Bayesian information criteria (EBIC; Chen & Chen, 2008; Epskamp, Cramer, Waldorp, Schmittmann, & Borsboom, 2012). Note however, that there are similar drawbacks to the application of the lasso penalty in graphical models as in SEM, specifically problems with consistency (see Williams, Rhemtulla, Wysocki, & Rast, 2019).

We can see an application of graphical models in Figure 7.7, where we estimate the conditional relationships between all 12 Grit items. From this, we can see a similarity to the results from factor analysis (see Table 7.3), where the items that loaded on the same latent variable have stronger conditional relationships, and thus are plotted in closer proximity in the graphical model. A more explicit tie between frameworks can be seen in exploratory graph analysis (Golino & Epskamp, 2017), where a graphical model is used to estimate the number of latent variables.

In graphical models a number of statistics are commonly computed. These relate to centrality, or deriving local information for each node (variable) and the strength of its relationship to other nodes. Centrality, in particular, has almost a direct relationship to factor loading strength in

FIGURE 7.7. Gaussian graphical model for the Grit data. Each edge represents the partial correlation between variables (nodes).

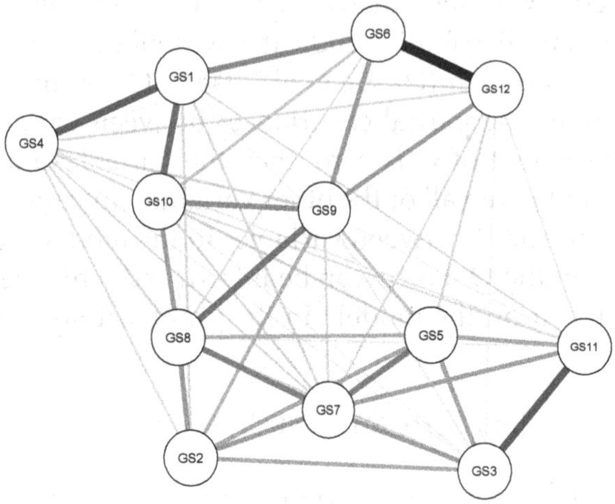

factor models (Hallquist, Wright, & Molenaar, 2019), while some research has developed network loadings to further highlight the similarity across methods (Christensen & Golino, 2021), making the theoretical distinctions between graphical models and SEM less clear. In our data, the correlation between centrality and the item R^2 values (sum of all factor loadings to that variable) in the CFA model above was 0.82, and 0.91 when using the results from the EFA with two latent variables.

7.7 Summary

In this chapter, we discuss a number of ways and methods for assessing variables to be used as predictors. Notably absent was a discussion of error in the outcome variable. Similar approaches can be used as explained above if the outcome is a scale score, including directly modeling the latent variable representation in an SEM model (see Chapter 8). However, just as with a single predictor variable, there is no way to overcome the error in an outcome variable when the aim is prediction. Finally, it is almost always preferable to use the individual items as opposed to scale scores when maximizing predictive performance is the goal. Along with this, we recommend assessing the reliability of individual items and scales to provide additional information into why some items/scales were more important, or why prediction was lower than expected.

7.7.1 Further Reading

- Reliability and validity are both complex topics, and have been written about extensively. See Furr (2011) for an introductory textbook. For more recent discussions of validity, see Kane (2013) or Flake, Pek, and Hehman (2017), and for reliability, see McNeish (2018).
- We only briefly discussed a handful of SEM fit indices. This is an extremely broad topic, as dozens of indices have been developed to assess the fit of SEMs. See McNeish and Wolf (2021) as well as Golino et al. (2021) for recent developments in this area.
- Our coverage of variable network models was relatively scant despite a recent increase in development in this area. While much of the research in this area is focused on modeling longitudinal data (see Epskamp et al., 2018), see Isvoranu Epskamp, Waldorp, and Borsboom (2022) and Borsboom et al. (2021) for recent reviews.
- While we briefly covered exploratory factor analysis, we recommend the book by Mulaik (2009) for more background, particularly from a technical perspective. For a more introductory textbook, see Beaujean (2014).
- To prevent an overoptimistic assessment of model fit when testing multiple EFA models (or PCA) with the aim of producing a "final" CFA model, it is impotant to separate the data used to create the model, and the data used to estimate the model fit. We discuss this further in Chapter 8 for general SEM, but for scale or factor model development, we recommend Fokkema and Greiff (2017).

7.7.2 Computational Time and Resources

Many of the methods detailed in the chapter involve modeling covariance matrices which can often be modeled relatively quickly (at most a few minutes). However, for many latent variable models that involve missingness, more complex constraints, or additional types of estimation, runtimes can be on the order of hours. For factor analysis and SEM, we recommend using both the `psych` and `lavaan` packages in `R`, as they are both easy to use and have been developed extensively. While `lavaan` (Rosseel, 2012) is a general SEM software, the `psych` (Revelle, 2020) package contains a variety of functions for factor analysis, reliability, and other psychometric operations. Further, both packages contain functionality for generating factor scores. Additionally, the `OpenMx` (Boker et al., 2011) package is an extremely flexible SEM program, and we will detail its use when paired with trees in Chapter 10. Finally, there are a host of packages for running variable network models. See the following site for reference to many of the most commonly used R packages in this area: http://sachaepskamp.com/R.

8
Machine Learning and Structural Equation Modeling

In Chapter 7 we introduced the concept of latent variables as a method to account for measurement error. We followed this introduction with detailing the consequence of measurement error, namely, in reducing our ability to predict an outcome of interest, as well as increase the instability of decision tree results. In this chapter we integrate concepts from Chapters 4 and 7 in using structural equation modeling (SEM) to account for measurement error while incorporating concepts more traditionally used in machine learning.

The preceding chapters (Chapters 4–6) focused primarily on predictive aims, and, to a lesser extent, descriptive aims in assessing relationships and variable importance. The idea of prediction in SEM has long been discussed and debated, because of the uncertainty regarding the application of SEM for purely predictive purposes, namely, casewise prediction. Given that SEM is a multivariate method that encompasses the estimation and modeling of covariance matrices, individual responses on X or Y variables are not necessary for the majority of models. With this in mind, and given that SEM cannot generate casewise predictions for some models (Evermann & Tate, 2016), alternatives such as partial least squares SEM (PLS-SEM) have been championed as viable alternatives to SEM (see Hair, Sarstedt, Ringle, & Mena, 2012 for an overview of the debate). Recently, specific forms of PLS-SEM have been shown to be equivalent to the use of factor score regression (Yuan & Deng, 2021). Finally, a recent paper demonstrated how to use SEM to generate casewise predictions, highlighting that it can be seen as an even less complex model for prediction than linear regression (de Rooij et al., 2022).

The aim of this chapter is not to explain how SEM can be used in a purely predictive domain. Instead, we discuss a number of strategies for moving the pendulum with how SEM is typically applied, from purely explanatory or descriptive applications, to increasingly incorporating aspects of prediction. This holds true for this chapter, as well as Chapters 9 and 10, where we no longer truly only have a singular outcome. To accomplish this, we break this chapter down into three main sections: latent variables as linear predictors, latent variables as linear outcomes, and nonlinear relationships in SEM. Although both linear and nonlinear relationships should be tested in a succession of models, we dissect the sections for pedagogical purposes, summarizing both frameworks at the conclusion of the chapter.

8.1 Key Terminology

- Maximum likelihood estimation. The most commonly used form of estimation in SEM since, with most common data characteristics in social and behavioral research, it has the best asymptotic (population) characteristics as long as assumptions (multivariate normality) hold (e.g., see Zhong & Yuan, 2011).
- Endogenous variable. A variable with at least one path directed toward it, meaning it is an outcome variable. Note that in SEM an endogenous variable can also have directed paths from it to other variables.
- Exogenous variable. A variable that is not predicted or has any directed paths to it. This is typically referred to as an *independent variable* in regression models.
- Measurement model. The part of an SEM that determines the composition of a latent variable, typically through a confirmatory factor analysis specification.
- Structural model. Part of an SEM that has directed or undirected paths between observed and/or latent variables. If a measurement model is not included, then it is typically referred to as *path analysis*. Mediation models that do not include the presence of latent variables are a subset of this.
- Multiple indicator multiple cause (MIMIC) model. An SEM model that incorporates a measurement model to represent latent variables, along with predictors of the latent variables.
- Interpretational confounding. When the meaning of a latent variable is confounded by the inclusion of a directed path from the latent variable to what is described as an outcome variable. In this situation, there is no distinction between a regression path and factor loading.

- Full versus limited information. In SEM, estimation can either entail the use of each entry in the dataset (casewise or full information) or by converting the full dataset to a covariance matrix (limited information). While using the covariance matrix is most often computationally simpler, more complex models often require full information estimation.

- Exploratory SEM. A hybrid of EFA and SEM that uses an EFA for the measurement model while allowing additional paths not typically used in EFA (such as regression paths and other constraints).

8.2 Latent Variables as Predictors

Presently, we will assume that the outcome of interest (e.g., distal outcome) is a singular, observed variable, either assumed to be continuous or binary (most of what we discuss generalizes to alternative distributions for an observed outcome). The main distinction between these types of outcomes is the type of estimation used. Just as in the distinction between linear and logistic regression, in structural equation modeling we can account for different types of outcomes by altering the form of estimation used. The default in most SEM software is maximum likelihood estimation (Jöreskog, 1969), and the extension full information maximum likelihood (for further detail on handling missing data in SEM and the types of missingness, see Enders, 2010), which allows for the inclusion of missing data. When the outcome is categorical, either binary or ordered polytomous[1], a number of estimation methods are available, with the most common being the use of some variant of weighted least squares with the probit link. This alters the parameters of the model and their interpretation in a very similar way as the interpretation is altered in moving from linear regression to either logistic or ordinal regression. We note, however, that this mainly applies to endogenous (variables with paths directed to them) and not exogenous (variables that only have paths emanating from them).

When our observed predictors of interest are greater than just a few (e.g., > 5), we have a number of distinct modeling options. Most often in social and behavioral research at least a subset of the predictors will come from the same scale, or be thought to measure similar constructs as other predictors. In deciding which modeling strategy is most appropriate, a number of additional factors need to to be considered. These include, but are not limited to:

[1]Software such as M*plus* can handle additional outcome types such as poisson, nominal, or censored.

1. Sample size
2. Number of predictors
3. Extent of empirical support for the theorized factor structures

With these factors, researchers have a number of different options. If the factor structure of the predictors is known to a large extent, researchers have three different modeling options: structural equation modeling, creating factor scores, or using the mean or sum of the predictors (grouping variables by latent factor) and entering these new scores into a linear (logistic) regression model. However, if the latent structure of the predictors is unknown or uncertain, researchers can either stay in the SEM framework and use exploratory SEM (ESEM; Asparouhov & Muthén, 2009; Marsh, Morin, Parker, & Kaur, 2014) or exploratory factor analysis to identify the clusters of predictors to use for factor scores or summed (mean) scores. We discuss the use of ESEM later in the chapter. While the degree of theoretical input can alter our assessment of the predictors, the interaction between our sample size and the number of predictors can cause similar problems as we often see in regression, particularly when the number of predictors is large and the sample size small. Later in this chapter we cover the use of regularization in SEM specifically for this research scenario.

8.2.1 Example

To demonstrate the use of latent variables as predictors, we will provide an empirical example with a categorical outcome, as things are relatively straightforward in calculating R^2 for a continuous outcome. On the other hand, it can be trickier to get estimated probabilities out from SEM software and calculating metrics such as area under the receiver operating characteristic curve (AUC). For this, we used the National Survey on Drug Use and Health (NSDUH; Substance Abuse and Mental Health Services Administration, 2021) from 2014, which was discussed previously in Chapter 4. As before, the dataset was subset to a sample of 2,000, with equal numbers of yes's and no's for suicidal thoughts. This dataset was further subset randomly into a training and test set (50–50), with missing values imputed. Nineteen variables were included in order to predict suicidal ideation (last 12 months; SUICTHINK). Predictors included questions assessing participants mental health in previous year, broadly falling into two categories: one set assessing symptoms of depression, anxiety, or emotional stress (variables starting with *DST*), and how emotions, nerves, or mental health interfered most with daily activities (variables starting with *IMP*). Additionally, there were four demographic variables (gender, ethnicity, relationship status, age; dummy coded). Of these 15 nondemographic predictors, we first used exploratory factor analysis to understand the latent structure.

For this factor analysis, we first fit a one-factor model. To select the number of latent variables we used the RMSEA fit index. The one factor model evidenced poor fit, achieving a value of 0.199 (90% CI 0.194, 0.205). Note that this model is equivalent to a one-factor CFA model, thus rotation is unnecessary. Next we fit a two-factor model. This model achieved an improved fit, with an RMSEA of 0.082 (90% CI 0.076, 0.088). Finally, a three-factor model further improved the fit, with an RMSEA of 0.066 (90% CI 0.059, 0.073), although not to a large extent. As the two-factor model did not fit much worse than the three-factor model, and the three-factor loadings made less substantive sense, with a third factor of all small factor loadings, we decided to choose the two-factor model as the final model. As the predictors all assess somewhat similar constructs, we would expect an oblique (correlated) rotation to be more appropriate than an orthogonal (uncorrelated) rotation. After rotation, the latent factors were correlated at -0.57, and had the loadings displayed in Table 8.1.

TABLE 8.1. Factor Loadings for Two Factors in the NSDUH Data

	factor1	factor2
DSTNRV12	-0.01	-0.73
DSTHOP12	-0.01	-0.93
DSTRST12	-0.08	-0.81
DSTCHR12	0.01	-0.88
DSTEFF12	0.08	-0.78
DSTNGD12	0.01	-0.89
IMPREMEM	-0.75	0.02
IMPCONCN	-0.83	0.01
IMPGOUT	-0.77	0.02
IMPPEOP	-0.73	0.04
IMPSOC	-0.77	0.02
IMPHHLD	-0.83	-0.01
IMPRESP	-0.84	-0.08
IMPWORK	-0.73	0.02
IMPDYFRQ	0.35	-0.32

Given the loadings, and the categories with which each variable falls under in the NSDUH codebook, we can label the first latent factor as *distress* and the second factor as *impairment*. This structure makes for a relatively clear simple structure, with the exception of IMPDYFRQ. This variable assesses "How many days in this week did you have difficulties?" This lends credence to how it assesses both topics of inquiry, and thus if we were specifying a CFA model based on this structure, IMPDYFRQ would load on both factors.

8.2.2 Application to SEM

For the empirical example in predicting suicidal ideation, we can form latent variables that represented sets of variables that were used as predictors, and instead of using factor scores as predictors, stayed in the SEM framework. This form of model is displayed in Figure 8.1.

FIGURE 8.1. SEM using the distress and impairment latent variables, along with 13 demographic variables, as predictors of suicidal ideation. In this, two-headed arrows represent variances (unique and residual) and covariances, while triangles represent means, and directed arrows represent factor loadings or regressions.

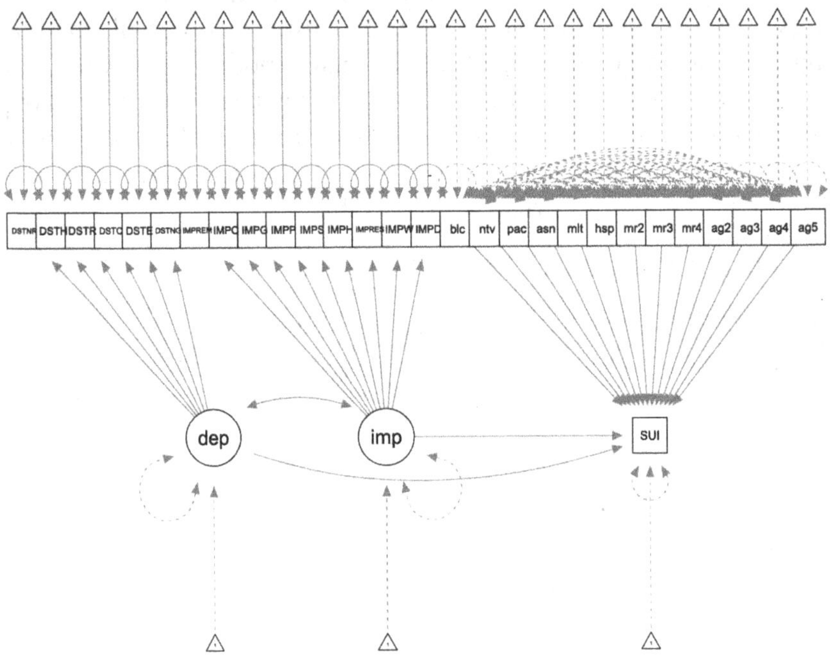

In this figure, a confirmatory factor analysis model was specified with simple structure (putting IMPDYFRQ on the *imp* latent variable), using only those variables that loaded strongly onto the distress factor as indicators for that factor, with the same holding true for the impairment latent variable. With these two latent variables as predictors, in addition to the 13 demographic variables, we estimated the model along with predicted probabilities for suicidal ideation. Given that our outcome is categorical, it is necessary to make sure that this is specified to the SEM software, using either a logit or probit link, necessitating different forms of estimation than is common for SEM. This alters aspects of the model formation, and can often take longer to run. For most SEM software, it is possible to get out

FIGURE 8.2. Representation of SEM with suicidal thinking as an outcome, highlighting that both representations are equivalent.

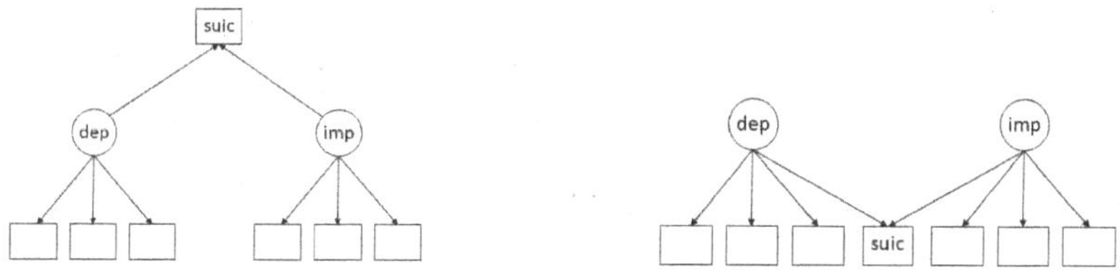

the estimated probabilities to evaluate model performance. For this example, extracting estimated probabilities from the training set with the SEM model resulted in an AUC of 0.80, a small decrease from the use of factor scores and observed variables. Although the causes for this decrease in prediction could be multifaceted, one explanation is that SEM estimation is attempting to optimize all of the parameter estimates to best fit the entire set of variables (i.e., the prediction of all endogenous variables), whereas a logistic regression model with factor scores is optimizing the regression weights to maximize prediction. If inference into the entirety of the model is of primary importance, then the SEM framework may be most appropriate. However, this may come with some decrease in our ability to predict a single variable.

8.2.3 Drawbacks

In much of our discussion regarding machine learning we have made a distinction between an outcome and a set of predictors. In SEM, the corollary distinction is between indicators of latent variables, predictors, and outcomes. In the model displayed in Figure 8.1, the set of demographic variables are predictors, where each of the two latent variables contains multiple indicators, and suicidal thoughts is the outcome. However, the distinction between indicators and outcomes is fuzzy (Burt, 1976; Levy, 2017). We illustrate this with an annotated depiction of our prior SEM, displayed in Figure 8.2.

In Figure 8.2, we can see a visual depiction of how regression paths from a latent variable to an observed outcome are equivalent to a factor loading, which is referred to as *interpretational confounding*. The important implication is that the outcome actually informs the composition of the latent variable, which can upwardly bias our assessment of prediction. More practically, the impairment latent variable is not only composed from aspects of the measurement model (indicators of the latent variable), but also a result of the outcome. This issue in separating indicators from outcomes in SEM has spurred a number of proposals, mostly focused on the use of two-step procedures: first creating factor scores and then inserting these into the SEM, thus ensuring that the composition of the latent variable is only a result of the indicators (see Levy, 2017, for additional detail).

8.3 Predicting Latent Variables

Just as it is common to have predictors that assess similar constructs in social and behavioral research, the same is often true for outcome of interest. For instance, if our goal is to try and predict a construct such as depression, it will often involve summarizing a participant's responses to a number of distinct questions coming from the same scale. In contrast to the common use of summed scores to create a single outcome, which makes an extremely restrictive assumption regarding each indicator variable (e.g., McNeish & Wolf, 2020), in this section we discuss the use of SEM. To demonstrate this, we will continue with our use of the Grit data, as discussed in Chapter 7. For this data, we will build off of our exploratory factor analysis, using the two latent variable formulation as an outcome model.

8.3.1 Multiple Indicator Multiple Cause (MIMIC) Models

Staying within the SEM framework, we can directly add a number of predictors to the model, with directed paths from each predictor to each of the latent variables. In this model, the latent Grit factors are influenced by both the indicators (weighted by the factor loadings) and the covariates (weighted by the regressions). To better understand this, we would have to lay out expectations for each of the observed indicators of the latent Grit factors. However, in more simplistic terms, we can just think of the latent Grit factors consisting of both the indicators and covariates in this model, each influencing the creation of the latent variables. In the literature, a distinction is often made between formative (just regressions) and reflective (just factor loadings) models, and combining these is called a *multiple indicators* (factor loadings), *multiple-causes* (regression parameters directed to the latent variable) *model* (MIMIC model; Jöreskog & Goldberger, 1975). This is why the resultant factor loadings can change when including the predictors in the model—the inclusion of predictors can change the meaning of the latent factors. More specific to our purposes, our first model will assess the influence of each predictor and its linear regression weight directed to each latent factor. The model is displayed in Figure 8.3.

FIGURE 8.3. MIMIC model using the 63 personality and demographic variables as predictors of both Grit factors.

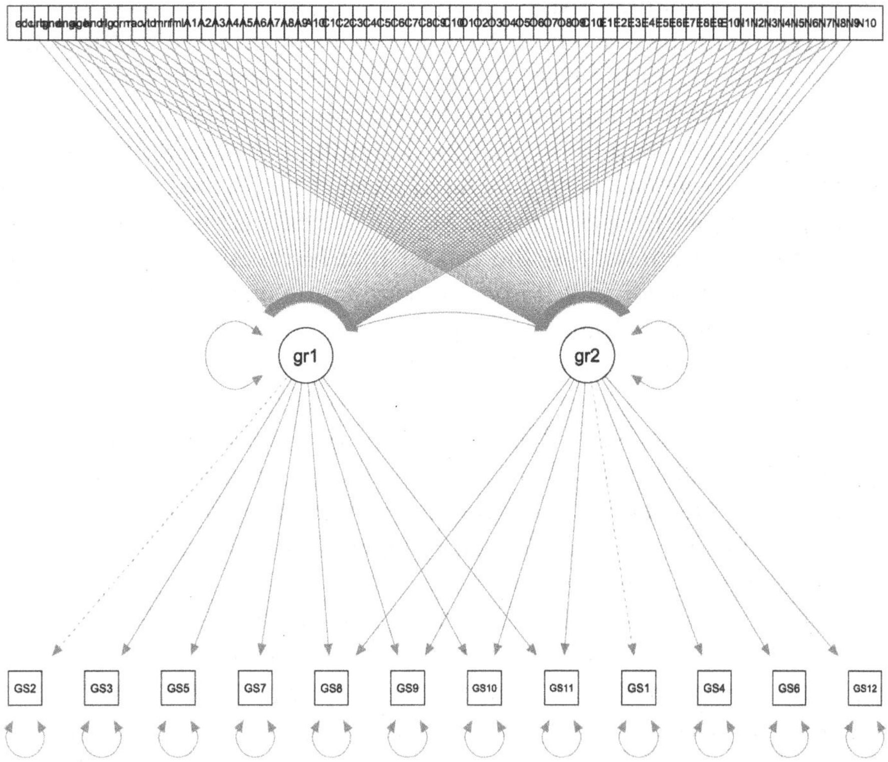

In this model, we have 10 predictors each from the extraversion, conscientiousness, openness, neuroticism, and agreeableness facets of the Big Five theory of personality. Additionally, we have measures of education, religion, age, race/ethnicity, and family (13 total). Once these predictors are included in the model, we can determine what percent of variance is accounted for in each latent variable. In this, the predictors explain 69.8% of $Grit_1$ (persistence) and 90.0% of $Grit_2$ (hard work). Note that this is calculated from the parameters within the SEM model, not by creating factor scores. To see the attenuation of effect that results from creating factor scores, we created factor scores for the training set. With these scores, the predictors explained 58.9% and 73.6% of the variance of both factors, respectively. Here we see the decrease in fit from adopting a two-step approach as compared to staying within the SEM framework.

8.3.2 Test Performance in SEM

One difficulty in using SEM, and not creating factor scores for latent variables, is that evaluating test set performance can be more difficult. This is mainly due to the existence of latent variables, and the fact that these must be estimated in the test set. It is critically important to ensure that the latent variable that was estimated in the training set is equivalent to the latent variable specified in the test set. Ensuring equality of measurement is referred to as *measurement invariance*, and it has a long history in the field of psychometrics (see Horn & McArdle, 1992). This involves adding constraints to parameters in the model that force estimates to be equal across datasets. Specifically, it involves estimating parameters freely in the training set, then constraining the parameters to these values in the test set. This forces the formulation of each latent variable, through constraints on the factor loadings, regression, mean, and variance parameters, to be equivalent across datasets. Particularly for endogenous latent variables, variances represent residual variances, or the amount of variability not accounted for by the regressors. This means that the residual variance can be freely estimated in the holdout sample, while all other parameters were estimated on the training sample.

Just as in other forms of training a model on one dataset and then testing it on a holdout set, it generally results in a worsening of fit.[2] Most notably, if the fit of the model in the test set degrades to a large degree, it could signal that there were discrepancies in measurement. This is more common when the datasets emanate from separate settings or across groups of observations. In our case, the datasets come from the same sample, with the exact same characteristics. Instead, degradation in fit would identify overfitting in our training set. This can be evaluated by creating estimated prediction in the test set (predicted probabilities in the case of a categorical outcome), after fixing all parameters to their training model values, only allowing the variance and covariance among latent variables to vary. Allowing the variance and covariance among latent variables to vary will allow us to assess the prediction of latent variables, as demonstrated later in this chapter, while not affecting the formation of each latent variable. Additionally, we can allow the intercept of the outcome variable to be estimated in the model, which results in four free parameters in our example model. Following this approach, we find R^2 values of 0.419 and 0.588, respectively. With the predicted factor scores, again using the training set to create the model, then predicting factor scores on the test set, we get R^2 values of

[2]When we say fit, we are referring to fit metrics such as RMSEA or CFI, not metrics based on casewise predictions, such as RMSE. Without creating factor scores, it is not possible to generate casewise predictions for latent variables on a test set.

0.196 and 0.414, respectively. Although both sets of analyses see a decrease in performance across training and test sets, the SEM model still has higher explained variance values. We note the large decrease in performance from assessment on the training set versus test set, particularly for $Grit_2$ which saw the R^2 decrease by 0.312. This decrement can most likely be attributed to the large number of predictors, inflating the R^2 estimate in the training sample.

8.4 Using Latent Variables as Outcomes and Predictors

Given the large number of predictors used in the previous example, the logical next step is to determine if a dimension reduction, based on the theoretical formulation of the predictors, can improve our interpretation, and possibly our prediction of both Grit latent variables. More specifically, what is to be gained by modeling the latent structure of each of the five facets of personality? Diagrammatically, this is shown in Figure 8.4.

In this model, we are able to hone in on a smaller number of parameters, namely, the regression coefficients from each of the personality latent variables to both Grit latent variables. The parameter estimates, both unstandardized and standardized, are displayed in Table 8.2.

In Table 8.2, it is clear that the conscientiousness latent variable is the most influential predictor of both Grit latent variables, with standardized coefficients of 0.57 and −0.60. As opposed to examining the influence of each indicator of each of the big five traits, we can now look at the specific contributions of each latent variable. What remains to be seen is what is lost by modeling the latent structure to the predictors. First off, our model evidenced mixed indicators of model fit, with an RMSEA of 0.051, and CFI and TLI of 0.74 and 0.73, respectively. Secondly, the percentage of variance accounted for in each of the Grit latent variables decreased from the model with only manifest predictors. Our latent variable predictor formulation explained 45.8% and 60.2% of the variance in Grit latent variables, respectively, while the manifest formulation explained 48.7% and 63.8% (note that these values are different from those in the earlier example in the chapter, as we used a larger sample size for this analysis). To overcome this level of model misfit, while also attempting to improve our prediction of Grit, we will test the use of regularized SEM.

TABLE 8.2. Parameter Estimates from the MIMIC Model with Personality Latent Variables and Demographics as Predictors

outcome	predictor	est	se	p	std
grit1	agree	-0.05	0.04	0.18	-0.04
grit1	consc	0.57	0.05	0.00	0.57
grit1	open	-0.16	0.05	0.00	-0.12
grit1	extra	-0.01	0.03	0.68	-0.01
grit1	neuro	-0.15	0.03	0.00	-0.20
grit1	education	0.03	0.02	0.19	0.04
grit1	urban	-0.03	0.03	0.29	-0.04
grit1	gender	0.06	0.04	0.14	0.09
grit1	engnat	-0.02	0.05	0.73	-0.02
grit1	age	0.00	0.00	0.46	0.00
grit1	hand	-0.03	0.05	0.59	-0.04
grit1	religion	0.01	0.01	0.04	0.02
grit1	orientation	-0.04	0.02	0.09	-0.05
grit1	race	-0.01	0.02	0.56	-0.01
grit1	voted	0.04	0.05	0.39	0.05
grit1	married	-0.01	0.04	0.77	-0.02
grit1	familysize	0.02	0.01	0.08	0.03
grit2	agree	0.12	0.03	0.00	0.14
grit2	consc	-0.46	0.04	0.00	-0.60
grit2	open	-0.21	0.04	0.00	-0.21
grit2	extra	-0.07	0.02	0.00	-0.12
grit2	neuro	0.03	0.02	0.19	0.04
grit2	education	-0.06	0.02	0.00	-0.10
grit2	urban	0.01	0.02	0.62	0.02
grit2	gender	-0.08	0.03	0.01	-0.14
grit2	engnat	0.11	0.03	0.00	0.20
grit2	age	-0.00	0.00	0.51	-0.00
grit2	hand	0.00	0.04	0.92	0.01
grit2	religion	-0.01	0.00	0.08	-0.01
grit2	orientation	0.04	0.02	0.03	0.06
grit2	race	-0.01	0.01	0.23	-0.03
grit2	voted	-0.01	0.03	0.71	-0.02
grit2	married	-0.03	0.03	0.29	-0.06
grit2	familysize	-0.01	0.01	0.30	-0.02

FIGURE 8.4. MIMIC model using latent variables for the five personality factors. Note that the demographic variables are not pictured.

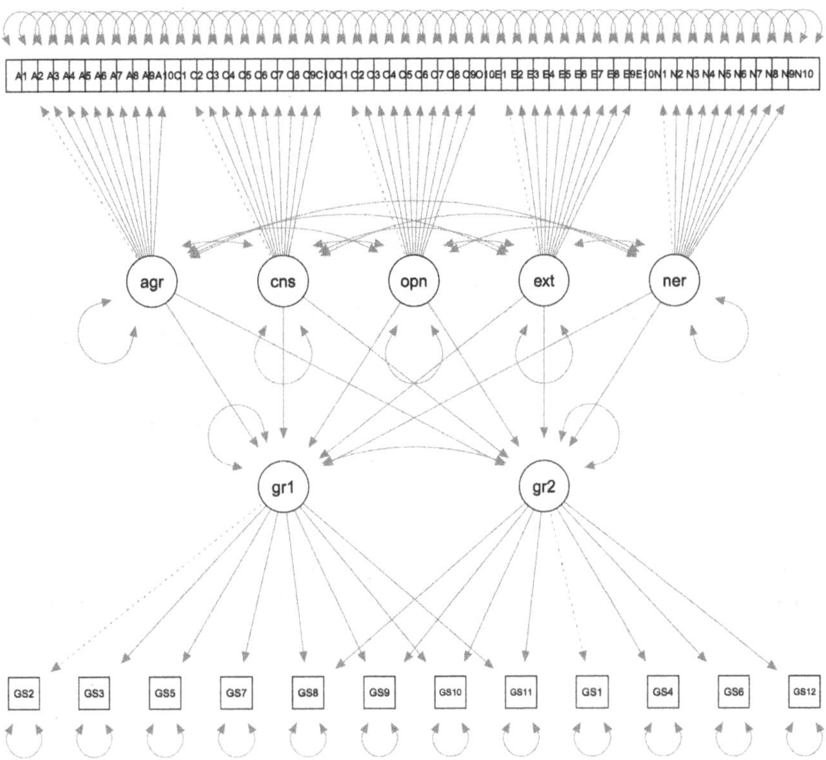

8.5 Can Regularization Improve Generalizability in SEM?

In Chapter 4, we looked at how the use of regularization, whether it be ridge, lasso, or any generalization, can reduce the complexity of our models and produce model estimates that result in higher predictive performance in holdout sets. In extending this to our prediction of latent Grit factors, we have two avenues where we can explore the utility of regularization. The first is using regularized regression in the second step with predicting factor scores, and the second option is building regularization directly into our SEM model estimation. This latter approach has been referred to as *regularized SEM* (Jacobucci, Grimm, & McArdle, 2016) or *penalized likelihood for SEM* (Huang et al., 2017). Equivalent in the results produced when using the same type of regularization, there are different software implementations of these approaches. For our application, we will use the `regsem` package (Li, Jacobucci, & Ammerman, 2021).

8.5.1 Regularized SEM

As maximum likelihood estimation (MLE) is the most common form of estimation for SEM, RegSEM adds a penalty function to the MLE for structural equation models (SEMs)

$$F_{regsem} = F_{ML} + \lambda P(\cdot), \tag{8.1}$$

where λ is the regularization parameter and takes on a value between zero and infinity. When λ is zero, MLE is performed, and when λ is infinity, all penalized parameters are shrunk to zero. $P(\cdot)$ is a general function for summing the values of one or more of the model's parameter matrices (i.e., a norm). Two common forms of $P(\cdot)$ include both the lasso ($\|\cdot\|_1$), which penalizes the sum of the absolute values of the parameters, and ridge ($\|\cdot\|_2$), which penalizes the sum of the squared values of the parameters. In comparison to regularized regression, where all predictors are typically penalized, in RegSEM it is more common to penalize only a subset of parameters. This takes place because there are dependencies between parameters in SEM, most notably the factor loadings and residual variances. Therefore, it is most typical to only penalize directed paths in SEM, either penalizing all or just a subset.

In our example, we may wish to penalize the regression parameters (which can be labeled (r11-r621 for those regressed on Grit1, and r12–r622 for those regressed on Grit2) from the covariates to both latent Grit factors. In total, there are 124 regression parameters, each of which could be penalized with the justification that by shrinking their estimates, we may produce a more generalizable solution in the test sample. Using lasso penalties, the absolute value of these 124 parameters would be summed and after being multiplied by the penalty λ, added to Equation 8.1, resulting in

$$F_{lasso} = F_{ML} + \lambda * \left\| \begin{matrix} r11 \\ r21 \\ \vdots \\ r621 \\ r12 \\ \vdots \\ r622 \end{matrix} \right\|_1 . \tag{8.2}$$

If we wished to perform ridge regularization, we could change the l_1 norm to the l_2. Additionally, many sparser alternatives are available (see Jacobucci, 2017, for more detail). Applying regularization to SEM carries with it similar requirements as in regression: the sequence of penalties must be selected as well as selecting a fit index to choose a final model. Very little research has gone into comparing different fit indices, and that limited research has supported the use of the Bayesian information criterion (Jacobucci et al., 2016; Huang et al., 2017). Alternatively, one could use cross-validation or bootstrapping, which is more computationally burdensome, but allows us to more explicitly test the model on a sample not used to estimate the model.

For our example, we used regularization for two purposes, one to produce more generalizable R^2 estimates and the other to perform variable selection among regression coefficients. We used lasso penalties ranging from 0 to 0.19 (20 total) and the BIC.

FIGURE 8.5. BIC values using lasso SEM.

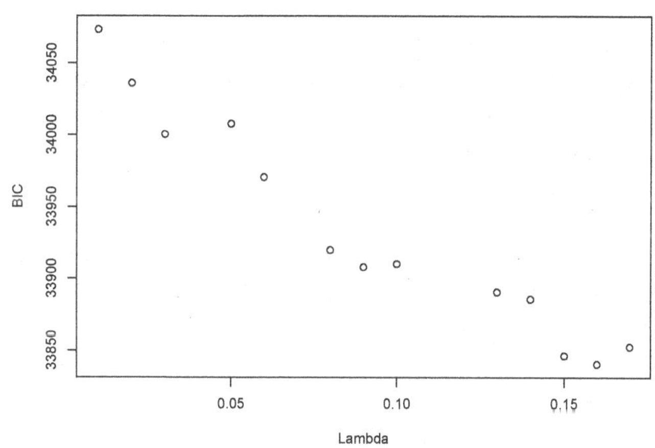

In Figure 8.5 we can see that as the penalties increase, the BIC generally decreases. This sequence of penalties corresponds to changes in the regression coefficients, as displayed in Figure 8.6. In this figure, as the penalty increases, there is mostly a monotonic shrinkage toward zero in coefficient size, with some parameters being set to zero at low penalties, and some never reaching zero. In smaller models, it is typical to test a vector of penalties that results in a range of coefficients from the MLE (unpenalized estimates) to all coefficients set to zero. In our example, the large model size produced difficulties in reaching convergence at higher

FIGURE 8.6. Parameter trajectory plot with a vertical line at the best fitting model.

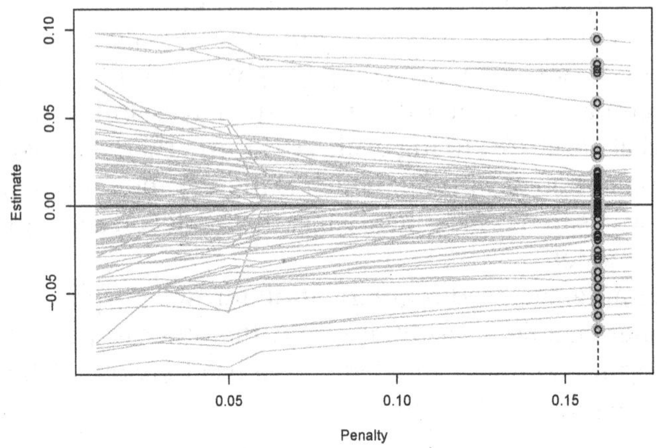

penalties, thus the range of λ was truncated to the highest penalty that still reached convergence.

Taking the lowest fit of these models, we can examine the R^2 values on both the training and test sets. Instead of choosing a final model to interpret, we examined the R^2 values from each of the 20 models, evaluated on both the training and test sets. Of these 20 models, 18 converged. These values are displayed in Figure 8.7.

FIGURE 8.7. R^2 values for *Grit1* and *Grit2*, respectively. Note that solid line denotes training set evaluation, dashed is test set. Note that we omit the R^2 values at higher values of lambda because they fall to zero.

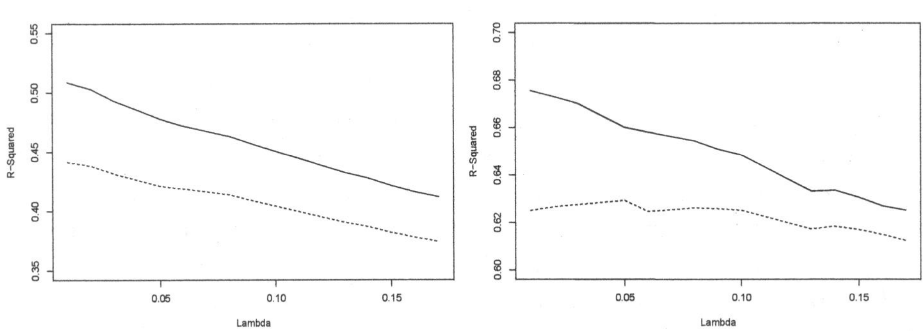

In both plots, there is a clear decrease to performance from the training to test sets, while the increase in penalties has less of an effect on R^2 in the test set than the training set. For $Grit_1$, the addition of lasso penalties results in a decrease in R^2 as evaluated in both the training and test datasets. This is always to be expected for the training set, as discussed in Chapter 3. A different picture emerges for $Grit_2$, with higher penalties resulting in a higher R^2 as evaluated on the test dataset. Although small, we can see that shrinking the regression paths directed to $Grit_2$ results in more generalizable prediction.

8.5.2 Exploratory SEM

In specifying a common factor model, it is common to use either a confirmatory factor analysis model if all of the factor loadings have an a priori justification, or specify an exploratory factor analysis model if uncertainty is inherent in the factor structure. Often, the prespecified CFA model will fit poorly as the imposed factor structure is too simplistic to adequately capture the covariance among variables, necessitating the use of a more flexible approach such as EFA. One major drawback of EFA is that it cannot be combined with other types of paths, such as regression or residual covariances, negating the use of this model for a prediction context. One method that overcomes this limitation, incorporating additional types of parameters while estimating an EFA model among specific variables, is *exploratory SEM* (ESEM; Asparouhov & Muthén, 2009). When using latent variables to predict an outcome of interest, the use of ESEM has shown good performance in the presence of small factor loadings that aren't specified in a CFA model, but captured by the EFA portion of the model (Mai, Zhang, & Wen, 2018). To determine if a more flexible specification of the latent variables underlying the personality variables can improve our prediction of Grit, we used ESEM while varying the number of latent variables extracted in the exploratory portion of the model. This model with five latent variables extracted from the personality variables is displayed in Figure 8.8.

FIGURE 8.8. MIMIC model using an EFA model to derive five latent variables as predictors of both grit factors. Note that the demographic variables are not pictured.

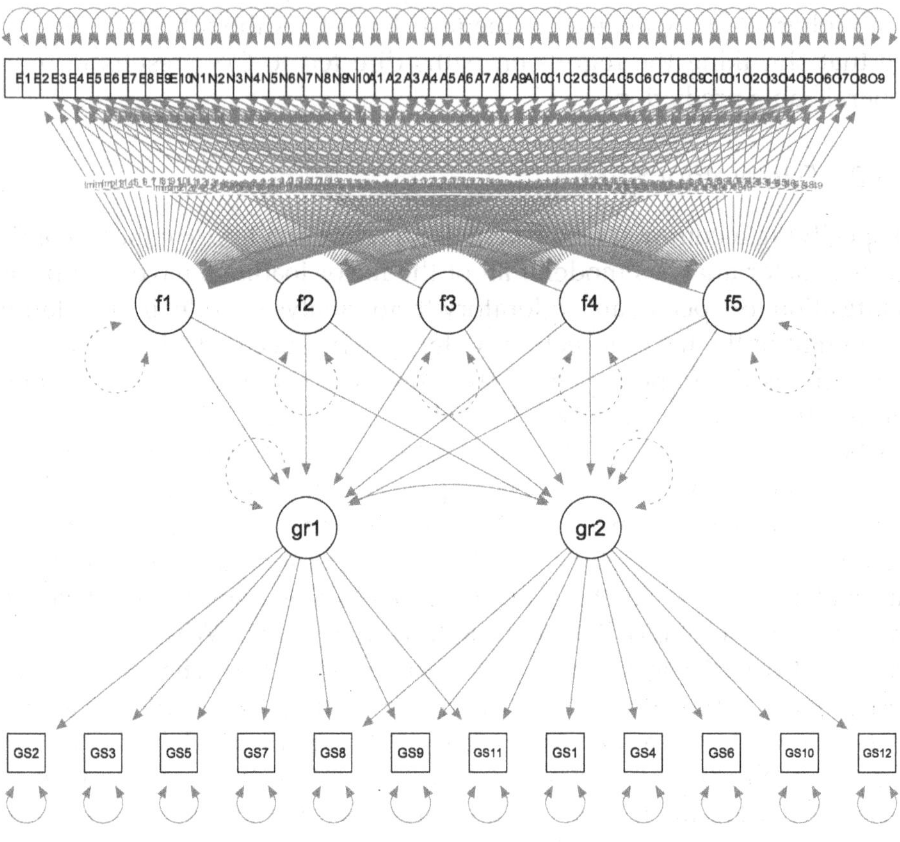

As a first attempt, we can extract three latent variables from the personality indicators. This model explained 32.4% and 39.6% of the variance respectively, in the Grit latent variables in the training set. Five latent variables improved our prediction, with 46.9% and 59.9% of the variance, respectively. At the upper limit, we tested the extraction of 10 latent variables, which explained 52.3% and 60.4% of the variance, respectively. The five exploratory latent variables explained similar amounts of variance as when specified with simple structure (no cross-loadings), while the 10 improved our prediction of $Grit_1$. However, these values were still far below the variance explained by manifest predictors (69.8% for $Grit_1$; 90.0% of $Grit_2$). Although the 10-factor model fit relatively well, with an RMSEA of 0.036 and CFI and TLI of 0.89 and 0.86, respectively, we can see that our improvement in prediction is marginal, particularly given the increase in number of parameters. Additionally, the interpretation of each personality latent variable is muddied by the number of latent variables and the sheer number of factor loadings for each.

We note that exploratory SEM can be seen as a method that blends explanatory and predictive aims through the integration of constraints with the flexibility afforded to EFA. From a prediction standpoint, the use of latent variables that do not contain constraints of the factor loadings as predictors will evidence some decrease in prediction relative to manifest variables; however, there is often some gain in interpretation due to the dimension reduction of the predictor space. As discussed in Chapter 2, we do not view explanation and prediction as opposing goals, and ideas/methods that fit more neatly into one side may be combined to better fit the aims of the study.

8.6 Nonlinear Relationships and Latent Variables

The methods that we have discussed in this chapter up until this point exist within the linear SEM framework. Thus the only types of nonlinearity that are natural to specify are with respect to observed variables, including interactions and quadratic terms. We do not discuss these further as they require manual creation prior to running the model, changing little about the actual model fitting procedure. We do note, however, that with larger numbers of variables, the number of possible interaction and quadratic effects increases quickly, which could require the use of regularization to reduce the dimensionality.

To specify fully nonlinear relationships, a few methods (outside of fully nonlinear growth models as in Grimm et al., 2016) are available. One is local SEM (Hildebrandt, Wilhelm, & Robitzsch, 2009) which examines the nonlinear relationships between moderator variables and specific parameters within an SEM model. This is similar to moderated nonlinear factor analysis (Bauer, 2017), where individual parameters are tested with one or more moderated variables in an attempt to identify invariance violations. However, both of these methods apply more at the individual parameter level, and would be inefficient for use in larger SEM models. Modeling nonlinear relationships between latent variables using latent product terms has spurred the development of a number of estimation methods to model these more complex models (Harring, Weiss, & Hsu, 2012). Two of the most popular approaches include product-indicator approaches (parametric approach; e.g., Kenny & Judd, 1984) and structural equation mixture models (semiparameteric; e.g., Bauer & Curran, 2004). However, interaction and quadratic terms among latent variables present a number of problems, namely, nonnormal distributions of the latent predictors, as well as the approaches being computationally expensive. A more recent approach that more seamlessly can incorporate nonlinear relationships is Bayesian SEM.

8.6.1 Bayesian SEM

Bayesian SEM (Lee & Song, 2012), which has received limited use in the past due to a lack of easy-to-use software and long run-times, has become an increasingly popular approach for estimating general SEM models. For the purposes of including nonlinear terms among latent variables, Bayesian estimation can simplify the process of estimating a model, which has been facilitated by a number of easier-to-use software packages being developed in the prior 10 years, such as `Stan` (Gelman, Lee, & Guo, 2015), Bayesian estimation in `Mplus` (Muthén & Asparouhov, 2012), and `blavaan` (Merkle & Rosseel, 2015). Additionally, Bayesian estimation has demonstrated improvements in scaling to larger numbers of product terms (Brandt, Cambria, & Kelava, 2018), while many of the traditional estimation methods are limited to 1–5 interactions or quadratic terms.

There are a number of commonalities across both Bayesian and frequentist SEM estimation. In the presence of large sample sizes and diffuse (noninformative priors), the results across estimation frameworks are often similar. Whereas parameters are estimated freely in frequentist SEM, Bayesian estimation allows for the use of informative priors, which can constrain the resulting posterior samples for each parameter estimate toward specific values, such as zero. This is similar to the use of regularization, where different types of regularization (shrinkage) priors can be used in both regression (e.g., Van Erp, Oberski, & Mulder, 2019) and SEM (Jacobucci & Grimm, 2018) to produce sparse results, just as in using frequentist types of regularization like the lasso. In contrast to testing a sequence of penalties as in lasso regularization, Bayesian regularization makes use of hierarchical priors, or a prior on a prior, necessitating the specification of only one model. An additional advantage of Bayesian estimation in SEM is that it is not reliant on covariance-based expectations, making more complex models, both in number of parameters and functional form of relationships, easier to specify and estimate. We demonstrate this below in extending our use of the MIMIC model for using Big Five personality to predict latent Grit factors.

8.6.2 Demonstration

For this demonstration, we build off of Figure 8.4, using the latent factors of agreeableness, conscientiousness, openness, extraversion, and neuroticism as predictors of two latent Grit factors. With this as a base model, we used the `rstan` package in `R` to run Bayesian estimation with `Stan` on three different models:

1. MIMIC model with $N(0,1)$ priors and just the five personality latent variables (10 total parameters) and 12 demographic variables (24 total parameters). This model should return similar parameter estimates to MLE.

2. MIMIC model with $N(0,1)$ priors and all possible linear, quadratic, and interaction terms among the five latent predictors (38 total parameters) and 12 demographic variables (24 total parameters).

3. Same models as #2, but using the hyperlasso prior on all of the 38 latent regression paths and $N(0,1)$ for the demographic predictors. The hyperlasso is one form of shrinkage prior (see Van Erp et al., 2019) that should shrink a subset of parameters to zero.

First, we compare the use of MLE (run with `lavaan`) and Bayesian with diffuse priors for all of the linear effects. This is displayed in Figure 8.9. Note that the demographic variables were not scaled prior to analysis (not done for interpretation and the lack of large effects), so they are not directly comparable to the personality latent variable coefficients, which were standardized.

In this figure, we can see almost identical parameter estimations across frequentist and Bayesian estimation. Additionally, the conscientiousness latent variable evidenced the largest effects, with coefficients in the area of 0.4 to 0.5 on $Grit_1$, and −0.4 to −0.5 on $Grit_2$. Additionally, each latent personality factor predicted at least one of the Grit latent variables. To determine whether there were interaction effects between variables, or quadratic effects for each latent variable, we added a set of predictors to each model. These models included all possible linear, quadratic, and interaction effects among latent variables for each of the Grit latent variables. To estimate these parameters, the size of the model (38 total linear, quadratic, and interaction effects), we could not use standard software, such as the `nlsem` package in R (the model failed to converge; Umbach, Naumann, Brandt, & Kelava, 2017). Instead, we specified the models in `Stan`, with two sets of priors on these coefficients. In the first model, we used the same diffuse priors ($N(0,1)$), whereas in the second model we used hyperlasso priors to shrink each of the coefficients toward zero (at different rates). The last prior may be beneficial for preventing overfitting, given the number of parameters, as well as increasing the clarity of interpretation. These results are displayed in Figure 8.10.

FIGURE 8.9. Parameter estimates from both the MLE and Bayesian models. Predictor names with ".1" refer to the coefficients for predicting $Grit_1$, whereas ".2" refers to $Grit_2$. Note that these are models with just linear regression paths from both the demographics and latent personality variables to each of the latent Grit variables. Standard error bars reflect two times the standard error (ML) or standard deviation of the samples for each parameter (Bayesian).

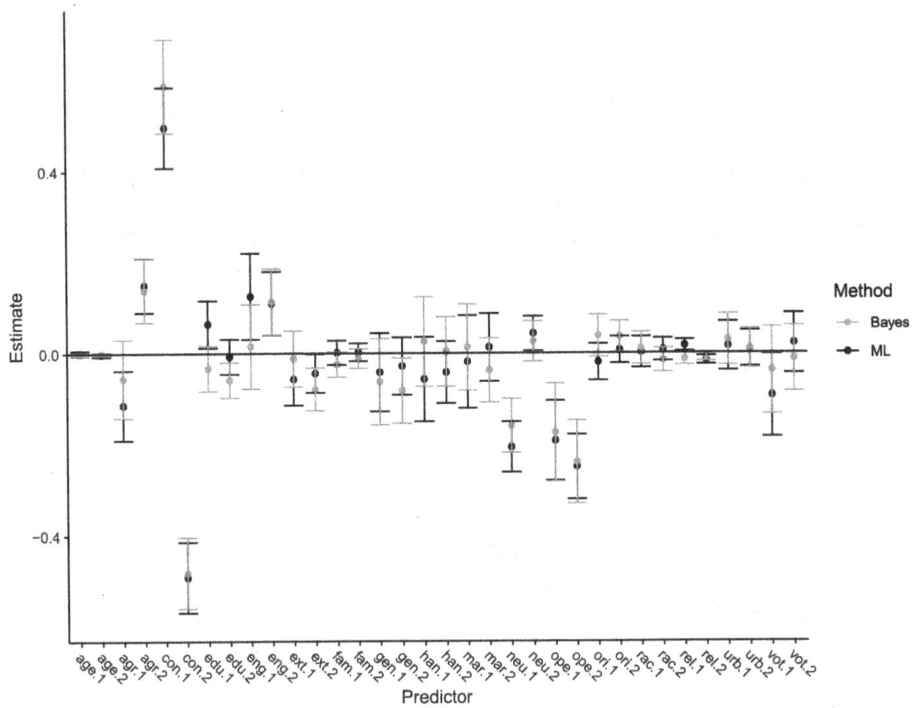

In this figure, we see uniform shrinkage for the coefficients from the hyperlasso model. However, few of these coefficients have mean estimates close to zero, denoting a form of variable selection. Instead, we see less variability to the parameter estimates, denoted by shorter credible intervals (the Bayesian form of confidence interval). For coefficients, we see the same pattern for linear effects, and a variety of significant interaction and quadratic effects, depending on which model is observed. For instance, some of the strongest interaction effects include conscientiousness, with both extraversion, and agreeableness for $Grit_1$. Additionally, there was a quadratic effect for conscientiousness on $Grit_2$, neuroticism on $Grit_1$, and openness on $Grit_2$.

FIGURE 8.10. Parameter estimates, excluding the demographic variables, for linear, quadratic, and interaction effects from each of the latent personality variables to both Grit latent variables. Both models used Bayesian estimation, whereas one model used diffuse priors ($Normal(0, 1)$), while the other used sparsity-inducing priors (hyperlasso). Standard error bars reflect two times standard deviation of the samples for each parameter.

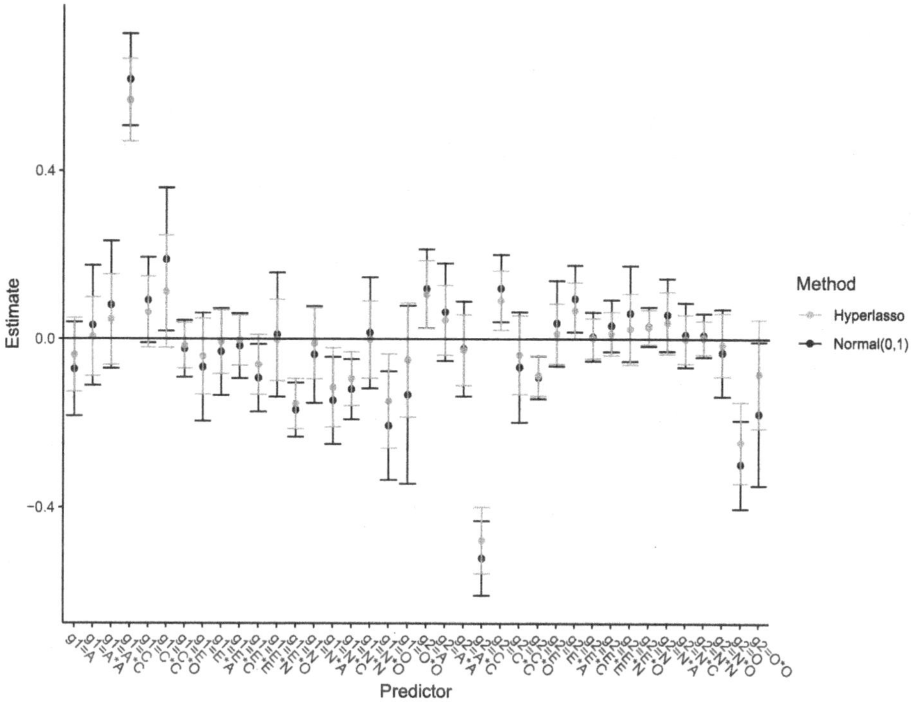

To visualize these effects, we saved the samples from the diffuse prior nonlinear model, using the mean estimates to derive the predicted regression lines for conscientiousness and neuroticism, displayed in Figure 8.11.

In each of these marginal plots, we see some degree of nonlinear relationship, a result of including the quadratic parameter in the model. While the positive quadratic parameter results in a less negative relationship between higher levels of conscientiousness and $Grit_2$, the opposite occurs between neuroticism and $Grit_1$, with a negative quadratic parameter resulting in a negative relationship at higher levels of neuroticism. As a next step, we could perform simple slope analyses to identify which points on each variable result in significant regression coefficients for each of the significant interactions effects. In our model, the interaction was signifi-

FIGURE 8.11. Marginal effects for conscientiousness on $Grit_2$ (left panel) and neuroticism on $Grit_1$ (right panel). Each of these use the mean factor score estimates for each latent variable, and the predicted regression line based on the mean parameter estimates.

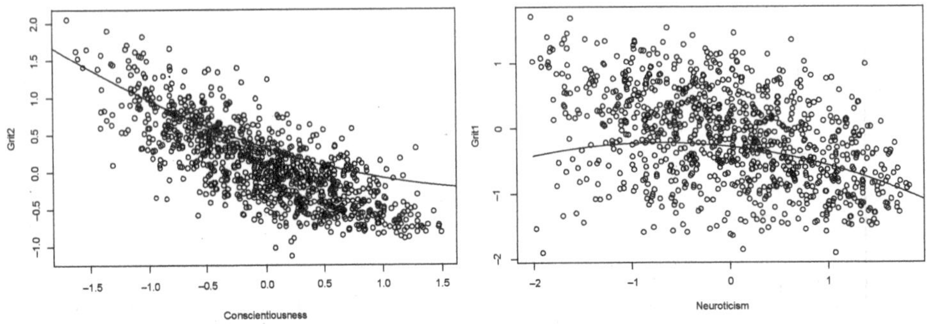

cant between neuroticism and conscientiousness with predicting $Grit_1$, and between extraversion and conscientiousness in predicting $Grit_2$.

In Bayesian estimation that includes the sampling of the factor scores, R^2 can be calculated from assessing the variance of the mean estimates, in comparison to the residual variability that is not explained by the regression parameters. More formally, we can represent this as:

$$FS \sim N(\mu, \psi^2) \tag{8.3}$$

$$\mu = \beta_0 + \beta_1 X_1 \tag{8.4}$$

$$R^2_{FS} = \frac{var(\mu)}{var(\mu) + \psi^2} \tag{8.5}$$

where ψ^2 is the residual variance and μ is the mean of the factor score. Also, μ is modeled by an intercept parameter, β_0, and a regression from a single predictor, β_1. In our model we modeled the mean of both latent Grit scores with additional sets of predictors, and with quadratic and interaction terms. The hyperlasso nonlinear model explained 50% and 65% of the variance for $Grit_1$ and $Grit_2$, while the diffuse nonlinear model explained 51% and 67% of the variance, which was a slight improvement over the 47% and 62% variance explained in the linear diffuse model (MLE was 46% and 60%, where the difference can be attributed to the sampling of the Bayesian estimation). This 4% and 5% respective improvement due to the interaction and quadratic terms is not negligible, and may represent theoretical significance depending on prior research.

Given the large increase in number of parameters, the question of overfitting remains. For our example, we did not see evidence for overfitting, even with the addition of interaction and quadratic effects. Our main assessment of overfitting was through the use of the hyperlasso, as this form of restrictive prior should shrink a number of coefficients to zero (or near zero) if the model is overparameterized. For both the diffuse and hyperlasso priors, the test set R^2 values were within the 95% credible intervals for the training set.

8.7 Summary

This chapter covered the application of dimension reduction and accounting for measurement error with structural equation modeling. Building off of Chapter 7, where we discussed the use of measurement models, we integrated additional complexity into an SEM model, notably with explicit outcome variables that were both observed and latent variables. This involved detailing models where the outcome is a latent variable, the predictors are latent variables, and a model has both. These complex forms of models can be easily fit in most software packages. Further, we detailed how concepts from machine learning can be integrated into these more complex forms of SEM, most notably regularization (Chapter 4). This requires the use of specialized R packages, but we expect regularization to be integrated into most general SEM packages in the near future.

While pairing regularization with SEM may be novel, we see it in line with recent innovations in the application of SEM above and beyond the traditional theory testing realm. While SEM is not a purely predictive method, aspects of prediction are increasingly being integrated into SEM, partially motivated by increases in dataset size and the resulting enlargement of SEM models. Moving forward, expect SEM development to continue in this vein, particularly as it relates to software development (fitting SEM models in neural network software) and on novel data types (such as text; see Chapter 11). Moving into the next two chapters, we will build off these more complex SEM models by integrating models that are modified to fit longitudinal data (Chapter 9) and specifically incorporate heterogeneity (Chapter 10).

8.7.1 Further Reading

- To learn more on the use of reflective versus formative SEM, see Howell, Breivik, and Wilcox (2007). Outside of the use of MIMIC models, SEM almost exclusively uses reflective indicators.
- In this chapter we almost completely avoided discussion of model fit in SEM. As benchmarks for the RMSEA, CFI, and TLI and good

fit, we used Hu and Bentler (1999). The evaluation of fit indices when adding regularization to SEM is an understudied topic. Part of the complication arises out of the complexity penalties in fit indices. In the case of the lasso, it is relatively easy to calculate the change in degrees of freedom as the penalty increases, whereas for other penalties (notably the ridge), this is less straightforward.

- While this chapter discussed the use of the relaxed lasso for inference into model estimates after variable selection was performed, recent research has focused on the development of alternative strategies (see Huang, 2020 for application in SEM).

- For background reading on Bayesian estimation, a number of great books are available on the fundamentals, including Kruschke (2014), Gelman et al. (2013), and McElreath (2020). For a more specific application of Bayesian estimation to psychometric models, see Levy and Mislevy (2016) or Depaoli (2021).

- We only provided an introduction to the application of regularization to SEM. For advances in this topic and more recent applications, see Li and Jacobucci (2020), Belzak and Bauer (2020), or Urban and Bauer (2020), for instance. The recent focus in this area is the application of regularization to new types of latent variable models, including item response theory (e.g., Sun, Chen, Liu, Ying, & Xin 2016), longitudinal (e.g., Ye, Gates, Henry, & Luo, 2020), and many others. A large challenge going forward is in scaling the algorithms to larger models, as it is common for most implementations to fail to converge when models include more than 100 parameters.

- The idea of incorporating cross-validation (CV) in SEM goes back to the 1980s (e.g., Cudeck & Browne, 1983). More recently, CV has seen very little application in SEM, which can be partly attributed to its increased computational complexity and that more traditional fit indices perform as well or better in selecting models (see Jacobucci et al., 2016 as well as Li & Jacobucci, 2020 for application with regularization). Additionally, it isn't straightforward as to which fit index CV should be paired with. It may be most appropriate to use CV (or bootstrapping) with the chi-square, although it can also be paired with fit indices such as the RMSEA.

- Particularly as it related to partial least squares, there has been debate regarding what prediction means in latent variable models. See Shmueli et al., (2016) for further discussion in this area and for alternative methods for evaluating predictive components of SEM models (e.g., Q^2).

8.7.2 Computational Time and Resources

Most structural equation models do not take more than a couple of seconds to run. However, when testing large models (e.g., more than 20 variables) or using different estimators to account for categorical variables, for instance, it can change the typical run-times to a couple of minutes. The addition of regularization necessitates testing a number of penalty values, along with constraining the model estimation, both factors that can drastically increase the computational complexity. For most of the models in this chapter, run-times were on the order of a few minutes to half an hour. Bayesian regularization typically takes much longer to run as it may require a large number of samples to converge to stable estimates. This can be sped up by using multiple chains, each of which can be run in parallel.

9 Machine Learning with Mixed-Effects Models

When working with a univariate outcome, calculating predicted values from any of the machine learning techniques discussed so far is straightforward, and assessing the usefulness of the model can be determined through cross-validation (k-fold or using a holdout sample). However, clustered data, data sampled from hierarchically structured units (i.e., children within schools, repeated measures data, employees within units), pose challenges to both the generation of predicted values and model evaluation due to the dependency present within the data. When analyzing clustered data using a theoretically driven model, an appropriate statistical model needs to be specified to distinguish the between-level effect from the within-level effect, obtain proper standard errors, and account for the potential imbalance present in clustered data (e.g., the number students sampled per school is different). While a variety of statistical models have been developed for the analysis of clustered data (i.e., fixed-effects regression models), we focus our attention on *mixed-effects models*, which are often referred to as *random coefficient models* in economics and *multilevel models* in the social and behavioral sciences.

9.1 Key Terminology

- Random effect. A parameter coefficient that is allowed to vary across clusters (people or schools). In this chapter's example, this means that both the intercept and slope are person specific.
- Fixed effect. A parameter coefficient that is the same for each unit (not allowed to vary across people or schools).
- Multilevel/hierarchical/mixed-effects models. Models that contain a mixture of fixed and random effects.

- Regularization. The application of penalties to shrink coefficients in the model. See Chapter 4 for additional details.
- Decision trees. An algorithm that recursively partitions values of covariates in order to place observations into hierarchically clustered groups. See Chapter 5 for additional details.

9.2 Mixed-Effects Models

The linear mixed-effects model can be written as

$$y_{ij} = x_{ijp}\beta_p + z_{ijq}u_{jq} + e_{ij} \tag{9.1}$$

where y_{ij} is the observed outcome score for observation i in cluster j, x_{ijp} is the pth predictor variable score for observation i in cluster j, β_p is the pth fixed-effects parameter, z_{ijq} is the qth predictor variable score for observation i in cluster j, u_{jq} is the qth random effect for cluster j, and e_{ij} is the residual for observation i in cluster j. The q random effects are not estimated, but assumed to follow a multivariate normal distribution with a mean vector of 0 and a unknown variance-covariance matrix. That is, $u_{jq} \sim N(\mathbf{0}, \mathbf{G})$, where $\mathbf{G}$ is a $q \times q$ covariance matrix. Typically, the residuals e_{ij} are assumed to follow a normal distribution with a mean of 0 and an unknown variance. That is, $e_{ij} \sim N(\mathbf{0}, \mathbf{R})$, where $\mathbf{R}$ is equal to $\mathbf{I}\sigma_e^2$. Lastly, the random errors are assumed to be uncorrelated with the random effects (i.e., $\text{cov}\left(e_{ij}, u_{jq}\right) = 0$).

As an example of a mixed-effects model, let's assume we're trying to predict mathematics achievement for students clustered in schools from a student-level predictor, teacher-rated externalizing behavior. Also, assume we allow each school to have a random effect for the intercept (random intercept) and a random effect for the slope for externalizing behavior (random slope). Such a model can be written as

$$math_{ij} = \left(\beta_{00} + u_{0j}\right) + \left(\beta_{10} + u_{1j}\right) \cdot ext_{ij} + e_{ij} \tag{9.2}$$

where $math_{ij}$ is the mathematics achievement score for student i in school j and ext_{ij} is the externalizing behavior score for student i in school j. In this model, β_{00} is the fixed effect for the intercept representing the predicted mathematics achievement score across schools when $ext_{ij} = 0$, u_{0j} is the random effect for the intercept for school j, which allows each school to have a different predicted level of mathematics achievement when $ext_{ij} = 0$, β_{10} is the average effect of externalizing behavior across schools, u_{1j} is the random effect for externalizing behavior for school j, which allows each school to have a different slope for the association between externalizing

FIGURE 9.1. Illustrative data with a random intercept and slope.

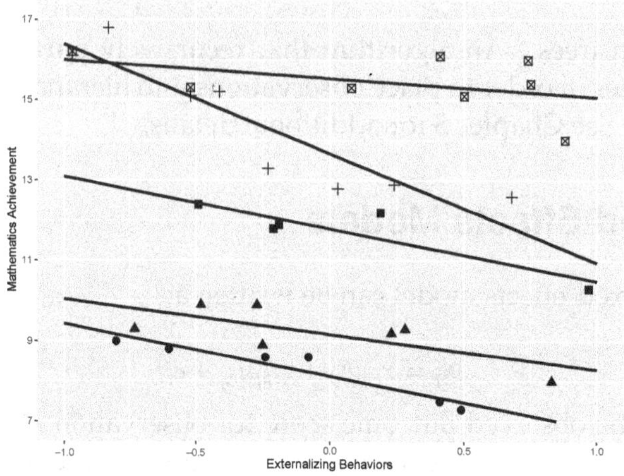

behavior and mathematics achievement, and e_{ij} is the residual for student i in school j.

Figure 9.1 is a hypothetical scatterplot for these data with different symbols used to represent different schools and regression lines for each school. The regression lines have different intercepts leading to different predicted mathematics achievement scores when externalizing behaviors equal zero (i.e., $\beta_{00} + u_{0j}$), and different slopes for the association between externalizing behavior and mathematics achievement in each school (i.e., $\beta_{10} + u_{1j}$). The model in Equation 9.2 could be extended to include additional student-level variables (e.g., social economic status) as well as school-level variables (e.g., school size). The school-level variables could affect the intercept (mathematics achievement when externalizing behavior equals zero) as well as the strength of the association (slope) between externalizing behavior (or any other within-cluster variable) and mathematics achievement.

In the social and behavioral sciences, the mixed-effects model in Equation 9.2 is often written with separate equations for the the observation-level (level-1) and cluster-level (level-2) models. That is, the observation-level model can be written as

$$math_{ij} = b_{0j} + b_{1j} \cdot ext_{ij} + e_{ij}, \tag{9.3}$$

where b_{0j} is the random intercept or predicted math score for school j when $ext_{ij} = 0$, b_{1j} is the random slope or predicted rate of change in $math_{ij}$ for a one-unit change in ext_{ij} in school j, and e_{ij} is the observation-level residual. The random intercept, b_{0j}, and slope, b_{1j}, from the observation-level model can then be specified as dependent variables in the cluster-level model as

$$\begin{aligned} b_{0j} &= \beta_{00} + u_{0j} \\ b_{1j} &= \beta_{10} + u_{1j} \end{aligned} \tag{9.4}$$

where β_{00} and β_{10} are fixed-effects parameters and u_{0j} and u_{1j} are the random effects. In this format, additional observation-level predictor variables are included in Equation 9.3 and cluster-level predictor variables are included in Equation 9.4.

9.3 Machine Learning with Clustered Data

Machine learning methods have been developed to handle clustered data because biased results can be found when the clustering of observations is not taken into consideration (Miller, McArtor, & Lubke, 2017). Machine learning methods for clustered data are particularly important when there is a mix of observation-level and cluster-level variables, and when sample sizes differ across the clusters. Thus, several R packages were developed to perform a variety of machine learning techniques with clustered data. We focus our attention on extensions of *recursive partitioning* and *regularized regression* for mixed-effects models, and illustrate these techniqes with longitudinal data.

9.3.1 Recursive Partitioning with Mixed-Effects Models

For the past few decades, researchers have developed recursive partitioning algorithms to examine individual change trajectories with mixed-effects models. Abdollel, LeBlanc, Stephens, and Harrison (2002) were the first to combine the linear mixed-effects model with a recursive partitioning algorithm to search for person-level (i.e., cluster-level) variables to explain heterogeneity in change trajectories. In this approach, person-level covariates partition the data into two nodes, a user-specified linear mixed-effects model is estimated within each node, and the −2 log-likelihood (−2*LL*) for each node is retained. The sum of the node-level −2*LL* is computed and compared to the −2*LL* when the data are not partitioned, with the partition of the data that minimizes the −2*LL* retained if the overall improvement in −2*LL* is greater than a user-provided criterion. While Abdollel and colleagues' focus was on studying determinants of change processes and cluster-level predictors, the integration of recursive partitioning and the linear mixed-effects model provided a framework to apply recursive partitioning to all types of clustered data and predictors (observation-level and cluster-level predictors).

Hajjem, Bellavance, and Larocqu (2011) and Sela and Simonoff (2012) extended Abdolell and colleagues' work with their work developing the RE-EM (random effects using the EM algorithm) tree algorithm. This work was focused on the prediction of observation-level scores as opposed to cluster-level differences and was designed to simultaneously handle observation-level predictors and cluster-level predictors. Thus, observations within the same cluster can be partitioned into different nodes. In this approach, indicator (dummy) variables are used to construct the decision tree in a mixed-effects model. Thus, there is a single set of random-effects parameters for all nodes. Given the differences between these approaches, the RE-EM algorithm has been shown to be better for prediction (Stegmann, Jacobucci, Serang, & Grimm, 2018), but lacks structure because indicator variables are used to form the decision tree structure. Abdollel's algorithm can be specified similarly to the RE-EM algorithm by having an empty random intercept model within each node; however, constraints on the variance of the random intercept across nodes cannot be implemented.

Several variants of the recursive partitioning algorithm for mixed-effects have been proposed. First, Fu and Simonoff (2015) extended the RE-EM tree (Sela & Simonoff, 2012) algorithm to account for variable selection bias (i.e., variables with more unique values are more likely to be chosen) using the conditional inference trees (ctree; Hothorn et al., 2006) algorithm. Another variant of recursive partitioning for longitudinal data is the mixed-effects model for longitudinal trees (MELTs) algorithm proposed by Eo and Cho (2014). The focus of this algorithm is on predictors of random slopes, which partitions the data based on cluster-level covariates. At each node, a linear mixed-effects model is fit, and the individual slopes for each individual are computed. The partition that minimizes the distance between the individuals' slopes and the mean slope at the node is chosen. Thus, this approach is viable when the focus is on finding moderators of observation-level associations. In the past few years, several extensions of these models have improved the utility and applicability of these models. For example, Fokkema, Smits, Zeileis, Hothorn, and Kelderman (2018) proposed the generalized linear mixed-effects model tree (GLMM tree) algorithm, which allows for non-Gaussian outcomes (e.g., count) and model-based (MOB; Zeileis, Hothorn, & Hornik, 2008) partitioning. In the GLMM tree algorithm the random-effects parameters are held invariant across nodes, which is similar to the RE-EM tree algorithm; however, GLMM tree allows for greater flexibility similar to the work by Abdollel et al. (2002). Stegmann, Jacobucci, Serang, and Grimm (2018) extended Abdollel et al.'s approach to allow for nonlinear mixed-effects models (e.g., exponential models) and Serang, Jacobucci, Grimm, Stegmann, and Brandmaier (2020a) integrated the CART algorithm with M*plus* to allow for more complex multilevel models within each node (e.g., multivariate outcomes).

Software

The first software package was developed by Abdolell et al. (2002), who utilized the macro language in `SAS` and the `PROC MIXED` (Singer, 1998) procedure. Their implementation was then developed into the `R` package `longRPart` (Stewart & Abdollell, 2012), which paired the classification and regression tree algorithm from `rpart` (Therneau & Atkinson, 2019) for use with the `lme` frunction from the `nlme` (Pinheiro et al., 2017) package. While this package is no longer available in `R`, Jacobucci, Stewart, Abdolell, Serang, and Stegmann (2017) updated this package, and it is available as the `longRPart2` package, which also allows for nonlinear mixed-effects models through the intergration with the `nlme` package (Pinheiro et al., 2017). The GLMM tree algorithm is available in the `glmertree` package, and combines the conditional inference tree algorithm from the `partykit` package (Hothorn et al., 2006) with the `lme4` (Bates, Maechler, Bolker, & Walker, 2015) package for mixed-effects models. The RE-EM tree algorithm from Sela and Simonoff (2012) is available in the `REEMtree` package, which uses the CART algorithm; however, adjustments can be made to integrate the conditional inference tree algorithm (see http://people.stern.nyu.edu/jsimonof/unbiasedREEM). Lastly the `MplusTrees` package (Serang et al., 2020) is available in `R`, which integrates `rpart` with M*plus*; however, the M*plus* software (Muthén, & Muthén, 2017) is necessary to use the `MplusTrees` package.

9.3.2 Algorithm

In this chapter, we focus on the standard recursive partitioning algorithm (from `rpart`) and allow for a researcher-specified mixed-effects model within each node (as opposed to the indicator approach in RE-EM tree). Given a mixed-effects model and a set of predictor (partitioning) variables, the algorithm proceeds in the following steps:

1. A stopping threshold k is specified, where k represents the minimum improvement in the $-2LL$ to retain a partition the data.

2. The mixed-effects model is estimated using the full sample and the $-2LL$ is retained. This is refered to as the *root* $(-2LL)$.

3. Set *base*$(-2LL)$ to *root* $(-2LL)$.

4. Given *a numeric* partitioning variable, w_{1i}, the data are partitioned based on each unique value c of the variable ($w_{1i} < c$ versus $w_{1i} \geq c$).

5. The mixed-effects model is estimated on each partition, the two $-2LL$ are obatined, and referred to as $node_1(-2LL)$ and $node_2(-2LL)$.

6. The $-2LL$ for the partition ($node\,(-2LL)$) is calculated as $node\,(-2LL) = node_1(-2LL) + node_2(-2LL)$.

7. Steps 4, 5, and 6 are repeated for each variable in the predictor set.

8. If $base\,(-2LL) - node\,(-2LL) < k$ for all partitions, then the algorithm is stopped and the data are not further partitioned.

9. If $base\,(-2LL) - node\,(-2LL) > k$ for some set of partitions, then the data are partitioned based on the predictor variable and value that resulted in the greatest improvement in $-2LL$ (e.g., $\min\,(node\,(-2LL))$).

10. Steps 3 through 9 are repeated within each node with $base\,(-2LL)$ set equal to $node_1(-2LL)$ and $node_2(-2LL)$ for each child node, respectively.

The stopping threshold k can be set to a specific value (e.g., 20) or based on the $root\,(-2LL)$. For example, $k = 0.01 \times root\,(-2LL)$, such that the improvement in model fit must be greater than 1% of the $-2LL$ when the model is estimated on the full sample. At a minimum, k should be set equal to $\chi^2_{0.95}\,(p)$, where p is the difference in the number of estimated parameters when partitioning the data.

9.4 Regularization with Mixed-Effects Models

A second machine learning technique that has been integrated into the mixed-effects modeling framework is regularization—primarily used with the lasso penalty for variable selection. In regularized mixed-effects models, the fixed-effects parameters are often penalized to examine which effects should be retained in the model; however, approaches have also penalized random-effects parameters to determine which slopes should be random and which slopes should be fixed (estimated without a random-effect component). The parameters in regularized mixed-effects models are found by minimizing the $-2LL$ with a penalty for the size of model parameters. That is, the -2 log-likelihood for the mixed-effects model is

$$-2LL = n\log\left(2\pi\sigma_e^2\right) + \log\left(|I + \mathbf{Z}\Phi\mathbf{Z}'|\right) + \frac{1}{\sigma_e^2}\left(y_i - \mathbf{X}\beta\right)'\left(I + \mathbf{Z}\Phi\mathbf{Z}'\right)\left(y_i - \mathbf{X}\beta\right) \tag{9.5}$$

where **X** and **Z** are known design matrices, β is a matrix of fixed-effects parameters, Φ is the variance-covariance matrix for the random effects, σ_e^2 is the observation level residual variance, n is the sample size and **I** is an identity matrix. In the lasso mixed-effects models,

$$f_{lasso} = -2LL + \lambda\, \Sigma_{p=1}^{P} \left|\beta_p\right| \tag{9.6}$$

where λ is the penalty and $\Sigma_{p=1}^{P} \left|\beta_p\right|$ is the sum of absolute values of the P fixed-effects parameter estimates. As the penalty, λ, increases, the fixed-effects estimates shrink and will eventually be set to 0. If the penalty is 0, then the fixed-effects parameters are not penalized and the estimates are equal to those obtained via a standard mixed-effects modeling program. The value of λ is varied from a low value to a high value and an optimal value is often chosen through cross-validation (i.e., k-fold cross-validation) or through an index of model fit that accounts for model complexity (e.g., Bayesian information criterion).

Software

There are multiple packages for incoroporating regularization into mixed-effects models. Specific to our goals is the method developed by Schelldorfer, Bühlmann, and van de Geer (2011) and implemented in the `R` package `lmmlasso` (Schelldorfer, 2011). For generalized linear mixed-effects models, there exists an extension (Schelldorfer, Meier, & Bühlmann, 2014) of the method developed by Schelldorfer et al. (2011) and implemented in the `glmmixedlasso` package (Schelldorfer, 2012). We note that Groll and Tutz (2014) developed a similar approach, which is implemented in the `glmmLasso` package (Groll, 2017), however, the fixed effects are penalized in this approach as opposed to random effects.

9.5 Illustrative Example

Longitudinal data are analyzed from the `ECLS-K`. Our goal is to determine whether this set of easily collected variables measured at the beginning of kindergarten can account for differences in the change trajectories for reading abilities assessed during the first two years of school.

The outcomes of interest are the reading *theta* scores from the public use dataset. These scores are estimated ability scores based on the reading questions asked and answered by the children. These scores ranged from −2.644 to 2.122 for the children assessed in kindergarten through first grade. Observed reading trajectories from a 1% random sample of children are contained in Figure 9.2. From this figure, we see that the trajectories are fairly linear over time, with large between-child differences in both performance at the beginning of kindergarten and the rate of change over time.

To begin, a linear mixed-effects model was fit to the reading scores with the time metric years beginning September 1, 1998, which was approximately the average first day of school in kindergarten, with the intercept centered at this date. This linear mixed-effects model can be written as

$$y_{ti} = (\beta_0 + u_{0i}) + (\beta_1 + u_{1i}) \cdot (x_{ti} - 0.25) + e_{ti} \tag{9.7}$$

where β_0 is the fixed effect for the intercept with u_{0i} as its associated random effect, β_1 is the fixed effect for the linear slope with u_{1i} as its associated random effect, x_{ti} is the timing metric (years beginning September 1, 1998), and e_{ti} is the time-dependent residual. We subtracted 0.25 from the timing metric variable so that the intercept is centered around the timing of the first assessment (approximately one quarter of the way through the kindergarten year). The random effects are assumed to follow a multivariate normal distribution with zero means and a fully specified covariance matrix, $u_{0i}, u_{1i} \sim N(0, \Psi)$. The time-dependent residual is assumed to be normally distributed with a zero mean and time-invariant variance σ_e^2.

As a basis for comparison, the linear mixed-effects model in Equation 9.7 was estimated using the `nlme` function in the `nlme` package. The $-2LL$ for the linear mixed-effects model was 33,056.9. We retain this information for now, and return to model fit information when discussing results from machine learning techniques. The fixed effect for the intercept was −0.89 and the fixed effect for the slope was 1.03, suggesting that, on average, children had a score of −0.89 in the fall of kindergarten and that score changed 1.03 points per year. This rate of change is fairly substantial given the random-effects parameters. The standard deviation of the random intercept was 0.52 and the standard deviation of the random slope was 0.16. Thus, the average yearly change represented approximately two standard deviations of the between-child differences in scores from the fall of kindergarten. The intercept and slope were negatively associated with an estimated correlation of −0.56. Finally, the standard deviation of the residual was 0.24.

9.5.1 Recursive Partitioning

The longitudinal data were run through the `longRPart2`, `glmertree`, and `REEMtree` packages to examine early predictors of the longitudinal reading scores using recursive partitioning algorithms. In `longRPart2` and

FIGURE 9.2. Longitudinal reading data.

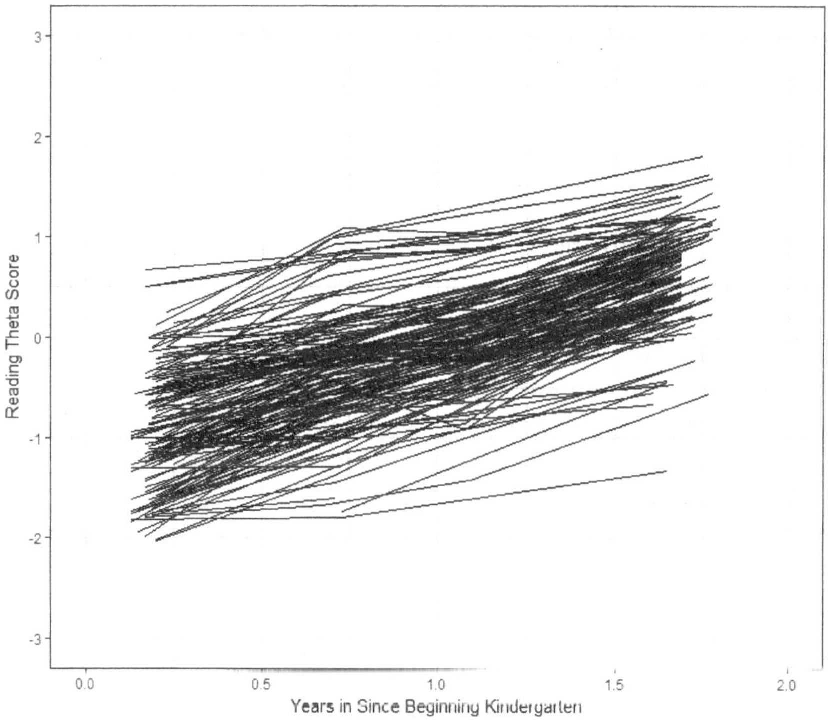

`glmertree`, a linear mixed-effects model with a random intercept and slope (for the timing metric variable) was estimated in each node. The notable difference between `longRPart2` and `glmertree` is that `glmertree` estimates a single set of random effects parameters (i.e., Φ and σ_e^2) for all nodes and `longRPart2` estimates the full mixed-effects model within each node. The stopping rules in `longRPart2` and `glmertree` were set to similar values with `MINSPLIT=500` (minimum number of observations to partition a node) and the improvement in $-2LL$ ($\approx$74). The demographic characteristics and parent rating variables were used as potential splitting variables. In `REEMtree`, a random intercept model was specified within each node with the timing variable, demographic characteristics, and parent rating variables used as potential splitting variables. A random slope (for the timing variable) can be specified in `REEMtree`; however, there is no associated fixed-effect for the slope. Thus, the random intercept model was specified.

longRPart2

The linear mixed-effects model was specified using the `lrp` function (`method= "lme"`) with the `cp`, which controls how much of an improvement in $-2LL$ is needed to retain the split, set to 0.002. This means that each split must reduce the $-2LL$ by 74.00 units (i.e., $0.00224 \cdot 33,037.9$), which is a fairly sizeable improvement in fit for a single split (note: when a split is made, the number of estimated parameters increases by six).

The decision tree from `longRPart2` is depicted in Figure 9.3. The decision tree highlights the variable splits and the deviance ($-2LL$) for the linear mixed-effects model in each node. The deviance values can be used to examine how much model fit improved due to the partition in the data. For example, the root deviance was 33,056.92 and the deviance after the first partition on father's education (`daded`) was 31,496.00 ($15,662.16 + 15,833.84$), an improvement of 1,560.92, which is a fairly large improvement in model fit. The `longRPart2` decision had seven terminal nodes.

The decision rules for each node are shown in Algorithm 3. In this text output from `longRPart2`, the nodes are numbered to correspond to Figure 9.3, the partitions of the data are hierarchically structured, and the values include the partition of the data (e.g., `daded < 4.5`), the sample size in the node (e.g., `16855`), the deviance (e.g., `15662.160`), and the mean value of the outcome for that node (e.g., `1.0613110`). This output is particularly helpful because the reported split values are accurately displayed. For example, the partition on approaches to learning (`app_ln`) was 3.125, whereas the splitting value in Figure 9.3 was 3.1. The variables used in the decision tree included *father's educational level* (`daded`), *poverty status* (`poor`), *mother's*

FIGURE 9.3. `longRPart2` tree.

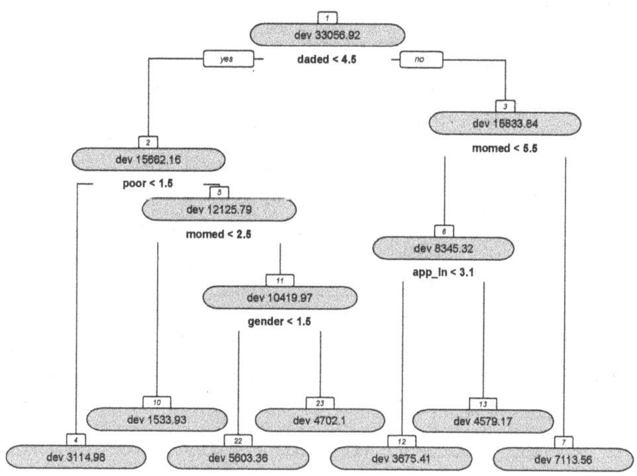

educational level (`momed`), *approaches to learning* (`app_ln`), which is a measure of attention and focus, and *gender* (`gender`).

Algorithm 3 `longRPart2` Decision Tree Nodes

```
1) root 36466 33056.920 1.0325550
2) daded < 4.5 16855 15662.160 1.0613110
4) poor < 1.5 3154  3114.981 1.0579940 *
5) poor >=1.5 13701 12125.790 1.0628380
10) momed < 2.5 1561  1533.931 1.1043460 *
11) momed >=2.5 12140 10419.970 1.0580860
22) gender < 1.5 6067  5603.362 1.0625080 *
23) gender >=1.5 6073  4702.098 1.0539520 *
3) daded >=4.5 19611 15833.840 1.0068780
6) momed < 5.5 10160  8345.322 1.0378900
12) app_ln < 3.125 4419  3675.407 1.0560330 *
13) app_ln >=3.125 5741  4579.168 1.0236320 *
7) momed >=5.5 9451  7113.559 0.9730953 *
```

In each terminal node, the linear mixed-effects model is fully estimated. Parameters for the terminal nodes (labeled node 4, 10, 22, 23, 12, 13, and 7) are contained in Table 9.1. The major difference between the terminal nodes was in the fixed-effect estimate for the intercept; however, we note that there are fairly sizable differences in the random-effects parameter estimates. For example, the standard deviation of the random intercept ranged from 1.48 to 2.35, and the correlation between the intercept and slope was negative

TABLE 9.1. Parameters Estimates of the Mixed-Effects Model in Each Terminal Node

Parameter	Node						
	4	10	22	23	12	13	7
$\hat{\beta}_0$	-1.31	-1.26	-1.05	-0.93	-0.95	-0.78	-0.60
$\hat{\beta}_1$	1.06	1.10	1.06	1.05	1.06	1.02	0.97
$\sqrt{\hat{\psi}_{00}}$	1.48	1.51	1.79	1.82	1.96	2.21	2.35
$\sqrt{\hat{\psi}_{11}}$	0.50	0.48	0.63	0.45	0.65	0.73	0.82
$\hat{\rho}_{10}$	0.12	0.01	-0.38	-0.63	-0.53	-0.66	-0.69
$\hat{\sigma}_e$	0.27	0.27	0.25	0.24	0.24	0.23	0.22

in some terminal nodes (Nodes 22, 23, 12, 13, and 7) and near zero in other terminal nodes (Nodes 4 and 10).

In addition to the decision tree and parameter estimates for each node, `longRPart2` provides variable importance indices from `rpart`. The most important variables were mother's education and father's education (variable importance $\approx$20% for mother's and father's education) with weaker importance values for poverty status ($\approx$10%), gender ($\approx$5%), and approaches to learning ($\approx$5%).

9.5.2 `glmertree`

The `lmertree` function from the `glmertree` package was specified with a minimum number of observations to partition a node set to 500 and an alpha level set to 1×10^{-16}. The small alpha level was used to limit the number of partitions given the large sample size. This alpha level leads to a necessary improvement in model (in a likelihood ratio test) equal to $\chi^2 \sim 73.5$ to retain a partition.

The resulting decision tree from `lmertree` is contained in Figure 9.4. This figure contains the partitioning variable in the node and the partitioning values on the connections between the nodes. Also contained in the node is a probability value for the partition. These probability values are based on permutation tests following the conditional inference tree approach (Hothorn et al., 2006), and are all $p < 0.001$ because of our stopping rule related to `alpha`. The first set of partitions from `lmertree` were highly similar to those made by `longRPart2` with the first few partitions based on father's education, poverty status, and mother's education.

The text output of the decision tree is contained in Algorithm 4. In this output, the node number is listed along with the partitioning variable and value. For each terminal node, the sample size is reported along with the estimate for the fixed effect of the intercept and slope for the node. For

FIGURE 9.4. `glmertree` decision tree.

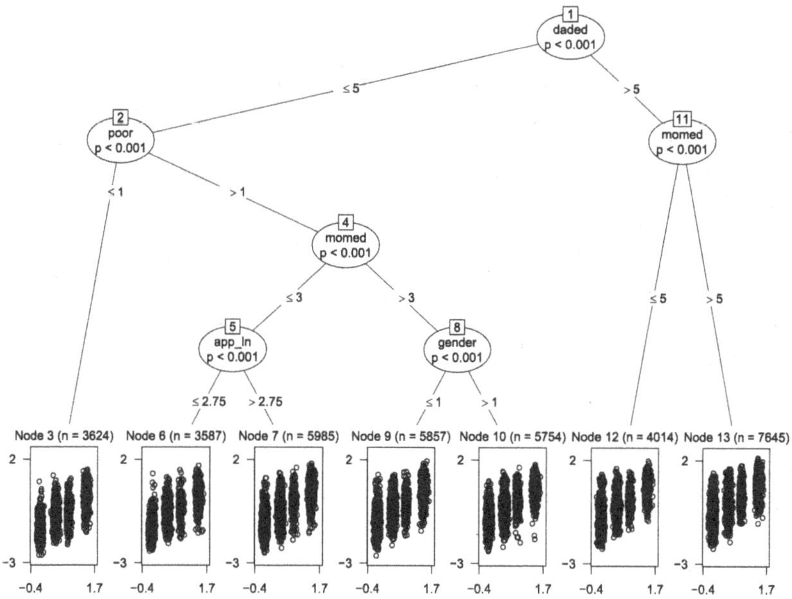

example, the first terminal node is number 3, which is obtained by `daded <= 5` and `poor <= 1`. In this terminal node, the sample size is 3,624 and the fixed-effect estimates for the intercept and slope were −1.29 and 1.06, respectively.

The terminal node parameter estimates from `lmertree` are contained in Table 9.2 with the fixed-effects parameter estimates followed by the random-effects parameter estimates. While there are fixed-effects parameter estimates for each node, there is a single set of random-effects parameter estimates for all nodes. The random-effects parameter estimates for the random intercept and slope from `lmertree` are notably smaller than those obtained from `longRPart2`. This is likely due to the additional partitions of the data from `lmertree` as well as the differences in the model specification.

9.5.3 `REEMtree`

The `REEMtree` function from the `REEMtree` package was used and specified with default stopping criteria (tree is constructed with cross-validation using a minimum `cp` parameter [`cp` from `rpart`] equal to 0.001). The partitioning variables included the demographic characteristics and parent rating variables as well as the timing variable (`time_c25`). The random effect for the intercept was specified.

Algorithm 4 An Abridged Output of `lmertree` Decision Tree Nodes

```
Fitted party:
[1] root
|   [2] daded <= 5
|   |   [3] poor <= 1: n = 3624
|   |     (Intercept)    time_c25
|   |      -1.285138    1.064815
|   |     [4] poor > 1
|   |     |   [5] momed <= 3
|   |     |   |   [6] app_ln <= 2.75: n = 3587
...

Number of inner nodes: 6
Number of terminal nodes: 7
Number of parameters per node: 2
Objective function (residual sum of squares): 1272.156
```

TABLE 9.2. `lmertree` Node Parameter Estimates

	Node Specific Estimates	
Node	Intercept	Slope
3	-1.29	1.06
6	-1.18	1.09
7	-1.00	1.07
9	-0.94	1.05
10	-0.81	1.02
12	-0.76	1.02
13	-0.57	0.97
	Whole Sample Estimates	
	Random Intercept Standard Deviation	0.47
	Random Slope Standard Deviation	0.15
	Correlation between Random Intercept and Slope	-0.52
	Residual Standard Deviation	0.24

The text for the decision tree is contained in Algorithm 5. Similar to `longRPart2`, the text listing of the nodes contains the node number (e.g., 8), the current split (e.g., `daded<5.5`), the sample size (e.g., `7821`), the deviance (e.g., `454.50770`), and the estimate for the fixed effect of the intercept (e.g., `-1.13617000`). An * at the end of the line indicates that the node is a terminal node. A benefit of the text, compared to the plot of the decision tree, is having fixed effects estimates for nonterminal nodes.

Algorithm 5 `REEMtree` Decision Tree Nodes

```
1) root 36466 16001.12000 -0.30273470
2) time_c25 <  0.875 25485 4735.33700 -0.65229520
4) time_c25 <  0.265 11545 984.38550 -1.02360900
8) daded <  5.5 7821 454.50770 -1.13617000 *
9) daded >= 5.5 3724 222.43020 -0.78725520 *
5) time_c25 >= 0.265 13940 840.91550 -0.34477590
10) daded < 5.5 9518 442.55190 -0.43242280
20) time_c25 <  0.68 8010 322.90660 -0.46977620 *
21) time_c25 >= 0.68 1508 48.96003 -0.23421640 *
11) daded >= 5.5 4422 167.86790 -0.15612290
22) time_c25 <  0.565 3730 119.60870 -0.19144810 *
23) time_c25 >= 0.565 692 18.74574 0.03340346 *
3) time_c25 >= 0.875 10981 924.47680 0.50853450
6) time_c25 <  1.135 861 37.87261 -0.04365325 *
7) time_c25 >= 1.135 10120 601.47300 0.55553620
14) daded <  5.5 6924 333.50000 0.47984130 *
15) daded >= 5.5 3196 141.99900 0.71962570 *
```

The first few partitions were all based on the timing variable. The first three partitions of data essentially splits the longitudinal data in the four assessment periods. That is, observations with the timing variable less than 0.265 (i.e., `time_c25 < 0.265`), observations with timing values between 0.265 and 0.875 (i.e., `0.265` ≤ `time_c25 < 0.875`), observations with timing values between 0.875 and 1.135 (i.e., `0.875` ≤ `time_c25 < 1.135`), and observations with timing values greater than 1.135 (i.e., `time_c25` ≥ `1.135`). After these partitions, *father's educational level* was used to partition the data in three of the four nodes. In all nodes, the partitioning values was 5.5, which is a value between "some college" and "bachelor's degree." The timing variable was then used to partition the data where the timing variable is between 0.265 and 0.875 after it was partitioned by father's education with a value of 5.5. In each terminal node, the estimated fixed effect for the intercept is the value reported in the decision tree.

The estimated parameters for the terminal nodes are contained in Table 9.3. As discussed, each terminal node has an estimated fixed effect for the intercept; however, there is a single set of random-effects parameters for the

TABLE 9.3. `REEMtree` Node Parameter Estimates

Node Specific Estimates	
Node	Intercept
8	-1.14
9	-0.79
20	-0.47
21	-0.23
22	-0.19
23	0.03
6	-0.04
14	0.48
15	0.72
Whole Sample Estimates	
Random Intercept SD	0.45
Residual SD	0.26

decision tree. The estimated standard deviation of the random intercept was 0.45 and the standard deviation of the residual was 0.26. The estimate for the standard deviation of the random intercept is similar to the value estimated in the glmertree package and the residual standard deviation is similar across all three packages for performing recursive partitioning with mixed-effects model. The `REEMtree` package estimates this model similarly to `glmertree`, such that the model is not separately estimated for each node, but estimated as a single model with dummy codes to indicate the node where the obervation falls. Thus, `glmertree` is very similar to `REEMtree`; however, `glmertree` is a bit more flexible in the specification of the within-node model (to include fixed effects for the slopes).

9.5.4 Regularization

The `lmmlasso` package in `R` was used to analyze the longitudinal reading data to perform lasso variable selection with linear mixed-effects models. The linear mixed-effects model was specified with the explanatory variables included as predictors of the intercept and slope (for the time variable, `time_c25`). The predictor variables were all standardized to have a mean of 0 and a standard deviation of 1 to account for differences in their scale. Following Grimm, Jacobucci, Stegmann, and Serang (2022), the effects from the explanatory variables to the intercept were penalized in the first stage and the effects from the explanatory to the slope were penalized in the second stage with the effects to the intercept retained from the first stage included.

Penalty values were examined in two stages. First, penalty values ranged from no penalty ($\lambda = 0$) to a value that set all effects to 0

($\lambda = 15,000$[1]), with penalty values incrementing in steps of 500. This first step provided an optimal range of values for λ, which was more closely examined in the second step. In the second stage, λ ranged from 3,500 to 6,500 in steps of 30. The optimal penalty value was chosen based on the BIC-500, a measure of model fit proposed by Grimm et al. (2022) and represents the value of the Bayesian information criterion for the model if the sample size was 500. This was proposed to balance model fit and the penalty for each parameter in the BIC, which is small for high sample sizes like we have in the ECLS-K data. We applied the same two-stage approach to determine an optimal value of λ when examining the effects to the slope.

The optimal λ value for the intercept was 5,000, which shrunk all of the effects to the intercept to zero with the exception of father's education and poverty status. These effects were then retained while the effects to the random slope were penalized to determine an optimal value of λ for these effects. In the first stage, λ values ranged from 0 to 8,000 in steps of 250. In the second stage we examined λ values between 2,500 and 7,000 in steps of 50. The λ value with the lowest BIC-500 was 7,000 with no effects to the slope retained. This is fairly common in mixed-effects models because there is much lower power to detect effects on random slopes compared to random intercepts. Thus, it may make sense to have different criteria to determine which effects to retain when predicting random slopes versus random intercepts, particularly if the goal is to retain parameters of a given effect size.

The lasso mixed-effects model retained two effects on the random intercept (*father's education* and *poverty status*) and no effects on the random slope when using the BIC-500 as the selection criterion. Now that certain effets were retained, a mixed-effect model was fit using the `lme` function from `nlme` package with only father's education and poverty status as predictors of the random intercept. This approach follows the relaxed lasso (Meinshausen, 2007), and lets us retain the natural scale of the variable (i.e., unstandardized); however, we did subtract 1 from the father's education and poverty status variables, so a value of 0 was observed. The parameters of this model are contained in Table 9.4. Father's education had a positive effect on the intercept and poverty status had a positive effect on the intercept (children above the federal poverty line had higher intercepts than those below the federal poverty line).

[1]Note that the scale of λ differs markedly from regression and SEM models as the scale of the fit function (log-likelihood) is on a larger scale.

TABLE 9.4. Parameter Estimates from the Relaxed Lasso

Parameter	Estimate (S.E.)	t-value	p-value
$\hat{\beta}_{00}$	-1.39 (0.013)	-105.77	$< .001$
$\hat{\beta}_{01}$ (father's education)	0.08 (0.002)	36.61	$< .001$
$\hat{\beta}_{02}$ (poverty status)	0.24 (0.01)	18.01	$< .001$
$\hat{\beta}_{10}$	1.03 (0.003)	390.76	$< .001$
$\sqrt{\hat{\psi}_{00}}$	0.47		
$\sqrt{\hat{\psi}_{11}}$	0.16		
$\hat{\rho}_{10}$	-0.53		
$\hat{\sigma}_e$	0.24		

9.6 Additional Strategies for Mining Longitudinal Data

In this chapter we focused on machine learning methods to examine cluster-level predictors in linear mixed-effects models. We did not focus on methods that could explore the nature of the association between observation-level variables. For example, in our illustrative work we assumed a linear association between reading achievement and time in school. Two popular machine learning algorithms that can be used to explore associations between observation-level variables in a mixed-effects modeling context are *piecewise splines models* and *generalized additive models*.

9.6.1 Piecewise Spline Models

Piecewise spline models are a commonly applied algorithm in single-level data. With single-level data, splines are able to model nonlinear relationships between a predictor and outcome by partitioning the predictor and fitting a simple model (typically a linear model) within each partition. The type of function fit within each partition of the predictor variable is referred to as the *basis* function. In addition to specifying the basis function, researchers typically need to specify the location of the knot point, or point on the predictor variable where the functions join, and the number of knot points. Although these aspects of piecewise spline models are typically specified by the researcher, multivariate adaptive regression splines (MARS; Friedman, 1991) were developed to automate variable selection, as well as the number and location of knot points. Typically, linear basis functions are used; however, higher-level terms (e.g., squared terms and product terms) can be included when performing variable selection.

The piecewise spline model with linear segments can be written as

$$\hat{y}_i = b_0 + \sum_{k=1}^{M} b_k(x_i - \tau_k)^*$$

where $(x_i - \tau_k)^*$ is either the negatively truncated function $(x_i - \tau_k)^-$ or the positively truncated function $(x_i - \tau_k)^+$, τ_k is the kth knot point, and b_k is the regression coefficient.

Going beyond the use of MARS, a number of variations on splines exist. First, there are cubic splines, natural cubic splines, restricted cubic splines, and smoothing splines that produce spline models with greater flexibility and smooth transitions at the knot point (see Harrell (2015) and Wang (2011) for more detail). Second, and relevant for this chapter is that spline models can be integrated into more complex models, such as mixed-effects models by allowing for the inclusion of random effects (Zhang, 1997, 1999, 2004). Zhang and He's (2009) MASAL algorithm combines linear mixed-effects models with the MARS algorithm to search for nonlinearity in associations between observation-level variables through the use of piecewise splines. The MASAL algorithm was available in `R` through the `masal` package, but the package is no longer available. However, a stand-alone version of the algorithm is available at https://publichealth.yale.edu/c2s2/software/masal/.

9.6.2 Generalized Additive Models

Generalized additive models (GAMs; Hastie & Tibshirani, 1986; Wood, 2017) fit a sum (the additive piece) of smooth functions, with the smooth function able to take on a number of flexible forms, including splines (smoothing, linear, cubic, etc.). GAMs can take the general form of

$$\hat{y}_i = f_1(x_{1i}) + f_2(x_{2i}) + f_3(x_{1i}x_{2i}) + f_4(x_{3i}) + f_3(x_{1i}x_{3i}) + f_3(x_{2i}x_{3i}) + f_3(x_{1i}x_{2i}x_{3i}) + \ldots$$

where each smoothing function $f()$ can take one of many forms and include either a single variable or multiple variables. The main distinction between GAMs and MARS is in the use of splines, where GAMs typically account for nonlinearities with smooth functions as opposed to only piecewise splines. This leads to a higher degree of complexity in GAMs compared to piecewise splines. The choice between the algorithms typically rests with the researcher to determine whether smooth or rough transition points make more theoretical sense.

GAMs have been extended in multiple ways. For example, GAMs can include autoregressive parameters (Bringmann et al., 2017) and the have been used for single-case designs (Sullivan, Shadish, & Steiner, 2015).

Additionally, GAMs have been extended to include random-effects parameters (generalized additive mixed models; GAMMs; McKeown & Sneddon, 2014). Within the `mgcv` package, the `gamm` function allows researchers to specify random effects within the model. In addition to the MGCV package, the `gamm4` package combines the `mgcv` package and the `lme4` package for fitting mixed-effects models. In GAMMs, researchers can specify whether the smoothing functions can differ across clusters. This allows for a host of flexible specifications that can take into account additional features of the data. Readers are referred to Wood (2017) for additional detail on GAMs.

9.7 Summary

The combination of mixed-effects models with machine learning algorithms is a powerful combination for performing variable selection and potentially examining nonlinear and interactive associations while accounting for the dependency in the data. However, further work is needed to determine how best to incorporate recursive partitioning and regularization into mixed-effects models. In recursive partitioning, `longRPart2` implements a multiple group approach, whereas `glmertree` and `reemtree` include terminal nodes as a categorical variable (`as.factor` in `R`), which only allows for fixed-effects parameters to differ across nodes. These differences in specification will lead to different tree structures and different conclusions, and we encourage researchers to use multiple approaches because it is likely that the approach that works best for a given research question is going to be data dependent. In terms of regularization, there are approaches that focus on the fixed-effects parameters as discussed here, but also approaches that attend to the random-effects parameters in an attempt to determine which, if any, random slopes should be included in the model. A remaining challenge for all of these approaches is model selection. While a form of cross-validation (e.g., multiple *k*-fold cross-validation) is often implemented in the regression context, the combination of machine learning methods and mixed-effects models leads to a computational burden that makes cross-validation very time consuming. Thus, researchers often use a fit index (e.g., BIC, $\Delta - 2LL$) for model selection; however, the choice of fit index and the criterion remains fairly arbitrary (see Grimm, Jacobucci, Stegmann, & Serang, 2022) and more research needs to be conducted in this realm.

9.7.1 Further Reading

- Increases in the collection of data using the experience sampling method (e.g., Larson & Csikszentmihalyi, 2014) or ecological momentary assessment (Shiffman, Stone, & Hufford, 2008), and more recently in passive smartphone data collection (see Reeves et al., 2019; Onnela & Rauch, 2016), have facilitated an increase in the application of machine learning to intensive data. Most notably, the outcome of interest is no longer a single variable, or a small number of variables as in multivariate methods (e.g., SEM). Instead, the outcome can be assessed over a 1,000 times. Additionally, the sample size no longer needs to be in the hundreds, as the number of assessments allows for modeling much smaller number of subjects (Molenaar, 2004). The application of machine learning to this type of data could be the subject of a book unto itself. As a result, we do not discuss this form of modeling further, instead pointing readers to Epskamp et al. (2018) for an overview of dynamic network modeling.

- Given that most longitudinal methods require the use of *long* data, applying *k*-fold CV would entail assigning the holdout partition based on random time points, while using responses from all respondents. Alternatively, multiple *k*-fold strategies exist that take into account the nested structure of the data. Two additional forms of CV, *stratified* and *grouped* (see the documentation for the `brms` package; Bürkner, 2017). Stratified CV attempts to equally partition the number of time points per ID, whereas grouped CV partitions the data by ID resulting in 20% (for 5-fold) of participants are placed in each partition. To partition by *time* as well, see Bulteel, Mestdagh, Tuerlinckx, and Ceulemans (2018) for a discussion.

- While covering the application of regularization and decision trees with mixed-effects models, we notably left out content regarding ensemble methods. This is mostly due to a lack of development in this area. However, there has been some recent research aimed at applying boosting and random forests for models with random effects. Notably, Miller, McArtor, and Lubke (2017) extend boosting for data that have a hierarchical structure, finding improved prediction and variable selection when incorporating grouping in the data. Similar extensions have been made for random forests (Hajjem et al., 2014).

- For a more in-depth overview on the use of mixed-effects models in social and behavioral research, we recommend the following resources depending on the type of data. For application in more traditional longitudinal data, see Grimm, Ram, and Estabrook (2017). See Bolger and Laurenceau (2013) for the specification of mixed-effects models in more intensive data collection studies. Finally, a newer area of application is in incorporating random effects into factor analysis or structural equation models. See Heck and Thomas (2015) for specific application to M*plus*.

9.7.2 Computational Time and Resources

The use of both regularization and trees with mixed-effects models can be computationally expensive. The main factor that drives how long the programs take to run is how long the initial base model takes to run. If the initial base mixed-effects model takes minutes to run, the addition of regularization and trees will likely lead to run-times in the hours. Particularly for tree models, the computational time can be long, with the main factor being the number of covariates and the number of unique values to each covariate. For an initial run of tree models it is recommended to include just a few covariates, preferably variables that have a few unique response options (e.g., binary variables). This will provide a reference for how long the full analysis could take. Additionally, for continous covariates, it is recommended to round to the nearest whole number as this can significantly cut down on the number of unique splits that the algorithm tests.

10

Searching for Groups

Researchers are often interested in assessing heterogeneity with respect to a model of interest. For instance, one extension of finite mixture models is growth mixture models, where the estimation of latent classes is performed with respect to parameters in a latent growth curve model. Finite mixture models have been extended in this way to a number of additional types of models (discussed below). A related approach that assesses the presence of groups with respect to a model of interest is structural equation model (SEM) trees (SEM trees; Brandmaier et al., 2013). In this algorithm, groups are derived through the use of decision trees and assessed with respect to any type of SEM. Whereas mixture models estimates latent classes, SEM trees extract groups based on values of covariate variables. For this chapter, we discuss the use of both mixture models and SEM trees, as we see these two algorithms as the most relevant methods for identifying heterogeneity in social and behavioral research. We accomplish this through highlighting their similarities and distinctions, concluding with a discussion of when either algorithm may be most appropriate.

10.1 Key Terminology

- Mixture model. A probabilistic model that identifies population heterogeneity through the use of latent classes.
- Structural equation model trees. An algorithm that pairs decision trees with structural equation models to identify subgroups among covariates of interest.
- Cluster analysis. An algorithm that identifies deterministic clusters of individuals in the sample of interest.
- Trees. The use of decision trees as a method for splitting the sample into distinct subgroups. See Chapter 5 for an overview of decision trees with a single outcome variable.

- Classes versus groups. In mixture models, the common terminology for the resulting probabilistic subgroups is classes, whereas in trees (SEM trees) it is groups.

- Invariance. The placement of equality constraints within a model to ensure that the same construct of interest is measured in the same way across time or groups.

In psychology and other behavioral sciences, researches often use data to infer group membership. For example, a researcher may administer the Center for Epidemiological Studies Depression Scale (CES-D), and use participants' responses to the items to distinguish two groups of participants, that is, participants with major depression and participants without major depression. Fundamentally, we are assessing whether the participants in our sample come from one population (homogeneity) or multiple distinct populations (heterogeneity). Often, this determination is based on whether each participant's total score (sum of item responses) is greater than a recommended cutoff score (e.g., > 16). The recommended cutoff score may be examined using decision theory analysis and receiver operating characteristic (ROC) curves, examining how the total score predicts a gold standard, such as a clinical evaluation. Once group membership is assigned, it can be used as an outcome or a predictor in subsequent analyses. This approach, while common, does not consider whether items are differentially associated with major depression and does not consider measurement error. Moreover, using a cutoff score to assign group membership is deterministic, and does not consider error in group assignment, which can affect the nature of associations with external variables (whether as an outcome or predictor variable). For these reasons, we examine the use of multiple statistical algorithms for assessing heterogeneity, taking a more algorithmic, and less theoretical, approach to identifying group membership.

In social and behavioral research, two of the most common approaches for identifying heterogeneity are *cluster analysis* (Everitt, Landau, Leese, & Stahl, 2011) and *finite mixture modeling* (McLachlan & Peel, 2004). In both of these approaches, multivariate data can be analyzed; however, finite mixture modeling has greater flexibility for modeling different types of data distributions (e.g., binary, ordinal, categorical, counts, continuous) and group membership is probabilistic (each participant is assigned a probability of belonging to each class). We therefore focus on finite mixture modeling in this chapter. Additionally, many great resources are available on cluster analysis, including James et al. (2013) and Aldenderfer and Blashfield (1984).

10.2 Finite Mixture Model

Finite mixture models are parametric models that combine multiple probability density functions. Generally, the finite mixture model with $k = 1$ to K unobserved (latent) classes can be written as

$$f(y_i) = \sum_{k=1}^{K} \phi_k \cdot f_k(y_i \mid \theta_k) \tag{10.1}$$

where $f(y_i)$ is the probability density function for the data y_i, ϕ_k is the proportion of the population in class k ($0 \leq \phi_k \leq 1$; $\sum_{k=1}^{K} \phi_k = 1$), and $f_k(y_i \mid \theta_k)$ is the probability density function for class k given model parameters of class k, θ_k.

To illustrate a mixture distribution, we've generated two normal distributions that differ in their means and standard deviations. These distributions were multiplied by their proportion in the (made-up) population (0.9 and 0.1), and then summed. The mixture probability density distribution is represented by the *gray* line in Figure 10.1, and the two class probability density distributions are represented by the *black* lines in Figure 10.1. In finite mixture modeling, the observed data would have a distribution following the *gray* line, and the goal would be to infer the presence of the two underlying distributions following the *black* lines. The estimated parameters in this example would include the mean and variance of the distribution for each class (i.e., four estimated parameters), as well as the mixing proportion. The mixing proportion is often estimated as an intercept with one class serving as the baseline category. Thus, five parameters would be estimated for a two-class model with an assumed normal distribution within each class. Once the model is estimated, the probability of each observation belonging to each class can be estimated based on the model's parameters. These probabilities are referred to as *posterior probabilities*.

A major area of flexibility in finite mixture modeling is the class-specific model. That is, different types of models can be specified at the class level, and this leads to different named models. For example, when a factor model is specified within each class, the model is referred to as a *factor mixture model* (Lubke & Muthén, 2005), and when a growth model is specified within each class, the model is referred to as a *growth mixture model* (Muthén & Shedden, 1999). Moreover, constraints can be imposed or relaxed on the class-specific models' parameters across classes, in certain programs, to test different model configurations. For example, in a factor mixture model, constraints can be imposed on the factor loadings and measurement intercepts, which would force class differences to be in the distributions of the common factor and unique factors. Another area of flexibility in finite mixture modeling

FIGURE 10.1. Illustration of mixture distribution.

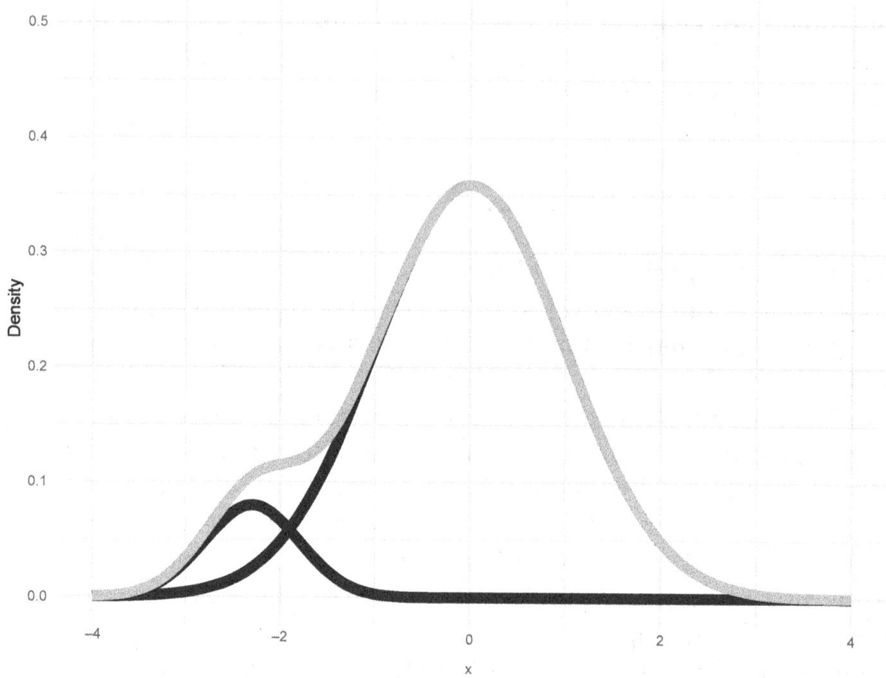

is the distributional form of the outcomes. While this does depend on the statistical program being utilized, finite mixture models can be specified with binary, ordinal, categorical, count, and continuous variables, as well as combinations of different distributional forms.

Prior to the development of a general latent variable modeling framework that incorporated finite mixture distributions (i.e., categorical latent variables), finite mixture models were employed, but there was little flexibility in their specification. This led to different names for models depending on the type of outcome being analyzed and the constraints imposed in the model. For example, latent class analysis (Collins & Lanza, 2009; Goodman, 1974; Lazarsfeld & Henry, 1968) is a finite mixture model with a single latent class variable, applied to binary or ordinal cross-sectional data, and specified with conditional independence. Thus, the binary/ordinal variables were assumed to be uncorrelated within each class and the latent categorical (class) variable was the *cause* of observed correlations in the population. In a latent class analysis, the estimated parameters include the thresholds separating the response categories of the observed variables for each class, and the intercept(s) for the latent class variable. Latent profile analysis (Gibson, 1959; Lazarsfeld & Henry, 1968) is a finite mixture model with a single latent class variable for cross-sectional continuous data that is specified with conditional independence. As in the latent class model, the variables in a latent profile analysis are assumed to be uncorrelated within a given class, with the cause of the correlations in the population due to the latent class variable. The parameters estimated in a latent profile analysis include the means and variances (or standard deviations) of the observed variables within each class and the intercept(s) for the latent class variable. Increased specification flexibility through the incorporation of the finite mixture model in the general latent variable framework led to more options for the specification of finite mixture models. For example, in latent profile analysis, the observed variables can be correlated within each class with variances and correlations constrained to be equal or freely estimated within each class. With certain programs (e.g., M*plus*, Muthén & Muthén, 1998–2017), there is flexibility with respect to the classes in which the constraints are applied. That is, in a 3-class latent profile model, equal variances and correlations can be specified for classes 1 and 2, with class 3 having variances and correlations freely estimated.

10.2.1 Search Procedure and Evaluation

In finite mixture modeling, the number of classes as well as the model and parameters for each class are unknown. Because of this, a comprehensive search is often employed. To simplify the search process, the model type within each class is often assumed to be known (e.g., single-factor confirmatory factor model). This leaves the number of classes and the model's parameters for each class as unknowns. To examine this model space, multiple models are estimated with a different number of classes and different parameter constraints (e.g., factor loadings of the single-factor model constrained to be equal versus freely estimated across classes). For example, Ram and Grimm (2009) laid out an approach for specifying growth mixture models. In this approach, a finite number (e.g., 4) of different model specifications is considered prior to analysis. These model specifications are theoretically derived and of interest to the researchers. Next, these model specifications are then estimated with an increasing number of classes. The number of classes are increased until the model fails to converge or model fit fails to improve. Once the set of models are estimated, they are compared in terms of model fit, model sensitivity, model implications, and classification quality to determine an optimal model or an optimal set of models.

Model comparison by model fit statistics has been a vital area of research in finite mixture modeling. This work often involves simulations, and researchers have made different recommendations regarding which model fit statistics should be employed for model comparison. This work also highlights how such recommendations can be sensitive to the population models considered, models specified, and sample sizes evaluated. We first review different model fit statistics and then discuss our recommendations. Finite mixture models are typically estimated using a form of maximum likelihood estimation, so the first model comparison statistics include information criteria, such as the Akaike information criterion (AIC), the Bayesian information criterion, and variants of these criteria, such as the sample size adjusted BIC and the corrected AIC (AICc). Information criteria combine the model's deviance (-2 log-likelihood [$-2LL$]) to assess how well the model captures the data and a penalty for the number of estimated parameters. Information criteria vary in the size of the penalty. For example, the AIC is $-2LL + 2p$, where $-2LL$ is the model's deviance and p is the number of estimated parameters, whereas the BIC is $-2LL + \ln(N) \cdot p$, where $\ln(N)$ is the natural log of the sample size. Thus, the penalty for an estimated parameter in the AIC is 2, and the penalty in the BIC is the natural log of the sample size. This leads to the BIC favoring more parsimonious models compared to the AIC when sample size is greater than seven. Information criteria can be used to compare both nested and nonnested models, that is, models with a different number of latent classes and different parameter specifications. When using information criteria for comparing models, the model obtaining the lower information criteria value is considered the superior fitting model.

The second group of model fit statistics is the approximate likelihood ratio tests. Finite mixture models that only differ in the number of classes are considered nested; however, the difference in their deviances under the null hypothesis are not asymptotically χ^2 distributed. Thus, corrections have been proposed, including the Vuong–Lo–Mendell–Rubin Approximate Likelihood Ratio Test and the Lo–Mendell–Rubin Adjusted Likelihood Ratio Test (Lo, Mendell, & Rubin, 2001). These likelihood ratio tests produce a test statistic and associated p-value, which compares the fit of the specified model (with K classes) with the fit of the same type of model with one fewer class (the $K - 1$ class model). In addition to these approximate likelihood ratio statistics, there is the Bootstrap Likelihood Ratio Test (BLRT; McLachlan, 1987). The BLRT repeatedly simulates data according to the specified model minus the smallest class, and then estimates the specified model and the model with one fewer class to obtain an empirical distribution of likelihood ratio under the null hypothesis. This distribution is then used as a comparison distribution to obtain the p-value for the observed likelihood ratio. A final approach is based on using k-fold cross-validation (Grimm, Mazza, & Davoudzadeh, 2017) for model selection. In this approach, the data are partitioned into k nonoverlapping folds with $k-1$ folds used to estimate the model parameters and the kth fold to obtain model fit information of the estimated model. This sequence is done k times and the resulting values and their distributions can be compared.

Simulation research (e.g., Grimm, Ram, Shiyko, & Lo, 2013; Nylund, Asparouhov, & Muthén, 2007; Tofighi & Enders, 2008) has failed to come to a definitive conclusion as to which model fit index performs best across a variety of models (e.g., latent class analysis, latent profile analyses, growth mixture models), sample sizes, number of classes, and class differences. Thus, our recommendation follows Ram and Grimm's (2009) study, which sequentially examines a variety of model fit information (i.e., information criteria → approximate likelihood ratio tests) and considers the substantive interpretation of the model parameter and the separation of latent classes (i.e., entropy). This sequence is then augmented by using k-fold cross-validation to examine the sensitivity of model estimation through multiple estimation with different folds of the data.

In addition to comparing the fit of the models with different constraints and classes, the quality of class assignment should be considered. This can be examined through the estimated posterior probabilities and the model's entropy. Often, the average posterior probabilities are calculated based on class assignment (i.e., most probable class assignment based on the individual posterior probabilities) and entropy is reported. Entropy is a summary statistic of the posterior probabilities of class membership across participants. Entropy (Asparouhov & Muthén, 2018) is defined as

$$Entropy = 1 + \frac{1}{N\ln(k)}\left(\sum_{i=1}^{N}\sum_{k=1}^{K} P(C_i = k|y_i)\ln(P(C_i = k|y_i))\right) \tag{10.2}$$

for $i = 1$ to N participants and $k = 1$ to K classes, where C_i is the latent class variable for participant i, and y_i is a vector of observed latent class indicators. When entropy is close to 1, then the posterior probabilities tend to be close to 1 or 0, which suggests that participants are well classified. When entropy is close to 0, it indicates that the latent class variable is more or less random. Some researchers have recommended a 0.80 threshold for entropy to consider a model; however, there are no strong theoretical grounds for this value.

Once an optimal model (or set of models) is determined, posterior probabilities of class membership can be estimated for each participant. Given the estimated parameters for each class, the likelihood of each participant belonging to each class can be estimated. These probabilities can then be taken into consideration when examining associations between class membership with predictors and outcomes of class membership (see Asparouhov & Muthén, 2014). Accounting for these posterior probabilities when examining associations of the latent class variable explains the uncertainty in class membership.

Implementation

Statistical programs to estimate mixture models have been around for many years; however, when initially developed these statistical programs were specific to the type of data analyzed (e.g., binary data) and model estimated (e.g., latent class model). The latent Gold (Vermunt & Magidson, 2003) program enabled the estimation of a variety of finite mixture models (e.g., latent class and latent profile models) with both categorical and continuous outcomes (with current extentions into longitudinal models, count variables, ordinal, and nominal variables) and the M*plus* program (Muthén & Muthén, 1998–2017) provided a comprehensive framework for the specification and estimation of a wide variety of models within each class (e.g., confirmatory factor model, growth model) with a variety of data types (e.g., binary data, ordinal data, count, continuous data) and combinations thereof, model constraints, multiple latent class variables, and different associations between the latent classes (e.g., latent transition analysis). In `R`, multiple packages are available to estimate finite mixture models, with most packages specific to the type of data analyzed and model estimated. For example, `poLCA` (Linzer & Lewis, 2011) can estimate latent class models, `mclust` (Scrucca, Fop, Murphy, & Raftery, 2016) can estimate latent profile models, and `lcmm` (Proust-Lima, Philipps, & Liquet, 2015) can estimate growth mixture models. One exception to this rule is the `OpenMx` package (Neale et al., 2016), where finite mixture models can be estimated and structural equation models with different constraints can be specified within each class. Additionally, `OpenMx` can handle binary, ordinal, and continuous data. A second exception is `mixtools` (Benaglia, Chauveau, Hunter, & Young, 2009), which is able to estimate finite mixture models with different parametric distributions (e.g., normal, multinomial, gamma) and different types of mixture models (e.g., latent profile analysis, mixture regression models).

10.2.2 Illustrative Example

The analyzed data were restricted to a random sample of 500 participants from the `Grit` data. While the Grit Scale was used as outcome variables, the 10 items for each construct in the IPIP were averaged to create a composite score for each of the five personality factors. These scores will be used as predictors of class membership.

The 12 Grit items were subjected to a latent class analysis. The Grit items were treated as ordinal and specified to be conditionally independent within each class (i.e., items were uncorrelated within each class). Thus, any association between the items was assumed to be due to the latent class variable and class differences in the probability of responding in each category. This model specification follows the standard specification of the latent class model. Models with 1 through 5 classes were estimated and no covariates were included in the model when determining the number of classes (see Stegmann & Grimm, 2018 for discussions about the incorporation of covariates when performing class enumeration). Each model was estimated 10 times with different sets of starting values because finite mixture models can be sensitive to starting values. Using multiple sets of starting values helps to identify the global maximum in the likelihood function, and also enables researchers to examine whether different starting values lead to the same set of parameter estimates. The latent class models were estimated using the `poLCA` package in `R`.

Results

The model fit statistics and entropy for the 1- through 5-class latent class models are contained in Table 10.1. The table contains the deviance, the number of estimated parameters, the AIC, the BIC, and the entropy. We note that the `poLCA` package does not provide the approximate likelihood ratio tests and cannot implement *k*-fold cross-validation, so this information is not provided here. The 1-class model contains 48 estimated parameters. The 48 estimated parameters include 4 thresholds separating the 5 response options for each of the 12 items of the Grit scale. The 1-class model provides baseline statistics that serve as the standard to improve upon when adding latent classes. The 2-class model has 97 parameters, which includes 48 estimated thresholds for each class, and the intercept (threshold) for the latent class variable that separates the two classes. The 2-class model was an improvement over the 1-class model based on the information criteria and has an entropy of 0.85, suggesting the two classes were fairly well separated. The 3-class model was an improvement over the 2-class model with lower AIC and BIC values. The entropy was 0.87 indicating that the three classes were well separated. The 4-class model had a lower AIC, but a higher BIC compared to the 3-class model. Thus, the information criteria were mixed when comparing the 3- and 4-class models. In our experience, the AIC is a better fix index when the sample size is fairly low, whereas the BIC is a better fit index with larger sample sizes. We, therefore, side with

TABLE 10.1. Model Fit Statistics for Latent Class Models

	Deviance	Parameters	AIC	BIC	Entropy
1-Class Model	17,636	48	17,732	17,934	–
2-Class Model	16,525	97	16,719	17,128	0.85
3-Class Model	16,184	146	16,476	17,091	0.87
4-Class Model	16,925	195	16,315	17,137	0.87
5-Class Model	15,721	244	16,209	17,238	0.86

TABLE 10.2. Parameter Estimates in the Probability Scale for Class 1 / Class 2 / Class 3

Item	*P* (1)	*P* (2)	*P* (3)	*P* (4)	*P* (5)
1	.00 / .03 / .01	.03 / .09 / .09	.17 / .36 / .46	.30 / .21 / .30	.50 / .32 / .13
2	.12 / .73 / .18	.22 / .14 / .41	.35 / .09 / .30	.21 / .03 / .11	.11 / .02 / .01
3	.08 / .60 / .12	.11 / .24 / .36	.26 / .12 / .25	.43 / .01 / .23	.12 / .02 / .01
4	.04 / .15 / .08	.12 / .24 / .34	.22 / .32 / .37	.32 / .15 / .21	.30 / .15 / .00
5	.08 / .74 / .16	.13 / .24 / .35	.29 / .00 / .28	.34 / .00 / .16	.16 / .02 / .05
6	.00 / .07 / .02	.00 / .18 / .15	.06 / .19 / .27	.21 / .28 / .37	.72 / .29 / .19
7	.02 / .54 / .03	.06 / .31 / .37	.26 / .07 / .38	.49 / .07 / .20	.18 / .00 / .02
8	.03 / .64 / .13	.10 / .20 / .45	.22 / .10 / .30	.43 / .07 / .12	.22 / .00 / .00
9	.00 / .13 / .01	.02 / .26 / .26	.17 / .35 / .49	.37 / .15 / .22	.44 / .11 / .02
10	.02 / .27 / .11	.06 / .29 / .32	.19 / .22 / .27	.23 / .10 / .22	.51 / .11 / .08
11	.14 / .47 / .02	.21 / .34 / .24	.31 / .15 / .45	.31 / .02 / .21	.03 / .02 / .08
12	.00 / .07 / .01	.02 / .14 / .13	.13 / .32 / .45	.28 / .19 / .33	.57 / .27 / .08

the BIC given our sample size, and report the results for the 3-class model. The 5-class model had a higher BIC than the 3-class and 4-class models suggesting that 5 classes were too many for these data.

In the 3-class model, approximately 50% of the sample was in class 1 with 20% in class 2 and 30% in class 3. The class-specific parameter estimates were translated to calculate the predicted probability of responding in each response category for each class. These probabilities are contained in Table 10.2. Given these predicted probabilities, we can begin to determine the nature of the three classes. Class 1 which is the largest class, tended to have high levels of Grit. On average, this class had the highest mean response on all items, except item number 11, which asked about the frequency of having an interest in new pursuits. Class 2 tended to have low mean responses to items that focused on interests and projects changing from year to year. Thus, Class 2 was more easily distracted and participants' level of commitment was more average. Class 3 had participants who responded in the low categories to questions about diligence and overcoming setbacks; however, this class tended to have participants whose interests changed less than Class 2.

The 3-class model was then extended to include predictors of class membership. The predictors of class membership were the Big Five personality factors from the IPIP. poLCA allows for the class membership to be predicted by measured variables; however, it's important to note that the inclusion of predictor variables can impact classification. Thus, a first check is to ensure that the classes have not meaningfully changed by the inclusion of the predictor variables. Approaches to include predictor variables without having them impact the class structure are available (Asparouhov & Muthén, 2014); however, these approaches aren't available in poLCA. The inclusion of the Big Five personality factors as predictor of class membership had minor effects on the latent class structure. The parameter estimates showed that participants who were more conscientious ($t = 7.25, p < 0.01$) and agreeable ($t = 4.18, p < 0.01$) and less neurotic ($t = 3.09, p < 0.01$) were more likely in Class 1 compared to Class 2, and participants who were high on openness ($t = 3.68, p < 0.01$) were more likely in Class 2 compared to Class 3.

10.2.3 Factor Mixture Models

In identifying heterogeneity, researchers often have multiple outcome variables of interest that they wish to use as a basis for examination. When these observed outcome variables come from the same or similar scales, or are the same variables assessed at different points in time, it often makes theoretical sense to place constraints on their covariance in the form of latent factors. One of the most general formulations is factor mixture models (Lubke & Muthén, 2005), where classes are estimated with respect to some form of factor model. This model represents a combination of latent variable types, a categorical latent variable used as the basis for grouping, and a continuous latent variable that summarizes the covariance among observed outcome variables. Thus, within each of the classes, a common factor model is estimated with at least a subset of parameters allowed to vary across classes.

A nice demonstration of factor mixture models is Arias, Garrido, Jenaro, and Arias (2020), where a two-class model is used to detect careless responding. Using survey data, they specified single-factor models for each scale within each class. While the residual variances and intercepts were specified to be equal across the two classes, differing factor loading matrices were used. In the majority class, each loading was constrained to 1, whereas in the careless responding class the loadings were constrained to 1 or −1, depending on whether the item was positive or negative valence. It was hypothesized that careless responders would fill out each item the same way regardless of valence, thus this loading matrix would capture these responses despite each negative valence item being reverse scored prior to analysis. They in fact found support for 4 – 10% of cases falling in the minority class that could be characterized as inattentive responders.

To demonstrate the use of factor mixture models, we used the same Grit data as above, so we can extend our search for heterogeneity to include the same two-factor model for the observed Grit indicators as detailed in Chapters 7 and 8. Although there isn't a perfect way to depict the application of mixtures to this CFA model, we provide a heuristic depiction in Figure 10.2.

FIGURE 10.2. Two-factor Grit CFA (left panel) and heuristic depiction of the factor mixture model (right panel). C represents the latent class variable, with the parameter estimates in the CFA varying across classes.

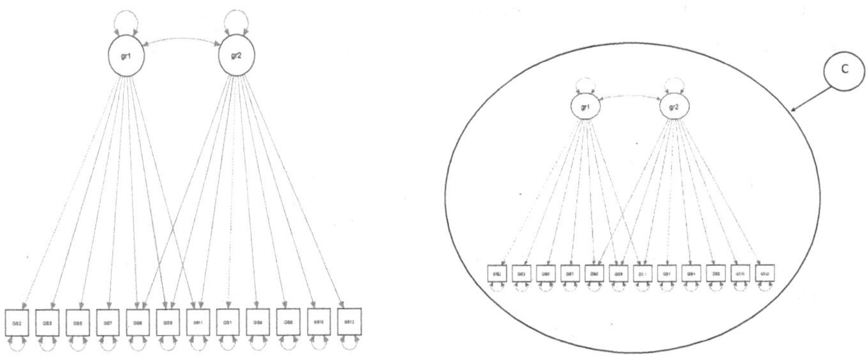

The most notable change in this model is that each parameter estimate has an added subscript, *k*, that denotes that each class has a separately estimated CFA model. Constraints can be placed on this, for instance, to only allow the factor covariance matrix to have class-specific estimates, while the factor loadings, observed variable intercepts, and variances are constrained to be the same across classes, thus drastically reducing the number of estimated parameters. A more commonly applied form of factor mixture model examines the direct effect of the latent class on the latent means. This involves constraining the mean of each latent variable to be zero in one class, while freely estimating the latent means in the other classes. This can be visually depicted as in Figure 10.3.

To apply this to the Grit data, we first start with estimating a two-class solution, only allowing the latent means to vary across classes. Note that since the observed variable intercepts are estimated, we need to constrain the latent means in one class to zero, thus allowing for a comparison across classes. We also estimate a model that allows the latent means, and variance-covariance matrix, to vary across classes. The model fit results are displayed in Table 10.3.

FIGURE 10.3. Factor mixture model that only allows the latent means to vary across classes.

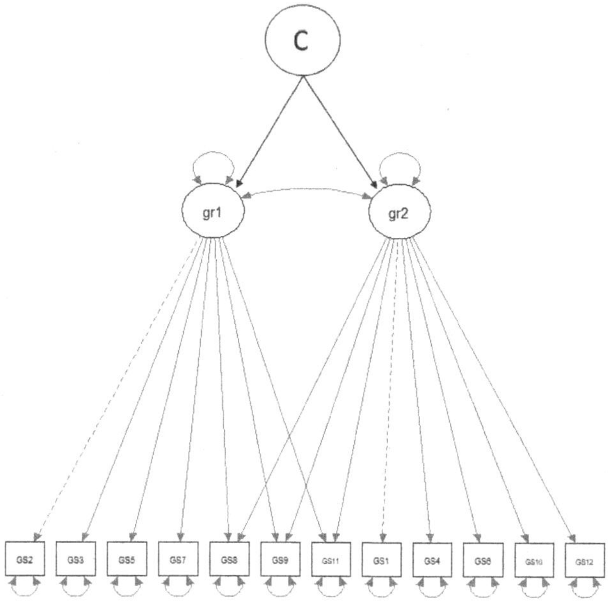

TABLE 10.3. Model Fit Statistics for Factor Mixture Models

	Deviance	Parameters	AIC	BIC	Entropy
1-Class Model	34263	40	34343	34540	–
2-Class Model Means	34212	43	34298	34509	0.62
2-Class Model All Latent	34140	46	34231	34457	0.66
3-Class Model Means	34152	46	34245	34470	0.62

We can see that the two-class means model improves upon the one-class model with respect to both the AIC and BIC, although the entropy value is relatively low. While allowing the factor variances and covariance to differ across classes improves all three metrics, one of the classes has a negative latent variance estimate, meaning an improper solution. Finally, the three-class means model improves upon the two-class means fit. We do not display more complex models given that the improper solutions persisted when adding more classes with all latent parameters varying, while additional classes in the means-only model did not improve the fit.

For pedagogical purposes, we can just focus our inference into the two-class means model. First, the mean of the categorical latent variable was estimated as −1.05, which in the log odds scale denotes a slightly imbalanced class distribution (zero means 50–50). The latent means for Class 2 were constrained to 0, while the latent means for Class 1 were estimated as −0.32 (0.10) for Grit1 and −0.98 (0.07) for Grit2. From this we can see that the first class was estimated to have lower average values of both forms of Grit in comparison to the second class. We note that this is a relatively constrained form of estimation, only allowing for three additional estimated parameters for each additional latent class. Researchers have the option to allow more parameters to vary across classes, however, this often comes at the expense of estimation difficulty. We refer readers to Clark et al. (2013) for further discussion.

10.2.4 Incorporating Covariates

In applying mixture models it is relatively straightforward to incorporate covariates. The complication is in whether it is desirable for the covariates to drive the class creation, or whether covariate effects should just be examined after the classes have been created. To be more concrete, we'll use FMMs as an example. If we wanted to incorporate covariates into the two-factor CFA model detailed in the prior section, letting them drive the composition of each latent class, it would probably be most natural to include the covariates as predictors of each latent variable, thus turning the CFA into a MIMIC model. In running this model, the formation of the latent classes could be a result of any part of the MIMIC model. In contrast, a number of methods have been developed that allow researchers to assess class differences on covariates after the class composition has been set. Chief among these is the three-step approach of Asparouhov and Muthén (2014), which first estimates the latent classes in Step 1. Uncertainty rates are calculated for each class in Step 2, then these are used as an outcome in a multinomial logistic regression with the covariates of interest as predictors in the Step 3.

TABLE 10.4. Parameter Estimates from the FMM. This uses class 2 as the reference category, thus is the effect of each covariate on belonging to class 1.

Variable	Estimate	SE	p-value
E	-0.745	0.215	0.001
C	-2.143	0.239	0.000
N	-0.126	0.179	0.481
O	-0.751	0.184	0.000
A	-0.834	0.174	0.000

Building upon our FMM results displayed in Table 10.3, we tested the effect of covariates on the two-class solution after the class composition was set. Note that in mixture models it is less common to incorporate large numbers of variables as covariates, as the estimation of mixture models is already tricky. With our data, we get inadmissible results by including all 62 variables. As a result, we created factor scores for each of the personality scales and only used these as covariates. This model converged, and resulted in the covariate effects displayed in Table 10.4.

Note that all of these parameter estimates are using Class 2 as the reference category, thus results in the table represent the effect of each covariate on the probability of belonging to Class 1. As our goal is not to interpret each parameter estimate, which would require exponentiating each as it is a logistic regression (as there are only two categories), we can just look at which covariates have significant effects. Four of the personality scales have significant effects (all but neuroticism). Given that each personality predictor was placed on the same scale (first each variable was standardized and then translated to factor scores, which have a mean of 0 and standard deviation of 1), we can also compare the magnitude of effects. Unsurprisingly, conscientousnous had the largest effect. The negative coefficient means that those high in conscientousnous were less likely to be in Class 1 as opposed to Class 2. This is in line with interpreting the latent means as estimated in Step 1. Class 1 had negative class means (Class 2 latent means were set to 0), thus Class 1 is lower on both forms of Grit.

10.3 Structural Equation Model Trees

In Chapter 9 we discussed the pairing of mixed effects models and decision trees as a mechanism for identifying groups in longitudinal data. In this section we provide an overview of pairing decision trees with SEM in the form of SEM trees (Brandmaier et al., 2013) and forests (Brandmaier et al., 2016). These two methods are within the same family of other multivariate methods developed as an integration between psychometrics and decision trees (Breiman et al., 1984), including the use of unconstrained covariance matrices as outcomes (Miller et al., 2016) and nonlinear mixed-effects models (Stegmann et al., 2018), among others. As SEM can be seen as a general family of models, namely, including a number of models for longitudinal data, SEM trees can be used in ways similar to those methods described in Chapter 9. For the purpose of this chapter, we just focus on the use of SEM for cross-sectional data.

An additional component of decision trees, outside of identifying nonlinear associations, is that observations are placed into terminal nodes, with each terminal node forming a subgroup. Given this, decision trees have also been used as a basis for identifying heterogeneity by grouping observations based on values of the predictors. Conceptualized as a form of exploratory multiple group modeling (Jacobucci et al., 2017), SEM trees pairs a structural equation model as an outcome with using decision trees to identify a grouping structure that improves the fit of the model. This grouping structure can be the result of one or more dichotomous splits on one predictor or multiple predictors, including interactions between predictors. These multiple dichotomous splits form step functions between the predictors in the tree and the outcome criteria, which is the deviance in the case of SEM trees. The use of step functions allows decision trees and SEM trees to fit highly nonlinear structures. However, the use of single decision trees results in the drawbacks of less than optimal prediction and instability of the structure. Just as decision trees have been generalized to random forests (Breiman, 2001a), fitting hundreds or thousands of trees using a subset of predictors for each tree, the same has occurred for generalizing SEM trees to SEM forests. Although an interpretable tree structure is lost, the effects of the predictors across the hundreds of trees can be condensed into variable importance metrics, allowing researchers to gauge the relative influence of each variable.

10.3.1 Demonstration

For demonstration purposes, we use the same Grit dataset as was used in the illustration above. For the SEM trees analyses, our outcome model is the two-factor model for the 12 Grit items as before. This model, with parameter estimates, is depicted in the left panel of Figure 10.2.

In contrast to directly incorporating covariates as predictors of each of the two latent variables, as in a MIMIC model, our covariates are used to derive subgroups that improve the fit of the model. This means that each of the covariates used in the SEM trees model will indirectly alter the parameter estimates in the model in the sense that the derived subgroups will differ with respect to all, or a subset, of the parameter estimates. To demonstrate this, we used the `semtree` package (Brandmaier, Prindle, & Arnold, 2020) with all of the covariates in the Grit dataset. With the default settings, outside of setting the maximum number of splits to one for demonstration purposes, the data were partitioned into two groups based on the C8 variable ("I shirk my duties.") with parameter estimates for the two groups depicted in the tree diagram contained in Figure 10.4.

FIGURE 10.4. Tree diagram for demonstrative SEM tree model. Loadings l2–l7 refer to the loadings from the first Grit latent variable and loadings l22–l88 refer to the loading from the second latent variable in the same order as in Figure 10.4.

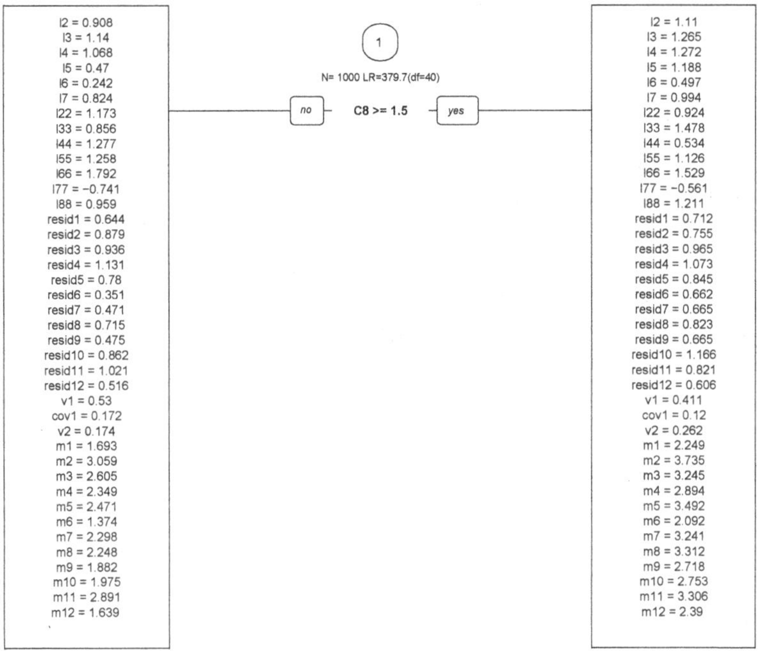

In this model, the split occurs between response options 1 and 2. Each resultant subgroup of individuals has a unique SEM (two-factor CFA model), which corresponds to different parameter estimates. Examining the parameter estimates can point us toward those aspects of the model that are driving the group differences. In the higher conscientiousness group (right set of parameter estimates, responding with values > 1 on C8), the factor loadings are higher for the first Grit latent variable, with the opposite occurring for the second Grit factor. The same could be done for the means of the indicators, examining whether groups have meaningful differences. In other types of SEMs models, differences in the parameter estimates across groups could be more informative. As an example, we could allow the slope loadings in a latent growth curve model to differ, resulting in varying expected trajectories over time across groups. In our analysis, our main point of inference is in explaining variability in the latent variables. Given this, we may only want to examine changes in the means and variances of each the latent variables (and assuming invariance of loadings and measurement intercepts).

10.3.2 Algorithm Details

The SEM trees algorithm is implemented in the `semtree` package (Brandmaier et al., 2022) in `R`. Prior to running SEM trees, researchers need to first fit the outcome model, which can take just about any form of SEM. The SEM can be tested and paired with `semtree` using either the `lavaan` (Rosseel, 2012) or `OpenMx` (Boker et al., 2011) packages. We note, however, that `semtree` was originally designed for pairing with `OpenMx` and in practice works better than when paried with `OpenMx` compared to with `lavaan`.

A number of different tuning parameters are available for the SEM trees algorithm. Although we term these options tuning parameters, we do not mean that researchers should test out multiple values of each. Instead, the tests should be based on best practices and theoretical considerations given the theoretical nature of identifying heterogeneity. One of these options is the splitting criterion (`method =` in `semtree.control()`). The default, *naive*, compares all possible split values across the predictor space, selecting the cutpoint that maximally improves the likelihood ratio. Cross-validation (`method = "crossvalidation"`; defaults to 5-fold CV) splits the data into partions, testing the improvement in fit due to each cutpoint on a holdout set of observations. In practice, this procedure can be extremely intensive from a computational standpoint. The procedure that we recommend in most research scenarios is the *fair* criterion. This method proceeds in two steps. The first step is to split the sample into two, using the first half of the sample to examine the improvement in fit associated with each cutpoint, associating a single best cutpoint for each predictor. In the second step, the second half of the sample is used to test the best cutpoint for each predictor. This procedure for selecting cutpoints can overcome some of the bias of most decision tree algorithms for selecting cutpoints from predictors with more response options (more possible cutpoints). Given this, we recommend using the fair criterion.

The second tuning parameter to consider setting is the minimum sample size. It is important to note that an SEM is estimated in each node, and depending on the complexity of the specified SEM, this could lead to testing complex SEMs with inadequate sample sizes. Therefore, we recommend setting a minimum sample size for each node (`min.N =` in `semtree.control()`), with 100 being a reasonable default for most SEMs.

This relates back to the starting sample size, meaning that SEM trees is fundamentally a large sample technique. Conversely, as with most decision tree algorithms, it can be common to produce overly large trees, thus inhibiting interpretation, particularly when starting with very large sample sizes (e.g., > 5,000). In these situations, it may be reasonable to set a maximum tree depth (`max.depth` in `semtree.control()`). For more detail on alternative specification options for SEM trees, see Brandmaier et al. (2013).

10.3.3 Focused Assessment

Given the nonlinearity present in trees, one point of assessment with SEM trees may be in the explanation or prediction of the latent variables in the model. Analogous to the use of linear predictors in a MIMIC model, while deviating from the focus on derived groups or classes as in a mixture model, this type of modeling requires a degree of alteration to be done properly. Most notably, this requires the placement of constraints to ensure that we are measuring the same construct in each resultant subroup. As in the above models, we were able to assess differences in factor loadings, means, and variances or covariances. In the case of examining differences in just the latent variables, we instead focus on the latent variable means, variances, and covariances, while placing constraints on other parts of the model to ensure that our interpretation of each latent variable stays consistent across nodes. This is known as *measurement invariance* (Meredith, 1993; Reise, Widaman, & Pugh, 1993). Although there are many variations to invariance testing, notably which set of parameters to constrain to be equal across groups, we focus on imposing a strict form of invariance by constraining all of the factor loadings, intercepts, and residual variances to be equal across groups. This can easily be done within the `semtree` package (using `global.invariance =` the name of parameters), only allowing the other parameters (latent variances and covariance) to vary across groups.

In mixture models, it is relatively easy to examine the mean of the latent variables across the derived classes. This is accomplished by specifying a reference class that has a latent mean of zero, thus freeing up the assessment of the latent means in other classes. If this constraint was not imposed, the latent means would be underspecified. This leads to complications in using SEM trees, as it isn't possible to specify a reference group. As a result, we have to get a little creative in order to examine the latent means across groups. The first step is centering the observed variables at zero. With this, the estimated intercepts in the model will be zero (or very close). Given this, we do not alter any other parts of the model by constraining the intercepts to zero since it matches the values at which they would be estimated. This allows for the estimation of the latent means to be identified. Note that in the base model this procedure will result in latent mean estimates of zero. However, this can be viewed as a grand mean to then be used as a comparison in the resulting SEM trees results, as each derived subgroup is likely to have an estimated latent mean to be different than zero. Thus, we can compare each mean estimate to zero to identify which subgroups have lower or higher estimated levels of each latent variable. Note that this procedure is not needed in most longitudinal SEMs, as the observed variable means are set to zero in order to push the changes in means over time to the latent level. In most cross-sectional data it is not appropriate to constrain the observed variable means to zero in the same way without first centering the variables.

Going back to our example, we imposed invariance constraints on the factor loadings and unique variances, while also setting the variable means to zero. With this, we can use each of the personality and demographic predictors to identify subgroups that are maximally different with respect to the latent means, variances, and covariance. Imposing invariance in the fitting process results in the tree structure displayed in Figure 10.5.

FIGURE 10.5. Strict invariance tree results. Only the factor variances (v1, v2), factor covariance (cov1), and factor means (lm1, lm2) were allowed to vary across groups.

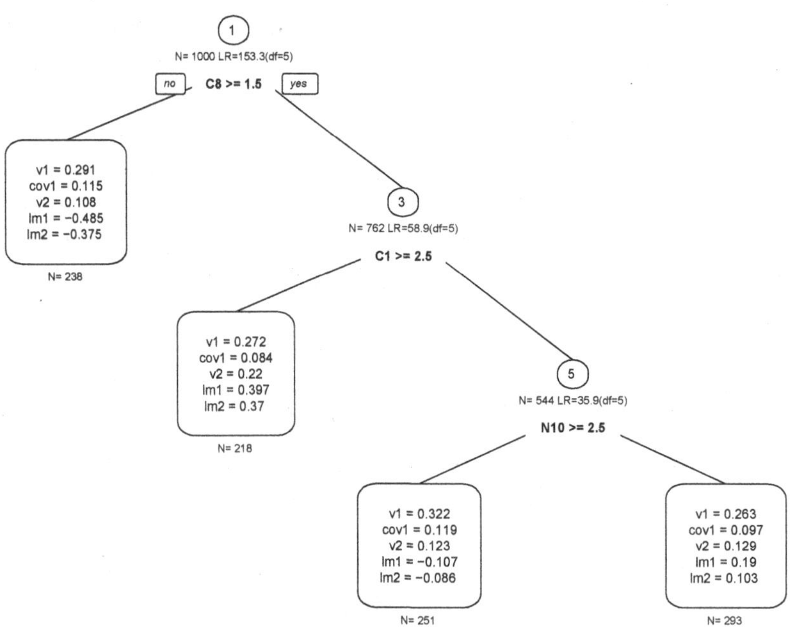

The first thing to note is that the first split is the same as in Figure 10.4, while additional splits occur on C1 ("I am always prepared"), as well as N10 ("I often feel blue"). Secondly, we can now focus on our explanation of the latent variables, specifically honing in on the means and variances. Given that the whole sample mean on each latent variable is zero, we can interpret each subgroup with reference to zero. Just as in Figure 10.4, those that endorse low values on C8 ("I shirk my duties."), meaning they are lower in conscientiousnous, have lower expected values of both facets of Grit, as the mean of each Grit latent variable is -0.49 and -0.38, respectively. Further, we see that the subgroup with the highest expected latent means is the one that endorses high values of C8, and low values of C1 (coded such that lower values means higher conscientiousnous). Further splits can be examined for the additional two groups based on the split on N10. The last thing to note is that the latent variances and covariance do not differ markedly across the subgroups, meaning that the heterogeneity within each subgroup is relatively similar.

10.3.4 SEM Forests

Many of the same drawbacks to decision trees mentioned in Chapter 5 also apply to SEM trees. It is worth noting that the purpose of SEM trees is less to predict an outcome and more to identify heterogeneity with respect to a statistical model. For this reason, less focus is placed on assessing model performance, particularly because it is not in a metric that is as easily interpreted as R^2 or accuracy. With the issue of decision trees being inherently unstable, it is often recommended to follow up the creation of a tree structure with assessing variable importance with random forests or boosting. The analog with respect to SEM trees is the application of SEM forests (Brandmaier et al., 2016). SEM forests applies the SEM trees algorithms hundreds of times, each time using a subset of covariates to create each tree (*mtry*; just as in random forests). A great example of the application of SEM forests as a supplement to SEM trees, particularly to validate the selection of variables for the tree structure is in Brandmaier et al. (2017). In practice, we would expect to see the same variables used to create the tree structure appear to have higher relative variable importance values in comparison to those variables not selected in the tree structure. In SEM forests, variable importance is calculated through permutation accuracy, which follows the procedure described in Chapter 6. In contrast to random forests, SEM forests' variable importance is based on the decrease in the log-likelihood, which is averaged across the set of trees to produce variable importance estimates for each variable.

FIGURE 10.6. Variable importance plot from the first SEM forests run. Note that only every other variable name is displayed on the *Y*-axis.

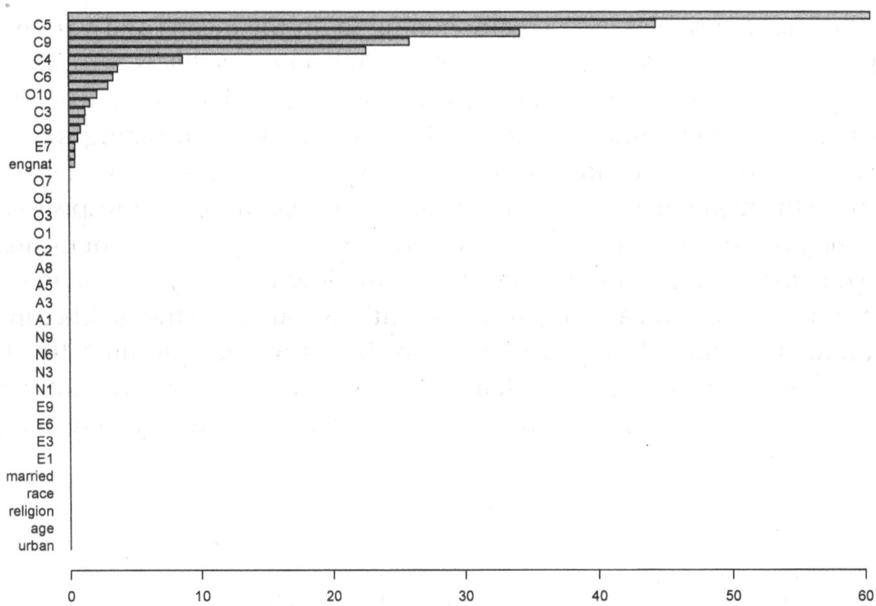

Like SEM trees, SEM forests can be applied using the `semtree` package. SEM forests adds a set of additional tuning parameters, most notably the number of trees and number of random selected covariates. Given the computational complexity to SEM trees, and thus SEM forests, we recommend only assessing a few tuning parameter values, mainly *mtry*. The number of trees can be set to 100 or 500, with more trees preferred with increasing numbers of covariates, while the testing of *mtry* should be based on the degree of correlation among covariates. Often times, the default of *mtry* (i.e., 2) works well; however, a low value of *mtry* may require more trees when there are more in the presence of more than 10 or so covariates. Higher values of *mtry* will tend to negate the influence of some covariates as there is less chance for them to be selected into the trees. We demonstrate this using the same BFI data as in the SEM trees example. For the first SEM forests run, we set *mtry* to 20 and the number of trees to 100. The resulting variable importance plot is displayed in Figure 10.6.

Here, we can see that the variables with the highest relative importance values mostly consist of a few conscientiousnous covariates, while many of the variables have values of near zero. In relation to the two SEM trees examples, C8 was the most important variable, thus providing some support for the stability of splits on that variable.

FIGURE 10.7. Variable importance plot from the second SEM forests run. Results are taken from 500 trees, with *mtry* set to 2. Note that only every other variable name is displayed on the *Y*-axis. C8 was the most important variable but its label was cutoff.

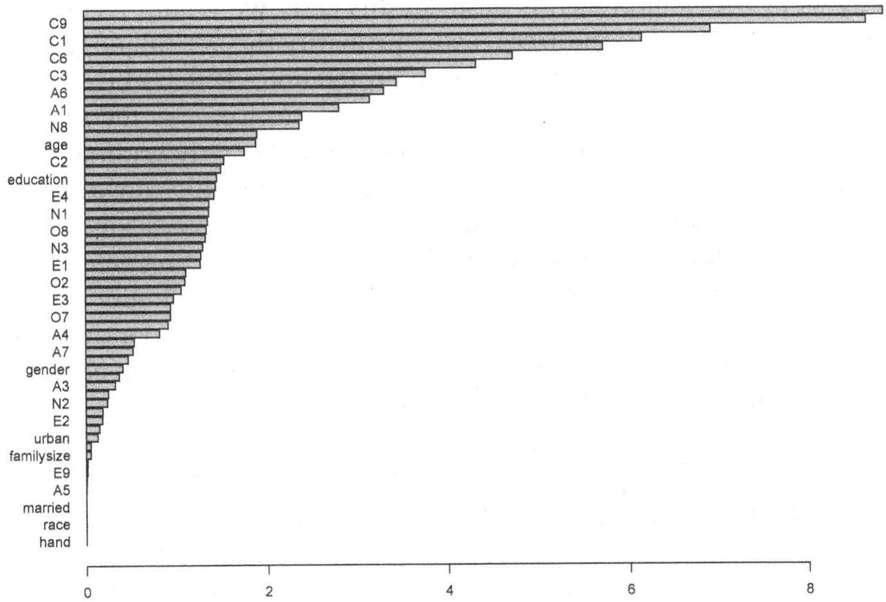

To see the effect of varying *mtry*, we completed an additional SEM forests run, this time setting *mtry* to 2, while also increasing the number of trees to 500. These results are displayed in Figure 10.7.

Here, there is a much more even distribution of importance values, hence the smaller values depicted on the *X*-axis. This can be attributed to only two variables being considered for the creation of each tree, which allows for the inclusion of many more variables. However, we wish to note that this is more in line with a marginal, as opposed to conditional, interpretation of variable importance. If researchers wish to give preference to variables that show effects given the testing of other covariates, using higher values of *mtry* may be preferrable.

10.4 Summary

The most important distinction between mixture models and the use of trees is whether researchers believe heterogeneity can be attributed to unobserved or observed variables. While covariates can be included in mixture models, it is typically preferrable to not have them drive the class creation, necessitating the use of three-step approaches. Given this, class construction is not specifically based on values of an observed variable, while trees, and specifically SEM trees, directly identifies groups based on covariate values. Oftentimes researchers may have some degree of uncertainty as to which approach is best. In this case, we would recommend running both mixtures and trees, using primarily theoretical judgment to discern which solution is chosen for interpretation. It is tricky to use fit criteria to compare the results from mixtures and trees, as the resulting models are not nested. While trees are constrained to only finding groups based on the unique values of covariates, mixtures are only constrained by the number of groups, thus making them inherently more flexible. Thus, it is expected that mixture models will evidence better fitting values of information criteria. We can summarize the benefits and limitations to each approach in a number of ways. Note that instead of limiting our discussion to SEM trees, we examined multivariate trees, which better envelopes the tree approaches described in the previous chapter.

As alluded to in this chapter, a number of algorithms are available to researchers for the identification or testing of heterogeneity. We notably ommitted a number of these, specifically cluster analysis, which can be used in a very similar way to that of mixtures (see Fraley & Raftery, 1998, for generalizations of cluster analysis to incorporate outcome models), with the distinction being whether classs membership is probabilistic (mixtures) or deterministic (cluster analysis). Additionally, while it was mentioned that decision trees specifically assigns group membership based on covariates, similar processes can be done with regression models (using a grouping variable in ANOVA or logistic regression for instance). We summarize the methods that have been covered in Table 10.5.

The main distinction in Table 10.5 is whether the grouping (heterogeneity) is thought to be unobserved in the case of mixture models, or observed in tree methods or multiple group SEM. Additionally, the more advanced methods can handle multiple variable types as outcomes, while SEM based methods constrain the relations among these variables in some form of latent variable model (or path analysis, for instance with a mediation model as an outcome). Finally, we have focused on the use of methods to search for heterogeneity, not test an a priori specified grouping structure. In this latter research scenario, multiple group SEM can be seen as a generalization of ANOVA, where a grouping structure is specified based on theoretical consideration and determining whether the levels to that group are, in fact, different with respect to the outcome (continuous variable in ANOVA, any type of SEM in multiple group SEM).

TABLE 10.5. Summarization of Techniques for Identifying or Testing Heterogeneity

Method	Heterogeneity Source	Outcome Model	Heterogeneity Theory
Latent class analysis	Unobserved	Categorical variables	Atheoretical
Latent profile analysis	Unobserved	Continuous variables	Atheoretical
Factor mixture model	Unobserved	Continuous and/or categorical variables constrained in a latent factor model	Atheoretical
Decision trees	Observed	A single continuous or categorical variable	Atheoretical
Multiple group SEM	Observed	Continuous and/or categorical variables in an SEM	Theoretical
SEM trees	Observed	Continuous and/or categorical in an SEM	Atheoretical

Multivariate Trees

- Best if there are meaningful covariates of interest.
- It is unknown what effect non-normality of the outcome variables can have on group formation.
- Can be computationally expensive when the number of covariates is large.
- In the presence of complex outcome models, it can be difficult to determine which parameters are meaningfully different across groups.
- The problems with decision trees, most notably instability.

Mixtures

- Heterogeneity is thought to be due to unobserved variables.
- Will fit better than multivariate trees.
- Non-normality can pose problems (see Bauer & Curran, 2004).
- Describing the makeup of each class is less straightforward than in multivariate trees.
- Can be difficult to choose among the constraints placed on class variance/covariance.

A ripe area for future research is in comparing these approaches and providing more guidance on when each algorithm may be most appropriate. Additionally, there is a recent focus on combining the benefits of each algorithm, making the comparison inherent in deriving groups (see Grimm et al., 2022), which is aided by new software developments (see Serang et al., 2020). We expect this to be a hot topic of inquiry in the near future.

10.4.1 Further Reading

- A number of methods have been developed to examine the effects of covariates in a mixture model after the classes are formed. For a more recent overview of the literature, see Stegmann and Grimm (2018).
- Recent research has focused on combining the use of mixture models and decision trees in searching for classes/groups, see Grimm et al. (2022) and the `MplusTrees` package in `R` for its implementation.

- Both mixture models and decision trees have been proposed as methods to identify violations of invariance in structural equation models. See Wang et al. (2021) for a recent applicaton of mixture models and Bollmann, Berger, and Tutz (2018) for an application of trees in item response theory (IRT) models. IRT can be seen as an equivalent statistical framework to SEM, of which there are analogous integrations with machine learning algorithms, most notably a rich literature on applying trees to detect measurement invariance violations (termed *differential item functioning*). The main distinction lies in the software implementations, of which a number of packages in R that pair trees and IRT models are available (e.g., De Boeck & Partchev, 2012).
- One common theme of this book that was not present in this chapter is the idea of cross-validation. While cross-validation has been applied in mixtures (Grimm et al., 2017) and SEM trees (`method = "cv"` in the `semtree` package), the computational time is prohibitive in both methods. Similar to pairing regularization with SEM, most of the focus of selecting a final model has been on the use of information criteria that include penalties for model complexity as a mechanism to approximate holdout sample fit.

10.4.2 Computational Time and Resources

For mixture models, we highly recommend using M*plus* as it has the most comprehensive set of tools available and is among the most computationally efficient piece of software for latent variable models. With this, the amount of time it takes to run mixture models is typically a result of the base model size (as in FMM) and the number of classes extracted. For the models in this chapter, most mixture models only took a few minutes to run. In contrast, SEM trees and SEM forests tend to take much longer. The main factor in run time is how long it takes to run the base SEM. Additionally, the number of covariates and maximum tree depth dictates the number of models that are tested. Typical run-times range from minutes to a couple of hours, whereas SEM forests tends to take on the order of multiple hours since it is repeating the process of running SEM trees 100 times (when number of trees is set to 100). SEM forests can be run in parallel in the `semtree` package, which can significantly cut down on the run-time.

Part IV

Alternative Data Types

11 Introduction to Text Mining

Although we typically work with quantitative numerical data, qualitative text data can be even more common. The text data can come from many different sources. For example, in research using surveys or questionnaires, free response items are frequently used to solicit feedback or response to open-ended questions such as "What else are you worried about?" (Rohrer, Brummer, Schmukle, Goebel, & Wagner, 2017). In diary studies, a daily record can be kept by the respondent at a researcher's request (Oppenheim, 1966). The record can include writing about the activities and feelings of a day. Text data can also come from the transcription of audio and video conversations from experiments (Bailey, 2008). Nowadays, social media sites provide even more text information that can be used to address new and innovative questions. For example, Jashinsky et al. (2014) analyzed more than 1.6 million tweets to identify at-risk for suicide tweets to suicide risk factors in real time. Studies also showed that Facebook posts and likes can be used to predict personality (Marshall, Lefringhausen, & Ferenczi, 2015; Wu, Kosinski, & Stillwell, 2015). Many statistical methods and techniques have been developed to analyze quantitative data. Although methods are available for text data analysis, researchers are less familiar with them. In this chapter, we will discuss several methods for dealing with text data.

11.1 Key Terminology

- Sentiment. Assessment the valence (positive/negative) of words used in a response or document.
- Topic. Latent dimensions extracted from a document or response.
- Dirichlet. A probability distribution used to model the relationship among latent topics in latent Dirichlet allocation (LDA).
- Document. An observation's text response. This can range from a single sentence to an entire book. Most applications in text mining do

not involve the responses of people, but instead books, newspapers, or other media.

- Stop words. Words such as "a," "and," or "the" that are typically removed from text prior to analysis.
- Tokenization. The process of splitting up responses into individual units, such as by character, word, or sentence.
- Stemming. Reducing individual words based on common stems. For example, turning "take" and "taking" into "tak."

11.2 Data

We focus on the analysis of the `Professor Ratings` data to show how to handle text data to answer real research questions. The data with student evaluation on college professors were scraped from an online website conforming to the site requirement. A tutorial on how to scrape online data can be found in Landers, Brusso, Cavanaugh, and Collmus, (2016). The whole dataset includes 27,939 teaching evaluations on a total of 999 professors.

11.2.1 Descriptives

The distribution of the number of evaluations received by professors is given in Figure 11.1, which is clearly skewed. The number ranges from 4 to 188, and, on average, each professor received 28 evaluations (the median is 21). The majority of professors received fewer than 50 evaluations.

The numbers of responses to each category of the teaching rating and "How hard did you have to work for this class?" are shown in Figure 11.2. The average score of the ratings of the professors is 3.85 and the average score for how hard a student worked is 2.88.

The comments from the students are in the free text format. For example, one such comment is given below. Note that some sensitive information such as the names of the professors and universities have been removed.

```
XXX is a good man, highly interested in and
    knowledgable about calculus. However,
    his teaching style involves hard exams,
    tons of homework, and very fast-paced
    lectures. He grades harshly and wants
    you to figure out the answers to your
    own questions. He is a good prof, but a
    hard one. Take him if you grasp new
    subject matter easily.
```

FIGURE 11.1. Distribution of the number of evaluations received by individual professors.

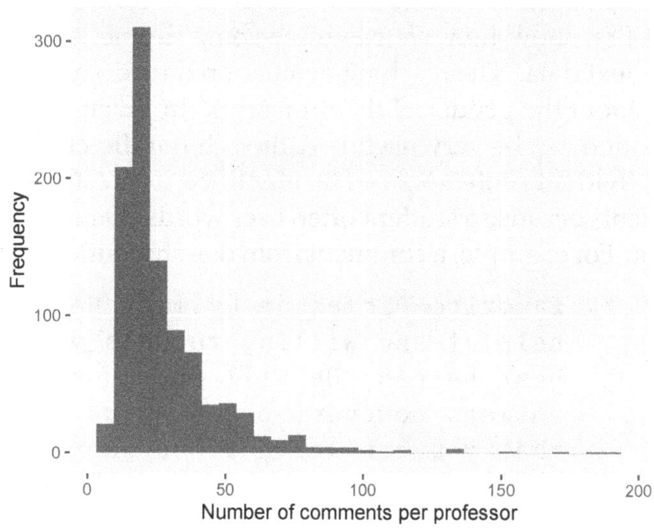

FIGURE 11.2. Distribution of response categories to two questions.

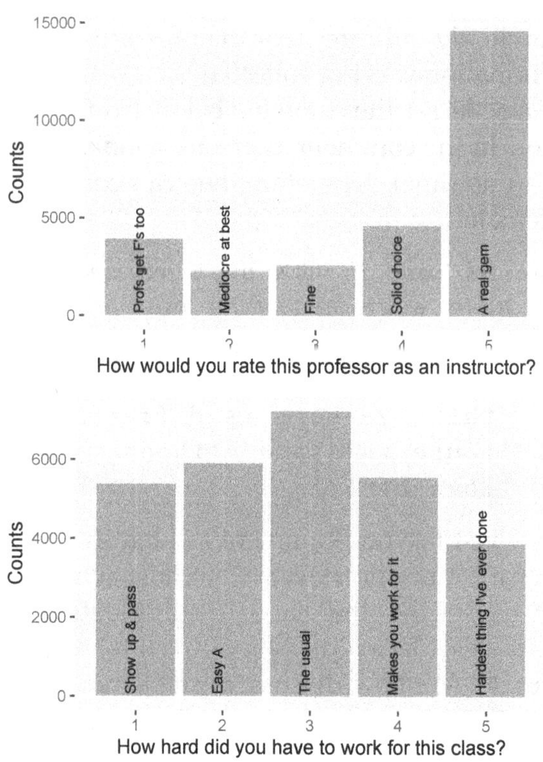

11.3 Basic Text Mining

Text data can contain a lot of information. Before we conduct more complex analysis, we first show how we can mine some simple, but useful, information from text data. The teaching evaluation data do not include direct information about the gender of the professors. In practical data analysis, such information can be very useful. Although not directly available, the gender of individual professors can be identified indirectly using the narrative comments because a student often uses words that reflect the gender of a professor. For example, a comment from one student was given below:

```
My favorite Professor by far. He is very
   helpful and willing to help you out the
   best he can. He will not just give you
   answers however, but help guide you so
   that you can learn it on your own. I
   definately recommend taking him for
   whatever math courses you can. He
   requires a lot of work, but it pays off
   in the run!
```

In the comment, the student used the pronouns "he" four times and "him" once. This clearly indicates that the professor is male even though the direct sex information was not collected.

As another example, see the comment below from another student on a different professor. In the comment, there are gender pronouns "she" (six times) and "her" (one time). Therefore, one can confidently assume that the professor is female.

```
She is one of the best voice teachers I
   have ever had. She may not be able to
   sing like she used to, but she sure
   knows how the voice works. And she knows
    that everyone is different so she doesn
   't use the same methods with everyone. I
    love her!!!
```

Certainly, if we just use one comment to identify the gender of a professor, it can have a lot of uncertainty especially when gender pronouns were not used often. One the other hand, if multiple students used the same gender pronouns to describe a professor, the results are cross-validated and can be more accurate. We now discuss, in steps, how to mine the gender information of all the 999 professors while illustrating the typical steps of text mining.

11.3.1 Text Tokenization

From the previous discussion, we know we can identify gender based on gender pronouns. However, the gender pronouns are embedded in the text. Therefore, the first step of the analysis is to identify and take out the gender pronouns. In text mining, one can break down a block of text into individual words, e.g., based on white space in the text. The process is called *tokenization* (e.g., Stavrianou, Andritsos, & Nicoloyannis, 2007; Weiss, Indurkhya, Zhang, & Damerau, 2010). For example, for the sentence "She is one of the best voice teachers I have ever had", after tokenization, we get the individual words as listed in Table 11.1. For this particular example, we also change all upper case letters to lowercase letters such as "She" becomes "she." In many situations, this is useful since one can simply ignore letter cases to treat the words as the same. In this example, the punctuation marks are also removed.

TABLE 11.1. Text Tokenization

	Word
1	she
2	is
3	one
4	of
5	the
6	best
7	voice
8	teachers
9	i
10	have
11	ever
12	had

Select the Gender Words

Since we are interested in identifying the gender of professors, only the words that reflect the gender information are useful. For example, for the words listed in Table 11.1, only the word "she" provides relevant information for our analysis. Therefore, in this step, we should identify such words. After a quick review of part of the comments in the data, we found the gender words listed in Table 11.2. For example, "he," "him," and "his" are associated with the male professors while "she," "her," and "hers" are associated with the female professors. Note that, in writing, the contractions such as "he's" and "she's" are also used. Once the words are identified, we keep these words only in our data for further analysis.

TABLE 11.2. Gender Related Words

Male	Female
he	she
him	her
his	hers
he's	she's
he'd	she'd
he'll	she'll
mr	mrs/ms/miss

FIGURE 11.3. Gender word frequency.

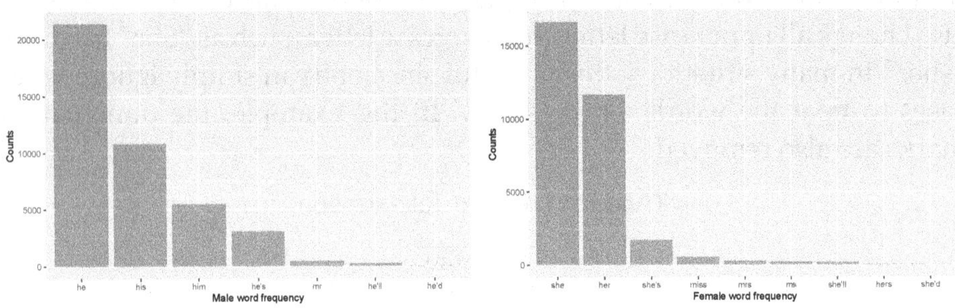

Frequency of Gender Words

After removing the nongender words, we have a dataset with the gender words in each of the 27,939 text comments. The combined frequency of each gender word for all professors is shown in Figure 11.3. Not surprisingly, for male, the words "he," "his", "him", and "he's" are used very frequently. For female, the words "she", "her", and "she's" are used most frequently. For example, "he" was used for a total of 21,372 times and "she" was used for 16,623 times. The frequency of each word is also listed in Table 11.3. Overall, more male words were used than female words. This might indicate there are more male professors than female professors in the data.

FIGURE 11.4. Number of gender words used in the comments of individual professors.

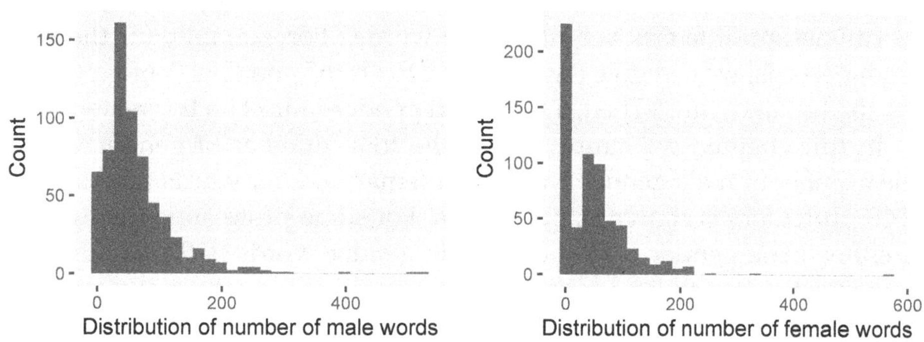

TABLE 11.3. Frequency of Gender Words Used in All Comments

Male		Female	
Word	Frequency	Word	Frequency
he	21,372	she	16,623
his	10,796	her	11,658
him	5,488	she's	1,687
he's	3,061	miss	525
mr	457	mrs	246
he'll	236	ms	179
he'd	15	she'll	166
		hers	27
		she'd	8
Total	41,425		31,119

The purpose is to identify the gender of each individual professor. Therefore, we also investigate how many gender words were used in comments for a given professor. Figure 11.4 shows the distribution of gender words used in the comments of individual professors. Both distributions are skewed. One reason could be that there were a very different number of comments (from 4 to 188) for the professors. For the distribution of female gender words, there are many professors with only one female gender word. In addition, for some professors, both male and female gender words were used in the comments.

A Gender Index

Based on the frequency of gender words, we can create a "gender index." A simple gender index can be the total number of gender words used in the comments for a given professor. In this way, we treat each gender word equally. In text comments, some words can be easily misspelled than others.

For example, for a female professor, one might misspell "she" as "he" in the comments. But "his" is hard to be misspelled as "her." Similarly for "mr" and "mrs", they might not be as reliable as "him" or "her." Therefore, we can assign different weights to the words. For example, for the male gender words, we can give a weight of 2 to "him" and "his," and a weight of 1 to "he" and "mr." Then, a weighted gender index can be created.

In this chapter, we simply count the total number of gender words. The number of male gender words and female gender words for a sample of 10 professors is shown in Table 11.4. For some professors, the number of either male gender words or female gender words is 0. In this case, we can label the professor as either a female or a male professor. For example, we can be very confident in saying that Professors 1, 2, 4, and 78 are male professors and Professors 27 and 79 are female professors. For the other four professors in the table, there are both male and female gender words in the comments. However, we can see that the difference in the numbers of male gender words and female gender words is quite large for all four professors. In this case, we might assume the small number of gender words were misspelled and label the professors based on the larger number of gender words. For example, we can label Professors 3 and 80 as male professors while Professors 79 and 84 as female professors.

TABLE 11.4. Gender Index for a Sample of Professors

ID	Male Gender Words	Female Gender Words	Gender
1	153	0	M
2	12	0	M
3	249	2	M
4	29	0	M
27	0	118	F
28	0	80	F
78	105	0	M
79	1	200	F
80	206	2	M
84	1	181	F

For this dataset, about 27.8% (278/999) of professors have both male gender words and female gender words. We plot the number of male and female words in Figure 11.5. For the vast majority of the professors, a clear division exists between the number of male gender words and the number of female gender words. Therefore, we can confidently label the professors as male or female based on the larger number of either male or female gender words.

Based on the above classification, there are 415 or 42% female professors and 584 or 58% male professors in the dataset. With the gender information,

FIGURE 11.5. Number of male and female words in comments on professors.

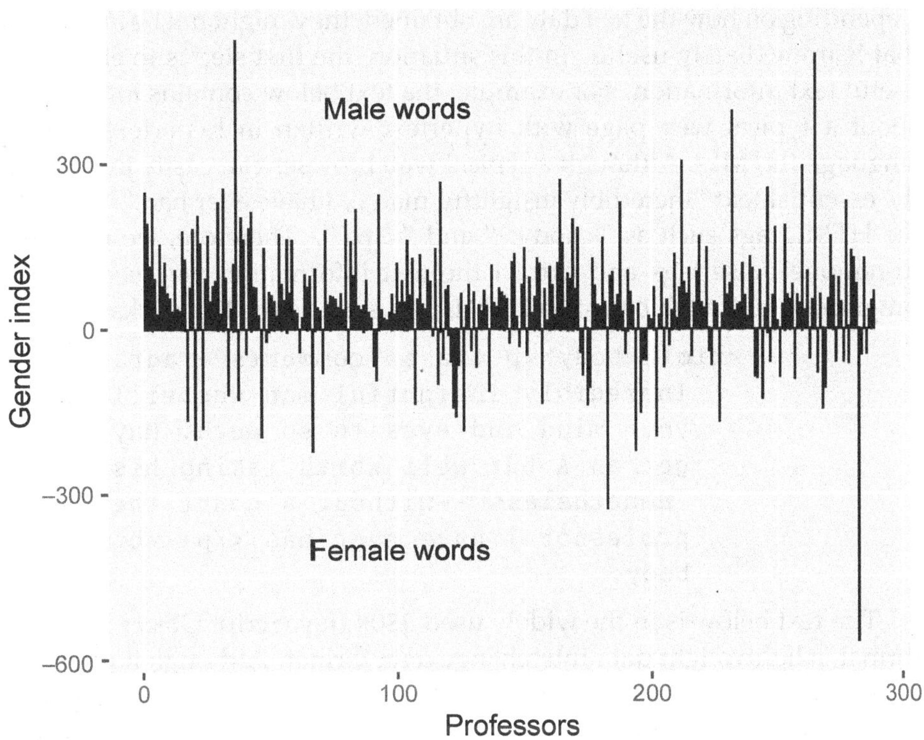

we can then conduct comparisons. For example, for the numerical rating of the professors, the average rating for male professors was 3.92 and for female professor was 3.76. The difference was 0.16 with a Cohen's *d* of 0.11. The difference was significant but the effect size was small. For the variable of how hard a student works on the class, the average score for the class taught by male professors was 2.877 and by female professors was 2.886. The difference was -0.009 with a Cohen's *d* of -0.007. The difference was insignificant and the effect size was essentially 0.

11.4 Text Data Preprocessing

In quantitative data analysis, data cleaning, such as correcting potential errors, is often necessary. The same is true for text data. Text data preprocessing is necessary in almost every situation. Depending on the data one works with, different preprocessing procedures can be used. In general, the following methods can be applied.

11.4.1 Extracting Text Information

Depending on how the text data are obtained, they might not be in a format that is immediately useful. In this situation, the first step is to extract the useful text information. For example, the text below contains information about a typical web page with hypertext written in hypertext markup language (HTML). Although a typical web browser can easily interpret it, the essential text "Incredibly insightful man ... I have ever had."[1] includes the HTML tags such as "<body>" and "</p>". Therefore, we first need to remove those tags and extract the text information we need. Many programs are available to strip HTML tags such as the `XML` package in `R`.

```
<html><body><p class="commentsParagraph">
   Incredibly insightful man who will open
   your mind and eyes to so much. May not
   get an A but well worth taking his class
    nonetheless---without a doubt the best
   professor I have ever had.</p></html></
   body>
```

The text below is in the widely used `JSON` (JavaScript Object Notation) format, a lightweight data-interchange data format. Although it might not appear easy to read for humans, it is easy for computers to parse and generate. For example, both Twitter and Facebook provide APIs (application programming interface) to scrape data from their websites. The scraped data are often stored in the JSON format. For example, below is a tweet from former President Trump. The JSON format data can be parsed into more readable text by many software programs such as the `R` package `jsonlite`.

```
[{"source": "Twitter for iPhone," "id_str":
    "1079888205351145472," "text": "HAPPY
   NEW YEAR! https://t.co/bHoPDPQ7G6," "
   created_at": "Mon Dec 31 23:53:06 +0000
   2018," "retweet_count": 33548, "
   in_reply_to_user_id_str": null, "
   favorite_count": 136012, "is_retweet":
   false}]
```

Removing Sensitive and Confidential Information

Text data can easily include identifiable, sensitive, or confidential information, such as name, home address, phone number, email address, credit

[1]You can copy the text into a text editor and save it to a file called test.html. Then, open the file in a web browser.

card number, or even Social Security number (SSN). Some or all such information generally should be removed before data analysis or data sharing. For the information with a clear pattern such as the email address and SSN, one can search and replace them by using regular expressions. For the text without a pattern such as names, one can first build a list of them and then remove them from the text through search and replace.

Handling Special Characters

Text data can also include special characters or words. For example, if the text is written in English, we would expect that it is comprised mostly of English words. However, it is possible that foreign languages are used in part of the text. An example is the collection of Facebook data in which multilingual users may use words from languages other than English in their posts. As another example, emojis are now widely used in social media and other forms of communication. When downloading tweets from Twitter, the Emojis are often saved as special characters such as in unicode. One can handle the special characters based on the purpose of analysis. For example, for text in foreign languages, one can often simply remove them. For emojis, they can also be removed directly. However, if the purpose of analysis is to understand the sentiment of texts, the emojis can provide useful information. In this case, the emojis can be coded or replaced with some unique and meaningful texts.

Abbreviations

Abbreviations and acronyms are often used in social media. For example, for the teaching evaluation data, "HW" was very frequently used as the abbreviation "homework." On Facebook, "BFF" is often used to describe a close friendship. Before analysis, these abbreviations should be taken care of so that they are not be treated differently from the words that they represent.

Spell Checking

Spelling errors are much more common in reviews and comments such as teaching evaluations than in formal writing. Correcting spelling errors can be time-consuming and tedious but can increase the analysis quality later on. The typical way to correct them is to first get a list of unique words, including the misspelled ones from all the text data. Then, we can use `Hunspell` (Ooms, 2017), a popular spell checker and morphological analyzer to find words that might be misspelled. After that, we ask Hunspell to suggest potential replacement words for the misspelled ones. Finally, we replace the misspelled words with the suggested correct words.

Word Stemming

Sometimes, different forms of a word that mean the same thing might be used. For example, "loves," "loving," and "loved" are all tenses of the word "love." "Better" and "best" are the comparative and the superlative adjectives of "good." In such situations, it is often useful to reduce the related words to their word stem, base, or root form, e.g., "love" and "good" in the above examples. Many algorithms are available to conduct word stemming dating back to the work by Lovins (1968). Programs such as `Hunspell` can be used to conduct word stemming.

11.4.2 Text Tokenization

In text analysis, tokenization is the process of breaking text into pieces such as words, keywords, phrases, symbols, and other elements called *tokens*. Tokens are often in the form of individual words, but they can also be sentences, paragraphs, or even chapters. They do not necessarily consist only of words. For example, they can be special characters such as punctuation marks and emojis, depending on the purpose of the analysis. The tokens from tokenization are machine readable and can then be analyzed.

We use the text in the listing below as an example. One way is to tokenize the text into individual sentences as tokens (see below). This is typically done by dividing the text based on the punctuation marks. Such tokenization can be useful in natural language processing where one is interested in the size of a paragraph and the length of a sentence. For this particular example, there are five sentences in the text. Note that it does not check whether a sentence is grammatically correct or not.

```
[1] "My favorite Professor by far."
[2] "He is very helpful and willing to help
    you out the best he can."
[3] "He will not just give you answers
   however, but help guide you so that you
   can learn it on your own."
[4] "I definately recommend taking him for
   whatever math courses you can."
[5] "He requires a lot of work, but it pays
    off in the run!"
```

The most widely used method for tokenization is to break text to individuals words as shown below. Typically in this process, one also converts upper case letters to lower case letters and strips punctuation marks and white space.

```
[1]  "my"        "favorite"    "professor"  "by"
[5]  "far"       "he"          "is"         "very"
[9]  "helpful"   "and"         "willing"    "to"
[13] "help"      "you"         "out"        "the"
[17] "best"      "he"          "can"        "he"
[21] "will"      "not"         "just"       "give"
[25] "you"       "answers"     "however"    "but"
[29] "help"      "guide"       "you"        "so"
[33] "that"      "you"         "can"        "learn"
[37] "it"        "on"          "your"       "own"
[41] "i"         "definately"  "recommend"  "taking"
[45] "him"       "for"         "whatever"   "math"
[49] "courses"   "you"         "can"        "he"
[53] "requires"  "a"           "lot"        "of"
[57] "work"      "but"         "it"         "pays"
[61] "off"       "in"          "the"        "run"
```

Word stemming can often be conducted when tokenizing to individual words. For example, the text below is tokenized to individual words. The words are also stemmed using the program `SnowballC` (Bouchet-Valat, 2020). For example, in the list, the word "very" was stemmed to "veri" and "pays" to pay.

```
[1]  "my"      "favorit"  "professor"  "by"
[5]  "far"     "he"       "is"         "veri"
[9]  "help"    "and"      "will"       "to"
[13] "help"    "you"      "out"        "the"
[17] "best"    "he"       "can"        "he"
[21] "will"    "not"      "just"       "give"
[25] "you"     "answer"   "howev"      "but"
[29] "help"    "guid"     "you"        "so"
[33] "that"    "you"      "can"        "learn"
[37] "it"      "on"       "your"       "own"
[41] "i"       "defin"    "recommend"  "take"
[45] "him"     "for"      "whatev"     "math"
[49] "cours"   "you"      "can"        "he"
[53] "requir"  "a"        "lot"        "of"
[57] "work"    "but"      "it"         "pay"
[61] "off"     "in"       "the"        "run"
```

In addition to tokenizing text into individual words, one can also split text into multiple words, which is called *n-grams*. For example, the following is based on 3-gram tokenization where every three words are grouped together. This is useful in studying the relationship among words.

```
[1] "my favorite professor"        "favorite professor by"
[3] "professor by far"             "by far he"
[5] "far he is"                    "he is very"
[7] "is very helpful"              "very helpful and"
[9] "helpful and willing"          "and willing to"
[11] "willing to help"             "to help you"
[13] "help you out"                "you out the"
[15] "out the best"                "the best he"
[17] "best he can"                 "he can he"
[19] "can he will"                 "he will not"
[21] "will not just"               "not just give"
[23] "just give you"               "give you answers"
[25] "you answers however"         "answers however but"
[27] "however but help"            "but help guide"
[29] "help guide you"              "guide you so"
[31] "you so that"                 "so that you"
[33] "that you can"                "you can learn"
[35] "can learn it"                "learn it on"
[37] "it on your"                  "on your own"
[39] "your own i"                  "own i definately"
[41] "i definately recommend"      "definately recommend taking
"
[43] "recommend taking him"        "taking him for"
[45] "him for whatever"            "for whatever math"
[47] "whatever math courses"       "math courses you"
[49] "courses you can"             "you can he"
[51] "can he requires"             "he requires a"
[53] "requires a lot"              "a lot of"
[55] "lot of work"                 "of work but"
[57] "work but it"                 "but it pays"
[59] "it pays off"                 "pays off in"
[61] "off in the"                  "in the run"
```

Many other methods for tokenization are available. For example, one can tokenize a text into individual letters. How to conduct the tokenization depends on the purpose of analysis.

11.4.3 Data Matrix Representation

Tokenization identifies the units of analysis. When a series of texts, collectively called a *corpus*, is available, we need to organize the tokens systematically for further analysis. As an example, we use the five sentences previously detailed above. Therefore, the text corpus consists of five units. After tokenization, we can use a document-term matrix (DTM) to represent the information in the text corpus. Other data representation methods are also available. A DTM is a matrix where the rows represent the documents, comments, sentences, or any other bodies of words. The columns are the tokens, terms, or words used in the document.

For example, if we treat each sentence as a document and then tokenize the sentences into individual words, we can get a DTM shown below (only part of the matrix is shown here to save space):

Terms										
Docs	but	by	can	far	favorite	he	help	it	the	you
1	0	1	0	1	1	0	0	0	0	0
2	0	0	1	0	0	2	1	0	1	1
3	1	0	1	0	0	1	1	1	0	3
4	0	0	1	0	0	0	0	0	0	1
5	1	0	0	0	0	1	0	1	1	0

The above DTM is constructed in the following way. First, the unique words in all documents (sentences) are identified and put into the columns of the matrix. Here, there are a total of 51 unique words in all five sentences. They are the terms in the matrix. Second, each row provides the information on whether a term/word appears in a sentence or how many times. For the first sentence/row, it has the words "by," "far," and "favorite" and in the matrix, the corresponding elements are 1. For words that appear in other sentences but not in this one, the corresponding elements are 0. For the second sentence, the word "he" appears twice, therefore, the number 2 is used in the matrix.

One can observe that in the matrix, many elements are zero. The whole matrix here is a 5 by 51 matrix. In total, there are 61 nonzero elements and 196 zero elements. Therefore, about 76% of the elements in the matrix are zero. This phenomenon is almost universally true for a DTM. In our example, the five sentences are quite short but they use many different words. This is especially true if the size of documents is not big but the number of documents is large.

A matrix with a significant amount of zeros is called a *sparse matrix*. On the contrary, if most of the elements are nonzero, it is a *dense matrix*. For a dense matrix, one has to store each element of it. But for a sparse matrix, we can usually store the information more efficiently by focusing on the nonzero elements. For example, one way is to use a triplet or coordinate (COO) form in which three vectors are used to represent the information in a matrix with two vectors storing the row and column numbers and the third vector storing the nonzero values. For the subset of DTM shown above, there are 20 nonzero values out of a total of 50 values. Using the triplet format, we have the following. Note that i is the row index, j is the column index, and v is the actual value in the original matrix.

	i	j	v
1	3	1	1
2	5	1	1
3	1	2	1
4	2	3	1
5	3	3	1
6	4	3	1

7	1	4	1
8	1	5	1
9	2	6	2
10	3	6	1
11	5	6	1
12	2	7	1
13	3	7	1
14	3	8	1
15	5	8	1
16	2	9	1
17	5	9	1
18	2	10	1
19	3	10	3
20	4	10	1

Another common way to store a sparse matrix is called *compressed sparse column* (CSC) format, which also represents a matrix by three vectors. One vector contains all the nonzero values. The second vector contains the row index of the nonzero elements in the original matrix. The third vector is of the length of the number of columns + 1. The first element is always 0. Each subsequent value is equal to the previous values plus the number of nonzero values on that column. For the above example, the CSC representation is shown below. Different from the above method, the three vectors can have different lengths.

```
i: 2 4 0 1 2 3 0 0 1 2 4 1 2 2 4 1 4 1 2 3
j: 0  2  3  6  7  8 11 13 15 17 20
v: 1 1 1 1 1 1 1 1 2 1 1 1 1 1 1 1 1 1 3 1
```

The advantage of using a sparse matrix becomes more obvious when a matrix is large. For example, for the teaching evaluation data, if we tokenize all the comments, we have a 27,939 (comments) by 18,216 (tokens/words) matrix. Only less than 0.2% of the elements are not zero. If we store all the values using a matrix in R, it takes about 3.8 Gb of computer memory. However, using the CSC format to store the nonzero values only, it just takes about 18.1 Mb of memory, saving more than 95% of the computer memory.

11.5 Basic Analysis of the Teaching Comment Data

We now discuss how we can conduct some basic analysis of the teaching comment data. We first tokenize the comments into individual words (unigrams) as tokens. Overall, the 27,939 comments used a total of 1,223,454 words and the number of unique words used in the comments is 18,216. Each comment on average used 43.8 words. The longest comment had 106 words and the shortest comment had only four words. The distribution of the number of words of all the comments is shown in Figure 11.6.

FIGURE 11.6. Number of words in individual written comments.

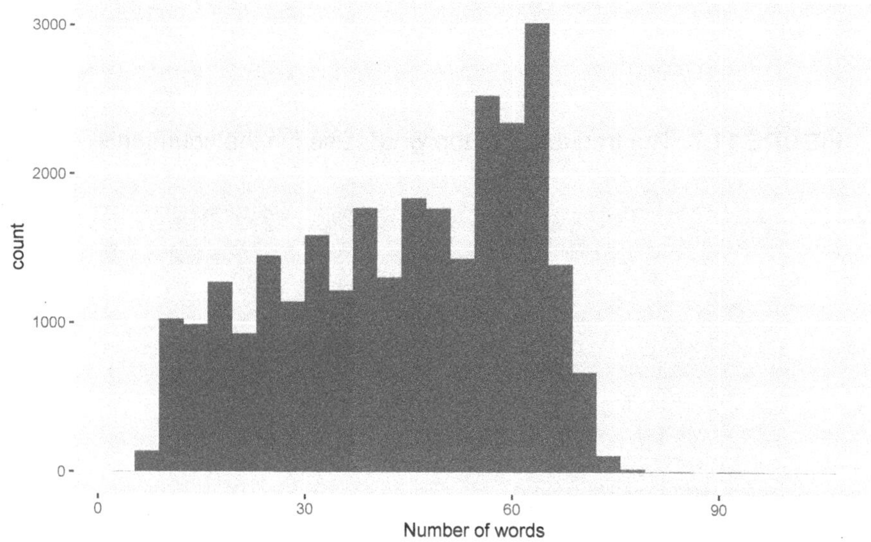

11.5.1 Word Frequency

To understand how students evaluate professors, we can first investigate what words are used in describing a professor. This can be done by finding the most commonly used words in the narrative comments. The 20 most used words are shown in Figure 11.7. They include "the," "and," "to," "a," "you," etc. The word "the" was used 41,864 times and the word "are" was used more than 10,000 times in the comments.

11.5.2 Stop Words

Although some words in Figure 11.7 are extremely common, they do not provide much useful information for analysis because they are used in all contexts. In order to better study a particular topic, we often simply remove these words not associated with the topic before analysis. Such words in text analysis are called *stop words*. There is no single universal list of stop words that can be used in all conditions. Actually, any group of words can be chosen as the stop words for a given purpose.

FIGURE 11.7. The frequency of top words used in the comments.

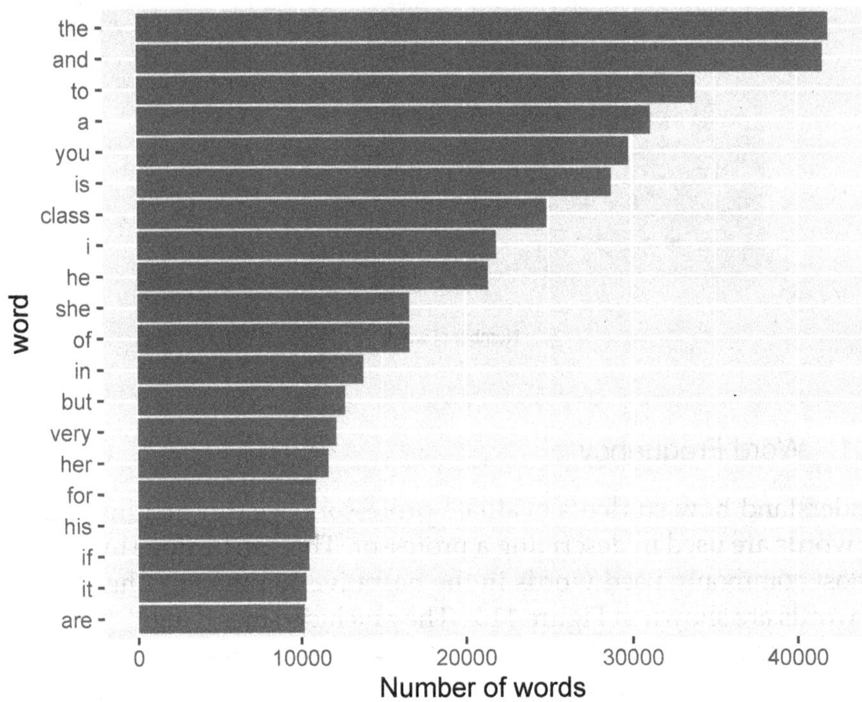

Since there is no particular stop word list for comments related to teaching evaluation, we build a stop word list based on three existing lists.

- SMART: This stop word list was built for the SMART information retrieval system at Cornell University (Salton, 1971). It consists of 571 words such as "able," "about," "your," and "zero."
- snowball: The snowball list is from the string processing language snowball. It has 174 words such as "than," "very," "so," and "you're."
- onix: This stop word list is probably the most widely used one among the three lists. It is from the onix system. This word list contains 429 words including "a," "do," "face," and "the."

FIGURE 11.8. The frequency of top words used in the comments after removing stop words.

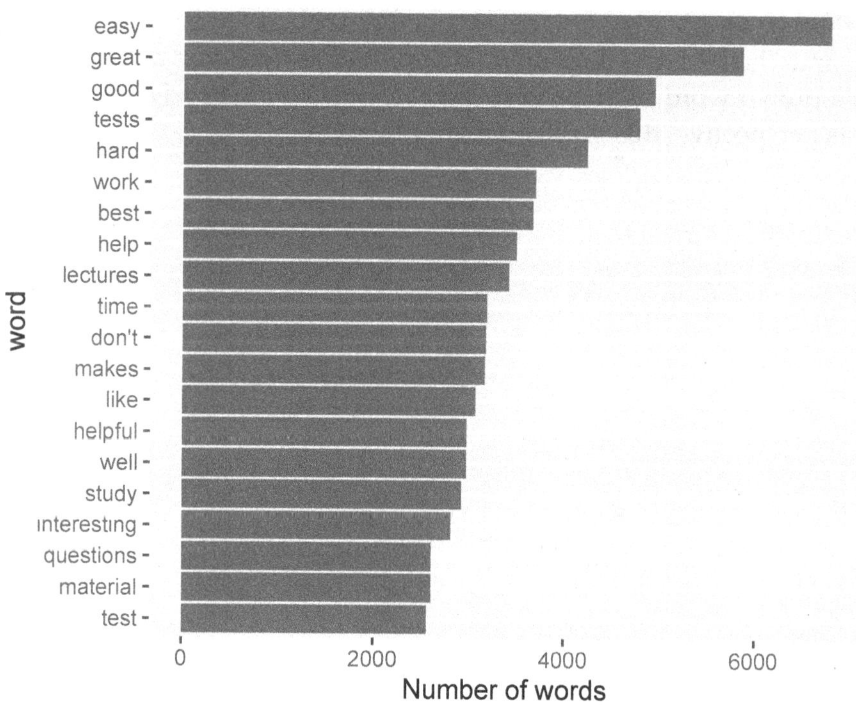

We first combined the three lists, which leads to a total of 1,149 words. We then went through the list to check if it fits the purpose of teaching evaluation and found that some words should not be removed as stop words. For example, the SMART list would remove the word "least." But in many comments, it is very useful for teaching evaluation. For example, in one comment, it said "This is the least organized professor." Similarly, the onix list suggests removing "best," which we think should be kept. After going through each of the 1,149 words, we identified a total of 568 words that can be safely removed. There are also words such as "professor,""teacher,"and "Dr" that are not in the three stop word lists. However, they are very commonly used in teaching evaluation and should be removed when necessary. Therefore, we also added some additional words into the stop word list. Through this procedure, we identify a total of 619 words as stop words for our analysis.

The top 20 most used words after removing the stop words are shown in Figure 11.8. They include "easy," "great," "good," "tests," and so on. Note both the words "tests" and "test" are in the list. Therefore, considering they can mean the same thing, we further stemmed the words.

The top 20 most used words after removing the stop words and stemming are shown in Figure 11.9. They include "help," "test," "easi," great," and so on. After stemming, the order of the top words changed. This is because some words were combined together such as "tests" and "test" to "test," and "help" and "helpful" to "help." Also note that a stem might not be a proper word such as "easi" and "lectur" in the list. From the data analysis perspective, this does not matter.

FIGURE 11.9. The frequency of top words used in the comments after removing stop words and stemming.

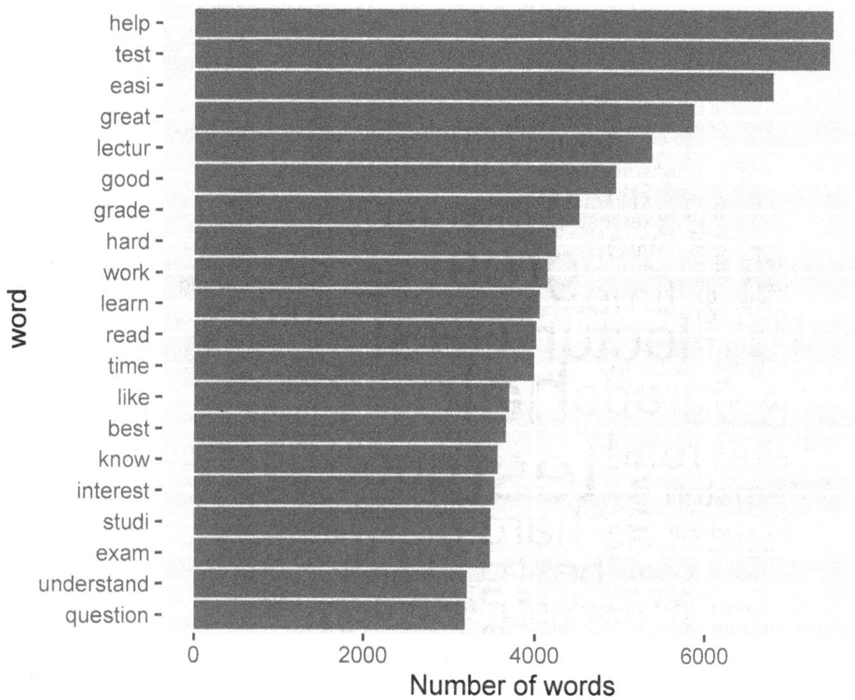

Word Cloud

Another way to visualize the word frequency is to generate a word cloud. A *word cloud* directly plots the words in a figure with the size of the words representing the frequency of them. For example, the top 200 most frequently used words are shown in the word cloud in Figure 11.10. From it, it is easy to see that "help," "test," and "easi" were the top three most widely used words. The words "exam," "question," and "interest" were also frequently used.

FIGURE 11.10. Word cloud of the top 200 words used in the comments.

11.5.3 n-gram Analysis

Previously, we focused on the analysis of individual words. Compared to an individual word, a group of words can provide additional information under certain conditions. For example, see the comment below. It starts with "not easy." If the comment was broken into individual words and one looks at "easy" only, the phrase "not easy at all" would have the opposite meaning. Similarly, in the same comment, "never" was used to modify "know." Therefore, for such situations, it is a better idea to treat the two words together.

> not easy at all , yes she is a good teacher and explained material well enough. BUT there is a LOT of material and you never

FIGURE 11.11. The frequency of top 2-grams used in the comments.

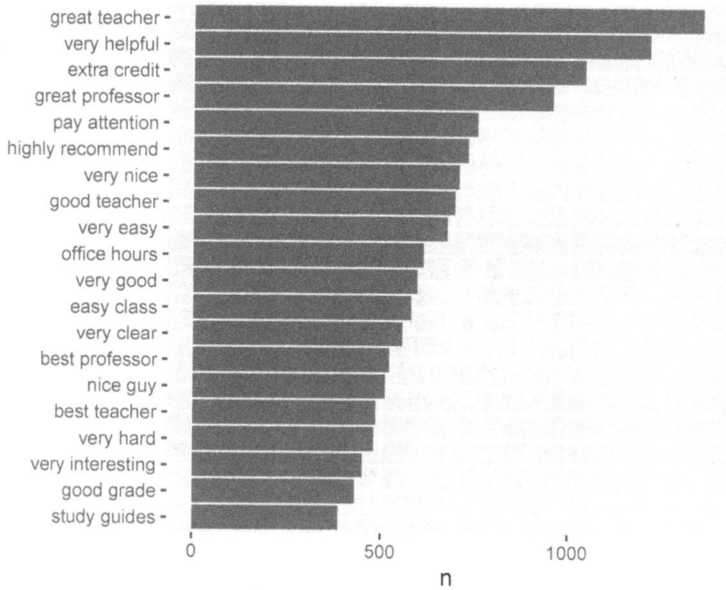

know what particularly would be on test . she asks on test not much but in details . be ready to read and memorize a huge amount of information

Earlier, we discussed on how to tokenize the text using n-gram. We now tokenize the comments into two words, also called 2-gram or bigram, and three words, also called 3-gram or trigram.

2-gram

As for the individual word analysis, the extremely common two-word phrases such as "he is" and "if you" might not be very informative for analysis. We can also remove those frequently used phrases based on stop words. In doing so, if either of the two words appears in the stop word list, we remove the two word phrase.

From Figure 11.11, the top three most frequent two-word phrases are "great teacher," "very helpful," and "extra credit." Each appeared more than 1,000 times in the comments. Note that one can combine phases such as "best professor" and "best teacher" through stemming.

Figure 11.12 shows the top 100 most frequently used two-word phrases. As expected, the 2-gram picks up the phrases such as "not hard," "not like,"

FIGURE 11.12. Word cloud of the top 100 bigrams used in the comments.

and "not helpful" that would have been missed in the analysis of individual words. In addition, one would also be able to distinguish "not helpful," "very helpful," and "extremely helpful."

3-gram

As for the 2-gram analysis, we can conduct 3-gram analysis by tokenizing the text into three words. Figure 11.13 shows the top 100 most frequently used three-word phrases. The most used three-word phrase is "very good teacher." Clearly, 3-gram analysis can provide some information that cannot be observed in unigram and bigram analysis. For example, we can see that "extra credit opportunities" is clearly important to students. In addition, the phrases "not very helpful" and "not very clear" would be characterized very differently if using 2-gram analysis.

FIGURE 11.13. Word cloud of the top 100 trigrams used in the comments.

Network Plot of the Word Relationship

In the previous 2-gram and 3-gram analysis, multiple words come together and one word might be associated more with specific words. The relationship of the words can be visualized through a network plot. Figure 11.14 shows the network plot of the 2-gram with more than 250 appearances in the comments. In the figure, each dot represents a word and the arrow between two words represents a 2-gram with the word at the end of the arrow being the second word. For example, the 2-gram "extra credit" can be seen in the figure. For this particular plot, the color and the width of the arrow also represent the frequency of the 2-grams. For example, the arrow for "great teacher" is the thickest and lightest, indicating it is the most frequent 2-gram in the data.

From the figure, we can see that the words "very" and "teacher" are associated with the largest number of words. In addition, "very" is often used to describe the other words such as "very clear" and "very funny." On the other hand, many words are used to describe "teacher" such as in "great teacher" and "worst teacher." The plot also shows the path of connection for more than two words. For example, at the top of the figure, we can see

FIGURE 11.14. Network plot of the word association of top used words.

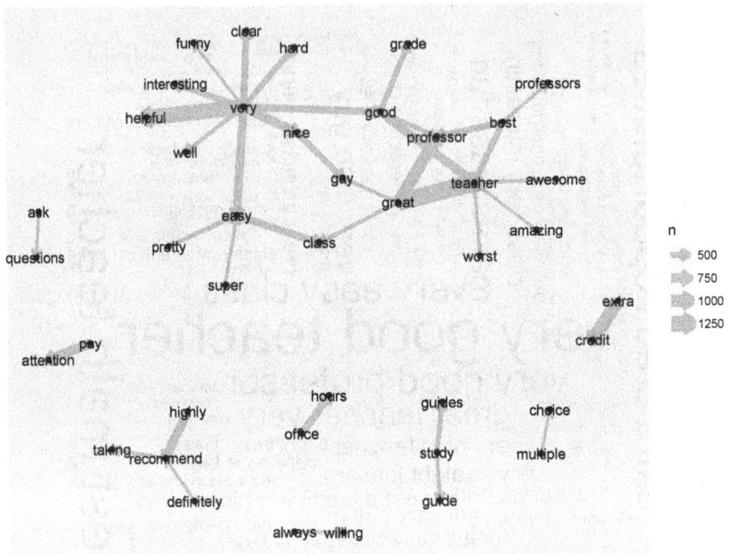

"highly recommend taking" and "definitely recommend taking." Another example is "very easy class."

11.6 Sentiment Analysis

Sentiment analysis, also known as *opinion mining* or *emotion AI*, is a method of text analysis to systematically identify and quantify the study affective state and subjective information in text. The basic idea is that the text reflects the emotional response to an event that a writer experiences (Tausczik & Pennebaker, 2010). For example, positive emotion words such as love, nice, and sweet are used in writing about a positive event, and negative emotion words such as hurt, ugly, and nasty are used in writing about a negative event (Kahn, Tobin, Massey, & Anderson, 2007). Most sentiment analyses focus on the polarity of a text, where polarity is a measure of the extent to which a text is more negative or more positive. However, methods are also available to look "beyond polarity" to identify dominant emotions such as joy, anger, and fear.

Although more complex methods such as latent semantic analysis and deep learning are available, the most common method for sentiment analysis still employs the knowledge-based or dictionary-based techniques. The dictionary-based techniques identify the sentiment of a text based on the presence of predetermined sentiment words such as happy, sad, afraid, and bored. Each of such word is labeled as negative, positive or neutral usually through crowd labeling. Once such words are identified, the sentiment is typically determined based on the sum or average score of these words.

11.6.1 Simple Dictionary-Based Sentiment Analysis

In dictionary-based sentiment analysis, one first builds a dictionary of sentiment words. In such a dictionary, each word is assigned an emotion or sentiment such as positive or negative or other categories such as happy, joy, fear, etc. The sentiment of each word can be best identified for a particular problem. For example, when studying positive and negative affects, one can ask people to identify whether a word shows positive or negative meanings. This chapter focuses on the use of existing sentiment dictionaries.

11.6.2 Word Sentiment

In the literature, there are several sentiment dictionaries or lexicons with identified word meanings that are widely used including AFINN, nrc, bing, and syuzhet.

AFINN

AFINN is a list of English words labeled by Finn A. Nielsen in 2009–2011 for positivity and negativity with an integer between −5 (most negative) and +5 (most positive) (Nielsen, 2011). The newest version of AFINN include 2,477 words and phrases. Some example words and their associated scores are given below. Example words are displayed in Table 11.5, with the word "robust" being labeled as positive with a score of +2 but "depressing" labeled as negative with a score −2.

TABLE 11.5. A Sample of 10 Words from the AFINN lexicon

word	score
robust	2
robber	−2
unloved	−2
hid	−1
ensuring	1
masterpiece	4
collapses	−2
eviction	−1
depressing	−2
disappointment	−2

nrc

The nrc lexicon categorizes words into positive or negative sentiments as well as eight different emotions, including anger, anticipation, disgust, fear, joy, sadness, surprise, and trust. The nrc lexicon was created by Mohammad and Turney (2010) through Mturk crowd labeling. We randomly selected 10 words as shown in Table 11.6. nrc includes a total of 6,468 words labeled as either positive (1) or negative (−1). For 4,463 words, their emotions were also labeled as one or more of the eight emotions. For example, "jump" was assigned the emotion "joy." The word "arsenic" had three emotions—disgust, fear, and sadness. Some words were not given any emotion.

TABLE 11.6. A Sample of 10 Words from the nrc Lexicon

word	score	
jump	1	joy
promotion	1	
working	1	
affable	1	
martingale	−1	
stools	−1	disgust
weatherproof	1	
leeches	−1	disgust, fear
arsenic	−1	disgust, fear, sadness
scotch	−1	

bing

The bing lexicon, developed by Hu and Liu, 2004a,b, categorizes words into positive and negative categories. The lexicon has 6,874 words and phrases with the majority of them coded as 1 (2,024 words) and −1 (4,824 words). The rest of the words were coded as 0, −1.05, and −2. A random selection of 10 words/phrases are listed in Table 11.7.

syuzhet

The syuzhet lexicon was developed in the Nebraska Literary Lab by Jockers (2017). The lexicon has a total of 10,738 words with 16 scores from −1 to 1. The number of words for each score is shown in Figure 11.15.

A sample of 10 words is listed in Table 11.8. For example, the word "warning" has a score −0.5 and the word "spirits" has a score 0.25. The words in this lexicon were extracted from a corpus of contemporary novels and therefore may work best for such text.

TABLE 11.7. A Sample of 10 Words from the bing Lexicon

word	score
paramount	1
durable	1
helps	1
repetitive	−1
disturbing	−1
spews	−1
polution	−1
too much	−2
staunchly	1
ill defined	−1

TABLE 11.8. A Sample of 10 Words from the syuzhet Lexicon

word	score
warning	−0.5
oddest	−0.5
extinguished	−0.25
pristine	1
spirits	0.25
illtreated	−1
illicit	−0.5
uneducated	−0.8
doubtfully	−0.5
prejudices	−1

Which sentiment lexicon to use in a particular study depends on the purpose of the study. Multiple lexicons can be combined to use in one study, too. Generally speaking, one should go through all the words in a chosen lexicon to add or remove relevant words.

FIGURE 11.15. The number of words in each of 16 score categories for the syuzhet lexicon.

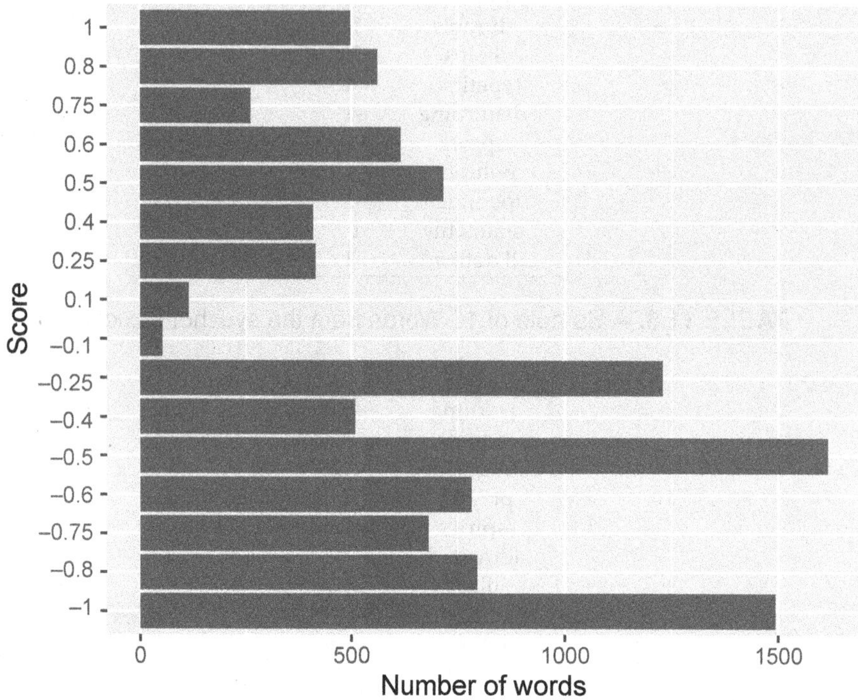

11.7 Conducting Sentiment Analysis

With a chosen sentiment lexicon, one can study the sentiment of a text. For a given text, one needs to first decide at what level a sentiment score is calculated. For example, one can get the sentiment of the whole text, a paragraph of the text, a sentence of the text, or individual words of the text. Therefore, we can tokenize the text into individual tokens and get the sentiment score for each token. For individual words, we can look them up in the sentiment lexicon and then use the sentiment scores directly. For a sentence, we can first identify and score the individual words that appear in the lexicon and then aggregate the scores of the individual words as the sentiment of the sentence. This can be done similarly for other units of text.

As an example, we first take a close look at the comment below.

```
My favorite Professor by far. He is very
    helpful and willing to help you out the
    best he can. He will not just give you
    answers however, but help guide you so
```

```
that you can learn it on your own. I
definately recommend taking him for
whatever math courses you can. He
requires a lot of work, but it pays off
in the run!
```

First, we can identify the sentiment words in the comment. Using different lexicons, we can get different words, as shown in Table 11.9. For example, using the lexicon AFINN, five different words are selected with "help" appearing twice. The lexicon syuzhet identified nine words. For all four lexicons, only positive words are found in the comment.

TABLE 11.9. The Sentiment Words in the Example Comment in the Above Listing

AFINN		nrc		bing		syuzhet	
Word	Score	Word	Score	Word	Score	Word	Score
favorite	2	favorite	1	favorite	1	favorite	0.75
helpful	2	professor	1	helpful	1	professor	0.4
help	2	helpful	1	willing	1	helpful	0.75
best	3	guide	1	best	1	willing	0.8
help	2	learn	1	recommend	1	best	0.5
recommend	2	recommend	1	work	1	guide	0.6
						learn	0.8
						recommend	0.5
						work	0.25

If we are interested in the overall sentiment of the comment, we can then add together the score for each word. For example, using the bing lexicon, the sentiment score for the comment is 6; and using the syuzhet lexicon, the sentiment score is 5.35. The comment includes five sentences, if splitting based on the period. Then the sentiment of each sentence can be similarly evaluated. If we use the syuzhet lexicon, the sentiment of each sentence is 1.15, 2.05, 1.40, 0.50, and 0.25, respectively. Note that although all lexicons pointed to a positive sentiment of the example comment, the magnitude of the sentiment cannot be determined simply by the score without defining a norm first.

11.7.1 Sentiment Analysis of Teaching Evaluation Text Data

The teaching evaluation dataset includes 27,939 comments on a total of 999 professors in terms of their teaching. For each comment, we can calculate its overall sentiment as illustrated earlier. Figure 11.16 shows the histogram of the sentiment scores of the 27,939 comments based on the bing lexicon. The average sentiment score is 1.68 with a standard deviation of 2.37. If 0 means a neutral comment, overall, the comments are positive.

FIGURE 11.16. The histogram of the sentiment scores of teaching evaluation comments based on the bing lexicon.

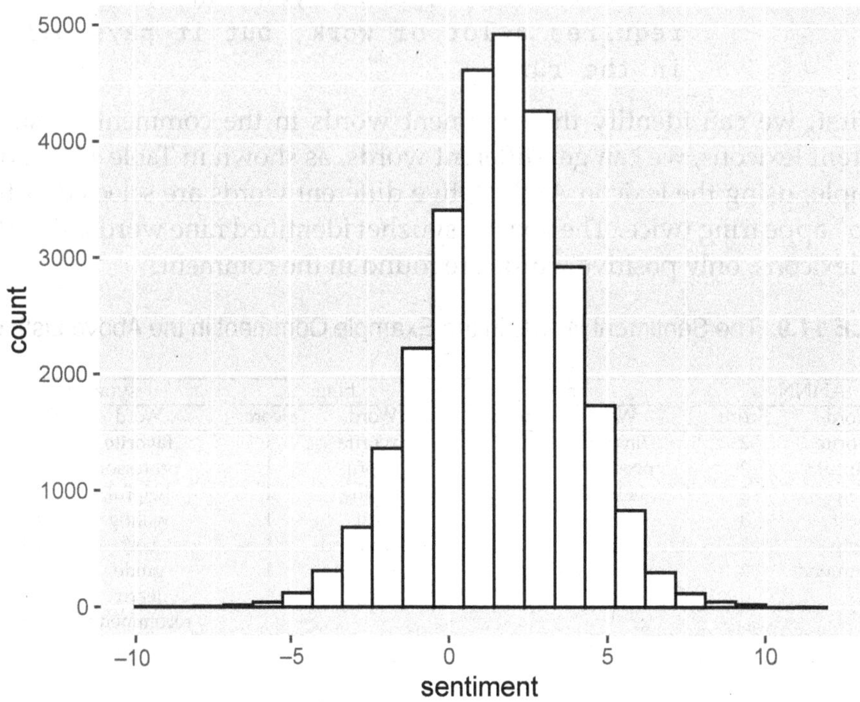

In the previous section, we generated a word cloud for the top words used in all the comments. Using the sentiment lexicon, we can further identify the positive and negative words or phases. Figure 11.17 shows the word clouds for the positive words on the left and for the negative words on the right. From this, we can see that the top used positive words in the comments are "easy," "great," "good," "interesting," and so on. The popular negative words include "hard," "difficult," "boring," "horrible," and so on. An interesting observation is that positive words are more concentrated where few words are used more frequently, but there are many more negative individual words that are used in the comments.

FIGURE 11.17. Word clouds of positive and negative words based on the bing lexicon.

One can also use other lexicon's for sentiment analysis. For example, the histogram of the sentiment scores based on the syuzhet lexicon is shown in Figure 11.18.

FIGURE 11.18. The histogram of the sentiment scores of teaching evaluation comments based on the syuzhet lexicon.

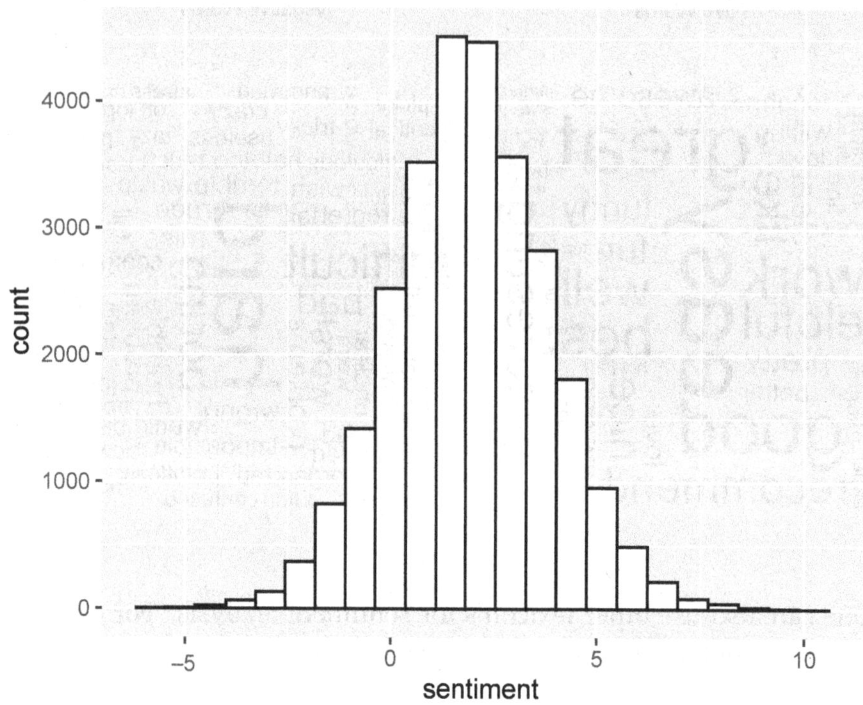

Figure 11.19 shows the scatterplot of the sentiment scores based on the bing and syuzhet lexicons. Clearly, the sentiment scores using the two lexicons very much agree with each other. In fact, the correlation is 0.852.

FIGURE 11.19. The positive correlation between the sentiment scores based on the bing and syuzhet lexicons.

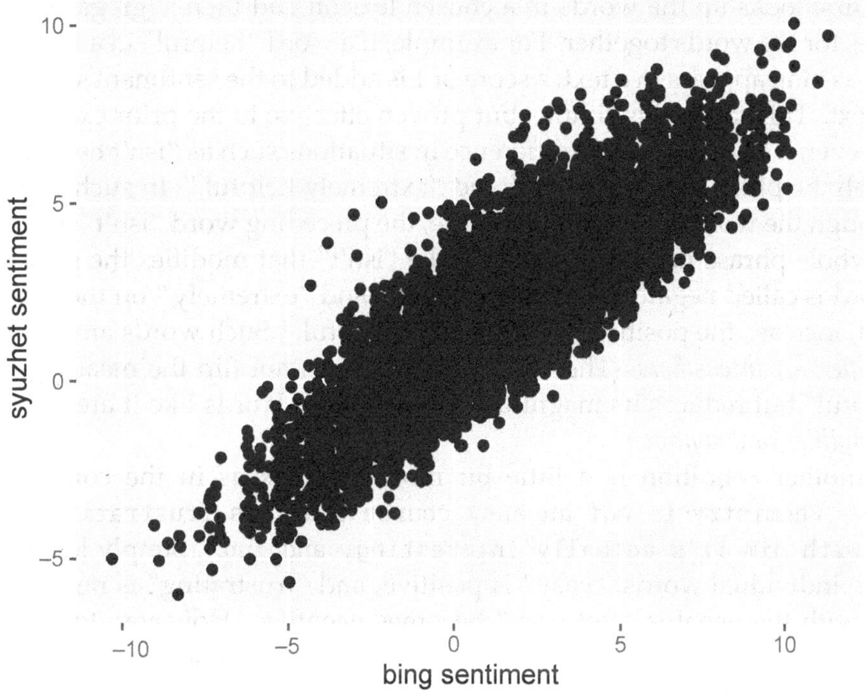

In the dataset, we also have a numerical rating on teaching performance as well as a rating on the difficulty of the class. We further investigated the correlation between the sentiment scores and the two variables as shown in Table 11.10. The correlation between the sentiment scores and the numerical ratings is 0.576 using the bing lexicon and 0.561 using the syuzhet sentiment. Based on the criteria set up by Cohen (1988), the correlation is large. In addition, we observed a negative correlation between the sentiment scores and the difficulty scores, and the correlation is medium according to Cohen (1988). Therefore, we might say the sentiment analysis has criterion validity or external validity if one trusts the numerical ratings.

TABLE 11.10. The Correlation Matrix between Sentiment Scores and Numerical Ratings

	Rating	Difficulty	bing sentiment	syuzhet sentiment
Rating	1			
Difficulty	−0.506	1		
bing sentiment	0.576	−0.323	1	
syuzhet sentiment	0.561	−0.303	0.852	1

11.7.2 Sentiment Analysis with Valence Shifters

The previous sentiment analysis was based on individual words or phrases. One first looks up the words in a chosen lexicon and then aggregates the scores for the words together. For example, if a word "helpful" in a lexicon such as bing appears in a text, a score of 1 is added to the sentiment score of the text. This method is simple, but proven effective in the prior example. However, it also ignores the difference in situations such as "isn't helpful," "barely helpful," "very helpful," and "extremely helpful." In such cases, although the word "helpful" is positive, the preceding word "isn't" makes the whole phrase negative. A word like "isn't" that modifies the sign of a word is called negator. The words "very" and "extremely," on the other hand, increase the positivity of the word "helpful." Such words are called *amplifiers* or *intensifiers*. The word "barely" does not flip the meaning of "helpful" but reduces its magnitude of positivity. Words like it are called *de-amplifier* or *downtoner*.

Another condition is a little bit more complex as in the comment here—"`Chemistry is not an easy course and it's frustrating, but with him it's actually interesting, and fun.`" Simply looking at the individual words, "easy" is positive, and "frustrating" is negative. But, with the negator, "not easy" becomes negative. However, together with the adversative conjunction "but" in the next sentence, the previous negative sentiment should not be considered as negative any more.

The above-mentioned types of words, including negator, amplifier, de-amplifier, and adversative conjunction, are collectively called *valence shifters*, which can alter or intensify the sentiment of words under evaluation. Valence shifters can be a serious problem. For example, for the teaching comments, about 20% of the time a negator appears together with the sentiment word using the bing lexicon (see Table 11.11). Therefore, to best capture the sentiment of a text, such valence shifters should be taken into consideration.

TABLE 11.11. The Co-occurrence Rate of Valence Shifters and the Sentiment Words Using the bing Lexicon

Valence shifter	Co-occurrence
negator	0.194
amplifier	0.297
de-amplifier	0.048
adversative	0.143

One way to handle this is to assign a weight to the sentiment score according to the type of shifters. For example, for the sentiment of a word with a negator, a weight of −1 can be used, which effectively reverses the

FIGURE 11.20. The histogram of the sentiment scores of teaching evaluation comments based on the bing lexicon with valence shifters.

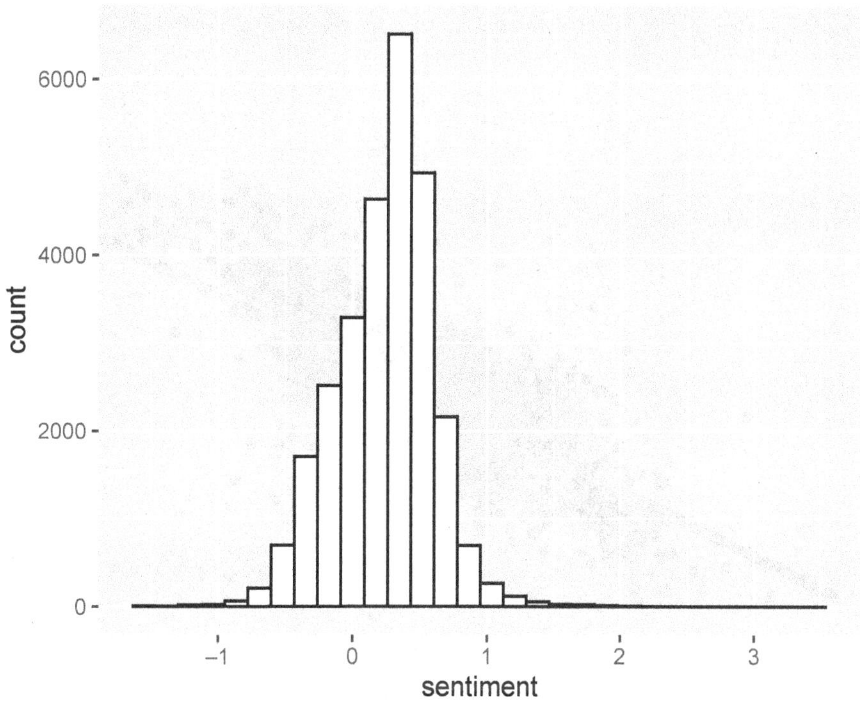

sentiment score. For amplifiers, a weight of 2 might be used to double the sentiment score of a positive or negative word. For de-amplifier, a weight between 0 and 1 can be used. The choice of the weights can be conditional on the research questions and the purpose of the research. For example, the R package `sentimentr` (Rinker, 2019) can conduct the sentiment analysis with valence shifters. In the package, the default weight for amplifier and de-amplifier is 0.8 and for adversative conjunction is 0.25.

Sentiment Analysis of Teaching Comments with Valence Shifters

We now reanalyze the teaching comments using sentiment analysis with valence shifters. The distribution of the sentiment scores for all comments is shown in Figure 11.20.

For comparison, we plot the scores with and without valence shifters in Figure 11.21. In the plot, the straight line has a slope of 1. If the two methods agree with each other, the data should fall around the line. From the plot, we can see that although the sentiment scores are positively correlated, they differ quite a bit. In fact, the correlation between the scores with and

FIGURE 11.21. Compassion of sentiment scores of the teaching evaluation comments with and without valence shifters.

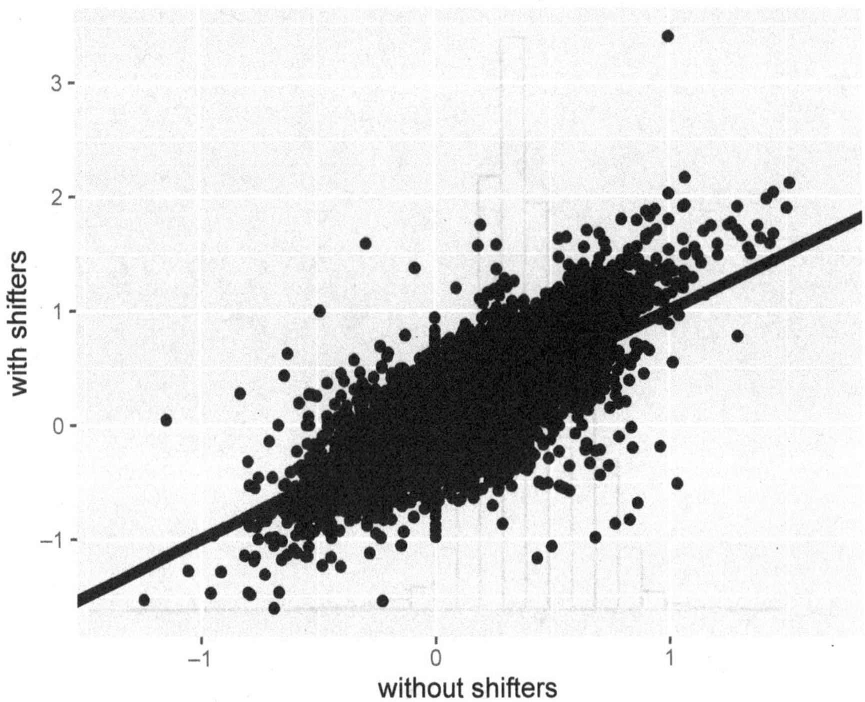

without valence shifters was about 0.86. Therefore, the consideration of valence shifters actually makes some difference in the sentiment scores.

Previously, we showed the the correlation between the numerical ratings of the professors and the sentiment scores based on the bing lexicon was about 0.576 (Table 11.10). The correlation now increased to 0.655 after taking into consideration of the valence shifters. If we assume the numerical ratings were accurate, we can conclude that the method with valence shifters works better in sentiment analysis.

11.7.3 Summary and Discussion

In this section, we showed that we can explore the sentiment of a text using the lexicon- or dictionary-based method. The method starts by choosing or building a sentiment lexicon. The sentiment lexicon consists of a list of words or phases and their corresponding sentiment scores. Ideally, the lexicon should be built based on the particular research question and context. For example, if the purpose is to understand the teaching evaluation based on student comments, then the lexicon should include the words that are relevant to teaching performance. The words can be selected through the joint work of students and teachers. Next, the words can be evaluated on whether they are positively and negatively related to teaching evaluations and then assigned a score. With the sentiment lexicon, one can then look up the words in a text and calculate a score for the text based on the scores of the words.

There are many existing sentiment lexicons that can be used for an initial quick sentiment analysis such as AFINN, nrc, bing, and syuzhet. Depending on which lexicon is used, the sentiment scores can differ. Even using the existing lexicons, one is also encouraged to adjust the lexicon accordingly, for example, adding or removing certain words and changing the associated sentiment scores. One can also combine several existing lexicons for sentiment analysis. The shifting of meanings of sentiment words because of modifiers or adversative conjunctions in general should and can be considered in sentiment analysis. Our example showed that the consideration of valence shifters did improve sentiment analysis.

Although this section has focused on the positive and negative polarity of the text, other types of emotion analysis can be conducted. Similarly, one can build a lexicon with different type of emotions. In fact, the nrc lexicon has eight different emotions, including anger, anticipation, disgust, fear, joy, sadness, surprise, and trust. For example, we selected 10 comments and obtained the emotions of them, as shown in Figure 11.22.

Other types of sentiment analysis can be conducted. The feature/aspect-based sentiment analysis can provide finer information than the sentiment analysis discussed in this chapter (Eirinaki, Pisal, & Singh, 2012; Qu & Zhang, 2020). In feature-based analysis, instead of getting a sentiment score for the whole text, different features can be first identified and then sentiment analysis can be conducted for each feature. For example, in student comments, one part of the comments might focus on the teaching style of a teacher but another part might focus solely on the personality of the teacher. Therefore, the method involved the additional step to find the features, where the topic modeling discussed in the next section can be used. Non-dictionary-based methods are also available for sentiment analysis. For example, machine learning methods can be used to build a model to predict the sentiment using labeled text. Then, the sentiment of new text can be derived based on the model.

FIGURE 11.22. Emotion composition of 10 selected student comments based on the nrc lexicon.

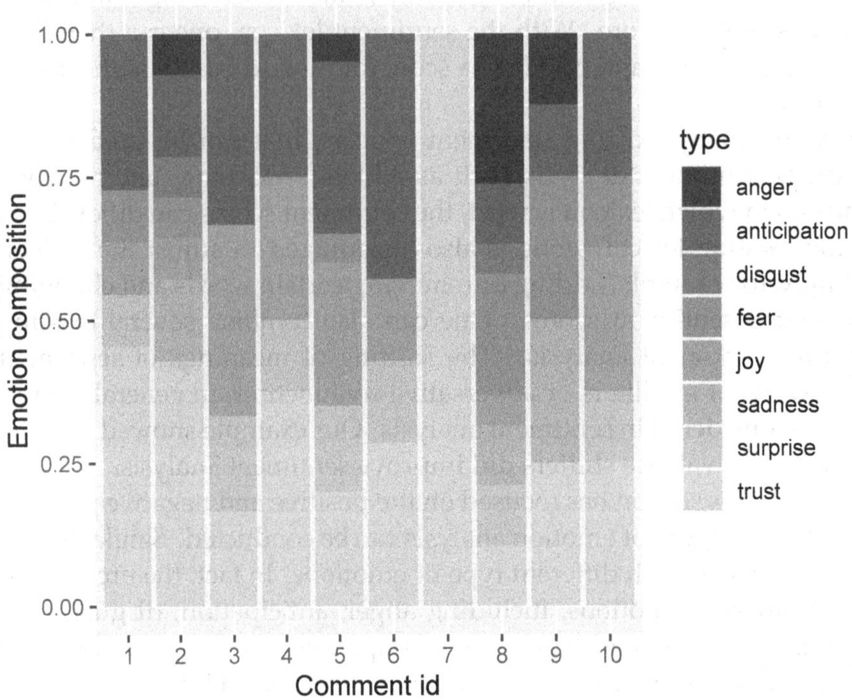

11.8 Topic Models

A body of text can be written around a specific topic or multiple topics. For example, in the teaching comments, one comment may focus on teaching effectiveness, another comment may simply talk about the personality of a teacher, and some comments may have both. Overall, we can view each comment as a combination or mixture of different topics. For example, the effectiveness of teaching and the personality of teachers can be viewed as two topics associated with teaching evaluation. Naturally, each topic is more associated with certain words or vocabularies. For example, when writing on teaching effectiveness, words like "prepared," "clarity," "organized," and so on, are expected to be used often. When describing personality, words such as "nice," "open," and "warm" might be more often used than the words for teaching effectiveness.

Topic modeling or topic models assess the topics and associated words in text. Latent Dirichlet allocation (LDA) is probably the most widely used method for topic modeling that allows the observed words to be explained by latent topics. It assumes that each document, for example, a teaching evaluation comment, is a mixture of a small number of topics and each word's presence in a document is associated with one of the document's topics.

11.8.1 Latent Dirichlet Allocation

LDA is a popular model for topic modeling. The model reflects the mechanism of writing a document such as a comment on evaluating teaching. In writing a comment, one might first think about the areas or aspects from which to evaluate a professor. For example, a student might focus more on the organization of the lectures or the difficulty of the tests. These can be viewed as two topics. Then the student would write around the two topics by picking words related to the topics.

We now discuss in more detail the LDA process in terms of document generation. Suppose we want to generate a collection of documents with a total of K topics. Documents within the collection can be viewed as independent of each other. For a given document, it can consist of one or all of the K topics with different probabilities. Let z_{km} be the kth ($k = 1, \ldots, K$) topic in the mth ($m = 1, \ldots, M$) document. z_{km} takes a value between 1 and K. The topics can be generated from a multinomial distribution

$$z_{km} \sim Multinomial(\boldsymbol{\theta}_m)$$

with the topic probability $\boldsymbol{\theta}_m = (\theta_{m1}, \theta_{m2}, \ldots, \theta_{mK})'$ for the document m. Note that $\sum_{k=1}^{K} \theta_{mk} = 1$. For example, if there are two topics, $K = 2$. For one document, the topic probabilities for the two topics can be 0.5 and 0.5; for another document, the topic probabilities could be 0.7 and 0.3. The topic probabilities can be viewed as proportions of words used to describe the different topics.

Once a topic is decided upon, one then organizes words around it. For example, if it is about the difficulty of the test, words such as "easy" and "difficult" might be more likely to be used. Let $w_{mn}, n = 1, \ldots, N_m; m = 1, \ldots, M$, be the nth word to be used in the mth document and N_m denoting the total number of words of the mth document. w_{mn} would take a value between 1 and V with V being the total number of unique words used in all the comments/documents. Specifically, a word is generated using

$$w_{mn} | z_{km} \sim Multinomial(\boldsymbol{\beta}_k)$$

where $\boldsymbol{\beta}_k = c(\beta_{k1}, \beta_{k2}, \ldots, \beta_{kV})'$ is the probability that a word is picked given the topic k is selected. Note that the probability is different for different words within different topics. For example, "easy" and "difficult" will have higher probabilities in the topic regarding the difficulty of the test than a topic related to the personality of the teachers.

LDA can also be understood from a bottom-up perspective. Consider a 100-word teaching comment with two topics—effectiveness of teaching and personality of the teacher. In the comment, 70 words are organized around the effectiveness of teaching and 30 words on the personality of the teacher. Therefore, the topic probabilities are 0.7 and 0.3 for the two topics. A much larger set, for example, 1,000 words, can be used to describe the two topics. The 100 words are actually selected from them based on the word probability associated with the topics.

Clearly, it is critical to specify $\boldsymbol{\theta}$ and $\boldsymbol{\beta}$. LDA assumes that both are generated from a Dirichlet distribution. For topic probability, it uses

$$\boldsymbol{\theta}_m \sim Dirichlet(\boldsymbol{\alpha}),$$

for each document m. For word probability, one can use

$$\boldsymbol{\beta}_k \sim Dirichlet(\boldsymbol{\delta}).$$

In the Dirichlet distribution, $\boldsymbol{\alpha}$ and $\boldsymbol{\delta}$ are either predetermined or parameters to be estimated.

In most scenarios, the parameters in LDA models are not known and need to be estimated. This is a reverse-engineering process to find the number of topics, the associated topic probabilities as well as word probabilities. Both frequentist and Bayesian methods are available to estimate the parameters. For example, Blei Ng, and Jordan (2003) proposed efficient approximate inference techniques based on variational methods and an EM algorithm for empirical Bayes parameter estimation.

11.8.2 Topic Modeling of the Teaching Evaluation Data

As an example, we explore what aspects or topics students focus on in evaluating their professors. Using the teaching comment data, we first combine the comments from students for each professor together. Therefore, the data include text data on a total of 999 professors. Before conducting topic modeling, the texts were preprocessed by removing stopwords, stemming, and removing very infrequent words. After processing, this resulted in 999 combined text comments with a total of 499,836 words, among which there were 3,064 unique words. Each unique word appears at least five times in the 999 comments.

Typical topic modeling involves (1) determining the number of topics, (2) finding terms associate with each topic, and (3) understanding the topic composition of each text document.

Determining the Number of Topics

In topic modeling, the number of topics was often unknown. Before estimating a topic model, we need first to empirically choose the best number of topics. To do it, we can use cross-validation (CV). For example, a c-fold cross-validation can be used. The basic idea of CV is to divide the data into c folds, or c subsets. Each time, we use $c - 1$ folds of data to fit a model and then use the left one fold of data to evaluate the model fit. This can be done for a given number of topics. Then, we can select the optimal number of topics based on a certain measure of the model fit.

In topic models, we can use a statistic (e.g., perplexity) to measure the model fit. The perplexity is the geometric mean of word likelihood. In c-fold CV, we first estimate the model, usually called the *training model*, for a given number of topics using $c - 1$ folds of the data and then use the left one fold of the data to calculate the perplexity.

FIGURE 11.23. Plot of the complexity for topic modeling of teaching comment data.

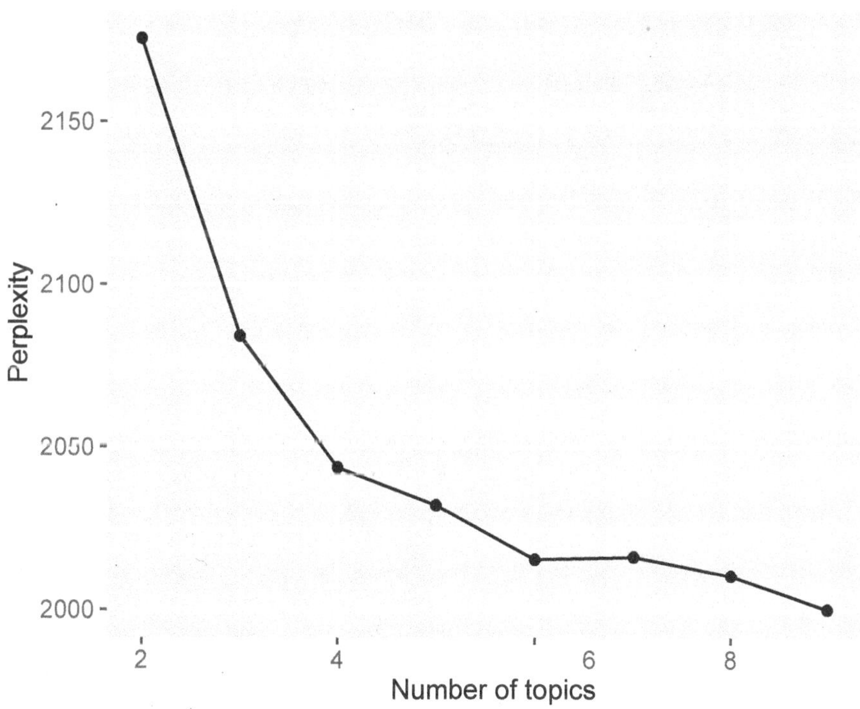

For the teaching comments, we conducted a 5-fold CV for the number of topics ranging from 2 to 9. The total perplexity with 2 to 9 topics is given in Figure 11.23. Overall, with the increase of the number of topics, the perplexity kept decreasing. However, the decrease seemed to slow down from six to seven topics. Therefore, we can choose six topics for analysis.

Terms Associated with Each Topic

Based on the six topics, we conducted the topic modeling of the teaching comment data. For the 3,064 unique words in the comments, each word has a probability to associate with each of the six topics. If each word has the same probability associated to a topic, then the probability would be 1/3064 = 0.03%. The top 10 words associated with each topic are listed in Table 11.12 and displayed in Figure 11.24.

For example, for topic 3, the probability for the word "lectur" to be associated with it is 3.29%, which is more than 100 times of the average probability of 0.03%. Note that the same word can be closely related to multiple topics. For example, for the word "class," it ranked as the top word for topics 1, 2, 4, 5, and 6. This tells us that when students talked about all six topics, they tended to use the word "class." But only when the third topic was mentioned, were they likely to use the word "lectur."

TABLE 11.12. The Top 10 Words Associated with Each Topic

Topic 1		Topic 2		Topic 3		Topic 4		Topic 5		Topic 6	
Word	Prob	Word	Prob	Word	Prob	Word	Prob	Word	Prob	Word	Prob
class	7.04%	class	6.06%	lectur	3.29%	class	5.01%	class	7.51%	class	5.33%
test	4.09%	not	4.42%	veri	2.78%	teacher	3.83%	veri	2.87%	veri	3.51%
easi	3.60%	hard	1.70%	test	2.62%	help	2.88%	great	2.43%	help	3.03%
veri	2.01%	like	1.52%	help	2.29%	math	2.75%	professor	2.40%	professor	2.53%
studi	1.73%	read	1.42%	exam	2.25%	veri	2.72%	interest	2.35%	work	2.45%
read	1.72%	grade	1.42%	class	1.97%	homework	2.12%	teacher	1.83%	student	2.18%
book	1.72%	don't	1.26%	professor	1.89%	not	2.12%	best	1.70%	teacher	2.12%
not	1.69%	veri	1.24%	studi	1.83%	teach	1.65%	easi	1.66%	great	1.73%
exam	1.55%	time	1.19%	not	1.81%	understand	1.63%	make	1.52%	assign	1.52%
quizz	1.38%	teacher	1.19%	materi	1.74%	easi	1.62%	funni	1.45%	learn	1.31%

FIGURE 11.24. The six topics and the associated top 10 items.

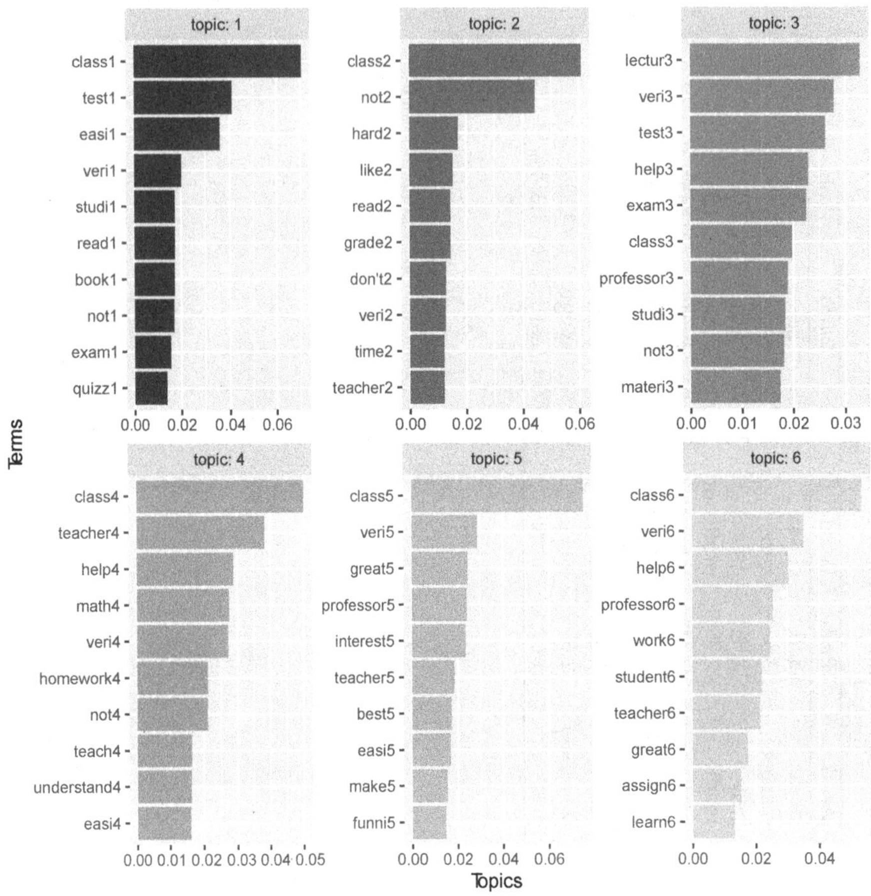

Topics Associated with Each Text

We can further investigate which topics a comment is composed of. Table 11.13 shows the topic probability of each topic for comments of five selected professors. For example, for Professor 1 in the table, about 55% of the comments were related to topic 2, meaning that 55% of words used in the comments are related to topic 2. Very few words in the comments were from topics 3 and 4. For Professor 5, the comments were primarily focused on topics 1, 2, and 3.

TABLE 11.13. Topic Probability of Each Topic in Comments of Selected Professors

Topics	Professor 1	Professor 2	Professor 3	Professor 4	Professor 5
1	4.00%	23.70%	0.02%	31.10%	30.00%
2	55.30%	42.90%	5.28%	0.03%	30.80%
3	0.07%	6.49%	25.30%	30.10%	39.10%
4	0.07%	0.22%	30.50%	0.03%	0.02%
5	30.20%	26.70%	6.79%	38.70%	0.02%
6	10.40%	0.01%	32.10%	0.03%	0.02%

Meaning of Topics and Classification of Text

Meaningfully naming the topics requires a thorough understanding of the problem under investigation. This can be done by the experts in a field assisted with the results from topic modeling. For example, for each topic, we can first identify the important words associated with it and then name the topic based on the meaning of the words. For example, for topic 3, "lectur" was a closely related word but did not appear as a top word for other topics. Therefore, maybe this topic was primarily about lecturing in teaching. In topic 5, the words such as "great," "best," "interest," and "fun" were frequent words and unique to this topic. Thus, the topic seemed to mainly concern the perception of teaching by the students. The meaning of other topics can be explored in a similar way.

Once we decide on the meaning of the topics, we can also classify the text into different topics based on the composition of topics. For the teaching comment data, we might group the professors according to their teaching styles. For example, for Professor 5, the majority of comments were related to topic 3. It indicates that they might be both good at lecturing or lecturing made them standout.

Topic Modeling Summary

In this section, we showed how to conduct topic modeling using the teaching evaluation data. The focus was on LDA. LDA can identify the topics in a text, the associated words with each topic, as well as topic composition of a text. In the literature, other methods for topic modeling are also available. For example, the correlated topics model (Blei & Lafferty, 2007) is an extension of the LDA model where correlations between topics are allowed. In addition, Mcauliffe and Blei (2008) proposed a supervised topic model that allows the topics to predict an observed outcome. More recently, Wilcox, Jacobucci, Zhang, and Ammerman (2023) extended the supervised topic model to allow the prediction of an observed outcome by the topics together with other covariates.

11.9 Summary

Although there are probably more qualitative text data than quantitative data, text data are relatively underutilized in social and behavioral research. In this chapter, we showed how one can extract and utilize information from text data. Through text analysis, one can gain insight into what otherwise might not be possible. For example, in the teaching evaluation data, no information on the gender of the professors was immediately available. However, we can still identify the gender of the professors based on the use of gender words such as he/she and him/her in the comments from the students. Although it is simple, this example illustrates how to conduct basic text analysis—identify and extract important information such as individual words and quantify them such as using frequency of the words.

Preprocessing in text analysis is much more critical than in quantitative data cleaning. Preprocessing should not be viewed as an isolated process but should be an integral part of the text data analysis. Preprocessing typically involves a variety of steps such as extracting text from unstructured data, removing sensitive and confidential information, handling special characters and abbreviations, spell checking and correction, removing stop words, and word stemming. Not all analyses necessarily need all the steps and some analyses might need additional preprocessing.

Tokenization can effectively break down a text to any unit for further analysis. Although it is most common to tokenize to individual words, many other ways of tokenization are possible and can be used according to the purpose of the analysis. Tokenization is often combined and repeated with preprocessing to best process the data into a format that is ready to be analyzed.

After tokenization, we typically express the text data in a document-term matrix. Such a matrix includes all the information we want to extract from the text. Each element in the matrix is typically a statistic regarding the tokens such as the frequency of a token in a comment. The matrix can be visualized or analyzed in a variety of ways. For example, we can visualize the word frequency through a bar plot or a word cloud. A network plot can be used to display the word associations. The process for the basic text analysis can be summarized in Figure 11.25.

After data cleaning, different text analysis methods can be applied. For example, sentiment analysis can be conducted to understand the sentiment of text. The sentiment information from the text can be further used in other analysis. For example, one can investigate what is related to the sentiment or how the sentiment is related to outcome variables of interest. More complex data analysis such as topic modeling can also be conducted

FIGURE 11.25. A simple diagram for basic text analysis.

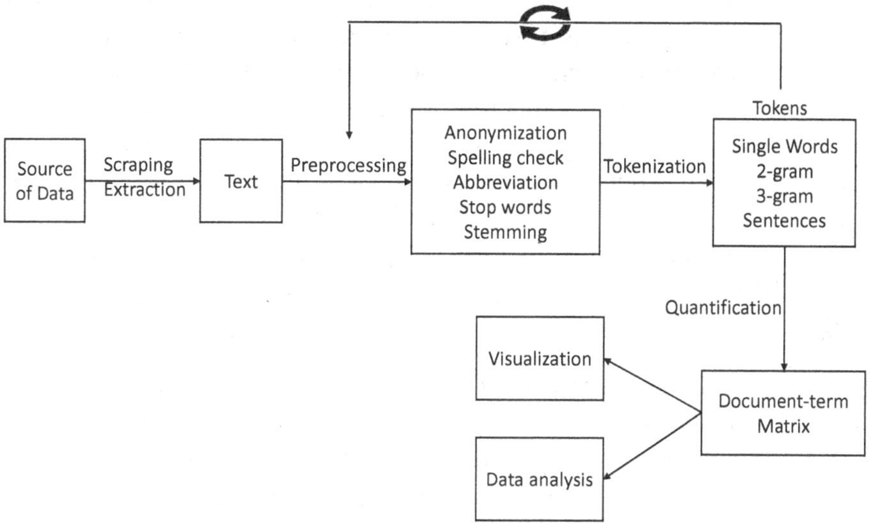

to identify the topics in texts to better understand the text information. This chapter serves an introduction to text analysis to get researchers familiar with the basic text analysis techniques. For more comprehensive treatment of text data, one can consult the seminal works such as Feldman et al. (2007) and Miner et al. (2012).

11.9.1 Further Reading

- One popular text mining method that was not covered in this chapter is latent semantic analysis (LSA; also known as latent semantic indexing; Deerwester, Dumais, Landauer, Furnas, & Harshman, 1990; Landauer, Foltz, & Laham, 1998) , a method that falls under the umbrella of topic modeling and is very similar to LDA. Essentially the difference between LSA and LDA can be boiled down to PCA versus LCA. Whereas PCA is a dimension reduction technique, mixture models such as LCA are generative models, meaning we are clustering words and documents by topic. Although very similar in practice, we see LDA applied to a greater extent and has spawned additional extensions which can be applicable to social and behavioral research. We do not dive further into this given space concerns, as well as the relative dearth of comparison.
- The most popular dictionary-based approach in psychological research is the Linguistic Inquiry and Word Count (LIWC; Pennebaker,

Francis, & Booth, 2001), which is implemented as a commercially available software program (Pennebaker, Boyd, Jordan, & Blackburn, 2015). LIWC analyzes text according to a dictionary comprised of 6,400 words, word stems, and emoticons, largely related to psychological processes (e.g., affective, social processes; Pennebaker et al., 2015). From this analysis, users get an output of scores on 90 components of the dictionary and linguistic/grammatical dimensions of their data. Particularly when the sample size is small or the response lengths are relatively short, use of dictionary-based approaches like the LIWC will likely result in better prediction than more complex algorithms.

- We discussed the analysis of text from a relatively simplistic point of view, mainly focusing on the individual words while negating the order in which they were used. The field of natural language processing has developed a number of more advanced approaches for modeling the sequence in which words are used, most commonly using various forms of neural networks (i.e., deep learning). We chose to not discuss this area of algorithmic development because many research applications in social and behavioral research do not have the amount of text necessary to take advantage of these more complex approaches. For readers interested in this, we recommend Chollet and Allaire (2017) for an introduction for deep learning with applications in R.

11.9.2 Computational Time and Resources

While the focus in this chapter was using R packages to process and analyze the data, Python has a richer set of tools for text data, as well as a larger array of resources. Most of the analyses conducted in this chapter can be run in a matter of seconds. Computational time scales with the complexity of the analysis, with the LDA, CTM, and sLDA analyses typically taking on the order of minutes or a few hours. The main factors in the amount of time these analyses take are the number of observations (documents) and the number of words in the DTM. Oftentimes it is common to remove both stop words and infrequently used words (e.g,. less than 10 times across all documents) to reduce the dimensionality of the DTM for the express purpose of reducing computational time. Scraping data can result in much larger datasets, thus potentially increasing the amount of time it takes to analyze. As with many of the prior chapters, it is recommended to try and parallelize as many of the computations as possible, either through built in arguments in each R package, or by explicitly creating your own script to run 5-fold CV in parallel, for instance.

12

Introduction to Social Network Analysis

Although the history of social network analysis can be traced back to 1930s (Moreno, 1934) when graphs were used to visualize social communities, it only became a popular interdisciplinary research topic in statistics, sociology, political science, and psychology in the past few decades (e.g., Che, Jin, & Zhang, 2020; Liu, Jin, & Zhang 2018; Saul & Filkov, 2007; Schaefer, Adams, & Haas 2013; Wasserman & Faust, 1994). The popularity of social network analysis is attributed to its distinct features in data and associated techniques that differ from traditional methods used in social and psychological research. The primary information of a social network is the interrelations (often called edges, ties, connections, links, or paths) among a group of participants (often called nodes, vertices, entities, actors, or individuals) (Wasserman & Faust, 1994). In this chapter, we introduce basic techniques for social network analysis including network visualization, basic network analysis, and network modeling. In particular, we will demonstrate how to apply these techniques through the analysis of a set of real network data introduced in the following section.

12.1 Key Terminology

- Node. Also referred to as vertices, entities, actors, or individuals. This refers to the actual people in the network.
- Edges. Also referred to as ties, connections, links, or paths. This refers to the inter-relationships between nodes.
- Binary network. Most common type of network in social network analysis. This refers to edges either being present or not present in the network. For our data, people are either friends or not friends. In other types of networks the edges can represents strength values, such as the commonly used partial correlation networks.

- Sparse. It is common for social networks to be sparse, meaning that most people are not related to most others.

- Network size. Number of nodes in a network.

- Density. Total number of edges divided by the number of possible edges.

The structural pattern of relationships of nodes is naturally the target of typical social network analysis. For instance, in a friendship network or a Facebook network, some people are closer to each other and thus form small friendship networks. The inherent patterns in dyadic ties are very informative and provide researchers rich opportunities to understand actors not only from their own attributes but also from the social environment around them.

Social network analysis has methodological advantages to other relational data analysis such as dyadic data analysis. In traditional dyadic data analyses, only data on dyads with relations are collected. Social network data, however, consist of both dyads with social relations and dyads without social relations. Therefore, they allow researchers to better understand dyadic relations. For example, sociologists and personality psychologists are often interested in the association between friendship and personalities (Asendorpf & Wilpers, 1998; Youyou, Stillwell, & Schwartz, 2017).

In the existing studies, only data on dyads with friendship relations are available and used in an analysis, as dyadic data without friendship are often not available.

Therefore, any conclusion may only reflect the situation with the friendship relation. Social network analysis, in contrast, can better understand an individual's behaviors through connections between entities/nodes/subjects in a bounded network (Otte & Rousseau, 2002).

Network analysis techniques have been applied in many disciplines. For example, in economic research, network techniques have been used to address how the social, economic, and technological worlds are connected (Easley & Kleinberg, 2010). In epidemiology, network analysis is used to analyze the emergence of infectious diseases, such as the severe acute respiratory syndrome (Berger, Drosten, Doerr, Stuurmer, & Preiser 2004). In political science, researchers have investigated how social networks influence individual political preferences (Lazer et al., 2010; Ryan, 2011). In sociology, Dean, Bauer, and Prinstein (2017) studied the factors leading to friendship dissolution within a social network. In education research, social network analysis has been used to detect and prevent bullying among students (Faris & Felmlee, 2011). In psychology, social network analysis can inform behavioral interventions using the information from a network (Maya-Jariego & Holgado, 2015).

12.2 Data

For the purpose of illustration, in this chapter, we will analyze a set of data collected by the Lab for Big Data Methodology at the University of Notre Dame. The data were collected from students in the Art and Design major in a four-year college in China. There were a total of 181 students in this major with six different study concentrations. The data collection was conducted in May 2017 after the approval of the Institutional Review Board (IRB) at the University of Notre Dame, when the students were at the end of their junior year. In this section, we will first introduce the information collected and then discuss network data structures to store the network data.

12.2.1 Data Collection

During the data collection, each student was given a roster of all the 181 students and was asked to report whether he/she was a friend on WeChat with all other students. WeChat is currently the most popular social network platform in China. Two students had to mutually accept each other as a friend to be connected by WeChat. Therefore, the information collected formed a WeChat network among the students.

In addition to the WeChat network data, other information on each student was also collected. A list of variables that will be used in this chapter and their summary statistics are given in Table 12.1.

TABLE 12.1. List of Variables

Name	Mean	Median	SD	Minimum	Maximum
Gender	Male 74 (45%)			Female 91 (55%)	
Age	21.64	22	0.855	18	24
GPA	3.273	3.285	0.488	1.173	4.22
BMI	21.51	20.31	3.848	15.4	39.52
Happy	19.72	19	3.51	10	28
Lonely	11.28	11	5.67	0	26
Depression	5.46	5	2.92	0	13
Smoke	Yes 43 (36%)			No 122 (64%)	
Alcohol	Yes 68 (41%)			No 97 (59%)	

Although the data collection process reached out to a total of 181 students, only 165 students provided their data. Therefore, the sample size is 165 here. There were about an equal number of male and female students

(45% vs. 55%) in the sample. The average age was 21.64 at the time of data collection. The average GPA of the students at the time was about 3.273. On average, each student had 161 friends on the WeChat social network platform.

According to the National Institutes of Health (NIH), the BMI of 67.3% of the students was in the ideal range of 18.5 and 24.9. About 18.2% were underweight and 11.5% were overweight. Only about 3% were considered obese (BMI > 30). About 36% percent of students smoked cigarettes, and about 41% drank alcohol in the past 30 days.

Finally, the following mental health data were collected. First, depression was measured by seven items modified from the Personal Health Questionnaire (Kroenke et al., 2009). Second, loneliness was measured by a revised UCLA loneliness scale with 10 items (Russell, Peplau, & Ferguson, 1978). Third, happiness was measured by the three item subjective happiness scale (Lyubomirsky & Lepper, 1999). The composite scores of the three measures are used in this chapter, and their summary statistics are given in Table 12.1.

12.2.2 Network Data Structure

In regular data analysis, the data are often organized as a rectangular matrix with each column representing a variable and each row representing a participant or subject. For network data, they are often represented as an adjacency matrix or an edge list matrix. The adjacency matrix, also called a *sociomatrix* or *connection matrix*, represents the network data as an $N \times N$ square matrix, with N being the total number of participants. Using the network lexicon, each participant is called a node or a vertex. For example, for the WeChat network, there are a total of 165 nodes. The WeChat network can be represented by a 165×165 square matrix, with each row and column being a student. For example, Table 12.2 shows the adjacency matrix of the first 10 students in the WeChat network data.

For the WeChat network, no self-loop is allowed, which means that a student cannot be a friend of himself or herself. Therefore, all the diagonal values of the adjacency matrix are 0. For the off-diagonal values, 1 indicates that two students are WeChat friends and 0 indicates they are not. In network analysis, the relationship is also called an *edge*. For the WeChat data, if Student A reports Student B as a WeChat friend, Student A should also be a WeChat friend of Student B. Therefore, the adjacency matrix is symmetric. Such a network is called an *undirected network*. However, if A views B as a friend but B does not view A as a friend, one would have a directed network. In this situation, the convention is that rows indicate the starting node or the "source," and columns indicate the ending node or the

TABLE 12.2. The Adjacency Matrix of 10 Students from the WeChat Network

	1	2	3	4	5	6	7	8	9	10
1	0	1	1	1	0	0	0	0	0	0
2	1	0	1	1	0	1	1	0	1	1
3	1	1	0	1	1	1	1	1	1	1
4	1	1	1	0	1	1	1	1	1	1
5	0	0	1	1	0	1	1	0	0	0
6	0	1	1	1	1	0	1	0	0	1
7	0	1	1	1	1	1	0	0	0	0
8	0	0	1	1	0	0	0	0	1	0
9	0	1	1	1	0	0	0	1	0	0
10	0	1	1	1	0	1	0	0	0	0

"target." The WeChat network is also a binary network, in which an edge either exists or not, representing by 1 or 0. Other values can be used to measure the strength of the edges. In this case, the adjacency matrix can take categorical and continuous values. Such a network is called a *weighted* or *valued* network.

The adjacency matrix can grow big quickly. For example, Facebook had more than 2.4 billion active users in 2019. To present the Facebook friends information, one would need a 2.4-billion by 2.4-billion adjacency matrix. However, on average, each Facebook user has around 338 Facebook friends. Therefore, the vast majority of the elements in the adjacency matrix would be 0 (about 99.99999%). A more economical way to store network data is to use the edge list matrix. In the simplest case, one only needs a $K \times 2$ rectangular matrix to store the network data, with K being the total number of edges in the network. The first column stores the index of the starting node and the second column stores the index of the ending node of an edge. Therefore, only the pair of nodes with a relationship will be stored. For example, for the network in Table 12.2, $K = 27$ for a total of 27 WeChat friend relationships among the 10 students. Therefore, the edge list matrix is the one shown in Table 12.3. The initial adjacency matrix needs to store $10 \times 10 = 100$ values. However, the edge list matrix only needs to store $27 \times 2 = 54$ values. For the whole WeChat network, the adjacency matrix is a 165×165 matrix and the edge list matrix is a $1,722 \times 2$ matrix, a saving of about 87% storage. For a sparse network matrix such as the Facebook example, the saving on storage is even more significant.

Node Covariates

In addition to the network data, other information is often available in a network study. The information can be related to the nodes or the edges. The former is called *node covariate, node attributes,* or *node features,* and the

TABLE 12.3. The Edge List Matrix of the Network in Table 12.2

Start	End
1	2
1	3
1	4
2	3
2	4
2	6
2	7
2	9
2	10
3	4
3	5
3	6
3	7
3	8
3	9
3	10
4	5
4	6
4	7
4	8
4	9
4	10
5	6
5	7
6	7
6	10
8	9

latter is called *edge covariates, edge attributes*, or *edge features*. For example, for the WeChat data, there are a total of 10 node covariates as shown in Table 12.1. The node covariates can be stored in a rectangular matrix as in regular data analysis.

Edge Covariates

In network data, edges may have their covariates, too. In the WeChat network, there is no edge covariate. However, if, in addition to the information on whether two students are WeChat friends, one also asks how frequently they interact on WeChat, the frequency is an edge covariate. For a network, multiple edge covariates can be available and used to define the properties of the edges. The edge covariates can be represented using an adjacency matrix or an edge list matrix. A hypothesized example with two edge covariates is given in Table 12.4.

TABLE 12.4. The Edge List Matrix of the Network with Edge Covariates

Start	End	Frequency	Color
1	2	24	blue
1	3	12	red
1	4	47	blue
2	3	19	red
2	4	2	red
2	6	96	red
2	7	0	blue
2	9	31	red
2	10	26	red
3	4	68	red
3	5	16	blue
3	6	14	blue
3	7	99	red
3	8	45	red
3	9	27	blue
3	10	57	blue
4	5	84	blue
4	6	5	blue
4	7	77	blue
4	8	76	blue
4	9	90	red
4	10	46	red
5	6	22	red
5	7	63	blue
6	7	8	red
6	10	20	red
8	9	42	blue

12.3 Network Visualization

Visualizing a network is not only the first step but also a critical step of social network analysis. For a long time, network analysis research focused on how to graphically represent a network. A large number of options are available to visualize a network—here we introduce the heat map and the network plot. Visualization makes the identification of the node relationships relatively easy.

12.3.1 Heat Map

A heat map can visualize any matrix of data, not only the network data. A heat map divides a plot area into small squares according to the number of rows and columns in the data matrix. Each square is colored according to the corresponding value in the matrix. For example, the heat map of the WeChat network is given in Figure 12.1. In this figure, the value 1 is represented by a black square and 0 by a gray square. Therefore, from the heat map, one can immediately see how many friendship relations there are in the WeChat network.

FIGURE 12.1. The heat map of the WeChat network data.

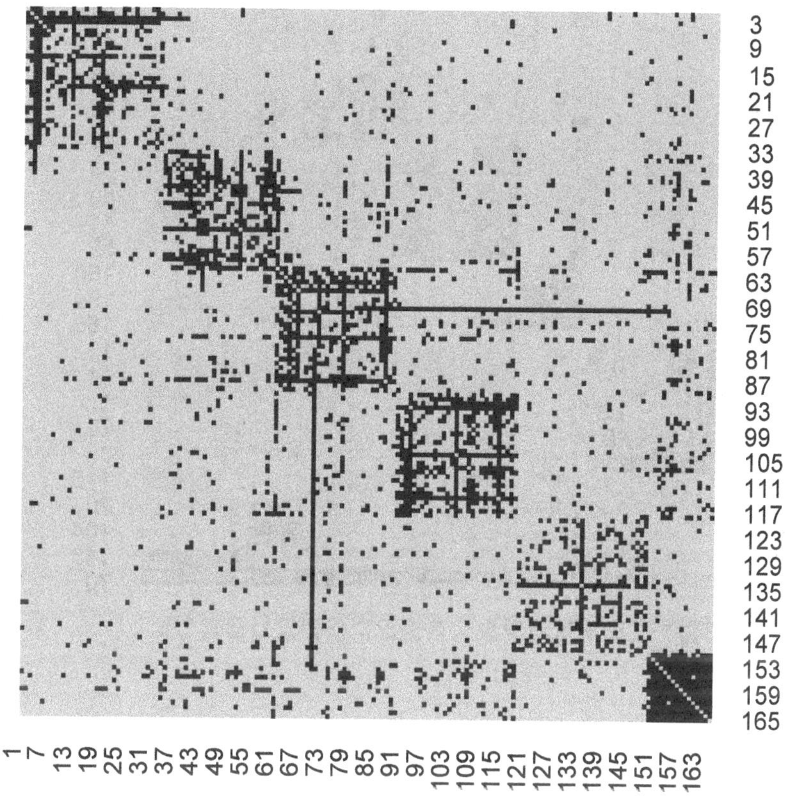

In Figure 12.1, the students are organized in the same order as in the WeChat network. Naturally, one would hope the students with more connections come together. Therefore, a heat map can be constructed by first reordering the data. Such a plot is given in Figure 12.2. From the heat map, a solid black block indicates that the students in that block are closely related to each other. One can also see that the students at the bottom have more WeChat friends because of the large number of black squares.

FIGURE 12.2. The heat map of the WeChat network data after ordering.

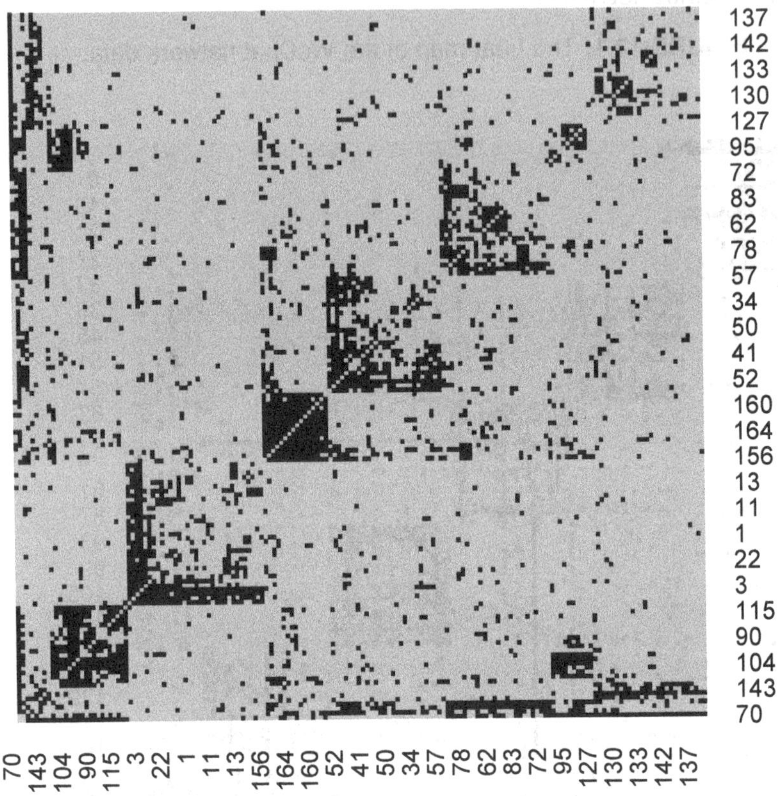

12.3.2 Network Plot

The network plot portrays the network in a graph. In a network plot, the nodes are placed in a two-dimensional space in a certain way. Two nodes are connected using a line if they are related. For example, the plot of the WeChat network is given in Figure 12.3. From the plot, we can roughly see three clusters of nodes (top, bottom left, and bottom right) in the network.

The critical issue in a network plot is to determine the position or layout of the nodes. Many methods have been developed for such a purpose (e.g., Brandes, Kenis, & Wagner, 2003; Fruchterman & Reingold, 1991; Kamada & Kawai, 1989). In general, a good method should minimize crossings between edges and maximize the symmetries (Di Battista, Eades, Tamassia, & Tollis, 1994). Different methods, or even the same method, can lead to different layouts of the nodes. A trial-and-error process is often used

FIGURE 12.3. The plot of the WeChat network.

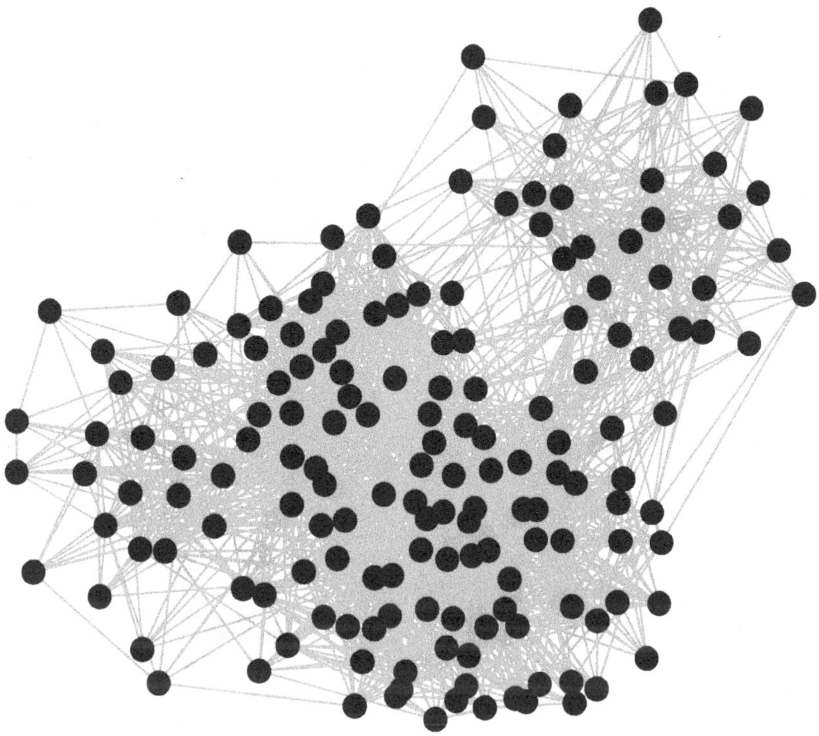

to generate a network plot that can reveal the important patterns of the network data without distortion. Figure 12.4 shows the network plots of the first 15 students in the WeChat network data based on four types of layout methods. Clearly, the layouts of the nodes are quite different.

Figure 12.4(a) is based on the Fruchterman and Reingold (FG) algorithm (Fruchterman & Reingold, 1991). The FG algorithm positions the nodes so that all the edges are of more or less equal length and with as few crossing edges as possible. It belongs to a large class of the force-directed layout algorithms. The idea of a force-directed layout algorithm is based on the force between any two nodes. The nodes can be viewed as steel rings and the edges are springs between them. The nodes are placed in some initial positions and let go so that the force of the springs will adjust to make the system reach a minimal energy state (Eades, 1984). The FG algorithm is

FIGURE 12.4. A plot of a subset of the WeChat network using different layout algorithms.

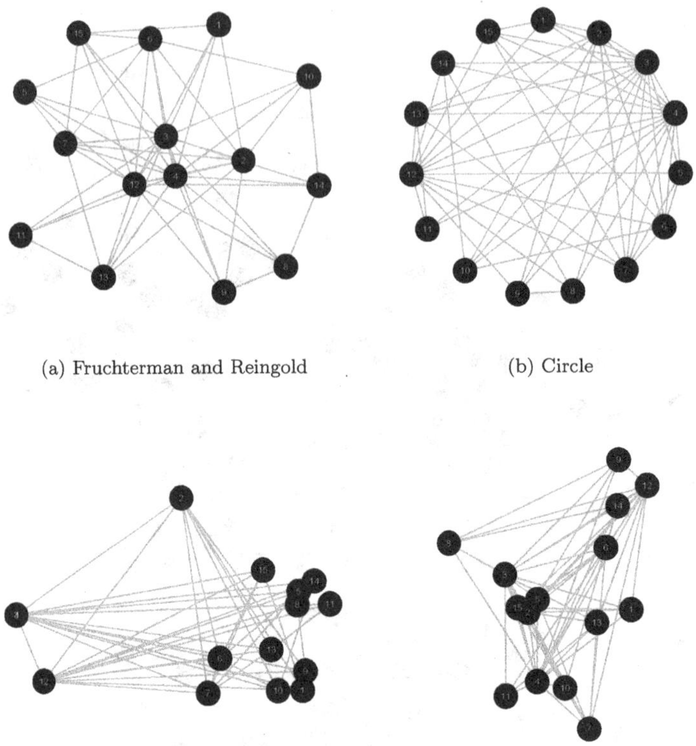

(a) Fruchterman and Reingold

(b) Circle

(c) MDS

(d) Random

probably the most widely used method in network plot because it is fast and often leads to aesthetically pleasing results.

Figure 12.4(b) positions the nodes in a circular layout. In the plot, all the nodes are placed on a circle, equally spaced. An advantage of the circular layout is its neutrality—no node is given a privileged position such as in center where the nodes are often assumed to be more important. The circular layout can be used by its own but can also be used in clusters in a larger network.

Figure 12.4(c) positions on the nodes based on multidimensional scaling (MDS). The basic idea of MDS is to represent proximities among nodes as distances between points in a two-dimensional space. Therefore, the closely related nodes appear close together in such a plot. It is useful for understanding networks as the distances between the nodes are Euclidean distances.

Figure 12.4(d) shows a network plot with a random layout of the nodes. In such a plot, the nodes are randomly placed at different locations.

12.4 Network Statistics

Information can be extracted from a network and stored as a network statistic. In this section, we introduce the widely used network statistics. The network statistics can be defined for a whole network, each node in the network, a dyad in the network, and so on.

12.4.1 Network Statistics for a Whole Network

The *network size* is the most basic statistic of a network, which is defined as the number of nodes in a network. For the WeChat network, there are 165 students in the network and, therefore, the network size is 165.

The *density* of a network is the total number of edges divided by the total number of possible edges, calculated based on the type of networks. For the WeChat network, it is an undirected network. The total number of possible edges is $165*(165-1)/2 = 13,530$. In the network, the total number of edges is 1,722. Therefore, the density of the network is $1,722/13,530 = 12.7\%$. The density measures the tendency for two nodes to be connected.

The *transitivity* is defined as the proportion of closed triangles to the total number of open and closed triangles. For a triad of three nodes, if they are all connected, there are three edges, which form a closed triangle. However, if there are only two edges with one side open, it forms an open triangle. For example, for the WeChat network, the transitivity is 35.5%. Transitivity predicts the likelihood that Student A and Student B are friends if both A and B are friends with Student C. This implies that a friend of my friend is not necessarily my friend, but is far more likely to be my friend than another randomly chosen person.

12.4.2 Network Statistics for Nodes

Network statistics can be defined for each node, which can then be averaged to use as a measure of the whole network. Such statistics are often developed around the concept of centrality to address the question of which are the most important nodes in a network.

Degree is a centrality measure that simply counts how many neighboring nodes a node has. For a directed network, *in-degree* is the number of incoming edges and *out-degree* is the number of outgoing edges. For an undirected network, in-degree is the same as out-degree. A node is important if it has many neighbors, and, therefore, a large degree. For the WeChat network, Student 70 has the largest degree—he/she has 85 WeChat friends out of a total of 164 students. Students 137 and 145 both have a degree of 6, the smallest in the network. Figure 12.5(a) shows the histogram the degree of all 165 students in the WeChat network. The histogram is right-skewed as observed in many social networks.

FIGURE 12.5. Distribution of selected node statistics.

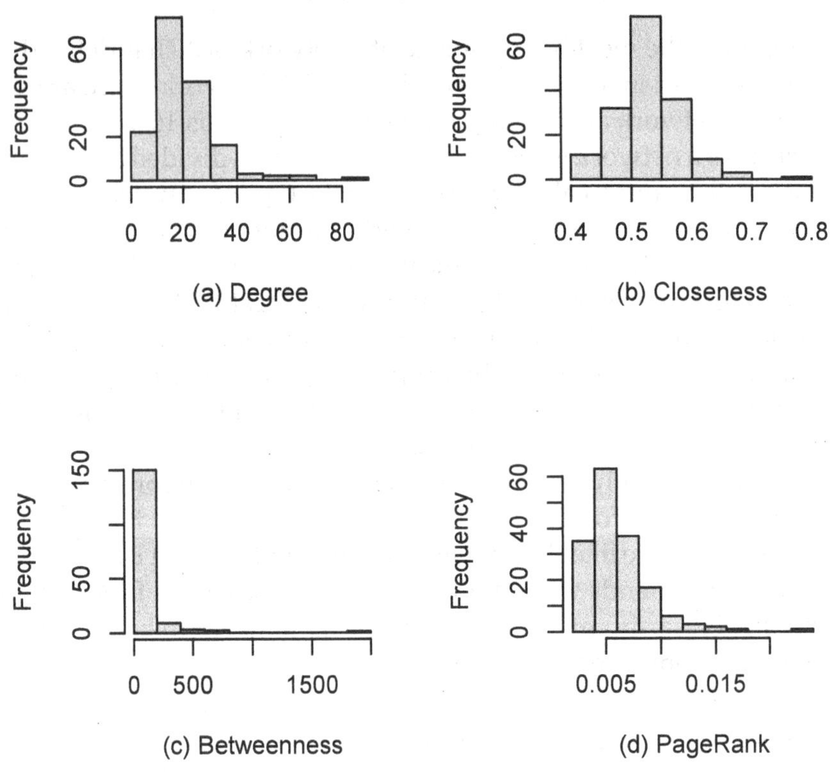

Closeness is another centrality statistic that measures the proximity of a node to all other nodes in a network, not only the nodes to which it directly connects (Freeman, 1978). A large value of closeness indicates that a node is close to the rest of nodes in the network, implying that the node has more opportunity to connect to others. For the WeChat network, Student 70 has the largest closeness while Student 15 has the smallest closeness. The histogram of the closeness of the network is shown in Figure 12.5(b).

Betweenness measures the extent to which a node lies on the paths between other nodes. Nodes with high betweenness influence how the information passes in the network. For some nodes, they may not have a large degree. However, they may be chokepoints through which information moves. If they are removed from the network, it can actually disrupt the communications among other nodes. A large betweenness indicates a more important node. For the WeChat network, Student 70 has the largest betweenness and Student 53 has the smallest. The histogram of the betweenness of the network is shown in Figure 12.5(c).

PageRank is most widely known for ranking the importance of web pages but is also a measure of the centrality of nodes in a network (Brin & Page, 1998). PageRank uses edges between nodes as a measure of importance. But unlike degree, it assigns a weight to the edge depending on the relative score of a node that it connects to. A large PageRank indicates an important node. For the WeChat network, Student 70 has the largest PageRank and Student 53 has the smallest. The histogram of the PageRank of the network is shown in Figure 12.5(d).

12.4.3 Network Statistics for Dyads

For a pair of nodes, a dyad, in the network, network statistics can also be defined. The shortest path is probably the most widely used one (West et al., 1996). The shortest path between two nodes in a network is a path with the minimum number of edges. For example, if there is an edge between Node A and Node B, the shortest path between them is 1. If Node A has to go through another node to reach Node B, then the shortest path between A and B is 2.

The shortest paths for all pairs of nodes in a network form a matrix. A heat map of the shortest paths of the WeChat network is given in Figure 12.6. In the plot, the darker color represents the larger shortest. Overall the largest shortest path is 4, implying that a student can get information to another student at most through three other students. The majority of dyads have a shortest path of 2 (67%) followed by 3 (30%). One of the most discussed network phenomena is the small-world effect. In most real networks, the typical shortest path is surprisingly short, in particular when compared with the number of nodes of the network (Milgram, 1967; Travers & Milgram, 1977). The WeChat network also reflects such an important observation in social network analysis.

FIGURE 12.6. The heat map of the shortest paths of the WeChat network.

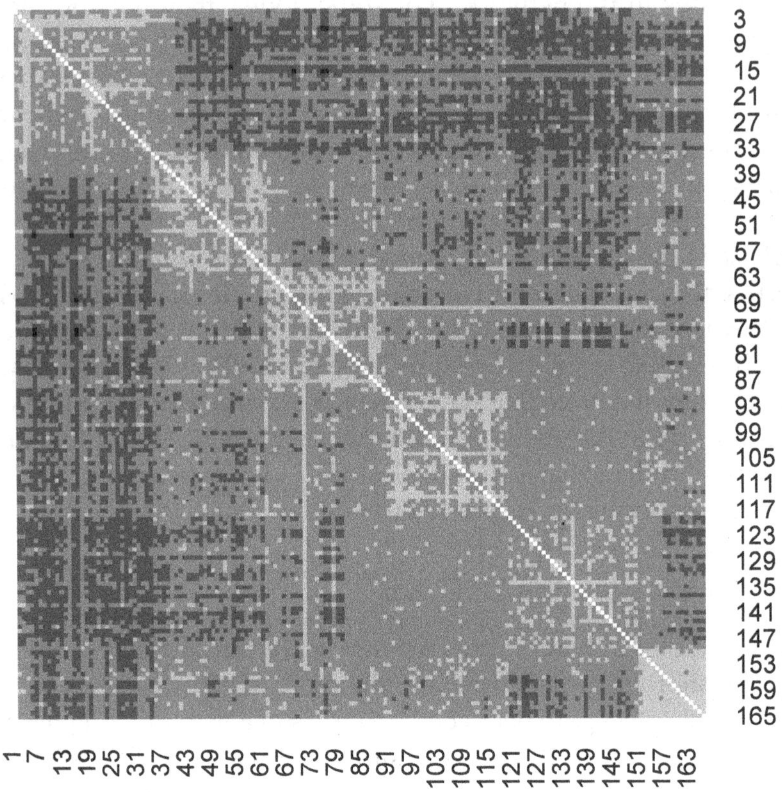

12.5 Basic Network Analysis

As a first step, one can extract information from a network and use it in a statistical model. For example, the degree statistic for the nodes can be used as a predictor, an outcome, or a moderator or mediator depending on the research question.

Suppose we are interested in understanding whether male and female students have the same centrality in the WeChat network. The t-test, as in traditional data analysis, can be applied here. Here, we choose PageRank as a measure of centrality. Since the distribution of PageRank is right-skewed as shown in Figure 12.5, the log transformation of PageRank was first conducted. After transformation, the average PageRank for male students is −5.21 and for female students is −5.18. The t-statistic for the Welch's

FIGURE 12.7. Comparison of the PageRank of male and female students.

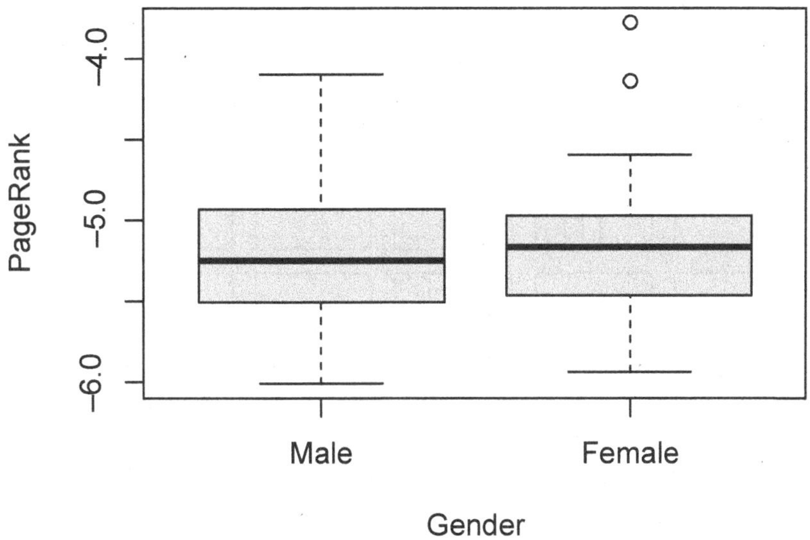

two-sample t-test is −0.43 with 142 degrees of freedom. The *p*-value for the t-test is 0.67. Therefore, we fail to reject the null hypothesis that the two groups have no difference. Figure 12.7 displays the boxplot of PageRank for both male and female students. It also shows there is no large difference between the two groups although the median of the female students is slightly higher than that of the male students.

Figure 12.8 shows the relationship between the centrality measure degree and academic performance (GPA), physical health (BMI), and emotion (happy and lonely). The correlations between degree and these variables are rather small and insignificant. This can also be observed in the scatterplots. The lack of correlation between the number of WeChat friends and other variables is not expected given the existing literature (e.g., Kim & Lee, 2011; Nabi, Prestin, & So, 2013). However, we also want to point out that the conclusions of the studies on the use of social media and well-being are not decisive in the literature (Kraut et al., 1998; Shaw & Gant, 2004)

More complex analyses can be conducted to test hypotheses with network data. As an example, we hypothesize that degree plays a mediating role between GPA, BMI, happiness, and loneliness. That is, GPA and BMI

FIGURE 12.8. Scatterplot and histogram of the selected variables. The top panel is the correlation.

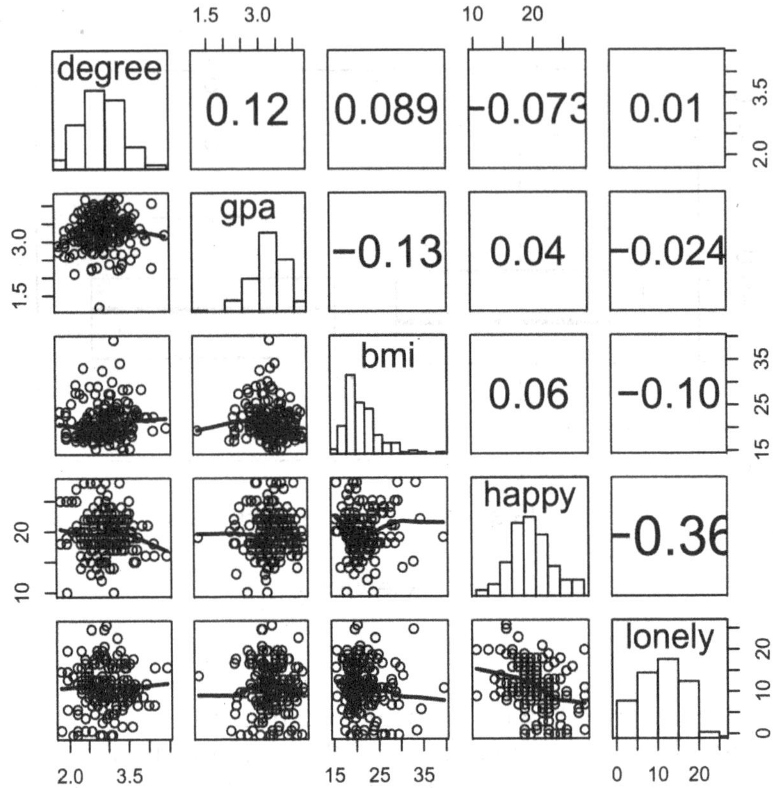

will predict degree and, in turn, predict happiness and loneliness. The path diagram for such a mediation model is given in Figure 12.9. For this model, the direct effect of GPA on happiness is c_1 and the indirect effect is a_1b_1 with the total effect $c_1 + a_1b_1$. Furthermore, the total indirect effect of GPA and BMI on happy through degree is $(a_1 + a_2)b_1$.

The results from the mediation analysis are summarized in Table 12.5. From this we can see that there was no mediation effect for degree on the relationship of GPA and BMI with happiness and loneliness. This is expected from the scatterplot in Figure 12.8, but it shows that the information extracted from a network can be used in traditional statistical analysis.

FIGURE 12.9. Path diagram of a mediation model.

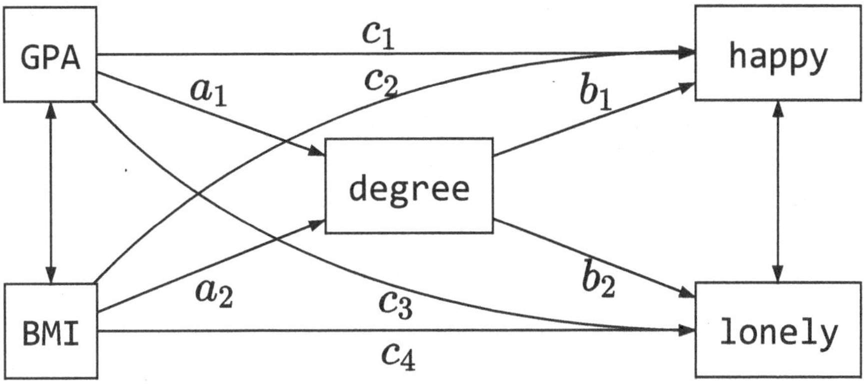

TABLE 12.5. Results from the Mediation Analysis

	Estimate	SE	Z-value	p-value
GPA -> Happy				
Direct	0.432	0.566	0.763	0.446
Indirect	−0.083	0.089	−0.929	0.353
Total	0.349	0.563	0.62	0.535
GPA -> Lonely				
Direct	−0.471	0.914	−0.515	0.606
Indirect	0.039	0.123	0.313	0.754
Total	−0.433	0.906	−0.477	0.633
BMI -> Happy				
Direct	0.069	0.072	0.964	0.335
Indirect	−0.008	0.01	−0.86	0.39
Total	0.061	0.071	0.849	0.396
BMI -> Lonely				
Direct	−0.161	0.116	−1.394	0.163
Indirect	0.004	0.013	0.31	0.756
Total	−0.157	0.115	−1.368	0.171

12.6 Network Modeling

The analysis in the previous section utilizes the information in a network indirectly. In this section, we introduce several models that can directly model a network.

12.6.1 Erdos–Rényi Random Graph Model

The Erdos–Rényi model (Erdos & Rényi, 1960; Gilbert, 1959) is the earliest and simplest, yet the most well-studied and famous statistical model of networks. Formally, if a random $N \times N$ adjacency matrix $\mathbf{A}$ follows an $ER(N, p)$ distribution, then for each element a_{ij} of the matrix, it follows a Bernoulli distribution identically and independently,

$$a_{ij} \sim Bernoulli(p)$$

where N is the size of the network and p is the probability of $a_{ij} = 1$. For the undirected network, we expect $i < j$. Note that here we follow the notation by Gilbert (1959), which is more commonly used. Erdos & Rényi (1960) defined the model in terms of the number of nodes and edges.

The model assumes that each edge has a fixed probability of being present or absent, independent of the other edges. Therefore, for networks with the same number of nodes and edges, they all have the same probability to be observed. As one can imagine, the Erdos–Rényi model would typically not fit a real-world network well. The network represented by the Erdos-Rényi model has low clustering, unlike many real social networks. The node degree of Erdos–Rényi networks approximately follows a Poisson distribution while observed networks often follow a power-law distribution. In real social networks, transitivity is often observed where persons who share a friend tend to be friends themselves. However, the Erdos–Rényi model assumes they are independent.

To estimate the unknown parameter p in the model, the maximum likelihood estimation (MLE) method can be applied. The likelihood function for the model is

$$L(p|\mathbf{A}) = \prod_{i<j} p^{a_{ij}}(1-p)^{1-a_{ij}}$$

for an undirected network. It is easy to see that for a network with M edges, the MLE estimator is

$$\hat{p} = \frac{M}{\binom{N}{2}} = \frac{M}{N(N-1)/2}.$$

For the WeChat network, we have $\hat{p} = 1722/13530 = 12.7\%$, which is equal to the density of the network.

12.6.2 Stochastic Block Model

The stochastic block model (Holland, Laskey, & Leinhardt, 1983) can be viewed as an extension of the Erdos–Rényi model. In a stochastic block model, the nodes are divided into disjoint groups or blocks. The blocks are often called *communities*. For any node, it can only belong to one block. The number of nodes in each block can be different.

Formally, the N nodes of a network are assigned into each of the K blocks $C_1, C_2, \ldots, C_K$ with the size $n_1, n_2, \ldots, n_K$. Each block follows a Erdos–Rényi model so that

$$a_{ij}^{kk} \sim Bernoulli(p_{kk})$$

where a_{ij}^{kk} is the edge with both i and j in the same block C_k and p_{kk} is the probability for $a_{ij}^{k} = 1$. For a node i in block C_k and a node j in block C_l, the edge also follows a Bernoulli distribution

$$a_{ij}^{kl} \sim Bernoulli(p_{kl})$$

where p_{kl} is the probability of having an edge between node i and node j. Therefore, within a block, two nodes have the same probability to be connected and for nodes across two blocks, they also have the same probability to be connected. Overall, we have a probability matrix for the K blocks as

$$\mathbf{P} = \begin{pmatrix} p_{11} & p_{12} & \cdots & p_{1K} \\ p_{21} & p_{22} & \cdots & p_{2K} \\ \vdots & \vdots & \ddots & \vdots \\ p_{K1} & p_{K2} & \cdots & p_{KK} \end{pmatrix}.$$

The probability matrix can be estimated with MLE. If the block membership is known, the estimation is straightforward. For example, for the WeChat network, if we form two block according to the gender of the students, we can get the following probability matrix

$$\mathbf{P} = \begin{matrix} & Male & Female \\ Male & 0.18 & 0.084 \\ Female & 0.084 & 0.15 \end{matrix}.$$

Therefore, assuming the edges are random, two male students have a probability of 0.18 to be WeChat friends, and two female students have a probability of 0.15 to be WeChat friends. For a male student and a female student, the probability for them to be WeChat friends is only 0.084.

If the members of the blocks are not known, they can be assigned through different algorithms such as the variational-EM (Mariadassou et al., 2010). The process is often referred to as *community detection* (Abbe, 2017). In determining the block members, the first step is to decide on the number of blocks. In this regard, the integrated completed likelihood (ICL) criterion can be used (Biernacki et al., 2000). A larger ICL indicates a better model.

The ICL for the stochastic block model with 1 to 15 blocks for the WeChat data is portrayed in Figure 12.10. From the plot, the model with 10 blocks gives the largest ICL. However, the model leads to four blocks with one, two, four, and five students, respectively. An examination of the ICL reveals that the ICL from the model with seven blocks is close to the model with 10 blocks. However, again, the model with seven blocks leads to a block with only four students. Therefore, we finally decide to use the model with six blocks with 37, 9, 33, 28, 31, and 27 students, respectively.

FIGURE 12.10. ICL of the stochastic block models with different numbers of blocks.

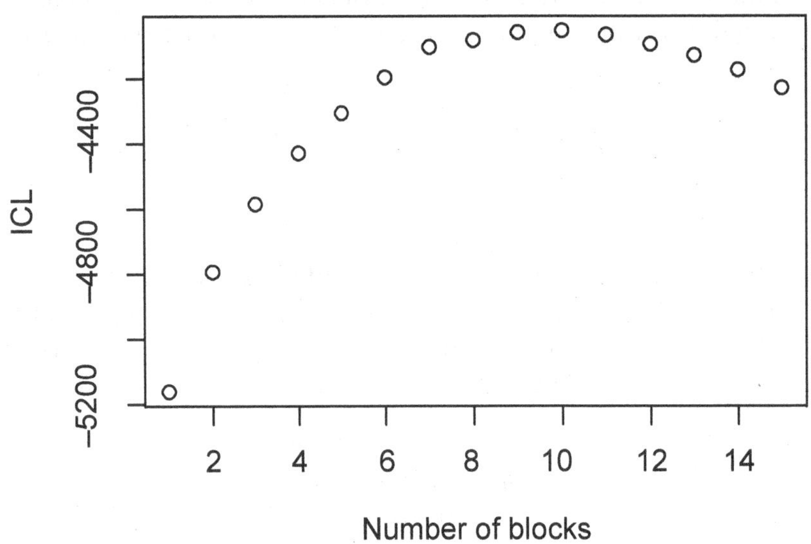

The block probability matrix for the six blocks is given in Table 12.6. For block 1, there are 37 students in it. Two students in this block have a probability of 0.312 to be WeChat friends. For block 2 with nine students, the density is 60.4%. If a student is in block 1 and another student is in block 2, they have a probability of 49.5% to be WeChat friends. However,

TABLE 12.6. Block Probability Matrix for the WeChat Data

	1	2	3	4	5	6	Size
1	0.312	0.495	0.018	0.066	0.029	0.055	37
2	0.495	0.604	0.082	0.359	0.221	0.355	9
3	0.018	0.082	0.403	0.02	0.015	0.034	33
4	0.066	0.359	0.02	0.528	0.032	0.041	28
5	0.029	0.221	0.015	0.032	0.302	0.042	31
6	0.055	0.355	0.034	0.041	0.042	0.493	27

students in block 1 have a much lower probability to be WeChat friends with students from blocks 3–6. Therefore, one would expect there are many connections in and between block 1 and block 2 but few connections from block 1 to blocks 3–6. Similarly, for block 3, based on the estimated probability, students in that block have few connections with students outside of the block.

The plot of the WeChat network with the identified block is given in Figure 12.11. The positions of the nodes of each block are consistent with the probability matrix in Table 12.6, as one would expect.

12.6.3 Exponential Random Graph Model

The exponential random graph models (ERGM) are a class of models that allow individual probabilities for edges and the inclusion of network covariates (Harris, 2013). It includes the Erdos–Rényi model as a special case and is probably the most widely used model for network modeling. Instead of working with individual edges, ERGM treats the whole network as a random variable.

Let $\mathbf{Y}$ represent a random network with N nodes, and $\mathbf{A}$ be an observed network. Both $\mathbf{Y}$ and $\mathbf{A}$ are an $N \times N$ matrix. The original ERGM can be expressed as

$$\Pr(\mathbf{Y} = \mathbf{A}) = \frac{\exp\left[\beta^t s(\mathbf{A})\right]}{c(\beta)} \propto \exp\left[\beta^t s(\mathbf{A})\right] \tag{12.1}$$

where $s(\mathbf{A})$ is a vector of statistics that can be derived from the observed network and/or the associated node and edge covariates. For example, the statistics can be the number of edges and triangles of a network, and can also be gender and age of the nodes in the network. β is a vector of coefficients associated with the statistics to be estimated. Finally, $c(\beta)$ is a normalizing constant.

As a way to easily interpret and estimate ERGM, the model in Equation 12.1 can be rewritten based on the change in network statistics (Ander-

FIGURE 12.11. The plot of the WeChat network.

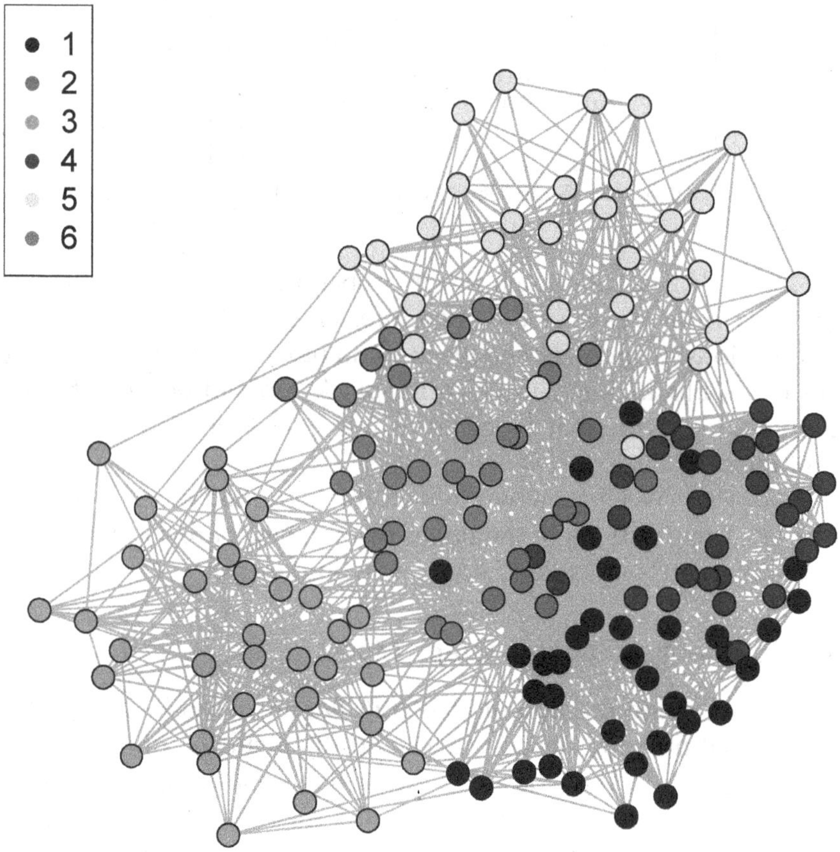

son, Wasserman, & Crouch, 1999; Hunter, Handcock, Butts, Goodreau, & Morris, 2008; Wasserman & Pattison, 1996) as below (for a binary network)

$$P(y_{ij} = 1 | Y_{ij}^C) \propto \exp\left[\sum_{k=1}^{K} \beta_k z_k^g(A_{ij})\right]$$

where $z_k^g(A)_{ij}$ is the change of a network statistic $s(\boldsymbol{A})$ when changing $a_{ij} = 0$ to $a_{ij} = 1$. Therefore, the ERGM essentially becomes a logistic regression model.

For illustration, consider a simple, yet often used baseline model in ERGM. Here, we model the network as a function of the number of edges. Since for any a_{ij} changes from 0 to 1, the change of the number of edges is 1. Therefore, the statistic is simply a constant and the model becomes an intercept only logistic model. For the WeChat network, the estimated coefficient $\hat{\beta}_1 = -1.925$ ($se = 0.026$, p-value≈ 0). The odds ratio is 0.146, indicating that, on average, the odds for two students to be WeChat friends is about 14.6% of the odds for two students not to be WeChat friends. From it, the probability for two students to be WeChat friends is 12.7%, the same as that from the Erdos–Rényi model.

In ERGM, many other terms can be included on the right-hand side of the model. Here, we discuss some of the terms related to the network, node covariates, and edge covariates. Note that the statistical terms are typically not independent, which can pose serious challenges in estimating ERGM (Robins et al., 2007).

12.6.4 Terms Related to the Network

In addition to the number of edges, many other statistics related to the network can be used in an ERGM. We list a few here.

- k-Star. Edge is a special case of a network structure called *stars* in which several nodes connect to a central node. We can include an item S_k, a star with one central node and k other nodes connecting to it. Clearly, an edge is S_1.
- Degree and density as defined earlier.
- Transitivity. It is equal to the number of triads in the network that are transitive.
- Triangle. The number of triangles in the network.

As an example, we fit a model with three terms—edge, S_2, and triangle—to the WeChat network. The results are given in Table 12.7. As in the earlier simple example, the results can be interpreted in terms of logistic regression. Therefore, the log odds of two students to be WeChat friends is

$$\begin{aligned}\text{logit}[p(a_{ij} = 1)] = &- 3.458 \times \text{change in the number of edges}\\ &- 0.019 \times \text{change in the number of 2-stars}\\ &+ 0.473 \times \text{change in the number of triangles.}\end{aligned}$$

For the coefficient for the 2-star, the odds ratio is $\exp(-0.019) = 0.982$. It indicates that if adding an edge to the WeChat network, the number of 2-stars increases by 1, while not adding any triangle, the odds for two students to be WeChat friends will decrease by about 1.8% (0.982 – 1). But if it increases one triangle in the network, the odds for two students to be WeChat friends will increase by about 60.6% (1.606 – 1).

TABLE 12.7. ERGM with Edge, 2-Star, and Triangle for the WeChat Network

	Estimate	s.e.	Z-value	p-value	Odds ratio
edges	−3.458	0.093	−37.066	<1e-04	0.031
2-star	−0.019	0.002	−8.274	<1e-04	0.982
triangle	0.473	0.011	43.463	<1e-04	1.606

12.6.5 Terms Related to Node Covariates

The ERGM can be used to investigate how node covariates are related to a network. Like the use of the statistics for the network, we can also include the terms derived from the node covariates in the model. For a node covariate $x_i, i = 1, \ldots, N$, we can define a function $h_{ij}(x_i, x_j)$ to use in ERGM (Hunter et al., 2008). The function h can be chosen for different types of node covariates (continuous vs. categorical) and the specific effects of interest.

For a continuous covariate x, the function below defines the *main factor effect* as the sum of the covariate of two nodes i and j,

$$h_{ij} = h(x_i, x_j) = x_i + x_j. \tag{12.2}$$

It can be used to investigate the effect of the total attributes of two nodes on the network such as the sum of GPA on the WeChat friendship.

Another widely used function for a continuous covariate is called the *absolute difference factor effect*,

$$h_{ij} = h(x_i, x_j) = |x_i - x_j|. \tag{12.3}$$

It describes the (dis)similarity of two nodes using the Manhattan distance. Because it is often expected that similar nodes tend to connect to each other, called the *homophily principle* (McPherson, Smith-Lovin, & Cook, 2001), this effect is often used in network analysis.

For a categorical covariate, we define the *nodal factor effect* according to the levels of the covariate as below,

$$h_{ij} = h(x_i, x_j) = \begin{cases} 2 & \text{if both nodes } i \text{ and } j \text{ have the specific factor level} \\ 1 & \text{if exactly one of } i, j \text{ has the specified factor level} \\ 0 & \text{if neither } i \text{ and } j \text{ has the specified factor level.} \end{cases} \tag{12.4}$$

For example, a nodal factor effect may be a female–female effect.

Other types of effects for categorical data can be defined based on the *homophily* of covariates. For the *uniform* homophily effect, it can use

$$h_{ij} = h(x_i, x_j) = \begin{cases} 1 & \text{if } i \text{ and } j \text{ have the same factor level} \\ 0 & \text{otherwise,} \end{cases} . \tag{12.5}$$

For example, for the covariate gender, when both students are male or female, $h = 1$, otherwise, $h = 0$. In contrast, for the *differential* homophily effect, the statistic is defined as

$$h_{ij} = h(x_i, x_j) = \begin{cases} 1 & \text{if both } i \text{ and } j \text{ have the specific factor level} \\ 0 & \text{otherwise.} \end{cases} \tag{12.6}$$

For instance, if both nodes i and j are males, then h_{ij} is 1, otherwise, it is 0. Note that for a categorical covariate with m levels, a maximum of m such effects can be defined.

For the WeChat network, we consider four covariates—GPA, BMI, gender, and whether a student smokes or not. For age, the main factor effect is used; for BMI, the absolute difference factor effect is considered; for gender, the uniform homophily effect is modeled; for smoking, the differential homophily effect is included. The results for the analysis are given in Table 12.8.

First, the estimated coefficient for GPA is 0.088 and significant. Since the main factor effect of GPA is evaluated, if the total GPA of two students is higher, the probability for the two students to be WeChat friends is higher. Second, for BMI, the effect is not significant. Therefore, even if two students have similar BMI, the likelihood for them to become friends does not significantly change. Third, for gender, the effect is positive and significant. This implies that if two students are both male or both female, they are more likely to become WeChat friends. Fourth, for smoking, we evaluate the differential homophily effect. For the effect of both students not smoking, the effect is not significant. However, the effect of both students smoking is positive and significant. Therefore, if both students smoke, the probability for them to be WeChat friends is greater. However, if neither student smokes, it does not increase or decrease the likelihood for them to be WeChat friends.

TABLE 12.8. ERGM with Node Covariates

	Estimate	s.e.	Z-value	p-value	Odds ratio
Edges	−2.917	0.257	−11.332	<1e-04	0.054
GPA	0.088	0.039	2.27	0.023	1.092
BMI	−0.005	0.007	−0.673	0.501	0.995
Gender	0.685	0.057	12.07	<1e-04	1.984
Not smoking	−0.025	0.059	−0.42	0.674	0.975
Smoking	0.663	0.093	7.114	<1e-04	1.940

12.6.6 Terms Related to the Edge Covariates

Edge covariates can also be included in ERGM. For example, the covariate could be another network. It can also be information derived from the network such as the shortest path.

12.6.7 Latent Space Model

Another class of network models is constructed around latent attributes rather than the observed attributes as in ERGM (Snijders, 2011). One such model is the latent Euclidean space model proposed by Hoff, Raftery, and Handcock(2002). In the model, each node is assumed to be associated with a latent position in a Euclidean space. The distance of two nodes in the latent space is related to how likely they are connected in the network.

Let $\mathbf{z}_i$ be a vector of latent positions of node i in the latent space. For nodes i and j, the Euclidean distance between them is:

$$d(i,j) = \sqrt{(z_i - z_j)^t(z_i - z_j)} = \sqrt{\sum_{d=1}^{D}(z_{i,d} - z_{j,d})^2} \tag{12.7}$$

where the symbol $(\cdot)^t$ is the transpose of a matrix or vector, D is the dimension of the Euclidean space, $\mathbf{z}_i = (z_{i,1}, z_{i,2}, \cdots, z_{i,D})^t$ and $\mathbf{z}_j = (z_{j,1}, z_{j,2}, \cdots, z_{j,D})^t$ are the latent positions of nodes i and j, respectively. With this distance function, the latent space model can be written as

$$\begin{cases} a_{ij} & \sim \text{Bernoulli}(p_{ij}) \\ \text{logit}[p(a_{ij})] & = \alpha + \beta' h_{ij} - d_{ij} \end{cases} \tag{12.8}$$

where α is an intercept, h_{ij} is a vector of covariates and β is the associated coefficients of the covariates. The covariates can be related to the nodes and/or edges of the network. The coefficient for d_{ij} is fixed as -1. Therefore, the closer two nodes are in the latent space, the higher the probability for them to be related after controlling the covariates in the model.

To fit the latent space model, we need to find the dimension of the latent space. One way to determine it is to compare models with different latent dimensions based on BIC. For example, for the WeChat network data, we fit the model below with $D = 1, \ldots, 9$:

$$\begin{cases} a_{ij} & \sim \text{Bernoulli}(p_{ij}) \\ \text{logit}[p(a_{ij})] & = \alpha - \sqrt{\sum_{d=1}^{D}(z_{i,d} - z_{j,d})^2} \end{cases}. \tag{12.9}$$

The BIC for the fitted model is plotted in Figure 12.12. Clearly, the model with 2 latent dimensions has the smallest BIC. This means that the WeChat friendship can be best explained using a two-dimensional latent space model.

FIGURE 12.12. BIC of the latent space models with different latent dimensions.

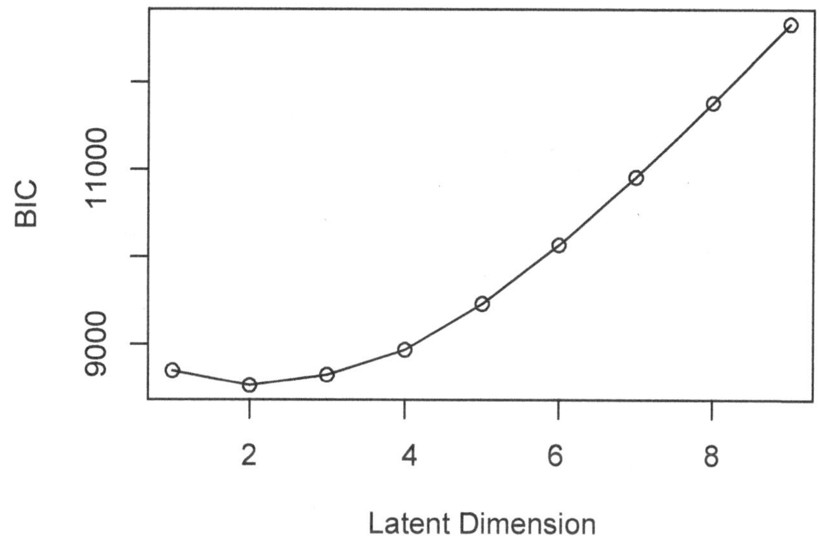

Based on the latent space model, the latent position of each student in the WeChat network can be estimated. Figure 12.13 shows the plot of the WeChat network based on the estimated latent positions. In the plot, if two students are close to each other, they are more likely to become WeChat friends.

FIGURE 12.13. Plot of the WeChat network based on the latent positions.

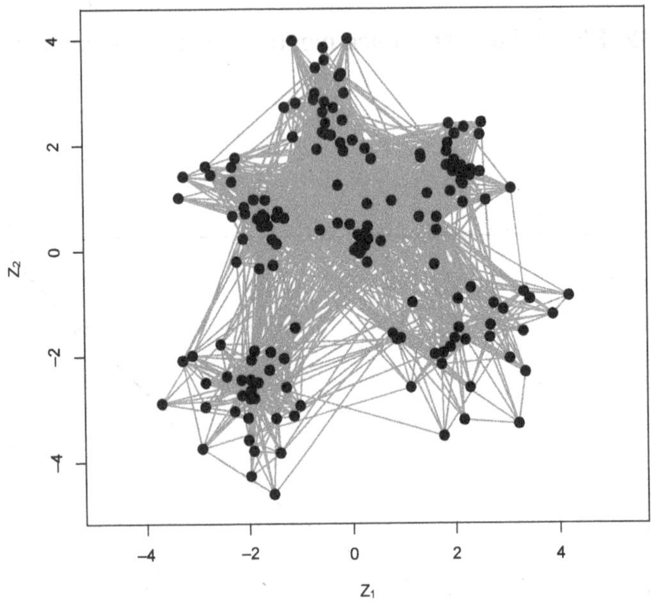

For illustration, we again include four covariates—GPA, BMI, gender, and whether a student smokes or not—in the latent space model. The parameter estimates for the model are given in Table 12.9. In estimating the model, the Markov chain Monte Carlo method is used. We also compared several models with different latent dimensions and found that the one with two latent dimensions fitted the WeChat data best.

TABLE 12.9. Latent Space Model with Covariates

		Credible interval		
	Estimate	2.5%	97.5%	Odds ratio
Intercept	1.284	0.446	2.197	3.611
GPA	−0.087	−0.221	0.035	0.916
BMI	−0.017	−0.037	0.001	0.983
Gender	0.964	0.835	1.101	2.623
Not smoking	−0.091	−0.238	0.057	0.913
Smoking	1.000	0.729	1.274	2.719

The results from the latent space model are similar to those from the ERGM. However, the estimates should be interpreted conditionally on the latent distance of the students in the latent space. Or we can interpret the results as if the effect of the latent space is controlled. In this model, students with the same gender and who both smoke are more likely to be WeChat friends.

12.7 Summary

In this chapter, we introduced the basic methods for network analysis. Network data are different from the traditional data in that the nodes are naturally interrelated. Network visualization is a critical component, and should always be the first step in network analysis. Although one can extract the information from a network and use it in a statistical model, many network modeling methods are available. For example, the exponential random graph models and latent space models are currently widely used.

12.7.1 Further Reading

- This chapter provides only a limited sample of the literature on social network analysis. For a more complete treatment of network analysis, one can consult with the review paper by Snijders (2011) and books such as Carrington, Scott, and Wasserman (2005); Scott (2017); Wasserman & Faust (1994). Many newly developed methods, such as network analysis with mediation Che et al. (2020); Liu et al. (2018) were not discussed in this chapter.

- The analysis in this chapter has focused on a binary, undirected social network. However, the methods can be easily adapted for valued, directed networks. Furthermore, network analysis is not limited to social networks, but can be and have been extended to many other networks such as psychological networks (Fried et al., 2017) and biological networks (Barabási, Gulbahce, & Loscalzo, 2011).

- The chapter only discussed cross-sectional networks. Longitudinal networks and associated analytical methods are available such as the temporal ERGM (Hanneke & Xing, 2007; Krivitsky & Handcock, 2014), the stochastic actor-oriented models (Snijders, Van de Bunt, & Steglich, 2010), and the dynamic network analysis (Sewell & Chen, 2015)

12.7.2 Computational Time and Resources

Network analysis can typically be conducted using `statnet`, a suite of `R` packages for the management, exploration, statistical analysis, simulation and visualization of network data (Krivitsky et al., 2022). It includes the `ergm` and `latentnet` packages used in this chapter. Depending on the estimation methods used by a particular model, an analysis can take a substantial amount of computational time. For example, for the latent space analysis took about 10 minutes, while the analysis in Table 12.8 took less than half a second on our desktop computer. The computing time also increases quickly with the increase of the network size.

References

Abbe, E. (2017). Community detection and stochastic block models: recent developments. *Journal of Machine Learning Research, 18*(1), 6446-6531.

Abdolell, M., LeBlanc, M., Stephens, D., & Harrison, R. V. (2002). Binary partitioning for contin-uous longitudinal data: Categorizing a prognostic variable. *Statistics in Medicine, 21*, 3395-3409.

Acito, F., & Anderson, R. D. (1980). A Monte Carlo comparison of factor analytic methods. *Journal of Marketing Research, 17*(2), 228-236.

Aiken, L. S., West, S. G., & Reno, R. R. (1991). Multiple regression: Testing and interpreting interactions. Sage.

Akaike, H. (1973). Information theory and an extension of the maximum likelihood principle. In B. N. Petrov & F. Csaki (Eds.), Second International Symposium on Information Theory (pp. 267-281). Akademiai Kiado.

Aldenderfer, M. S., & Blashfield, R. K. (1984). A review of clustering methods. *Cluster Analysis*, 33-61.

Alexander, D. L., Tropsha, A., & Winkler, D. A. (2015). Beware of R 2: Simple, unambiguous assessment of the prediction accuracy of QSAR and QSPR models. *Journal of Chemical Information and Modeling, 55*(7), 1316-1322.

Alvarez-Iglesias, A., Hinde, J., Ferguson, J., & Newell, J. (2016). An alternative pruning based approach to unbiased recursive partitioning. *Computational Statistics & Data Analysis, 106*, 90-102.

Anderson, C. (2008, June 23). The end of theory: The data deluge makes the scientific method obsolete. Wired. www.wired.com/science/discoveries/magazine/16-07/pb_theory

Anderson, C. J., Wasserman, S., & Crouch, B. (1999). A p* primer: Logit models for social networks. *Social Networks, 21*(1), 37-66.

Apley, D. W. (2016). Visualizing the effects of predictor variables in black box supervised learning models. arXiv. https://arxiv.org/abs/1612.08468

Archer, K. J. (2010). rpartOrdinal: An R package for deriving a classification tree for predicting an ordinal response. *Journal of Statistical Software, 34*, 7.

Arias, V. B., Garrido, L. E., Jenaro, C., & Arias, B. (2020). A little garbage in, lots of garbage out: Assessing the impact of careless responding in personality survey data. *Behavior Research Methods, 52*(6), 2489-2505.

Asendorpf, J. B., & Wilpers, S. (1998). Personality effects on social relationships. *Journal of Personality and Social Psychology, 74*(6), 1531-1544.

Asparouhov, T., & Muthén, B. (2009). Exploratory structural equation modeling. *Structural Equation Modeling, 16* (3), 397-438.

Asparouhov, T., & Muthén, B. (2014). Auxiliary variables in mixture modeling: Three-step approaches using M plus. *Structural Equation Modeling, 21* (3), 329-341.

Asparouhov, T., & Muthén, B. (2018). *Variable-specific entropy contribution.* Muthén & Muthén.

Athey, S. (2018). The impact of machine learning on economics. In A. Agrawal, J. Gans, & A. Goldfarb (Eds.), *The economics of artificial intelligence: An agenda* (pp. 507-547). University of Chicago Press.

Austin, P. C. (2008). Bootstrap model selection had similar performance for selecting authentic and noise variables compared to backward variable elimination: A simulation study. *Journal of Clinical Epidemiology, 61* (10), 1009-1017.

Austin, P. C., & Steyerberg, E. W. (2015). The number of subjects per variable required in linear regression analyses. *Journal of Clinical Epidemiology, 68* (6), 627-636.

Austin, P. C., & Tu, J. V. (2004). Automated variable selection methods for logistic regression produced unstable models for predicting acute myocardial infarction mortality. *Journal of Clinical Epidemiology, 57* (11), 1138-1146.

Bailey, J. (2008). First steps in qualitative data analysis: Transcribing. *Family Practice, 25* (2), 127-131.

Barabasi, A.-L., Gulbahce, N., & Loscalzo, J. (2011). Network medicine: A network-based approach to human disease. *Nature Reviews Genetics, 12* (1), 56-68.

Bates, D., Maechler, M., Bolker, B., & Walker, S. (2015). Fitting linear mixed-effects models using lme4. *Journal of Statistical Software, 67,* 1-48.

Batista, G. E., Prati, R. C., & Monard, M. C. (2004). A study of the behavior of several methods for balancing machine learning training data. *ACM SIGKDD Explorations Newsletter, 6* (1), 20-29.

Bauer, D. J. (2017). A more general model for testing measurement invariance and differential item functioning. *Psychological Methods, 22* (3), 507-526.

Bauer, D. J., & Curran, P. J. (2004). The integration of continuous and discrete latent variable models: Potential problems and promising opportunities. *Psychological Methods, 9* (1), 3.

Beauducel, A., Harms, C., & Hilger, N. (2016). Reliability estimates for three factor score predictors. *International Journal of Statistics and Probability, 5* (6), 94-107.

Beaujean, A. A. (2014). *Latent variable modeling using R: A step-by-step guide.* Routledge.

Behrens, J. T. (1997). Principles and procedures of exploratory data analysis. *Psychological Methods, 2* (2), 131-160.

Belzak, W., & Bauer, D. J. (2020). Improving the assessment of measurement invariance: Using regularization to select anchor items and identify differential item functioning. *Psychological Methods, 25* (6), 673-690.

Benaglia, T., Chauveau, D., Hunter, D., & Young, D. (2009). mixtools: An R package for analyzing finite mixture models. *Journal of Statistical Software, 32* (6), 1-29.

Benjamini, Y., & Hochberg, Y. (1995). Controlling the false discovery rate: A practical and powerful approach to multiple testing. *Journal of the Royal Statistical Society: Series B (Methodological), 57* (1), 289-300.

Berger, A., Drosten, C., Doerr, H., Stuurmer, M., & Preiser, W. (2004). Severe acute respiratory syndrome (SARS)-paradigm of an emerging viral infection. *Journal of Clinical Virology, 29* (1), 13-22.

Berk, R. A. (2008). *Statistical learning from a regression perspective.* Springer.

Bernecker, S. L., Zuromski, K. L., Gutierrez, P. M., Joiner, T. E., King, A. J., Liu, H., . . . & Ursano, R. J. (2019). Predicting suicide attempts among soldiers who deny suicidal ideation in the Army Study to Assess Risk and Resilience in Servicemembers (Army STARRS). *Behaviour Research and Therapy, 120,* 103350.

Bien, J., Taylor, J., & Tibshirani, R. (2013). A lasso for hierarchical interactions. *Annals of Statistics, 41,* 1111-1141.

Bien, J., & Tibshirani, R. (2014). *hierNet: A lasso for hierarchical interactions.* https://cran.r-project.org/web/packages/hierNet/index.html

Biernacki, C., Celeux, G., & Govaert, G. (2000). Assessing a mixture model for clustering with the integrated completed likelihood. *IEEE Transactions on Pattern Analysis and Machine Intelligence, 22* (7), 719-725.

Blei, D. M., & Lafferty, J. D. (2007). A correlated topic model of Science. *Annals of Applied Statistics, 1* (1), 17-35.

Blei, D. M., Ng, A. Y., & Jordan, M. I. (2003). Latent dirichlet allocation. *Journal of Machine Learning Research, 3,* 993-1022.

Boker, S., Neale, M., Maes, H., Wilde, M., Spiegel, M., Brick, T., . . . & Fox, J. (2011). OpenMx: An open source extended structural equation modeling framework. *Psychometrika, 76* (2), 306-317.

Bolger, N., & Laurenceau, J. P. (2013). *Intensive longitudinal methods: An introduction to diary and experience sampling research.* Guilford Press.

Bollen, K. A. (1989). *Structural equations with latent variables.* Wiley.

Bollen, K. A., & Pearl, J. (2013). Eight myths about causality and structural equation models. In S. L. Morgan (Ed.), *Handbook of causal analysis for social research* (pp. 301-328). Springer.

Bollmann, S., Berger, M., & Tutz, G. (2018). Item-focused trees for the detection of differential item functioning in partial credit models. *Educational and Psychological Measurement, 78* (5), 781-804.

Borra, S., & Di Ciaccio, A. (2010). Measuring the prediction error: A comparison of cross-validation, bootstrap and covariance penalty methods. *Computational Statistics & Data Analysis, 54* (12), 2976-2989.

Borsboom, D., Cramer, A. O. J., Schmittmann, V. D., Epskamp, S., & Waldorp, L. J. (2011). The small world of psychopathology. *PLoS ONE, 6* (11), e27407.

Borsboom, D., Deserno, M. K., Rhemtulla, M., Epskamp, S., Fried, E. I., McNally, R. J., . . . & Waldorp, L. J. (2021). Network analysis of multivariate data in psychological science. *Nature Reviews Methods Primers, 1* (1), 1-18.

Borsboom, D., Mellenbergh, G. J., & Van Heerden, J. (2003). The theoretical status of latent variables. *Psychological Review, 110* (2), 203-219.

Bouchet-Valat, M. (2020). *SnowballC: Snowball stemmers based on the C 'libstemmer' UTF-8 library.* https://CRAN.R-project.org/package=SnowballC

Boulesteix, A. L., & Strobl, C. (2009). Optimal classifier selection and negative bias in error rate estimation: An empirical study on high-dimensional prediction. *BMC Medical Research Methodology, 9* (1), 85.

Box, G. E. (1976). Science and statistics. *Journal of the American Statistical Association, 71* (356), 791-799.

Brandes, U., Kenis, P., & Wagner, D. (2003). Communicating centrality in policy network drawings. *IEEE Transactions on Visualization and Computer Graphics, 9* (2), 241-253.

Brandmaier, A. M., Prindle, J. J., & Arnold, M. (2020). *semtree: Recursive partitioning for structural equation models.* https://CRAN.R-project.org/package=semtree

Brandmaier, A. M., Prindle, J. J., Arnold, M., & Van Lissa, C. J. (2022). *semtree: Recursive partitioning for structural equation models.* https://CRAN.R-project.org/package=semtree

Brandmaier, A. M., Prindle, J. J., McArdle, J. J., & Lindenberger, U. (2016). Theory-guided exploration with structural equation model forests. *Psychological Methods, 21* (4), 566-582.

Brandmaier, A. M., Ram, N., Wagner, G. G., & Gerstorf, D. (2017). Terminal decline in well-being: The role of multi-indicator constellations of physical health and psychosocial correlates. *Developmental Psychology, 53* (5), 996-1012.

Brandmaier, A. M., von Oertzen, T., McArdle, J. J., & Lindenberger, U. (2013). Structural equation model trees. *Psychological Methods, 18* (1), 71-86.

Brandt, H., Cambria, J., & Kelava, A. (2018). An adaptive Bayesian lasso approach with spike-and-slab priors to identify multiple linear and non-linear effects in structural equation models. *Structural Equation Modeling: A Multidisciplinary Journal, 25* (6), 946-960.

Breheny, P., & Huang, J. (2009). Penalized methods for bi-level variable selection. *Statistics and Its Interface, 2* (3), 369-380.

Breheny, P., & Huang, J. (2015). Group descent algorithms for nonconvex penalized linear and logistic regression models with grouped predictors. *Statistics and Computing, 25* (2), 173-187.

Breiman, L. (1996a). Bagging predictors. *Machine Learning, 24* (2), 123-140.

Breiman, L. (1996b). Heuristics of instability and stabilization in model selection. *Annals of Statistics, 24* (6), 2350-2383.

Breiman, L. (2001a). Random forests. *Machine Learning, 45* (1), 5-32.

Breiman, L. (2001b). Statistical modeling: The two cultures. *Statistical Science, 16* (3), 199-215.

Breiman, L., Friedman, J., Olshen, R., & Stone, C. (1984). *Classification and regression trees.* Wadsworth & Brooks/Cole.

Breiman, L., & Spector, P. (1992). Submodel selection and evaluation in regression: The X-random case. *International Statistical Review, 60* (3), 291-319.

Brin, S., & Page, L. (1998). The anatomy of a large-scale hypertextual web search engine. *Computer Networks and ISDN Systems, 30* (1-7), 107-117.

Bringmann, L. F., Hamaker, E. L., Vigo, D. E., Aubert, A., Borsboom, D., & Tuerlinckx, F. (2017). Changing dynamics: Time-varying autoregressive models using generalized additive modeling. *Psychological Methods,* 22, 409-425.

Brodmann, K. (1994). *Localization in the cerebral cortex* (L. J. Garey, Trans.). Smith-Gordon. (Original work published 1909)

Brown, T. A., Di Nardo, P. A., Lehman, C. L., & Campbell, L. A. (2001). Reliability of DSM-IV anxiety and mood disorders: Implications for the classification of emotional disorders. *Journal of Abnormal Psychology, 110* (1), 49-58.

Browne, M. W. (2000). Cross-validation methods. *Journal of Mathematical Psychology, 44* (1), 108-132.

Bryk, A. S., & Raudenbush, S. W. (1987). Application of hierarchical linear models to assessing change. *Psychological Bulletin, 101,* 147-158.

Buda, M., Maki, A., & Mazurowski, M. A. (2018). A systematic study of the class imbalance problem in convolutional neural networks. *Neural Networks, 106,* 249-259.

Bühlmann, P. (2006). Boosting for high-dimensional linear models. *Annals of Statistics, 34* (2), 559-583.

Bühlmann, P., & Hothorn, T. (2007). Boosting algorithms: Regularization, prediction and model fitting. *Statistical Science, 22* (4), 477-505.

Bühlmann, P., Peters, J., & Ernest, J. (2014). CAM: Causal additive models, high-dimensional order search and penalized regression. *Annals of Statistics, 42* (6), 2526-2556.

Bulteel, K., Mestdagh, M., Tuerlinckx, F., & Ceulemans, E. (2018). VAR (1) based models do not always outpredict AR (1) models in typical psychological applications. *Psychological Methods, 23* (4), 740.

Burke, T. A., Ammerman, B. A., & Jacobucci, R. (2019). The use of machine learning in the study of suicidal and non-suicidal self-injurious thoughts and behaviors: A systematic review. *Journal of Affective Disorders, 245,* 869-884.

Bürkner, P. C. (2017). brms: An R package for Bayesian multilevel models using Stan. *Journal of Statistical Software, 80,* 1-28.

Burt, R. S. (1976). Interpretational confounding of unobserved variables in structural equation models. *Sociological Methods & Research, 5* (1), 3-52.

Byrt, T., Bishop, J., & Carlin, J. B. (1993). Bias, prevalence and kappa. *Journal of Clinical Epidemiology, 46* (5), 423-429.

Cabrera, F. (2020). Does IBE require a "model" of explanation? *British Journal for the Philosophy of Science 71* (2), 727-750.

Carpenter, B., Gelman, A., Hoffman, M. D., Lee, D., Goodrich, B., Betancourt, M., . . . & Riddell, A. (2017). Stan: A probabilistic programming language. *Journal of Statistical Software, 76* (1), 1-32.

Carrig, M. M., Manrique-Vallier, D., Ranby, K. W., Reiter, J. P., & Hoyle, R. H. (2015). A nonparametric, multiple imputation-based method for the retrospective integration of data sets. *Multivariate Behavioral Research, 50* (4), 383-397.

Carrington, P. J., Scott, J., & Wasserman, S. (Eds.). (2005). *Models and methods in social network analysis* (Vol. 28). Cambridge University Press.

Carroll, R. J., Ruppert, D., Stefanski, L. A., & Crainiceanu, C. M. (2006). *Measurement error in nonlinear models: A modern perspective.* Chapman & Hall/CRC.

Cattell, R. B. (1966). Psychological theory and scientific method. In R. B. Cattell (Ed.), *Handbook of multivariate experimental psychology* (pp. 1-18). Rand McNally.

Chalmers, A. F. (2013). *What is this thing called science?* Hackett.

Chang, J. (2015). *lda: Collapsed Gibbs sampling methods for topic models.* https://CRAN.R-project.org/package=lda

Chapman, B. P., Weiss, A., & Duberstein, P. R. (2016). Statistical learning theory for high dimensional prediction: Application to criterion-keyed scale development. *Psychological Methods, 21* (4), 603-620.

Chawla, N. V., Bowyer, K. W., Hall, L. O., & Kegelmeyer, W. P. (2002). SMOTE: Synthetic minority over-sampling technique. *Journal of Artificial Intelligence Research, 16,* 321-357.

Che, C., Jin, I. H., & Zhang, Z. (2020). Network mediation analysis using model-based eigenvalue decomposition. *Structural Equation Modeling, 28* (1), 148-161.

Chen, J., & Chen, Z. (2008). Extended Bayesian information criteria for model selection with large model spaces. *Biometrika, 95* (3), 759-771.

Chen, T., & Guestrin, C. (2016, August). Xgboost: A scalable tree boosting system. In *Proceedings of the 22nd ACM SIGKDD International Conference on Knowledge Discovery and Data Mining* (pp. 785-794). Association for Computing Machinery.

Chen, T., & He, T. (2023). *xgboost: Extreme gradient boosting.* https://cran.r-project.org/web/packages/xgboost/vignettes/xgboost.pdf

Chen, Y., & Yang, Y. (2021). The one standard error rule for model selection: Does it work? *Stats, 4* (4), 868-892.

Chickering, D. M. (2003). Optimal structure identification with greedy search. *Journal of Machine Learning Research, 3,* 507-554.

Choi, N. H., Li, W., & Zhu, J. (2010). Variable selection with the strong heredity constraint and its oracle property. *Journal of the American Statistical Association, 105,* 354-364.

Chollet, F., & Allaire, J. J. (2017). *Deep learning with R.* Manning.

Christensen, A. P., & Golino, H. (2021). On the equivalency of factor and network loadings. *Behavior Research Methods, 53* (4), 1563-1580.

Christodoulou, E., Jie, M. A., Collins, G. S., Steyerberg, E. W., Verbakel, J. Y., & van Calster, B. (2019). A systematic review shows no performance benefit of machine learning over logistic regression for clinical prediction models. *Journal of Clinical Epidemiology, 110,* 12-22.

Clark, S. L., Muthén, B., Kaprio, J., D'Onofrio, B. M., Viken, R., & Rose, R. J. (2013). Models and strategies for factor mixture analysis: An example concerning the structure underlying psychological disorders. *Structural Equation Modeling, 20* (4), 681-703.

Cohen, J. (1983). The cost of dichotomization. *Applied Psychological Measurement, 7* (3), 249-253.

Cohen, J. (1988). *Statistical power analysis for the behavioral sciences* (2nd ed.). Erlbaum.

Cohen, J., Cohen, P., West, S. G., & Aiken, L. S. (2003). *Applied multiple regression/correlation analysis for the behavioral sciences* (3rd ed.). Routledge.

Cohen, P., West, S. G., & Aiken, L. S. (2014). *Applied multiple regression/correlation analysis for the behavioral sciences.* Psychology Press.

Cole, P. M., Bendezu, J. J., Ram, N., & Chow, S. M. (2017). Dynamical systems modeling of early childhood self-regulation. *Emotion, 17* (4), 684-699.

Collins, L. M., & Lanza, S. T. (2009). *Latent class and latent transition analysis: With applications in the social, behavioral, and health sciences* (Vol. 718). Wiley.

Cortes, C., & Vapnik, V. (1995). Support-vector networks. *Machine Learning, 20* (3), 273-297.

Costantini, G., Epskamp, S., Borsboom, D., Perugini, M., Mottus, R., Waldorp, L. J., & Cramer, A. O. (2015). State of the aRt personality research: A tutorial on network analysis of personality data in R. *Journal of Research in Personality, 54*, 13-29.

Craver, C. F. (2006). When mechanistic models explain. *Synthese, 153* (3), 355-376.

Cronbach, L. J. (1951). Coefficient alpha and the internal structure of tests. *Psychometrika, 16* (3), 297-334.

Cronbach, L. J., & Meehl, P. E. (1955). Construct validity in psychological tests. *Psychological Bulletin, 52* (4), 281-302.

Cudeck, R., & Browne, M. W. (1983). Cross-validation of covariance structures. *Multivariate Behavioral Research, 18*(2), 147-167.

Darlington, R. B., & Hayes, A. F. (2017). *Regression analysis and linear models: Concepts applications, and implementation.* Guilford Press.

Davis, J., & Goadrich, M. (2006, June). The relationship between precision-recall and ROC curves. In *Proceedings of the 23rd International Conference on Machine Learning* (pp. 233-240). ACM.

De Boeck, P., & Partchev, I. (2012). IRTrees: Tree-based item response models of the GLMM family. *Journal of Statistical Software, 48* (1), 1-28.

de Rooij, M., Karch, J. D., Fokkema, M., Bakk, Z., Pratiwi, B. C., & Kelderman, H. (2022). SEM-based out-of-sample predictions. *Structural Equation Modeling, 30* (1), 132-148.

Dean, D. O., Bauer, D. J., & Prinstein, M. J. (2017). Friendship dissolution within social networks modeled through multilevel event history analysis. *Multivariate Behavioral Research, 52* (3), 271-289.

DeCastro, B. R. (2019). Cumulative ROC curves for discriminating three or more ordinal outcomes with cutpoints on a shared continuous measurement scale. *PloS ONE, 14* (8), e0221433.

Deerwester, S. C., Dumais, S. T., Landauer, T. K., Furnas, G. W., & Harshman, R. A. (1990). Indexing by latent semantic analysis. *JASIS, 41* (6), 391-407.

Deng, L., Yang, M., Marcoulides K. M., (2018). Structural equation modeling with many variables: A Systematic review of issues and developments. *Frontiers in Psychology, 9,* 580.

Depaoli, S. (2021). *Bayesian structural equation modeling.* Guilford Press.

Devlieger, I., Mayer, A., & Rosseel, Y. (2016). Hypothesis testing using factor score regression: A comparison of four methods. *Educational and Psychological Measurement, 76* (5), 741-770.

Devlieger, I., & Rosseel, Y. (2017). Factor score path analysis: An alternative for SEM? *Methodology, 13* (Suppl. 1), 31-38.

Devlieger, I., Talloen, W., & Rosseel, Y. (2019). New developments in factor score regression: Fit indices and a model comparison test. *Educational and Psychological Measurement, 79* (6), 1017-1037.

DeYoung, C. G., & Krueger, R. F. (2020). To wish impossible things: On the ontological status of latent variables and the prospects for theory in psychology. *Psychological Inquiry, 31* (4), 289-296.

Di Battista, G., Eades, P., Tamassia, R., & Tollis, I. G. (1994). Algorithms for drawing graphs: An annotated bibliography. *Computational Geometry, 4* (5), 235-282.

Ding, Y., & Simonoff, J. S. (2010). An investigation of missing data methods for classification trees applied to binary response data. *Journal of Machine Learning Research, 11* (1), 131-170.

Duarte, C. W., Klimentidis, Y. C., Harris, J. J., Cardel, M., & Fernandez, J. R. (2011). A hybrid Bayesian network/structural equation modeling (BN/SEM) approach for detecting physiological networks for obesity-related genetic variants. In *2011 IEEE International Conference on Bioinformatics and Biomedicine Workshops.* Institute of Electrical & Electronics Engineers.

Duckworth, A. L., Peterson, C., Matthews, M. D., & Kelly, D. R. (2007). Grit: Perseverance and passion for long-term goals. *Journal of Personality and Social Psychology, 92* (6), 1087-1101.

Duckworth, A. L., & Quinn, P. D. (2009). Development and validation of the Short Grit Scale (GRIT-S). *Journal of Personality Assessment, 91* (2), 166-174.

Dwyer, D. B., Falkai, P., & Koutsouleris, N. (2018). Machine learning approaches for clinical psychology and psychiatry. *Annual Review of Clinical Psychology, 14*, 91-118.

Eades, P. (1984). A heuristic for graph drawing. *Congressus Numerantium, 42*, 149-160.

Easley, D., & Kleinberg, J. (2010). *Networks, crowds, and markets: Reasoning about a highly connected world.* Cambridge University Press.

Efron, B., Hastie, T., Johnstone, I., & Tibshirani, R. (2004). Least angle regression. *Annals of Statistics, 32* (2), 407-499.

Efron, B., & Tibshirani, R. (1986). Bootstrap methods for standard errors, confidence intervals, and other measures of statistical accuracy. *Statistical Science, 1* (1) 54-75.

Eirinaki, M., Pisal, S., & Singh, J. (2012). Feature-based opinion mining and ranking. *Journal of Computer and System Sciences, 78* (4), 1175-1184.

Elith, J., Leathwick, J. R., & Hastie, T. (2008). A working guide to boosted regression trees. *Journal of Animal Ecology, 77*, 802-813.

Enders, C. K. (2010). *Applied missing data analysis.* Guilford Press.

Enders, C. K., & Tofighi, D. (2008). The impact of misspecifying class-specific residual variances in growth mixture models. *Structural Equation Modeling, 15*, 75-95.

Eo, S. H., & Cho, H. (2014). Tree-structured mixed-effects regression modeling for longitudinal data. *Journal of Computational and Graphical Statistics, 23* (3), 740-760.

Epskamp, S., Cramer, A. O., Waldorp, L. J., Schmittmann, V. D., & Borsboom, D. (2012). qgraph: Network visualizations of relationships in psychometric data. *Journal of Statistical Software, 48*, 1-18.

Epskamp, S., van Borkulo, C. D., van der Veen, D. C., Servaas, M. N., Isvoranu, A. M., Riese, H., & Cramer, A. O. (2018). Personalized network modeling in psychopathology: The importance of contemporaneous and temporal connections. *Clinical Psychological Science, 6*, 416-427.

Erdos, P., & Renyi, A. (1960). On the evolution of random graphs. *Publication of the Mathematical Institute of the Hungarian Academy of Sciences, 5* (1), 17-60.

Everitt, B. S., Landau, S., Leese, M., & Stahl, D. (2011). *Cluster analysis.* Wiley.

Evermann, J., & Tate, M. (2016). Assessing the predictive performance of structural equation model estimators. *Journal of Business Research, 69,* 4565- 4582.

Fan, J., & Li, R. (2001). Variable selection via nonconcave penalized likelihood and its oracle properties. *Journal of the American Statistical Association, 96* (456), 1348-1360.

Faris, R., & Felmlee, D. (2011). Status struggles: Network centrality and gender segregation in same and cross-gender aggression. *American Sociological Review, 76* (1), 48-73.

Fawcett, T. (2006). An introduction to ROC analysis. *Pattern Recognition Letters, 27* (8), 861-874.

Feldman, R., & Sanger, J. (2007). *The text mining handbook: Advanced approaches in analyzing unstructured data.* Cambridge University Press.

Fernandez-Delgado, M., Cernadas, E., Barro, S., & Amorim, D. (2014). Do we need hundreds of classifiers to solve real world classification problems? *Journal of Machine Learning Research, 15* (1), 3133-3181.

Fife, D. A., & Rodgers, J. L. (2022). Understanding the exploratory/confirmatory data analysis continuum: Moving beyond the "replication crisis." *American Psychologist, 77* (3), 453-466.

Fisher, A., Rudin, C., & Dominici, F. (2019). All models are wrong, but many are useful: Learning a variable's importance by studying an entire class of prediction models simultaneously. *Journal of Machine Learning Research, 20* (177), 1-81.

Flack, V. F., & Chang, P. C. (1987). Frequency of selecting noise variables in subset regression analysis: A simulation study. *The American Statistician, 41* (1), 84-86.

Flake, J. K., Pek, J., & Hehman, E. (2017). Construct validation in social and personality research: Current practice and recommendations. *Social Psychological and Personality Science, 8* (4), 370-378.

Fokkema, M., & Greiff, S. (2017). How performing PCA and CFA on the same data equals trouble. *European Journal of Psychological Assessment, 33* (6), 399-402.

Fokkema, M., Smits, N., Zeileis, A., Hothorn, T., & Kelderman, H. (2018). Detecting treatment-subgroup interactions in clustered data with generalized linear mixed-effects model trees. *Behavior Research Methods, 50,* 2016-2034.

Foster, E. D., & Deardorff, A. (2017). Open science framework (OSF). *Journal of the Medical Library Association, 105* (2), 203.

Fox, J. (2015). *Applied regression analysis and generalized linear models.* Sage.

Fraley, C., & Raftery, A. E. (1998). How many clusters? Which clustering method?: Answers via model-based cluster analysis. *Computer Journal, 41* (8), 578-588.

Freeman, L. C. (1978). Centrality in social networks conceptual clarification. *Social Networks, 1* (3), 215-239.

Freitas, A. A. (2014). Comprehensible classification models: A position paper. *ACM SIGKDD Explorations Newsletter, 15* (1), 1-10.

Freund, Y., & Schapire, R. E. (1995). A decision-theoretic generalization of on-line learning and an application to boosting. In *European Conference on Computational Learning Theory* (pp. 23-37). Springer.

Freund, Y., & Schapire, R. E. (1996). Experiments with a new boosting algorithm. *Machine Learning: Proceedings of the Thirteenth International Conference, 96*, 148-156.

Freund, Y., & Schapire, R. E. (1997). A decision-theoretic generalization of on-line learning and an application to boosting. *Journal of Computer and System Sciences, 55*, 119-139.

Fried, E. I., & Robinaugh, D. J. (2020). Systems all the way down: Embracing complexity in mental health research. *BMC Medicine, 18* (1), 205.

Fried, E. I., van Borkulo, C. D., Cramer, A. O., Boschloo, L., Schoevers, R. A., & Borsboom, D. (2017). Mental disorders as networks of problems: A review of recent insights. *Social Psychiatry and Psychiatric Epidemiology, 52* (1), 1-10.

Friedman, J. H. (1991). Multivariate adaptive regression splines. *Annals of Statistics, 19*, 1-67.

Friedman, J. H. (2001). Greedy function approximation: A gradient boosting machine. *Annals of Statistics, 29*, 1189-1232.

Friedman, J., Hastie, T., & Tibshirani, R. (2000). Additive logistic regression: A statistical view of boosting (with discussion and a rejoinder by the authors). *Annals of Statistics, 28* (2), 337-407.

Friedman, J., Hastie, T., & Tibshirani, R. (2007). Sparse inverse covariance estimation with the graphical lasso. *Biostatistics, 9* (3), 432-441.

Friedman, J., Hastie, T., & Tibshirani, R. (2010). *A note on the group lasso and a sparse group lasso.* arXiv. https://arxiv.org/abs/1001.0736

Fruchterman, T. M., & Reingold, E. M. (1991). Graph drawing by force-directed placement. *Software: Practice and Experience, 21* (11), 1129-1164.

Fu, W., & Simonoff, J. S. (2015). Unbiased regression trees for longitudinal and clustered data. *Computational Statistics & Data Analysis, 88*, 53-74.

Fuller, W. A. (1987). *Measurement error models*. Wiley.

Furr, M. (2011). *Scale construction and psychometrics for social and personality psychology*. Sage.

Gatz, F. M., Gosling, S. D., & Rentfrow, P. J. (2022). Small effects: The indispensable foundation for a cumulative psychological science. *Perspectives on Psychological Science, 17* (1), 205-215.

Gelman, A. (2004). Exploratory data analysis for complex models. *Journal of Computational and Graphical Statistics, 13* (4), 755-779.

Gelman, A., Carlin, J. B., Stern, H. S., Dunson, D. B., Vehtari, A., & Rubin, D. B. (2013). *Bayesian data analysis*. CRC Press.

Gelman, A., Lee, D., & Guo, J. (2015). Stan: A probabilistic programming language for Bayesian inference and optimization. *Journal of Educational and Behavioral Statistics, 40* (5), 530-543.

Gibson, W. A. (1959). Three multivariate models: Factor analysis, latent structure analysis, and latent profile analysis. *Psychometrika, 24* (3), 229-252.

Gigerenzer, G. (2004). Mindless statistics. *Journal of Socio-Economics, 33* (5), 587-606.

Gilbert, E. N. (1959). Random graphs. *Annals of Mathematical Statistics, 30* (4), 1141-1144.

Glymour, C., Scheines, R., Spirtes, P., & Kelley, K. (1987). *Discovering causal structure*. Academic Press.

Golbraikh, A., & Tropsha, A. (2002). Beware of q2! *Journal of Molecular Graphics and Modelling, 20* (4), 269-276.

Goldstein, A., Kapelner, A., Bleich, J., & Pitkin, E. (2015). Peeking inside the black box: Visualizing statistical learning with plots of individual conditional expectation. *Journal of Computational and Graphical Statistics, 24* (1), 44-65.

Golino, H. F., & Epskamp, S. (2017). Exploratory graph analysis: A new approach for estimating the number of dimensions in psychological research. *PloS ONE, 12* (6), e0174035.

Golino, H., Moulder, R., Shi, D., Christensen, A. P., Garrido, L. E., Nieto, M. D., . . . & Boker, S. M. (2021). Entropy fit indices: New fit measures for assessing the structure and dimensionality of multiple latent variables. *Multivariate Behavioral Research, 56* (6), 874-902.

Goodfellow, I., Bengio, Y., & Courville, A. (2016). *Deep learning* (Vol. 1, No. 2). MIT Press.

Goodman, L. A. (1974). Exploratory latent structure analysis using both identifiable and unidentifiable models. *Biometrika, 61* (2), 215-231.

Goodrich, B., Gabry, J., Ali, I., & Brilleman, S. (2022). *rstanarm: Bayesian applied regression modeling via Stan*. https://mc-stan.org/rstanarm/

Goorbergh, R. V. D., van Smeden, M., Timmerman, D., & Van Calster, B. (2022). *The harm of class imbalance corrections for risk predic-*

tion models: Illustration and simulation using logistic regression. arXiv. https://arxiv.org/abs/2202.09101

Green, S. B. (1991). How many subjects does it take to do a regression analysis? *Multivariate Behavioral Research, 26* (3), 499-510.

Grice, J. W. (2001). Computing and evaluation factor scores. *Psychological Methods, 6*, 430-450.

Grimm, K. J., & Jacobucci, R. (2018). *Individually varying time metrics in latent change score models. Advances in longitudinal models for multivariate psychology: A festschrift for Jack McArdle.* Routledge.

Grimm, K. J., Jacobucci, R., Stegmann, G., & Serang, S. (2022). Explorations of individual change processes and their determinants: A novel approach and remaining challenges. *Multivariate Behavioral Research, 57* (4), 525-542.

Grimm, K. J., Mazza, G. L., & Davoudzadeh, P. (2017). Model selection in finite mixture models: A k-fold cross-validation approach. *Structural Equation Modeling, 24* (2), 246-256.

Grimm, K. J., Ram, N., & Estabrook, R. (2017). *Growth modeling: Structural equation and multilevel modeling approaches.* Guilford Press.

Grimm, K. J., Ram, N., & Shiyko, M. P. (2013). A simulation study of the ability of growth mixture models to uncover growth heterogeneity. In J. J. McArdle & G. Ritschard (Eds.), *Contemporary issues in exploratory data mining in the behavioral sciences* (pp. 194-211). Routledge.

Grimm, K. J., Stegmann, G., Jacobucci, R., & Serang, S. (in press). Big data in developmental psychology. In S. E. Woo, L. Tay, & R. W. Proctor (Eds.), *Big data methods for psychological research: New horizons and challenges.* American Psychological Association.

Grimmer, J. (2015). We are all social scientists now: How big data, machine learning, and causal inference work together. *PS: Political Science & Politics, 48* (1), 80-83.

Groll, A. (2017). *glmmLasso: Variable selection for generalized linear mixed models by L1-penalized estimation.* https://CRAN.R-project.org/package=glmmLasso

Groll, A., & Tutz, G. (2014). Variable selection for generalized linear mixed models by L1-penalized estimation. *Statistics and Computing, 24*, 137-154.

Gromping, U. (2009). Variable importance assessment in regression: Linear regression versus random forest. *The American Statistician, 63* (4), 308-319.

Grubinger, T., Zeileis, A., & Pfeiffer, K. P. (2014). evtree: Evolutionary learning of globally optimal classification and regression trees in R. *Journal of Statistical Software, 61*, 1-29.

Gunn, H. J., Hayati Rezvan, P., Fernandez, M. I., & Comulada, W. S. (2022). How to apply variable selection machine learning algorithms with multiply imputed data: A missing discussion. *Psychological Methods*.

Haibe-Kains, B., Adam, G. A., Hosny, A., Khodakarami, F., Waldron, L., Wang, B., . . . & Broderick, T. (2020). Transparency and reproducibility in artificial intelligence. *Nature, 586* (7829), E14-E16.

Haig, B. D. (2014). *Investigating the psychological world: Scientific method in the behavioral sciences*. MIT Press.

Haig, B. D. (2019). Big data science: A philosophy of science perspective. In S. E. Woo, R. Proctor, & L. Tay (Eds.), *Big data methods for psychological research: New horizons and challenges*. American Psychological Association.

Hair, J. F., Sarstedt, M., Ringle, C. M., & Mena, J. A. (2012). An assessment of the use of partial least squares structural equation modeling in marketing research. *Journal of the Academy of Marketing Science, 40* (3), 414-433.

Haixiang, G., Yijing, L., Shang, J., Mingyun, G., Yuanyue, H., & Bing, G. (2017). Learning from class-imbalanced data: Review of methods and applications. *Expert Systems with Applications, 73*, 220-239.

Hajjem, A., Bellavance, F., & Larocque, D. (2014). Mixed-effects random forest for clustered data. *Journal of Statistical Computation and Simulation, 84* (6), 1313-1328.

Hallquist, M. N., Wright, A. G., & Molenaar, P. C. (2019). Problems with centrality measures in psychopathology symptom networks: Why network psychometrics cannot escape psychometric theory. *Multivariate Behavioral Research, 56* (2), 199-223.

Hamaker, E. L., Mulder, J. D., & van IJzendoorn, M. H. (2020). Description, prediction and causation: Methodological challenges of studying child and adolescent development. *Developmental Cognitive Neuroscience, 46*, 100867.

Hand, D. J. (2006). Classifier technology and the illusion of progress. *Statistical Science, 21* (1), 1-14.

Hanneke, S., & Xing, E. P. (2007). Statistical network analysis: Models, issues, and new directions. In *Lecture notes in computer science* (pp. 115-125). Springer.

Haris, A., Witten, D., & Simon, N. (2016). Convex modeling of interactions with strong heredity. *Journal of Computational and Graphical Statistics, 25*, 981-1004.

Harrell, Jr., F. E. (2015). *Regression modeling strategies: With applications to linear models, logistic and ordinal regression, and survival analysis*. Springer.

Harring, J. R., Weiss, B. A., & Hsu, J. C. (2012). A comparison of methods for estimating quadratic effects in nonlinear structural equation models. *Psychological Methods, 17* (2), 193-214.

Harris, J. K. (2013). *An introduction to exponential random graph modeling* (Vol. 173). Sage.

Hastie, T., & Tibshirani, R. (1986). Generalized additive models. *Statistical Science, 1*, 297-318.

Hastie, T., Tibshirani, R., & Friedman, J. (2009). *The elements of statistical learning*. Springer.

Hastie, T., Tibshirani, R., & Tibshirani, R. (2020). Best subset, forward stepwise or lasso?: Analysis and recommendations based on extensive comparisons. *Statistical Science, 35* (4), 579-592.

Hayes, A. F. (2017). *Introduction to mediation, moderation, and conditional process analysis: A regression-based approach*. Guilford Press.

He, Y. (2006). *Missing data imputation for tree-based models*. University of California, Los Angeles.

Heck, R. H., & Thomas, S. L. (2015). *An introduction to multilevel modeling techniques: MLM and SEM approaches using Mplus*. Routledge.

Helwig, N. E. (2017). Adding bias to reduce variance in psychological results: A tutorial on penalized regression. *Quantitative Methods for Psychology, 13* (1), 1-19.

Hildebrandt, A., Wilhelm, O., & Robitzsch, A. (2009). Complementary and competing factor analytic approaches for the investigation of measurement invariance. *Review of Psychology, 16* (2), 87-102.

Hoerl, A. E., & Kennard, R. W. (1970). Ridge regression: Biased estimation for nonorthogonal problems. *Technometrics, 12* (1), 55-67.

Hoff, P. D., Raftery, A. E., & Handcock, M. S. (2002). Latent space approaches to social network analysis. *Journal of the American Statistical Association, 97* (460), 1090-1098.

Hofner, B., Boccuto, L., & Goker, M. (2015). Controlling false discoveries in high-dimensional situations: Boosting with stability selection. *BMC Bioinformatics, 16* (1), 144.

Hofner, B., & Hothorn, T. (2017). *stabs: Stability selection with error control*. https://CRAN.R-project.org/package=stabs

Hofstadter, A. (1951). Explanation and necessity. *Philosophy and Phenomenological Research, 11* (3), 339-347.

Holland, P. W., Laskey, K. B., & Leinhardt, S. (1983). Stochastic blockmodels: First steps. *Social Networks, 5* (2), 109-137.

Holm, E. A. (2019). In defense of the black box. *Science, 364* (6435), 26-27.

Holzinger, K. J., & Swineford, F. (1939). *A study in factor analysis: The stability of a bi-factor solution* (Supplementary Educational Monographs, Vol. 48). University of Chicago Press.

Hong, M., Jacobucci, R., & Lubke, G. (2020). Deductive data mining. *Psychological Methods, 25* (6), 691-707.

Horn, J. L. (1965). A rationale and test for the number of factors in factor analysis. *Psychometrika, 30*, 179-185.

Horn, J. L., & McArdle, J. J. (1992). A practical and theoretical guide to measurement invariance in aging research. *Experimental Aging Research, 18* (3), 117-144.

Hornung, R. (2021). *ordinalForest: Prediction and variable ranking with ordinal target variables*. https://CRAN.R-project.org/package=ordinalForest

Hosseini, M., Powell, M., Collins, J., Callahan-Flintoft, C., Jones, W., Bowman, H., & Wyble, B. (2020). I tried a bunch of things: The dangers of unexpected overfitting in classification of brain data. *Neuroscience & Biobehavioral Reviews, 119*, 456-467.

Hothorn, T., Hornik, K., & Zeileis, A. (2006). Unbiased recursive partitioning: A conditional inference framework. *Journal of Computational and Graphical Statistics, 15*, 651-674.

Hothorn, T., & Zeileis, A. (2015). partykit: A modular toolkit for recursive partioning in R. *Journal of Machine Learning Research, 16*, 3905-3909.

Howell, R. D., Breivik, E., & Wilcox, J. B. (2007). Reconsidering formative measurement. *Psychological Methods, 12* (2), 205-218.

Hu, L. T., & Bentler, P. M. (1999). Cutoff criteria for fit indexes in covariance structure analysis: Conventional criteria versus new alternatives. *Structural Equation Modeling, 6* (1), 1-55.

Hu, M., & Liu, B. (2004a). Mining and summarizing customer reviews. In *Proceedings of the Tenth ACM SIGKDD International Conference on Knowledge Discovery and Data Mining* (pp. 168-177). Association for Computing Machinery.

Hu, M., & Liu, B. (2004b, July). Mining opinion features in customer reviews. In *Proceedings of the 19th National Conference on Artificial Intelligence* (pp. 755-760). Association for Computing Machinery.

Huang, J., Breheny, P., & Ma, S. (2012). A selective review of group selection in high-dimensional models. *Statistical Science, 27* (4), 481-499.

Huang, P. H. (2020). Postselection inference in structural equation modeling. *Multivariate Behavioral Research, 55* (3), 344-360.

Huang, P. H., Chen, H., & Weng, L. J. (2017). A penalized likelihood method for structural equation modeling. *Psychometrika, 82* (2), 329-354.

Hunter, D. R., Handcock, M. S., Butts, C. T., Goodreau, S. M., & Morris, M. (2008). ergm: A package to fit, simulate and diagnose exponential-family models for networks. *Journal of Statistical Software, 24* (3), nihpa54860.

Isvoranu, A. M., Epskamp, S., Waldorp, L., & Borsboom, D. (Eds.). (2022). *Network psychometrics with R: A guide for behavioral and social scientists.* Routledge.

Jacobucci, R. (2017). *dtree: Decision trees* (version 0.2.3) [Software]. https://cran.r-project.org/web/packages/dtree/index.html

Jacobucci, R., & Grimm, K. J. (2018). Comparison of frequentist and Bayesian regularization in structural equation modeling. *Structural Equation Modeling, 25* (4), 639-649.

Jacobucci, R., & Grimm, K. J. (2020). Machine learning and psychological research: The unexplored effect of measurement. *Perspectives on Psychological Science, 15* (3), 809-816.

Jacobucci, R., Grimm, K. J., & McArdle, J. J. (2016). Regularized structural equation modeling. *Structural Equation Modeling, 23*, 555-566.

Jacobucci, R., Grimm, K. J., & McArdle, J. J. (2017). A comparison of methods for uncovering sample heterogeneity: Structural equation model trees and finite mixture models. *Structural Equation Modeling, 24*, 270-282.

Jacobucci, R., & Li, X. (2022). Does minority case sampling improve performance with imbalanced outcomes in psychological research? *Journal of Behavioral Data Science, 2* (1), 59-74.

Jacobucci, R., Littlefield, A. K., Millner, A. J., Kleiman, E. M., & Steinley, D. (2021). Evidence of inflated prediction performance: A commentary on machine learning and suicide research. *Clinical Psychological Science, 9* (1), 129-134.

Jacobucci, R., Stewart, S., Abdolell, M., Serang, S., & Stegmann, G. (2017). *longRPart2: Recursive partitioning of longitudinal data* (version 0.0.1) [Software]. https://cran.r-project.org/web/packages/longRPart2/index.html

Jaeger, R. G., & Halliday, T. R. (1998). On confirmatory versus exploratory research. *Herpetologica*, pp. S64-S66.

James, G., Witten, D., Hastie, T., & Tibshirani, R. (2013). *An introduction to statistical learning* (Vol. 112). Springer.

Jashinsky, J., Burton, S. H., Hanson, C. L., West, J., Giraud-Carrier, C., Barnes, M. D., & Argyle, T. (2014). Tracking suicide risk factors through twitter in the us. *Crisis, 35* (1), 51-59.

Jockers, M. L. (2017). *Syuzhet: Extract sentiment and plot arcs from text.* https://github.com/mjockers/syuzhet

Jolly, E., & Chang, L. J. (2019). The flatland fallacy: Moving beyond low-dimensional thinking. *Topics in Cognitive Science, 11* (2), 433-454.

Joreskog, K. G. (1969). A general approach to confirmatory maximum likelihood factor analysis. *Psychometrika, 34* (2), 183-202.

Joreskog, K. G., & Goldberger, A. S. (1975). Estimation of a model with multiple indicators and multiple causes of a single latent variable. *Journal of the American Statistical Association, 70*, 631-639.

Kahn, J. H., Tobin, R. M., Massey, A. E., & Anderson, J. A. (2007). Measuring emotional expression with the linguistic inquiry and word count. *American Journal of Psychology, 120* (2), 263-286.

Kamada, T., & Kawai, S. (1989). An algorithm for drawing general undirected graphs. *Information Processing Letters, 31* (1), 7-15.

Kane, M. T. (2013). Validating the interpretations and uses of test scores. *Journal of Educational Measurement, 50* (1), 1-73.

Kendler, K. S. (2005). Toward a philosophical structure for psychiatry. *American Journal of Psychiatry, 162* (3), 433-440.

Kendler, K. S. (2017). DSM disorders and their criteria: How should they inter-relate? *Psychological Medicine, 47* (12), 2054-2060.

Kendler, K. S. (2019). From many to one to many–The search for causes of psychiatric illness. *JAMA Psychiatry, 76* (10), 1085-1091.

Kenny, D. A., & Judd, C. M. (1984). Estimating the nonlinear and interactive effects of latent variables. *Psychological Bulletin, 96* (1), 201-210.

Kim, J., & Lee, J.-E. R. (2011). The Facebook paths to happiness: Effects of the number of Facebook friends and self-presentation on subjective well-being. *CyberPsychology, Behavior, and Social Networking, 14* (6), 359-364.

Kim, M., Lamont, A. E., Jaki, T., Feaster, D., Howe, G., & Van Horn, M. L. (2016). Impact of an equality constraint on the class-specific residual variances in regression mixtures: A Monte Carlo simulation study. *Behavior Research Methods, 48*, 813-826.

Kimmelman, J., Mogil, J. S., & Dirnagl, U. (2014). Distinguishing between exploratory and confirmatory preclinical research will improve translation. *PLoS Biology, 12* (5), e1001863.

King, M. W., & Resick, P. A. (2014). Data mining in psychological treatment research: A primer on classification and regression trees. *Journal of Consulting and Clinical Psychology, 82* (5), 895-905.

Koch, R., Azen, C., Friedman, E., Hanley, W., Levy, H., Matalon, R., . . . & De La Cruz, F. (2003). Research design, organization, and sample characteristics of the maternal PKU collaborative study. *Pediatrics, 112* (Suppl. 4), 1519-1522.

Kohavi, R. (1995). A study of cross-validation and bootstrap for accuracy estimation and model selection. *International Joint Conference on Artificial Intelligence, 14* (2), 1137-1145.

Kraut, R., Patterson, M., Lundmark, V., Kiesler, S., Mukophadhyay, T., & Scherlis, W. (1998). Internet paradox: A social technology that reduces social involvement and psychological well-being? *American Psychologist, 53* (9), 1017-1031.

Krivitsky, P. N., & Handcock, M. S. (2014). A separable model for dynamic networks. *Journal of the Royal Statistical Society: Series B (Statistical Methodology), 76* (1), 29-46.

Krivitsky, P. N., Handcock, M. S., Hunter, D. R., Butts, C. T., Klumb, C., Goodreau, S. M., & Morris, M. (2003-2022). Statnet: Tools for the statistical modeling of network data. *Journal of Statistical Software, 24* (1), 1-11.

Kroc, E., & Zumbo, B. D. (2020). A transdisciplinary view of measurement error models and the variations of X = T+ E. *Journal of Mathematical Psychology, 98*, 102372.

Kroenke, K., Strine, T. W., Spitzer, R. L., Williams, J. B., Berry, J. T., & Mokdad, A. H. (2009). The PHQ-8 as a measure of current depression in the general population. *Journal of Affective Disorders, 114* (1), 163-173.

Krstajic, D., Buturovic, L. J., Leahy, D. E., & Thomas, S. (2014). Cross-validation pitfalls when selecting and assessing regression and classification models. *Journal of Cheminformatics, 6* (1), 10.

Kruschke, J. (2014). *Doing Bayesian data analysis: A tutorial with R, JAGS, and Stan*. Academic Press.

Kuhn, M. (2008). Caret package. *Journal of Statistical Software, 28* (5), 1-26.

Kuhn, M., & Johnson, K. (2013). *Applied predictive modeling* (Vol. 26). Springer.

Landauer, T. K., Foltz, P. W., & Laham, D. (1998). An introduction to latent semantic analysis. *Discourse Processes*, 25, 259-284.

Landers, R. N., Brusso, R. C., Cavanaugh, K. J., & Collmus, A. B. (2016). A primer on theory-driven web scraping: Automatic extraction of big data from the internet for use in psychological research. *Psychological Methods, 21* (4), 475-492.

Larson, R., & Csikszentmihalyi, M. (2014). The experience sampling method. In M. Csikszentmihalyi, *Flow and the foundations of positive psychology* (pp. 21-34). Springer.

Lazarsfeld, P. F., & Henry, N. W. (1968). *Latent structure analysis*. Houghton Mifflin.

Lazer, D., Rubineau, B., Chetkovich, C., Katz, N., & Neblo, M. (2010). The coevolution of networks and political attitudes. *Political Communication, 27* (3), 248-274.

Lee, B. K., Lessler, J., & Stuart, E. A. (2010). Improving propensity score weighting using machine learning. *Statistics in Medicine, 29* (3), 337-346.

Lee, S. Y., & Song, X. Y. (2012). *Basic and advanced Bayesian structural equation modeling: With applications in the medical and behavioral sciences.* Wiley.

Levy, R. (2017). Distinguishing outcomes from indicators via Bayesian modeling. *Psychological Methods, 22* (4), 632-648.

Levy, R., & Mislevy, R. J. (2016). *Bayesian psychometric modeling.* CRC Press.

Lewis, D. D., Yang, Y., Rose, T. G., & Li, F. (2004). Rcv1: A new benchmark collection for text categorization research. *Journal of Machine Learning Research, 5*, 361-397.

Li, X., & Jacobucci, R. (2020). *Regularized structural equation modeling with stability selection.* PsyArXiv. https://psyarxiv.com/t4d5y/

Li, X., Jacobucci, R., & Ammerman, B. A. (2021). Tutorial on the use of the regsem package in R. *Psych, 3* (4), 579-593.

Lieberman, M. D., & Cunningham, W. A. (2009). Type I and Type II error concerns in fMRI research: Re-balancing the scale. *Social Cognitive and Affective Neuroscience, 4* (4), 423-428.

Lin, H. W., Tegmark, M., & Rolnick, D. (2017). Why does deep and cheap learning work so well? *Journal of Statistical Physics, 168* (6), 1223-1247.

Lindsay, D. S. (2015). Replication in *Psychological Science. Psychological Science, 26* (12), 1827-1832.

Linzer, D. A., & Lewis, J. B. (2011). poLCA: An R package for polytomous variable latent class analysis. *Journal of Statistical Software, 42* (10), 1-29.

Liu, H., Jin, I. H., & Zhang, Z. (2018). Structural equation modeling of social networks: Specification, estimation, and application. *Multivariate Behavioral Research, 53* (5), 714-730.

Lo, Y., Mendell, N. R., & Rubin, D. B. (2001). Testing the number of components in a normal mixture. *Biometrika, 88* (3), 767-778.

Lobo, J. M., Jimenez-Valverde, A., & Real, R. (2008). AUC: A misleading measure of the performance of predictive distribution models. *Global Ecology and Biogeography, 17* (2), 145-151.

Lockhart, R., Taylor, J., Tibshirani, R. J., & Tibshirani, R. (2014). A significance test for the lasso. *Annals of Statistics, 42* (2), 413-468.

Lovins, J. B. (1968). Development of a stemming algorithm. *Mechanical Translation & Computational Linguistics, 11* (1-2), 22-31.

Lubke, G. H., & Muthén, B. (2005). Investigating population heterogeneity with factor mixture models. *Psychological Methods, 10* (1), 21-39.

Lykken, D. T. (1968). Statistical significance in psychological research. *Psychological Bulletin, 70*, 151-159.

Lyubomirsky, S., & Lepper, H. S. (1999). A measure of subjective happiness: Preliminary reliability and construct validation. *Social Indicators Research, 46* (2), 137-155.

MacKinnon, D. P., & Luecken, L. J. (2008). How and for whom?: Mediation and moderation in health psychology. *Health Psychology, 27* (2, Suppl.), S99.

Mai, Y., Zhang, Z., & Wen, Z. (2018). Comparing exploratory structural equation modeling and existing approaches for multiple regression with latent variables. *Structural Equation Modeling, 25* (5), 737-749.

Mariadassou, M., Robin, S., & Vacher, C. (2010). Uncovering latent structure in valued graphs: A variational approach. *Annals of Applied Statistics, 4* (2), 715-742.

Marsh, H. W., Morin, A. J., Parker, P. D., & Kaur, G. (2014). Exploratory structural equation modeling: An integration of the best features of exploratory and confirmatory factor analysis. *Annual Review of Clinical Psychology, 10*, 85-110.

Marshall, T. C., Lefringhausen, K., & Ferenczi, N. (2015). The big five, self-esteem, and narcissism as predictors of the topics people write about in Facebook status updates. *Personality and Individual Differences, 85*, 35-40.

Marsman, M., Borsboom, D., Kruis, J., Epskamp, S., van Bork, R. V., Waldorp, L. J., . . . & Maris, G. (2018). An introduction to network psychometrics: Relating Ising network models to item response theory models. *Multivariate Behavioral Research, 53* (1), 15-35.

Maxwell, S. E., Delaney, H. D., & Kelley, K. (2017). *Designing experiments and analyzing data: A model comparison perspective*. Routledge.

Maxwell, S. E., Lau, M. Y., & Howard, G. S. (2015). Is psychology suffering from a replication crisis? What does "failure to replicate" really mean? *American Psychologist, 70* (6), 487-498.

Maya-Jariego, I., & Holgado, D. (2015). Network analysis for social and community interventions. *Psychosocial Intervention, 24* (3), 121-124.

Mazumder, R., & Hastie, T. (2012). The graphical lasso: New insights and alternatives. *Electronic Journal of Statististics, 6*, 2125-2149.

McArdle, J. J. (2012). Exploratory data mining using CART in the behavioral sciences. In H. Cooper (Ed.), *APA handbook of research methods in psychology* (pp. 405-421). American Psychological Association.

McArdle, J. J., Ferrer-Caja, E., Hamagami, F., & Woodcock, R. W. (2002). Comparative longitudinal structural analyses of the growth and decline of multiple intellectual abilities over the life span. *Developmental Psychology, 38*, 115-142.

Mcauliffe, J. D., & Blei, D. M. (2008). Supervised topic models. In M. I. Jordan, Y. LeCun, & S. A. Solla (Eds.), *Advances in neural information processing systems* (pp. 121-128). MIT Press.

McClure, K., Jacobucci, R., & Ammerman, B. A. (2021). *Are items more than indicators?: An examination of psychometric homogeneity, item-*

specific effects, and consequences for structural equation models. PsyArXiv. https://psyarxiv.com/n4mxv/

McElreath, R. (2020). *Statistical rethinking: A Bayesian course with examples in R and Stan.* Chapman & Hall/CRC.

McFarland, D. A., Lewis, K., & Goldberg, A. (2016). Sociology in the era of big data: The ascent of forensic social science. *The American Sociologist, 47* (1), 12-35.

McKeown, G. J., & Sneddon, I. (2014). Modeling continuous self-report measures of perceived emotion using generalized additive mixed models. *Psychological Methods, 19,* 155-174.

McLachlan, G. J. (1987). On bootstrapping the likelihood ratio test statistic for the number of components in a normal mixture. *Journal of the Royal Statistical Society: Series C (Applied Statistics), 36* (3), 318-324.

McLachlan, G. J., & Peel, D. (2004). *Finite mixture models.* Wiley.

McNeish, D. M. (2015). Using lasso for predictor selection and to assuage overfitting: A method long overlooked in behavioral sciences. *Multivariate Behavioral Research, 50* (5), 471-484.

McNeish, D. (2018). Thanks coefficient alpha, we'll take it from here. *Psychological Methods, 23* (3), 412.

McNeish, D., & Wolf, M. G. (2020). Thinking twice about sum scores. *Behavior Research Methods, 52* (6), 2287-2305.

McNeish, D., & Wolf, M. G. (2021). Dynamic fit index cutoffs for confirmatory factor analysis models. *Psychological Methods.*

McPherson, M., Smith-Lovin, L., & Cook, J. M. (2001). Birds of a feather: Homophily in social networks. *Annual Review of Sociology, 27,* 415-444.

Meehl, P. E. (1990). Appraising and amending theories: The strategy of Lakatosian defense and two principles that warrant it. *Psychological Inquiry, 1* (2), 108-141.

Meinshausen, N. (2007). Relaxed lasso. *Computational Statistics & Data Analysis, 52* (1), 374-393.

Meinshausen, N., & Bühlmann, P. (2006). High-dimensional graphs and variable selection with the lasso. *Annals of Statistics, 34* (3), 1436-1462.

Meinshausen, N., & Bühlmann, P. (2010). Stability selection. *Journal of the Royal Statistical Society: Series B (Statistical Methodology), 72* (4), 417-473.

Menardi, G., & Torelli, N. (2014). Training and assessing classification rules with imbalanced data. *Data Mining and Knowledge Discovery, 28* (1), 92-122.

Meredith, W. (1993). Measurement invariance, factor analysis and factorial invariance. *Psychometrika, 58* (4), 525-543.

Meredith, W., & Tisak, J. (1990). Latent curve analysis. *Psychometrika, 55,* 107-122.

Merkle, E. C., & Rosseel, Y. (2015). blavaan: Bayesian structural equation models via parameter expansion. arXiv. https://arxiv.org/abs/1511.05604

Milborrow, S. (2019). *earth: Multivariate adaptive regression splines.* https://CRAN.R-project.org/package=earth

Milborrow, S. (2022). *_rpart.plot: Plot 'rpart' Models: An Enhanced Version of 'plot.rpart'_.* R package version 3.1.1, <https://CRAN.R-project.org/package=rpart.plot>

Milgram, S. (1967). The small world problem. *Psychology Today, 2* (1), 60-67.

Miller, P. J., Lubke, G. H., McArtor, D. B., & Bergeman, C. S. (2016). Finding structure in data using multivariate tree boosting. *Psychological Methods, 21* (4), 583-602.

Miller, P. J., McArtor, D. B., & Lubke, G. H. (2017). *metboost: Exploratory regression analysis with hierarchically clustered data.* arXiv. https://arxiv.org/abs/1702.03994

Miner, G., Elder IV, J., Fast, A., Hill, T., Nisbet, R., & Delen, D. (2012). *Practical text mining and statistical analysis for non-structured text data applications.* Elsevier.

Mitchell, M. (2009). *Complexity: A guided tour.* Oxford University Press.

Mohammad, S. M., & Turney, P. D. (2010). Emotions evoked by common words and phrases: Using mechanical turk to create an emotion lexicon. In *Proceedings of the NAACL HLT 2010 Workshop on Computational Approaches to Analysis and Generation of Emotion in Text* (pp. 26-34). Association for Computational Linguistics.

Molenaar, P. C. (2004). A manifesto on psychology as idiographic science: Bringing the person back into scientific psychology, this time forever. *Measurement, 2,* 201-218.

Molnar, C. (2019). *Interpretable machine learning.* Lulu.com.

Moreno, J. L. (1934). *Who shall survive?: A new approach to the problem of human interrelations.* Nervous and Mental Disease Publishing.

Morgan, J. N. (2005). History and potential of binary segmentation for exploratory data analysis. *Journal of Data Science, 3* (2), 123-136.

Morgan, J. N., & Sonquist, J. A. (1963). Problems in the analysis of survey data, and a proposal. *Journal of the American Statistical Association, 58* (302), 415-434.

Moshontz, H., Campbell, L., Ebersole, C. R., IJzerman, H., Urry, H. L., Forscher, P. S., . . . & Castille, C. M. (2018). The Psychological Science Accelerator: Advancing psychology through a distributed collaborative network. *Advances in Methods and Practices in Psychological Science, 1* (4), 501-515.

Mottus, R., & Rozgonjuk, D. (2019). Development is in the details: Age differences in the Big Five domains, facets, and nuances. *Journal of Personality and Social Psychology, 20* (4), 1035-1048.

Mottus, R., Wood, D., Condon, D. M., Back, M., Baumert, A., Costantini, G., . . . & Murray, A. L. (2020). Descriptive, predictive and explanatory personality research: Different goals, different approaches, but a shared need to move beyond the Big Few traits. *European Journal of Personality, 34* (6), 1175-1201.

Mulaik, S. A. (1972). *The foundations of factor analysis*. McGraw-Hill.

Mulaik, S. A. (2009). *Foundations of factor analysis*. CRC Press.

Muthén, B., & Asparouhov, T. (2012). Bayesian structural equation modeling: A more flexible representation of substantive theory. *Psychological Methods, 17* (3), 313-335.

Muthén, B., & Shedden, K. (1999). Finite mixture modeling with mixture outcomes using the EM algorithm. *Biometrics, 55*, 463-469.

Muthén, L. K., & Muthén, B. O. (1998-2017). *Mplus user's guide* (7th ed.). Authors.

Muthén, L. K., & Muthén, B. O. (2017). *Mplus: Statistical analysis with latent variables: User's guide* (Version 8). Authors.

Nabi, R. L., Prestin, A., & So, J. (2013). Facebook friends with (health) benefits?: Exploring social network site use and perceptions of social support, stress, and well-being. *Cyberpsychology, Behavior, and Social Networking, 16* (10), 721-727.

National Center for Education Statistics. (2009). *Combined user's manual for the ECLS-Eighth-grade and K-8 full sample data files and electronic codebooks*. U.S. Department of Education.

Navarro, D. (2013). *Learning statistics with R: A tutorial for psychology students and other beginners: version 0.5*. University of Adelaide.

Neale, M. C., Hunter, M. D., Pritikin, J. N., Zahery, M., Brick, T. R., Kirkpatrick, R. M., . . . Boker, S. M. (2016). OpenMx 2.0: Extended structural equation and statistical modeling. *Psychometrika, 81* (2), 535-549.

Nielsen, F. A. (2011). *A new ANEW: Evaluation of a word list for sentiment analysis in microblogs*. ArXiv. https://arxiv.org/abs/1103.2903

Nosek, B. A., Ebersole, C. R., DeHaven, A. C., & Mellor, D. T. (2018). The preregistration revolution. *Proceedings of the National Academy of Sciences, 115* (11), 2600-2606.

Nowok, B., Raab, G. M., & Dibben, C. (2016). synthpop: Bespoke creation of synthetic data in R. *Journal of Statistical Software, 74* (11), 1-26.

Nylund, K. L., Asparouhov, T., & Muthén, B. O. (2007). Deciding on the number of classes in latent class analysis and growth mixture modeling:

A Monte Carlo simulation study. *Structural Equation Modeling, 14* (4), 535-569.

Onnela, J. P., & Rauch, S. L. (2016). Harnessing smartphone-based digital phenotyping to enhance behavioral and mental health. *Neuropsychopharmacology, 41*, 1691-1696.

Ooms, J. (2017). *hunspell: High-performance stemmer, tokenizer, and spell checker for R.* https://CRAN.R-project.org/package=hunspell.

Oppenheim, A. N. (1966). *Questionnaire design and attitude measurement.* Basic Books.

Osborne, R. T., & Suddick, D. E. (1972). A longitudinal investigation of the intellectual differentiation hypothesis. *Journal of Genetic Psychology, 121*, 83-89.

Otte, E., & Rousseau, R. (2002). Social network analysis: A powerful strategy, also for the information sciences. *Journal of information Science, 28* (6), 441-453.

Pearl, J. (1988). *Probabilistic reasoning in intelligent systems: Networks of plausible inference.* Elsevier.

Pearl, J. (2019). The seven tools of causal inference, with reflections on machine learning. *Communications of the ACM, 62* (3), 54-60.

Pearl, J. (2000). Causal inference without counterfactuals: Comment. *Journal of the American Statistical Association, 95* (450), 428-431.

Pedersen, T. L., Benesty, M. (2019). *lime: Local interpretable model-agnostic explanations.* https://CRAN.R-project.org/package=lime

Pennebaker, J. W., Boyd, R. L., Jordan, K., & Blackburn, K. (2015). *The development and psychometric properties of LIWC2015.* University of Texas at Austin.

Pennebaker, J. W., Francis, M. E., & Booth, R. J. (2001). *Linguistic inquiry and word count: LIWC 2001.* Erlbaum.

Philipp, M., Rusch, T., Hornik, K., & Strobl, C. (2018). Measuring the stability of results from supervised statistical learning. *Journal of Computational and Graphical Statistics, 27* (4), 685-700.

Piironen, J., & Vehtari, A. (2016). *On the hyperprior choice for the global shrinkage parameter in the horseshoe prior.* arXiv. https://arxiv.org/abs/1610.05559

Pinheiro, J., Bates, D., DebRoy, S., Sarkar, D., Heisterkamp, S., Van Willigen, B., & Maintainer, R. (2017). *Package 'nlme'. Linear and nonlinear mixed effects models.* https://cran.r-project.org/web/packages/nlme/index.html

Polley, E., LeDell, E., Kennedy, C., & van der Laan, M. (2019). *Super-Learner: Super Learner Prediction.* https://CRAN.R-project.org/package=SuperLearner

Proust-Lima, C., Philipps, V., & Liquet, B. (2015). *Estimation of extended mixed models using latent classes and latent processes: The R package lcmm.* arXiv. https://arxiv.org/abs/1503.00890

Psillos, S. (2002). *Causation and explanation* (Vol. 8). McGill-Queen's Press.

Qu, W., & Zhang, Z. (2020). An application of aspect-based sentiment analysis on teaching evaluation. In Z. Zhang, K.-H. Yuan, Y. Wen, & J. Tang (Eds.), *New developments in data science and data analytics: Proceedings of the 2019 Meeting of the International Society for Data Science and Analytics.* ISDSA Press.

R Core Team. (2017). *R: A language and environment for statistical computing* [Computer software manual]. www.R-project.org

R Core Team. (2020). *R: A language and environment for statistical computing.* R Foundation for Statistical Computing. www.R-project.org

Raad, B. D. E., & Perugini, M. E. (2002). *Big five factor assessment: Introduction.* Hogrefe & Huber.

Ram, N., & Grimm, K. J. (2009). Methods and measures: Growth mixture modeling: A method for identifying differences in longitudinal change among unobserved groups. *International journal of behavioral development, 33* (6), 565- 576.

Reeves, B., Ram, N., Robinson, T. N., Cummings, J. J., Giles, C. L., Pan, J., & Gagneja, A. (2019). Screenomics: A framework to capture and analyze personal life experiences and the ways that technology shapes them. *Human-Computer Interaction, 36* (2), 150-201.

Reise, S. P., Bonifay, W. E., & Haviland, M. G. (2013). Scoring and modeling psychological measures in the presence of multidimensionality. *Journal of Personality Assessment, 95,* 129-140.

Reise, S. P., Widaman, K. F., & Pugh, R. H. (1993). Confirmatory factor analysis and item response theory: Two approaches for exploring measurement invariance. *Psychological Bulletin, 114* (3), 552-566.

Revelle, W. (2020). *psych: Procedures for personality and psychological research.* https://cran.r-project.org/web/packages/psych/index.html

Revelle, W., Wilt, J., & Rosenthal, A. (2010). Individual differences in cognition: New methods for examining the personality-cognition link. In A. Gruszka, G. Matthews, & B. Szymura (Eds.). *Handbook of individual differences in cognition* (pp. 27-49). Springer.

Rhemtulla, M., van Bork, R., & Borsboom, D. (2018). Worse than measurement error: Consequences of inappropriate latent variable measurement models. *Psychological Methods, 25* (1), 30-45.

Ribeiro, M. T., Singh, S., & Guestrin, C. (2016, August). Why should I trust you?: Explaining the predictions of any classifier. In *Proceedings of the*

22nd ACM SIGKDD International Conference on Knowledge Discovery and Data Mining (pp. 1135-1144). Association for Computing Machinery.

Ridgeway, G. (2017). *gbm: Generalized boosted regression models.* https://CRAN.R-project.org/package=gbm

Rinker, T. W. (2019). *Package 'sentimentr': Calculate text polarity sentiment.* https://cran.r-project.org/web/packages/sentimentr/sentimentr.pdf

Ripley, B (2023). *tree: Classification and regression trees.* https://CRAN.R-project.org/package=tree

Robins, G., Pattison, P., Kalish, Y., & Lusher, D. (2007). An introduction to exponential random graph (p*) models for social networks. *Social Networks, 29* (2), 173-191.

Rohrer, J. M., Brummer, M., Schmukle, S. C., Goebel, J., & Wagner, G. G. (2017). "What else are you worried about?": Integrating textual responses into quantitative social science research. *PloS ONE, 12* (7), e0182156.

Rosseel, Y. (2012). lavaan: An R package for structural equation modeling. *Journal of Statistical Software, 48* (2), 1-36.

Russell, D., Peplau, L. A., & Ferguson, M. L. (1978). Developing a measure of loneliness. *Journal of Personality Assessment, 42* (3), 290-294.

Ryan, J. B. (2011). Social networks as a shortcut to correct voting. *American Journal of Political Science, 55* (4), 753-766.

Saito, T., & Rehmsmeier, M. (2015). The precision-recall plot is more informative than the ROC plot when evaluating binary classifiers on imbalanced datasets. *PLoS ONE, 10.*

Salton, G. (1971). *The SMART Retrieval System: Experiments in automatic document processing*. Prentice-Hall.

Saucier, G., & Iurino, K. (2020). High-dimensionality personality structure in the natural language: Further analyses of classic sets of English-language trait-adjectives. *Journal of Personality and Social Psychology, 119* (5), 1188-1219.

Saul, Z. M., & Filkov, V. (2007). Exploring biological network structure using exponential random graph models. *Bioinformatics, 23* (19), 2604-2611.

Schaefer, D. R., Adams, J., & Haas, S. A. (2013). Social networks and smoking: Exploring the effects of peer influence and smoker popularity through simulations. *Health Education & Behavior, 40* (1, Suppl.), 24S-32S.

Scheel, A. M., Tiokhin, L., Isager, P. M., & Lakens, D. (2021). Why hypothesis testers should spend less time testing hypotheses. *Perspectives on Psychological Science, 16* (4), 744-755.

Schelldorfer, J. (2011). *lmmlasso: Linear mixed-effects models with lasso.* https://CRAN.R-project.org/package=lmmlasso

Schelldorfer, J. (2012). *glmmixedlasso: Generalized linear mixed models with lasso*. https://R-Forge.R-project.org/projects/lmmlasso/

Schelldorfer, J., Buhlmann, P., & van de Geer, S. (2011). Estimation for high-dimensional linear mixed-effects models using l1-penalization. *Scandinavian Journal of Statistics, 38*, 197-214.

Schelldorfer, J., Meier, L., & Buhlmann, P. (2014). Glmmlasso: An algorithm for high-dimensional generalized linear mixed models using l1-penalization. *Journal of Computational and Graphical Statistics, 23*, 460-477.

Schmitt, N. (1996). Uses and abuses of coefficient alpha. *Psychological Assessment, 8* (4), 350-353.

Schwarz, G. (1978). Estimating the dimension of a model. *Annals of Statistics, 6*, 461-464.

Scott, J. (2017). *Social network analysis*. Sage.

Scott, S. B., Whitehead, B. R., Bergeman, C. S., & Pitzer, L. (2013). Understanding global perceptions of stress in adulthood through tree-based exploratory data mining. In J. McArdle & G. Ritschard (Eds.), *Contemporary issues in exploratory data mining in the behavioral sciences* (pp. 371-404). Routledge.

Scrucca, L., Fop, M., Murphy, T. B., & Raftery, A. E. (2016). mclust 5: Clustering, classification and density estimation using Gaussian finite mixture models. *The R Journal, 8* (1), 289.

Segal, M. R. (2004). *Machine learning benchmarks and random forest regression*. Center for Bioinformatics and Molecular Biostatistics, University of California, San Francisco.

Sela, R. J., & Simonoff, J. S. (2012). RE-EM trees: A data mining approach for longitudinal and clustered data. *Machine Learning, 86*, 169-207.

Serang, S., Grimm, K. J., & Zhang, Z. (2019). On the correspondence between the latent growth curve and latent change score models. *Structural Equation Modeling, 26*, 623-635.

Serang, S., Jacobucci, R., Grimm, K. J., Stegmann, G., & Brandmaier, A. M. (2020a). *MplusTrees: Decision trees with structural equation models fit in 'Mplus'*. https://CRAN.R-project.org/package=MplusTrees

Serang, S., Jacobucci, R., Stegmann, G., Brandmaier, A. M., Culianos, D., & Grimm, K. J. (2020b). MplusTrees: Structural equation model trees using M plus. *Structural Equation Modeling, 28* (1), 127-137.

Sewell, D. K., & Chen, Y. (2015). Latent space models for dynamic networks. *Journal of the American Statistical Association, 110* (512), 1646-1657.

Shaw, L. H., & Gant, L. M. (2004). In defense of the internet: The relationship between internet communication and depression, loneliness, self-esteem, and perceived social support. *Internet Research, 28* (3), 157-171.

Shiffman, S., Stone, A. A., & Hufford, M. R. (2008). Ecological momentary assessment. Annual *Review of Clinical Psychology, 4,* 1-32.

Shimizu, S., Hoyer, P. O., Hyvärinen, A., & Kerminen, A. (2006). A linear non-Gaussian acyclic model for causal discovery. *Journal of Machine Learning Research, 7,* 2003-2030.

Shmueli, G. (2010). To explain or to predict? *Statistical Science, 25* (3), 289-310.

Shmueli, G., Ray, S., Estrada, J. M. V., & Chatla, S. B. (2016). The elephant in the room: Predictive performance of PLS models. *Journal of Business Research, 69* (10), 4552-4564.

Shrout, P. E., & Rodgers, J. L. (2018). Psychology, science, and knowledge construction: Broadening perspectives from the replication crisis. *Annual Review of Psychology, 69,* 487-510.

Silge, J., & Robinson, D. (2016). tidytext: Text mining and analysis using tidy data principles in R. *Journal of Open Source Software, 1* (3), 37.

Sim, J., & Wright, C. C. (2005). The kappa statistic in reliability studies: Use, interpretation, and sample size requirements. *Physical Therapy, 85* (3), 257-268.

Simmons, J. P., Nelson, L. D., & Simonsohn, U. (2011). False-positive psychology: Undisclosed flexibility in data collection and analysis allows presenting anything as significant. *Psychological Science, 22* (11), 1359-1366.

Singer, J. D. (1998). Using SAS PROC MIXED to fit multilevel models, hierarchical models, and individual growth models. *Journal of Educational and Behavioral Statistics, 23,* 323-355.

Singer, J. D., & Willett, J. B. (2003). *Applied longitudinal data analysis: Modeling change and event occurrence.* Oxford University Press.

Skrondal, A., & Laake, P. (2001). Regression among factor scores. *Psychometrika, 66,* 563-575.

Snedecor, G. W., & Cochran, W. G. (1980). *Statistical methods.* Iowa State University Press.

Snijders, T. A. (2011). Statistical models for social networks. *Annual Review of Sociology, 37,* 131-153.

Snijders, T. A., Van de Bunt, G. G., & Steglich, C. E. (2010). Introduction to stochastic actor-based models for network dynamics. *Social Networks, 32* (1), 44-60.

Stavrianou, A., Andritsos, P., & Nicoloyannis, N. (2007). Overview and semantic issues of text mining. *ACM Sigmod Record, 36* (3), 23-34.

Stegmann, G., & Grimm, K. J. (2018). A new perspective on the effects of covariates in mixture models. *Structural Equation Modeling, 25*(2), 167-178.

Stegmann, G., Jacobucci, R., Serang, S., & Grimm, K. J. (2018). Recursive partitioning with nonlinear models of change. *Multivariate Behavioral Research, 53*, 559-570.

Stewart, S., & Abdolell, M. (2012). *longRPart: Recursive partitioning of longitudinal data using mixed-effects models.* https://cran.r-project.org/src/contrib/Archive/longRPart/

Steyerberg, E. W. (2019). *Clinical prediction models: A practical approach to development, validation, and updating*. Springer.

Strobl, C., Boulesteix, A. L., Kneib, T., Augustin, T., & Zeileis, A. (2008). Conditional variable importance for random forests. *BMC Bioinformatics, 9*, 1-11.

Strobl, C., Malley, J., & Tutz, G. (2009). An introduction to recursive partitioning: Rationale, application, and characteristics of classification and regression trees, bagging, and random forests. *Psychological Methods, 14* (4), 323-348.

Substance Abuse and Mental Health Services Administration. (2021). *National Survey on Drug Use and Health.* https://www.samhsa.gov/data/data-we-collect/nsduh-national-survey-drug-use-and-health

Sullivan, K. J., Shadish, W. R., & Steiner, P. M. (2015). An introduction to modeling longitudinal data with generalized additive models: Applications to single-case designs. *Psychological Methods, 20*, 26-42.

Sun, J., Chen, Y., Liu, J., Ying, Z., & Xin, T. (2016). Latent variable selection for multidimensional item response theory models via L_1 regularization. *Psychometrika, 81* (4), 921-939.

Tausczik, Y. R., & Pennebaker, J. W. (2010). The psychological meaning of words: Liwc and computerized text analysis methods. *Journal of Language and Social Psychology, 29* (1), 24-54.

Temple Lang, D. (2020). *XML: Tools for parsing and generating XML within R and S-Plus.* https://rdrr.io/cran/XML/

Therneau, T., & Atkinson, B. (2019). *rpart: Recursive partitioning and regression trees.* https://CRAN.R-project.org/package=rpart

Therneau, T. M., & Atkinson, E. J. (1997). *An introduction to recursive partitioning using the RPART routines* (Vol. 61). Mayo Foundation.

Therneau, T. M., Atkinson, E. J., & Ripley, B. (2015). CART: Recursive partitioning and regression trees. http://CRAN.R-project.org/package=CART

Tibshirani, R. (1996). Regression shrinkage and selection via the lasso. *Journal of the Royal Statistical Society, Series B (Methodological), 58* (1), 267-288.

Tibshirani, R. (1997). The lasso method for variable selection in the Cox model. *Statistics in Medicine, 16* (4), 385-395.

Tibshirani, R. (2011). Regression shrinkage and selection via the lasso: A retrospective. *Journal of the Royal Statistical Society, Series B (Statistical Methodology), 73* (3), 273-282.

Tofighi, D., & Enders, C. K. (2008). Identifying the correct number of classes in growth mixture models. In G. R. Hancock (Ed.), *Advances in latent variable mixture models* (pp. 317-341). Information Age.

Travers, J., & Milgram, S. (1977). An experimental study of the small world problem. *Sociometry, 32* (4), 179-197.

Tukey, J. W. (1962). The future of data analysis. *Annals of Mathematical Statistics, 33* (1), 1-67.

Tukey, J. W. (1977). *Exploratory data analysis*. Addison-Wesley.

Tutz, G., & Groll, A. (2010). Generalized linear mixed models based on boosting. In T. Kneib & G. Tutz (Eds.), *Statistical modelling and regression structures* (pp. 197-215). Springer.

Umbach, N., Naumann, K., Brandt, H., & Kelava, A. (2017). Fitting nonlinear structural equation models in R with package nlsem. *Journal of Statistical Software, 77*(7), 1-20.

Urban, C. J., & Bauer, D. J. (2020). *A deep learning algorithm for high-dimensional exploratory item factor analysis.* arXiv. https://arxiv.org/abs/2001.07859

Van De Schoot, R., Winter, S. D., Ryan, O., Zondervan-Zwijnenburg, M., & Depaoli, S. (2017). A systematic review of Bayesian articles in psychology: The last 25 years. *Psychological Methods, 22* (2), 217-239.

Van der Laan, M. J., Polley, E. C., & Hubbard, A. E. (2007). Super learner. *Statistical Applications in Genetics and Molecular Biology, 6* (1).

Van Doorn, J., Verhoef, P. C., & Bijmolt, T. H. (2007). The importance of non-linear relationships between attitude and behaviour in policy research. *Journal of Consumer Policy, 30* (2), 75-90.

Van Erp, S., Oberski, D. L., & Mulder, J. (2018). Shrinkage priors for Bayesian penalized regression. *Journal of Mathematical Psychology, 89*, 31-50.

van Kesteren, E. J., & Oberski, D. L. (2019). Exploratory mediation analysis with many potential mediators. *Structural Equation Modeling, 26* (5), 710-723.

van Rooij, I., & Baggio, G. (2021). Theory before the test: How to build high-verisimilitude explanatory theories in psychological science. *Perspectives on Psychological Science, 16* (4), 682-697.

Van Rossum, G., & Drake, F. L. (2009). *Python 3 reference manual.* CreateSpace.

Varma, S., & Simon, R. (2006). Bias in error estimation when using cross-validation for model selection. *BMC Bioinformatics, 7* (1), 1-8.

Velicer, W. F., & Jackson, D. N. (1990). Component analysis versus common factor analysis: Some issues in selecting an appropriate procedure. *Multivariate Behavioral Research, 25,* 1-28.

Vermunt, J. K., & Magidson, J. (2003). *Latent Gold 3.0.* www.statisticalinnovations.com

Wagenmakers, E. J., Wetzels, R., Borsboom, D., van der Maas, H. L., & Kievit, R. A. (2012). An agenda for purely confirmatory research. *Perspectives on Psychological Science,* 7(6), 632-638.

Wainer, J., & Cawley, G. (2021). Nested cross-validation when selecting classifiers is overzealous for most practical applications. *Expert Systems with Applications,* 182, 115222.

Wang, M. W., & Stanley, J. C. (1970). Differential weighting: A review of methods and empirical studies. *Review of Educational Research, 40* (5), 663-705.

Wang, Y. (2011). *Smoothing splines: Methods and applications.* CRC Press.

Wang, Y., Kim, E., Ferron, J. M., Dedrick, R. F., Tan, T. X., & Stark, S. (2021). Testing measurement invariance across unobserved groups: The role of covariates in factor mixture modeling. *Educational and Psychological Measurement, 81* (1), 61-89.

Wasserman, S., & Faust, K. (1994). *Social network analysis: Methods and applications* (Vol. 8). Cambridge University Press.

Wasserman, S., & Pattison, P. (1996). Logit models and logistic regressions for social networks: I. An introduction to Markov graphs andp. *Psychometrika, 61* (3), 401-425.

Weiss, S. M., Indurkhya, N., Zhang, T., & Damerau, F. (2010). *Text mining: Predictive methods for analyzing unstructured information.* Springer.

West, D. B. (1996). *Introduction to graph theory* (Vol. 2). Prentice-Hall.

Westfall, J., & Yarkoni, T. (2016). Statistically controlling for confounding constructs is harder than you think. *PloS ONE, 11* (3), e0152719.

Widaman, K. F. (1993). Common factor analysis versus principal component analysis: Differential bias in representing model parameters? *Multivariate Behavioral Research, 28* (3), 263-311.

Widaman, K. F., & Grimm, K. J. (2013). Exploratory analysis of effects of prenatal risk factors on intelligence in children of mothers with phenylketonuria. In J. J. McArdle & G. Ritschard (Eds.), *Contemporary issues in exploratory data mining in the behavioral sciences* (pp. 450-470). Taylor & Francis.

Wilcox, K. T., Jacobucci, R., Zhang, Z., & Ammerman, B. A. (2023). Supervised latent Dirichlet allocation with covariates: A Bayesian structural and measurement model of text and covariates. *Psychological Methods.*

Williams, D. R., Rhemtulla, M., Wysocki, A. C., & Rast, P. (2019). On nonregularized estimation of psychological networks. *Multivariate Behavioral Research, 54* (5), 719-750.

Wolpert, D. H. (1996). The lack of a priori distinctions between learning algorithms. *Neural Computation, 8* (7), 1341-1390.

Wood, S. N. (2017). *Generalized additive models: An introduction with R.* Chapman & Hall/CRC.

Wu, Y., Kosinski, M., & Stillwell, D. (2015). Computer-based personality judgments are more accurate than those made by humans. *Proceedings of the National Academy of Sciences, 112* (4), 1036-1040.

Xu, Y., & Goodacre, R. (2018). On splitting training and validation set: A comparative study of cross-validation, bootstrap and systematic sampling for estimating the generalization performance of supervised learning. *Journal of Analysis and Testing, 2* (3), 249-262.

Yarkoni, T., & Westfall, J. (2017). Choosing prediction over explanation in psychology: Lessons from machine learning. *Perspectives on Psychological Science, 12* (6), 1100-1122.

Ye, A., Gates, K., Henry, T. R., & Luo, L. (2020). Path and directionality discovery in individual dynamic models: A regularized unified structural equation modeling approach for hybrid vector autoregression. *Psychometrika, 86* (2), 404-441.

Youyou, W., Stillwell, D., Schwartz, H. A., & Kosinski, M. (2017). Corrigendum: Birds of a feather do flock together: Behavior-based personality-assessment method reveals personality similarity among couples and friends. *Psychological Science, 28* (3), 276-284.

Yuan, K. H., & Chan, W. (2002). Fitting structural equation models using estimating equations: A model segregation approach. *British Journal of Mathematical and Statistical Psychology, 55* (1), 41-62.

Yuan, K. H., & Deng, L. (2021). Equivalence of partial-least-squares SEM and the methods of factor-score regression. *Structural Equation Modeling, 28* (4), 557-571.

Yuan, M., & Lin, Y. (2006). Model selection and estimation in regression with grouped variables. *Journal of the Royal Statistical Society, Series B (Statistical Methodology), 68* (1), 49-67.

Yuan, M., & Lin, Y. (2007). Model selection and estimation in the gaussian graphical model. *Biometrika, 94* (1), 19-35.

Zeileis, A., Hothorn, T., & Hornik, K. (2008). Model-based recursive partitioning. *Journal of Computational and Graphical Statistics, 17* (2), 492-514.

Zhang, H. P. (1997). Multivariate adaptive splines for analysis of longitudinal data. *Journal of Computational and Graphical Statistics, 6,* 74-91.

Zhang, H. P. (1999). Analysis of infant growth curves using multivariate adaptive splines. *Biometrics, 55,* 452-459.

Zhang, H. P. (2004) Multivariate adaptive splines in the analysis of longitudinal and growth curve data. *Statistical Methods in Medical Research, 13,* 63-82.

Zhang, H. P., & He, Y. (2009). *Multivariate adaptive splines for analysis of longitudinal data.* https://publichealth.yale.edu/c2s2/software/masal/

Zhang, Z., & Wang, L. (2017). *Advanced statistics using R.* ISDSA Press.

Zhong, X., & Yuan, K. H. (2011). Bias and efficiency in structural equation modeling: Maximum likelihood versus robust methods. *Multivariate Behavioral Research, 46* (2), 229-265.

Zhou, Y., & McArdle, J. J. (2015). Rationale and applications of survival tree and survival ensemble methods. *Psychometrika, 80* (3), 811-833.

Zou, H., & Hastie, T. (2005). Regularization and variable selection via the elastic net. *Journal of the Royal Statistical Society: Series B (Statistical Methodology), 67*(2), 301-320.

Author Index

B

C

D

E

F

G

H

I

J

K

L

M

N

O

P

Q

T

U

V

W

X

Y

Z

Subject Index

Note. *f* or *t* following a page number indicates a figure or a table.

B

F

G

H

Q

R

V

W

About the Authors

Ross Jacobucci, PhD, is Assistant Professor in Quantitative Psychology at the University of Notre Dame. His research is in the development and application of machine learning for clinical research, specifically suicide and nonsuicidal self-injury. He is also an active developer of open-source software for the R statistical environment, with five packages that implement some form of machine learning. For more information, see his website, *www.rjacobucci.com.*

Kevin J. Grimm, PhD, is Professor of Psychology at Arizona State University. Dr. Grimm's research interests include multivariate methods for the analysis of change, multiple group and latent class models for understanding divergent developmental processes, nonlinearity in development, machine learning techniques for psychological data, and mathematics and reading ability development. His research has been funded by the National Science Foundation, the National Institute of Education, and the Institute of Education Sciences. Dr. Grimm received the Early Career Research Award from the Society of Multivariate Experimental Psychology in 2017. He is an author of *Growth Modeling: Structural Equation and Multilevel Modeling Perspectives,* which received the inaugural Barbara Byrne Book Award from the Society of Multivariate Experimental Psychology in 2021. While at the University of California, Davis, Dr. Grimm received the Award for Excellence in Service to Graduate Students from the Graduate Student Association and was nominated for the Excellence in Education Award from the Associated Students of the University of California, Davis.

Zhiyong Zhang, PhD, is Professor in Quantitative Psychology in the Department of Psychology at the University of Notre Dame, where he directs the Lab for Big Data Methodology (*https://bigdatalab.nd.edu*). Dr. Zhang has conducted research in the areas of Bayesian methods, structural equation modeling, longitudinal data analysis, and missing data and nonnormal data analysis. His recent research involves the development of new methods and software for social network and text analysis. He is the founding editor of the Journal of Behavioral Data Science.